/orld

DATE DUE	RETURNED

CONTENTS

Hearst's bank robbery for the Symbionese Liberation Army, to the bomb planted by the Weather Underground at the Capitol Rotunda. The Weather Underground bombings were meant to send a message that said "we" can and will strike anywhere, *and beware*: the revolution is coming and you can either—to paraphrase Weather Underground leader Bernardine Dohrn—fight on the side of the oppressed or the oppressor.

After the first jet crashed into the World Trade Center, and as Al Qaeda militants who were gathered around television sets were beginning to celebrate, Osama bin Laden is reputed to have told them to "just wait. . . ." Wait, that is, for the second jet, the finale, the last act. The attack made use of a kind of performativity and seems to have been at least in part inspired by Hollywood disaster movies, as some have pointed out. The second attack was timed with an eye to maximal television coverage. The attack and its global mediation were supposed to send a message about the vulnerability of America, intimidating the superpower and encouraging anti-American activists (now of a disaffected fundamentalist Islamist stripe) to join in jihad.

Karlheinz Stockhausen, in his well-publicized and controversial comments following the attack, allowed himself to consider the event as a pure performance (in terms of rehearsal, performance, composition, audience), a kind of serious high art. What I found most troubling in his remarks was not that he used the term "great" or that he admired the discipline of the terrorists, but that he could distance himself sufficiently at that moment to *deal* with the attack as performance intellectually, rather than empathetically as an immense tragedy that would ripple out for years in grief and pain.

Although my dalliance with the violent wing of the antiwar movement lasted only a couple of years, this all seemed frighteningly current to me in the aftermath of 9/11. The perpetrators of 9/11 and their sympathizers justified the violence because it "brought the war home" to America, and they have argued that no one living in America is innocent—arguments that were familiar to me. I had once been complicit in a way of thinking that excused or rationalized the loss of innocent lives in the exercise of terror for political ends, and I had countenanced the aestheticization of violent political action in the real world *as* performance. As I coped with my grief and shock following 9/11, I also had to deal with an unsettling sense of complicity and guilt, a failure of my humanism. And what continued to frighten me was simply this: If I, as someone who might *otherwise* be described as ethically and morally strong and who lived a comfortable, middle-class life in America, could drift so far in support of violent ends, might there not be millions of disaffected youth among the extremely marginalized of the world, among people who had suffered so much at the hands of a global system, who would be easy recruits for terror?

CONSTRUCTIVE AND DESTRUCTIVE INTERFERENCE: INTERVENTION AND SCHOLARLY CITIZENSHIP

Having come into the academy from activist and public arts work, I always found applied or public ethnomusicology, or as I prefer to call it, engaged ethnomusicology, to be a comfortable fit, even when I didn't know what to call it. I believed, and have argued, however, that the responsibility to intervene in the world doesn't emanate only, or even primarily, from our relationship to groups with whom we work (the "reciprocity" responsibility), but from our role as scholars, as potential public intellectuals, within institutions of higher learning. We have the opportunity to use our training, experience, knowledge, and insights to contribute to public debates and to advise. Our responsibility to profess doesn't stop at the classroom door.

We know that music can be a powerful instrument in the march toward peace and justice as well as in the rush to war, so we need to ask how we as scholars can clarify that possibility and, in our interventions, amplify it. We know that music can aid in the recovery from trauma, so we need to encourage our societies to respect this capacity in music. We know that involving children in music leads to their becoming healthier, better adjusted, more disciplined, and self-aware adults, so we should work to make music thrive again in schools, families, and communities. And of course, all of us need to bring our critical abilities to the task of understanding how music is implicated in conflict, justice, intercultural understanding, and peace. The sustained sound from 9/11, rippling through all of our lives so many years afterward, can help to remind us of how important this responsibility is.

REFERENCES

Averill, Gage. 2001. "Soundly Organized Humanity" (Invited response to Roundtable on 9/11 and War in Afghanistan). *ECHO* 3(2). http://www.echo.ucla.edu/volume3-issue2/contributors.html#averill.

Schechner, Richard. 2006. "A Polity of Its Own Called Art." In *Artistic Citizenship: A Public Voice for the Arts,* edited by Mary Schmidt Campbell and Randy Martin, 33–41. New York: Routledge.

From the mountains, to the prairies,

To the oceans white with foam—

God bless America, my home sweet home!

God bless America, my home sweet home!

The power of the moment was undeniable. At the same time, the emotional charge of this performance defies easy categorization. At the most transparent level, one could interpret the legislators (who the previous day had been locked in bitterly partisan battles over U.S. tax policy and the Social Security program) as responding to the trauma of the attacks by constructing, through musical performance, a palpable, visceral model of a unified community. The literal unity of their unison voices extended in an easy metaphorical arch to encompass the absent members of Congress, the government, the dispersed rescuers and victims, and that most overdetermined of imagined communities, the nation. Televised live across the country and rebroadcast internationally, the performance deployed the incantatory power of song—a song exhorting God to bestow blessings upon the nation, no less—to restore faith in the United States' ability to withstand the extreme act of physical and, importantly, symbolic violence that it had experienced that morning. The nation's power, called into question by the sudden destruction of a prominent architectural metonym of American economic might and the damaging assault on the seat of its military strength, was thus reasserted through the performance of music.[2] But if the symbolic restoration of the status quo effected by the singing of "God Bless America" comforted many listeners, others may have detected in the intonation of a patriotic song that achieved national popularity during World War II an ominous whiff of the military response that was to come.[3] Indeed, as I watch the performance today, five years later, it seems clear that the singers, Janus-like, are directing their voices toward two audiences: one face turned inward to console the citizenry, a second directed defiantly outward toward unknown antagonists. (Interestingly, in both cases the message appears to have been the same: "We are still here.") This strange and spontaneous performance, drawing simultaneously on the iconicity of the united chorus, the indexical associations of patriotic music, and the symbolic attributes of political authority, delivered its message to its disparate audiences more emphatically than the words that preceded it ever could.

* * *

Music and violence are frequently found locked in a tight dialectical embrace, with the former alternately mitigating, eliding, inciting, preventing, and at times embodying the latter. Using music to create narrative cohesion in the face of the entropic sting of violent acts, as in the rendition of "God Bless America" above, is one of the more common permutations of this relationship, though certainly not the only one. A growing body of scholarship seeks to shed light on the cultural and political work music accomplishes in violent contexts, as well as on the various distortions systemic violence produces on the music people make.[4]

The present volume contributes to this general project by examining, on an international level, music production and reception in the wake of September 11, 2001. The weeks and months following 9/11 witnessed the production of a wide range of musical reactions to the attacks and to their eventual violent aftermath in Afghanistan and Iraq. These densely layered cultural texts-in-performance emanated from and resonated within a diverse and shifting set of political, economic, and social horizons. Moreover, and predictably, they staked out radically different positions vis-à-vis the events of 9/11. In tracing these reactions and situating them in time and space, the authors of this volume collectively present a vivid albeit necessarily incomplete picture of a complex array of musical performances, the structural changes that enabled them, the discourses that surrounded them, and the ideological terrain upon which they were positioned. In short, they offer readers a provisional map of music in the post-9/11 world.

A NEW EPOCH?
ON THE HISTORICAL SIGNIFICANCE OF 9/11

The assumption embedded in that last statement and reflected in this volume's title—namely, that there is such a thing as a "post-9/11 world"—requires some clarification. On its face, this formulation smacks of precisely the American arrogance and exceptionalism that have frequently been cited as contributing to global animosity against the United States (e.g., Spanos 2003, Zuber 2006). As Eric Hershberg and Kevin W. Moore have argued, casting 9/11 as "a watershed event of world-historical importance" positions the United States at "the epicenter of global transformation," feeding the logic that "if the United States would never be the same again after September 11 . . . neither would the rest of the world" (2002: 1). This critique notwithstanding, prominent figures from across the ideological spectrum, from George Bush to Jean Baudrillard, have framed 9/11 as an event of epochal significance. The latter figure has described the 9/11 attacks, somewhat rapturously, as putting into motion "a global catastrophic process" (2002: 405). To Baudrillard, the global war on terror is "a World War, not the third,"—he gives the Cold War this designation—"but the fourth and only, truly global one, since its stake is globalization itself" (406).

Ultimately, one does not have to regard 9/11 as "arguably the most potent symbolic event since the crucifixion of Christ" (Butterfield 2002) or "the greatest work of art that is possible in the whole cosmos" (Karlheinz Stockhausen) in order to recognize the event's far-reaching repercussions.[5] It is clear that the casualties on 9/11, tragic as they were, are dwarfed in number by the victims of mass violence among other populations around the world in the twentieth and even twenty-first centuries. But it is equally clear that the size of the calamity, measured in innocent dead, is not the factor that has rendered 9/11 so momentous a date. Rather, it was the globally recognized symbolic dimension to the attacks on the world's sole superpower, coupled with the asymmetry and open-endedness of the military responses and the complicated transnational reactions these responses have inspired, that fueled the notion that a global paradigmatic shift had taken place. While the dynamics of 9/11 may evoke memories of Pearl Harbor—an unexpected attack that provoked America's entry into a world conflict—its geopolitical implications are more comparable in scale to the global realignment and reevaluation of history that occurred at the end of the Cold War. Indeed, if it was once conventional to talk of the "short twentieth century" that began with World War I and came to a close with the fall of the Soviet Union in 1991 (Hobsbawm 1996, cf. Kocka 1995), 9/11 and its aftermath appear to have brought the "long twentieth century" to its fraught conclusion.

REVERBERATIONS: MAKING MUSIC AFTER 9/11

What does this provisional "post-9/11 world" look like? More to the point, what does it sound like? The twelve contributors to this volume address this question from two broad vantage points, which are reflected in the volume's bipartite structure. The essays of Part One, "Music, the United States, and the Mass Media After 9/11," document the burst of domestic musical activity that occurred in the weeks and months following the attacks. During this period, musicians located throughout the American pop mainstream produced a varied body of songs that generated a multitude of often-conflicting 9/11 narratives. In Chapter 1, Reebee Garofalo provides a broad overview of this mass-mediated soundscape, after which Kip Pegley and Susan Fast (Chapter 2), Bryan

Garman (Chapter 4), and Peter Schmelz (Chapter 6) grapple with a number of the musical performances that emanated from it. Pegley and Fast deconstruct "America: A Tribute to Heroes," the first and most prominent post-9/11 commemorative concert, in order to better understand the ways in which the event "attempted to forge a unified American community, wherein 'appropriate' gendered and racialized behaviors were modeled." Garman teases out a number of references to Christian theology in Bruce Springsteen's post-9/11 performances, and reads these performances as providing a "model of charity" for Americans that contrasted sharply with the more vitriolic musical polemics of some of Springsteen's contemporaries. Schmelz takes on one of these musical calls for retribution, Darryl Worley's "Have You Forgotten?" and reveals the extent to which this song (and country music more generally) trumpeted "support [for the] dominant political actions and ideologies" of the day, and lent credence to the specious assertion of an alliance between Osama bin Laden and Saddam Hussein.

In addition to these examinations of post-9/11 mass-mediated musical reactions, one essay in this section scrutinizes distortions in the fabric of the mass media itself. Martin Scherzinger's discussion of "new sites and forms of censorship" in the musical mainstream (Chapter 5) focuses on the "pathological watchfulness" exerted by corporations and individual artists after 9/11, which in turn created "restricting circumstances" for music production in the United States even in the absence of overt government censorship.

Other authors in this half of the collection focus their attention on domestic musical reactions to 9/11 that occurred beyond the horizons of the popular music mainstream: in the underground rap and punk scenes (Garofalo), within the "invisible" genre of TV news music (James Deaville, Chapter 3), and in the domain of classical music (Peter Tregear, Chapter 7). Garofalo finds that the ethos of protest that was once associated with popular music as a whole has migrated to the periphery, where political critique remains a salient, if controversial, presence among some rap and punk musicians. Deaville compares television news music on both sides of the 49th parallel in order to reveal the speed with which U.S. and Canadian news agencies adopted different narrative trajectories for their 9/11 coverage. And Tregear analyzes the broad spectrum of art music that was performed in commemoration of the victims of 9/11 and reflects on the paradoxical manner in which the performance of German canonical works resulted in the projection of an idealized image of American nationhood.

Many if not all of the domestic musical reactions treated in the first half of this volume will be familiar to readers who were in the United

States or had access to the U.S. mainstream media in the months following 9/11. By contrast, the essays in the second half, "Music and 9/11 Beyond the United States," introduce a sonic world that will be startlingly new to most readers, and serve as proof of the degree to which the events of 9/11 were, in Jonathan Ritter's words, "reread and reinterpreted through the lenses of decidedly local cultural practices" by people outside the United States. Ritter's essay (Chapter 8) reflects on the theoretical issues that obtain in a decentered world of globalized violence and shows how these issues are crystallized in a body of songs dealing with Osama bin Laden that were composed and performed in a Quechua-speaking village in the Peruvian Andes. In a similar fashion, bin Laden proved a viable protagonist for composers of Spanish-language *corridos* on both sides of the U.S.-Mexico border, as John McDowell's essay (Chapter 10) illustrates. Larry Blumenfeld (Chapter 9) documents the ways in which festival organizers in Morocco and the Senegalese musician Youssou N'Dour have endeavored to promote ecumenical dialogue while also creating a public image of nonfundamentalist Islamic engagement with the post-9/11 world. In contrast, James Grippo (Chapter 11) provides a sobering look at 9/11's aftermath in the Middle East in his examination of the music of Sha'bān 'Abd al-Raḥīm, an Egyptian popular singer whose recent songs articulate a harsh critique of American and Israeli policies in the region and present a radically revisionist history of 9/11. Lastly, within her broad assessment of music in pre- and post-9/11 Afghanistan, Veronica Doubleday (Chapter 12) discusses an Afghan singer who has used music as a vehicle for denouncing the actions of bin Laden, the Taliban, and their Pakistani patrons. Along with the essays in the first half of the book, these ethnographically informed examinations present a picture of globalization-in-motion, as a local terrorist incident is transformed through music into an event of global concern.

While these essays point to the powerful ways in which music composition and performance configured and were configured by emergent narratives in the wake of the attacks, other factors hint at the need to proceed cautiously with the blanket application of "post-9/11 world" as a transnational frame. As Doubleday illustrates, September 11 is not seen as a significant date in Afghanistan; it is dwarfed in importance by the date later in 2001 when the Taliban were ousted from Kabul. More problematic, perhaps, is that the vast bulk of musical reactions to 9/11 have proven highly ephemeral. Ritter, for example, found that by 2005 the empathetic songs metaphorically linking the victims of 9/11 to local tragedies in the Peruvian Andes were no longer in circulation. McDowell draws similar conclusions about the attenuation of 9/11 *corridos*. And if Schmelz makes the case that in Darryl Worley's

"Have You Forgotten?" "the Iraq war had its anthem," current Billboard charts indicate that the war, which has entered its fourth year at this writing, has left its anthem behind. For these and other reasons, our use of the term "post-9/11 world" should be seen as conditional, not a reified boundary but a useful rhetorical conceit, deployed here to delimit our topic and lend it an analytical focus.

DISCURSIVE READING: FINDING COMMONALITIES AND POINTS OF CONTRAST

Originally conceived by Ritter and myself as an ethnomusicological study (along with both editors, Doubleday and Grippo are ethnomusicologists), this volume has grown into a thoroughly interdisciplinary project, which includes essays written by musicologists (Deaville, Fast, Pegley, Schmelz, Tregear), a music theorist (Scherzinger), a folklorist (McDowell), a scholar of popular music and communication (Garofalo), a scholar of American studies (Garman), and a music journalist (Blumenfeld). Such diversity could make for discursive cacophony, were it not for the common themes that wind their way through the authors' contributions, connecting seemingly disparate essays and creating a productive tension that, we hope, both animates and lends cohesion to the volume.

As discussed above, the essays in the book's first half collectively evoke the nexus of art, politics, economics, and violence in the post-9/11 United States, bringing into focus the ways in which music was deployed, variously, to heal a massive societal trauma, hasten the "rush to war," and warn against the effects of extremism—all within the comfortable capitalist matrix of U.S. hegemony. If a single composite story were to be drawn from these essays, it might be a story of fluidity, of the seamless ways in which various sectors of the music industry reassembled themselves to address the new, volatile commercial and political atmosphere of the post-9/11 United States. The essays in the second half, by contrast, tell a different story, one in which musical responses to remote terrorist acts were used to metaphorically link far-flung populations in a world of transnationally mediated violence, while simultaneously anchoring them to local viewpoints, histories, and concerns. This sensation of "inhabiting multiple places at once . . . of seeing the larger picture stereoscopically with the smaller" is the hallmark of cosmopolitanism (Pollock et al. 2000: 587). While treated most explicitly by Ritter, the essays of Blumenfeld, McDowell, Grippo, and Doubleday all demonstrate the extent to which a cosmopolitan orientation has permeated even the most seemingly remote and traditional societies. The realization that one's local existence is shot through with traces of distant worlds often generates more ambivalence than joy, however. Grippo's essay on Egyptian *sha'bi* introduces us to a rather extreme manifestation of this anxiety, but it is present in all of the other essays in this half of the volume as well. The prevalence of cosmopolitan tensions in a book on 9/11 should not be surprising: as Howard Stein (2003) has reminded us, the terrorists were cosmopolitans, too.

While the sequence of essays thus adheres to a certain expositional logic, we also encourage readers to experiment with reading the essays in other configurations, placing them in dialogue with one another to bring subtle commonalities and contrasts to the fore. For example, reading Schmelz's essay on Darryl Worley's "Have You Forgotten?" next to Grippo's discussion of Egyptian *sha'bi* music reveals a common emphasis on musical nationalism while also lending a cross-cultural perspective to the pair. Placing these essays in dialogue with Ritter's and McDowell's examinations of songs that display a more empathetic and/or circumspect view of 9/11 pulls into sharper focus the ideological spectrum along which such musical responses are arranged. Likewise, Peter Tregear's discussion of classical music after 9/11 can be read against Schmelz's essay on Darryl Worley to throw into high relief issues of class, ethnicity, and nationalism within the United States, as members of two social strata stake out partially overlapping ground for imagining a post-9/11 America, through radically different musical means.

While these authors draw similar themes from different musics, others approach a single musical performance from multiple directions. For example, the seminal "America: A Tribute to Heroes" concert that took place on September 21, 2001, is analyzed in depth by Pegley and Fast as an attempt to reconfigure an imagined community that had been distorted by the trauma; by Garman as the context for Bruce Springsteen's first post-9/11 performance; and by Garofalo as an "understated, reverential event" embodying a "gentle patriotism" that contrasted starkly with the more bellicose jingoism on display at the "Concert for New York City" held one month later.

In a final example of discursive consonance, several essays in the volume deal with post-9/11 changes to the environment in which music is produced and received, primarily in the United States, but also in places like Afghanistan, where the U.S.-led military campaign has produced a number of far-reaching, and occasionally contradictory, effects for local musicians. Scherzinger's essay on censorship and Doubleday's exploration of the rapidly evolving music scene in Afghanistan speak to these structural shifts, as does Garofalo's overview of changes to the U.S. popular music industry after 9/11. Scherzinger's argument—that subtle societal pressures, often mediated by corporations, resulted in a marked increase of public censure and internal self-censorship in domestic music production and performance—is given historical depth by Garofalo, who draws our attention to the broad transformation of popular music's ideological charge, from one privileging "rebellion, defiance, protest, opposition, and resistance" to one "used in the service of mourning, healing, patriotism, and nation building." By contrast, Doubleday explains how the (partial) ousting of the Taliban regime in late 2001 produced a (fragile) relaxation in rules governing music performance and an influx of exiled Afghan musicians who hoped to resume their musical activities in this newly permissive environment. As she points out, however, any gains in this sphere have been significantly hampered by the weight of several decades of unremitting, extreme violence; the mounting number of local victims to the continuing military conflict; and continued societal ambivalence toward music-making—all of which have sapped the vitality of the post-9/11 Afghan music scene.

A DISCIPLINARY OPENING: OPPORTUNITIES AND OBLIGATIONS FOR POST-9/11 MUSIC SCHOLARSHIP

I close this introduction with a reflection on the historical moment in which this volume was produced and the place of music scholarship in the post-9/11 world. Currently, the disquieting effects of the interpenetration of economies, cultures, and ideologies commonly referred to as globalization, set against a background of entrenched regional animosities and punctuated by snowballing acts of extreme violence cast as retributive justice, have led to pervasive rhetoric in the United States describing contemporary global relations in the stark terms of Samuel Huntington's (1996) "clash of civilizations." In a recent paper on the embattled state of multiculturalism in the wake of 9/11, David Palumbo-Liu characterized this trend as an "imbrication of nationalist and civilizational thinking" in which "national interests" are projected as synonymous with "civilizational imperatives," and where the word "civilization" is employed as a transparent euphemism for religion (2002: 10). The effect of this rhetorical strategy is to boil the world's complexity down into a zero-sum oppositional relation between Self and Other (cf. Radano and Bohlman 2000: 5–10). It is important to note here that the rhetoric of Al Qaeda is disconcertingly similar, if less euphemistic, casting the world in terms of the religious faithful versus the infidels. In a phantasmagoric reproduction of the Cold War struggle between superpowers, the current conflict is presented by both sides as global in scope, open-ended in length, and apocalyptic in consequence.

By reducing the options for maneuvering through this environment to the binary minimum of "us" and "them," nationalist dogma on one side and religionist dogma on the other are effectively bleeding the nuance out of experience. In tense and momentous times such as these, the place of music scholarship, or even its relevance, may seem less than clear to some.

At the same time, an increasing number of scholars are arguing that our current state of affairs lends a new urgency to the traditional mission of the humanities. In a recent lecture titled "Terror: A Speech After 9/11," Gayatri Chakravorty Spivak proposed that the best hope for navigating between the Scylla and Charybdis of post-9/11 fundamentalisms lies in the humanities' "persistent attempt at an uncoercive rearrangement of desires" (2004: 81), the slow cultivation of an ethic that "listen[s] to the other as if it were a self, neither to punish nor to acquit" (83). Similarly, Palumbo-Liu has argued for a return to humanism, and more specifically to "critical multiculturalism," defined as "multiculturalism that focuses on the material historical productions of difference rather than on 'culture' as a ready-made thing" (2002: 110). The contributors to *Music in the Post-9/11 World* participate in these broad mandates. In doing so, they take up the challenge that Gage Averill posed to himself after living through 9/11 in New York: "to criticize the nefarious uses to which the power of music is put, to continue to campaign against censorship and political regulation of music, and to encourage the rich exploration of music as a connective tissue in human interaction and as a medium that makes clearer our shared humanity" (2001).

One can proclaim the need for music scholarship in the post-9/11 world without harboring quixotic illusions of scholarship's potential to save it. Indeed, the collective position of the authors of this volume is far from utopian: their essays reflect a grim realization of the powerful ideologies that polarize the attitudes and even consciousness of large populaces around the globe. Skeptical of the odds of success in their attempts to counter the inexorable logic of violence and retribution, imperialism and jihad, they nonetheless continue to listen, generously and critically, to musical voices in the post-9/11 world. In so doing, they hold open a discursive space, however small, in which new musical, social, and political worlds can be imagined.

REFERENCES

Averill, Gage. 1997. *A Day for the Hunter, a Day for the Prey: Popular Music and Power in Haiti.* Chicago: University of Chicago Press.

———. 2001. "Soundly Organized Humanity." *ECHO: A Music-Centered Journal* 3(2). http://www.echo.ucla.edu/volume3-issue2/sept11_roundtable/averill_response.html.

Baudrillard, Jean. 2002. "L'esprit du Terrorisme." Translated by Michel Valentin. *The South Atlantic Quarterly* 101(2): 403–15.

Bell, John. 2003. "Performance Studies in an Age of Terror." *The Drama Review* 47(2): 6–8.

Bohlman, Philip. 1993. "Musicology as a Political Act." *Journal of Musicology* 11(4): 411–36.

Borneman, John. 2002. "Genital Anxiety." *Anthropological Quarterly* 75(1): 129–137.

Butterfield, Bradley. 2002. "The Baudrillardian Symbolic, 9/11, and the War of Good and Evil." *Postmodern Culture* 13(1).

Gussow, Adam. 2002. *Seems Like Murder Here: Southern Violence and the Blues Tradition.* Chicago: University of Chicago Press.

Hershberg, Eric, and Kevin Moore. 2002. "Introduction: Place, Perspective and Power—Interpreting September 11." In *Critical Views of September 11: Analyses From Around the World,* edited by Eric Hershberg and Kevin Moore, 1–19. New York: The New Press.

Hobsbawm, Eric. 1996. *The Age of Extremes: A History of the World 1914–1991.* New York: Vintage Books.

Huntington, Samuel. 1996. *The Clash of Civilizations and the Remaking of World Order.* New York: Simon & Schuster.

Kocka, Jürgen. 1995. "The Short Twentieth Century from a European Perspective." *History Teacher* 28(4): 471–77.

LaFreniere, Bree. 2000. *Music Through the Dark: A Tale of Survival in Cambodia.* Honolulu: University of Hawaii Press.

Lentricchia, Frank and Jody McAuliffe. 2002. "Groundzeroland." *The South Atlantic Quarterly* 101(2): 349–59.

Longinovic, Tomislav. 2000. "Music Wars: Blood and Song at the End of Yugoslavia." In *Music and the Racial Imagination,* edited by Ronald Radano and Philip V. Bohlman, 622–43. Chicago; London: University of Chicago Press.

McDowell, John. 2000. *Poetry and Violence: The Ballad Tradition of Mexico's Costa Chica.* Urbana: University of Illinois Press.

Palumbo-Liu, David. 2002. "Multiculturalism Now: Civilization, National Identity, and Difference Before and After September 11th." *boundary 2* 29(2): 109–27.

Pettan, Svanibor, ed. 1998. *Music, Politics and War: Views from Croatia.* Zagreb: Institute of Ethnology and Folklore Research.

Pollock, Sheldon, Homi Bhabha, Carol Breckenridge, and Dipesh Chakrabarty. 2000. "Introduction: Cosmopolitanisms." *Public Culture* 12(3): 577–89.

Radano, Ronald, and Philip V. Bohlman. 2000. "Introduction: Music and Race, Their Past, Their Presence." In *Music and the Racial Imagination,* edited by Ronald Radano and Philip V. Bohlman, 1–53. Chicago; London: University of Chicago Press.

Ritter, Jonathan. 2006. "A River of Blood: Music, Memory, and Violence in Ayacucho, Peru." Ph.D. diss., University of California, Los Angeles.

Scruggs, T. M. 2002. "Socially Conscious Music Forming the Social Conscience: Nicaraguan Musica Testimonial and the Creation of a Revolutionary Moment. In *From Tejano to Tango: Essays on Latin American Popular Music,* edited by Walter Aaron Clark, 41–69. New York and London: Routledge.

Shapiro-Phim, Toni. 2002. "Dance, Music, and the Nature of Terror in Democratic Kampuchea." In *Annihilating Difference: The Anthropology of Genocide,* edited by Alexander Laban Hinton, 179–93. Berkeley and Los Angeles: University of California Press.

Schechner, Richard. 2006. *Performance Studies: An Introduction.* 2nd ed. New York; London: Routledge.

Spanos, William V. 2003. "A Rumor of War: 9/11 and the Forgetting of the Vietnam War." *boundary 2* 30(3): 29–66.

Spivak, Gayatri Chakravorty. 2004. "Terror: A Speech after 9-11." *boundary 2* 31(2): 81–111.

Stein, Howard. 2003. "Days of Awe: September 11, 2001 and its Cultural Psychodynamics." *Journal for the Psychoanalysis of Culture and Society* 8(2): 187–99.

Zuber, Devin. 2006. "Flanerie at Ground Zero: Aesthetic Countermemories in Lower Manhattan." *American Quarterly* 58(2): 269–99.

NOTES

1. Some, of course, have argued that the first performances on that day were the attacks themselves. See Schechner 2006: 263–84, cf. Averill 2001.

2. Several scholars have interpreted the attack on the World Trade Center in distinctly Freudian terms, positing that the terrorists succeeded in performing a symbolic castration of the nation. See, for example, Borneman 2002: 136–37, and Stein 2003: 193.

3. Composed on a U.S. Army base in 1918 by a Jewish emigrant from Siberia as part of a now-defunct musical, Irving Berlin's song was shelved for twenty years before gaining a new life through Kate Smith's Armistice Day performance of 1938. However, the song attained nationwide popularity only after it was performed, again by Kate Smith, in the 1943 film, "This Is the Army." Sung against a montage of clips of military equipment being assembled, this rendition added a thick layer of wartime associations to the piece's reception history.

4. The literature on the relationship between music and violence is rapidly expanding. Some important recent works include Averill 1997, Bohlman 1993, Gussow 2002, LaFreniere 2000, Longinovic 2000, McDowell 2000, Pettan 1998, Ritter 2006, Scruggs 2002, and Shapiro-Phim 2002.

5. Stockhausen made this statement at a press conference held in Hamburg on September 16 to publicize his twenty-eight-hour performance cycle titled *Licht*. Stockhausen's statement was generally vilified in the press; the composer has argued that it was taken out of context (Bell 2003: 7). The translation used here is taken from Frank Lentricchia and Jody McAuliffe's (2002) discussion of the controversy.

Part One:

Music, the United States, and the Mass Media After 9/11

1

POP GOES TO WAR, 2001–2004:

U.S. POPULAR MUSIC AFTER 9/11

Reebee Garofalo

Mainstream popular music in the United States has always provided a window on national politics. The middle-of-the-road sensibilities of Tin Pan Alley told us as much about societal values in the early twentieth century as rock and roll's spirit of rebellion did in the fifties and sixties. To cite but one prominent example, as the war in Vietnam escalated in the mid-sixties, popular music provided something of a national referendum on our involvement. In 1965 and 1966, while the nation was sorely divided on the issue, both the antiwar "Eve of Destruction" by Barry McGuire and the military ode "The Ballad of the Green Berets" by Barry Sadler hit number one within months of each other. As the war dragged on through the Nixon years and military victory seemed more and more remote, however, public opinion began to turn against the war, and popular music became more and more clearly identified with the antiwar movement.

Popular music—and in particular, rock—has nonetheless served contradictory functions in American history. While popular music fueled opposition to the Vietnam War at home, alienated, homesick GIs eased the passage of time by blaring those same sounds on the battlefield (as films such as *Apocalypse Now* and *Good Morning, Vietnam* accurately document). Rock thus was not only the soundtrack of domestic opposition to the war; it was the soundtrack of the war itself. This phenomenon was not wasted on military strategists, who soon began routinely incorporating music into U.S. military "psychological operations." When the United States invaded Grenada in 1983, one of the first military objectives was to take over the government-run radio station. Just before Manuel Noriega was arrested in Panama, the military "blasted" him out of his compound with barrages of high-volume rock. The United States has used rock more recently in similar ways throughout the Middle East. In some sense, then, rock has become the sound that the U.S. military uses to announce its presence in foreign lands. Still, until recently, popular music—or what I would identify more precisely as the rock and rap axis of popular music—has been linked primarily with liberal to left-wing issues and causes.

In the mid-eighties and nineties, a new chapter in the politics of American popular music opened with a series of globalized fund-raising concerts and politicized rock and rap songs, all addressing a range of social issues that included hunger and starvation in Africa, apartheid, the deteriorating environment, homelessness, child abuse, racism, AIDS, industrial plant closings, and U.S. intervention in Central America, to name but a few. Providing a counterpoint to this liberal humanitarian impulse, the Parents Music Resource Center, joined by a number of conservative Christian organizations, waged a campaign against popular music to promote their vision of a more wholesome culture. In this way popular music became a primary site of contestation over American values and identities, with conservatives (and some prominent liberals) opposing prevailing musical practices at every turn.

Then came September 11, 2001. The terrorist attacks that leveled the World Trade Center towers, blew a hole in the side of the Pentagon, and crashed a plane in a Pennsylvania field shook the United States out of its sense of security, elicited sympathy (however short-lived) from nations around the world, and plunged the economy into a prolonged tailspin. The role of contemporary popular music also changed dramatically as it adjusted to this new political reality. If popular music had previously been associated with rebellion, defiance, protest, opposition, and resistance, it would now be used in the service of mourning, healing, patriotism, and nation building. In this new order, the dissent—and in particular the antiwar protest music—that helped provide the basis for the national debate on Vietnam was nowhere to be found on mainstream media during the invasions of Afghanistan and Iraq. If anything, country anthems that pushed the envelope in support of government policy seemed more likely to capture the popular imagination.

As Martin Cloonan has argued, "post 9/11 it became increasingly hard for musicians to express dissent, not because music had lost its power to be able to do this, but because of a changed political climate."[1] This new political context included decisive conservative control over all three branches of government, legislation and executive practices that privileged national security over civil liberties, and concentration and consolidation in the music industry itself that narrowed the diversity of voices in the musical marketplace. The purpose of this essay is to document the events that have ushered in this new context within the American mediascape, and discuss their effects on freedom of expression generally and on popular music as a social indicator in particular. I focus on five aspects of this recent history: (1) initial popular music responses to 9/11; (2) the role of country music in endorsing military action; (3) the new conservative activism of corporate radio; (4) musicians' responses to government disincentives to political protest; and (5) fledgling attempts by progressive musicians to engage the political process.

INITIAL RESPONSES

While the initial shock of 9/11 briefly transformed all media into news outlets—and, for a time, even held out the possibility that hard news might replace the tabloid fare consumers had come to expect—people soon returned to music to minister to their emotional (if not their intellectual) needs. In fact, the music industry was among the first to mount an institutional response to the tragic events. In addition to massive individual contributions—Dr. Dre, for example, personally donated one million dollars to the victim-relief effort and countless others earmarked proceeds from tour dates—the music/entertainment community turned to the ensemble benefit concerts and all-star recordings that had become tried and true fund-raising strategies since Live Aid and "We Are the World."

Prior to the attacks, U2's Bono had already recruited hip-hop producer Jermaine Dupree and artists Christina Aguilera, Backstreet Boys, Mary J. Blige, Wyclef Jean, Michael Stipe, and others to record an ensemble version of Marvin Gaye's 1971 classic "What's Goin' On" for Artists Against AIDS Worldwide. In the aftermath of 9/11, they added the United Way's September 11 Fund as a beneficiary. Arista re-released Whitney Houston's stirring 1991 Super Bowl performance of "The Star-Spangled Banner," with proceeds earmarked for New York firefighters. The Houston single shot up charts, peaking at number six, and sustained enough momentum to finish 2002 as the ninth most popular song of the year. Columbia rushed production on a compilation album called *God Bless America,* featuring a cross section of artists such as Celine Dion, Bruce Springsteen, Mariah Carey, Lee Greenwood, Bob Dylan, and Frank Sinatra, with "a substantial portion of the proceeds" earmarked for The Twin Towers Fund. Michael Jackson ultimately failed to release an ensemble recording of his new composition "What More Can I Give," which included

Destiny's Child, Backstreet Boys, Tom Petty, and Seal, among many others, but the song was performed at the October 22 "United We Stand" benefit in Washington, D.C., which raised $3 million.

Concerts to benefit the victims of 9/11 were organized with remarkable efficiency and cooperation among all sectors of the music business. The first and most impressive of these, staged on September 21, just ten days after the attacks, was "America: A Tribute to Heroes." The event included twenty-two performing artists and fifty actors staffing telephones, and was transmitted over the big four commercial networks, as well as thirty cable channels, without credits or commercial interruptions. The Tribute raised $160 million from its East Coast broadcast alone, making it the largest single fund-raising event in history, even before the DVD and compilation CD were released. A month later, on October 21, the "Concert for New York City" was held in Madison Square Garden. Produced by VH-1, Cablevision, Miramax, and AOL, and headlined by Paul McCartney, the concert featured a number of British and American rock acts, and generated $30 million for the New York Fire Department. Finally, the Beastie Boys organized "New Yorkers Against Violence," a two-night fund-raiser at the Hammerstein Ballroom that brought together Moby, Michael Stipe, Bono, Mos Def, and the Strokes. Significantly, it was the only U.S.-based 9/11 event of its kind that was explicitly committed to nonviolence.

A comparison between "America: A Tribute to Heroes" and the "Concert for New York City," produced just one month apart, reveals the trajectory of the new social role for popular music in the post-9/11 context. In the month that separated these two events, the United States invaded Afghanistan. The character of these two events thus marked the transition from the initial shock immediately following 9/11, when the nation was plunged into grief, to the more calculated and vengeful search for those responsible.

"America: A Tribute to Heroes" was an understated, reverential event, which captured the national mood during a brief moment of what I would call "gentle patriotism." In an effort to achieve the proper tone, the tribute's dominant aesthetic was that of *MTV Unplugged,* within which the event scheduled a diversity of performers including Bruce Springsteen, Bon Jovi, Mariah Carey, Alicia Keys, Faith Hill, the Dixie Chicks, Sting, Paul Simon, Limp Bizkit, Sheryl Crow, and Wyclef Jean, among others. As Kip Pegley and Susan Fast note elsewhere in this volume, the event downplayed the star power of these performers to create a sense of community that included the performers and television viewers at home. Within the generally respectful atmosphere, a number of performers articulated sentiments that hinted at the mixed concerns and competing agendas that characterized the initial response to the attacks. Will Smith introduced Mohammad Ali as a Muslim in a segment that included footage of Muslim children in America expressing fears of retaliation. In their defense, Stevie Wonder chastised those who "hate in the name of God or Allah" in his intro to "Love's in Need of Love Today." The only overtly conservative commentary was offered by Clint Eastwood, who referred to 9/11 as "the twenty-first century's day of infamy." If Tom Petty's toned down, but still somewhat aggressive, rendition of "I Won't Back Down" was a call to arms for the nationalist project that was about to get underway, it was offset by Neil Young's stirring performance of John Lennon's "Imagine," which conjured up visions of a world with neither religions nor countries and "nothing to fight or die for." And if something like Celine Dion's bloated arrangement of "God Bless America" was considered obligatory for a moment like this, noticeably absent was "The Star-Spangled Banner" with its "rockets' red glare" and "bombs bursting in air." It should also be noted that the all-cast version of "America the Beautiful" led by Willie Nelson that closed the show included the second verse, which calls on America to "Confirm thy soul in self-control/Thy liberty in law."

If "America: A Tribute to Heroes" attempted to be a muted, measured response to the tragedy of 9/11, the "Concert for New York City" was a grand, commercialized, public extravaganza staged at Madison Square Garden that announced to the world, as host Billy Crystal said in his opening remarks, "that we're not afraid to go out"—this in contrast to the "America" tribute, which, for security reasons, was staged in undisclosed locations. Crystal then introduced "6,000 special guests"— all the firefighters, policemen, and emergency workers for whom the show was produced, who were present in uniform and assigned to the best seats in the house—in contrast to the "America" tribute, which had no live audience. While the "America" tribute tended to obscure celebrity, the New York concert welcomed it with all its attendant fanfare, as each media personality, actor, political figure, and performer was introduced by name. Crystal set the political tone for the event with his introductory comment that "We're showing everybody that we don't hide in caves like cowards," a sentiment later echoed by former president Bill Clinton. The concert also offered a platform to other political figures ranging from Tom Daschle and Hillary Clinton to George Pataki and Rudy Giuliani.

Musically, the concert was a tribute to white, male, guitar-based rock in both its line-up and performance styles. The increased testosterone level of the music was a clear indicator of the change in mood, emotional tone, and political will that was taking place in the United States. While some measure of diversity was provided by rapper Jay-Z (who had to be explained to the audience by Mark Wahlberg) and Destiny's Child (who were introduced in a sexually demeaning way by Chris Kattan), the bill was dominated by British and American rockers including Billy Joel, Bon Jovi, John Mellencamp, David Bowie, Eric Clapton, The Who, Mick Jagger and Keith Richards, Elton John, and Paul McCartney. Though there were more American performers overall, the press treated the show as if it was another British Invasion, which resonated well with Britain's support for U.S. policy over the next few years.

As the headliner, Paul McCartney—who was often identified erroneously in the press as the organizer of the event—closed the show. McCartney's very presence was significant as the primary link between the first British Invasion and the present alliance between Britain and the United States. He performed three Beatles songs—"I'm Down," "Yesterday," and "Let It Be"—and showcased his new song "Freedom," which he reportedly wrote as he was sitting in a plane on a New York runway when the World Trade Center was hit. "Freedom" includes the cautionary line: "Anyone who tries to take it away, they'll have to answer." In five short weeks talk of helping and healing had begun to give way to the rhetoric of revenge and retribution. Of all the speakers and performers who appeared at the concert, only the actor Richard Gere attempted to deliver a message of moderation when he talked about "the possibility of taking . . . all this horrendous energy that we're feeling . . . and turn[ing] it into compassion and to love and to understanding." He was roundly booed for his trouble.

The theme of revenge for the September 11 attacks was foreshadowed in Bon Jovi's performance of "Wanted Dead or Alive," which echoed President Bush's pronouncements regarding the capture of Osama bin Laden. But it was The Who that put it over the top. Who better to give vent to the anger in the room than the group that practically invented the symbolic release of violent emotion as part of their stage act? Opening their set with classic Pete Townshend power chords on "Who Are You"—now a query to the terrorists—the group performed their high-energy single in front of a Union Jack background, as if to recall their use of the British flag as a pop-cultural icon in the 1960s and to let the audience know that Britain was still in the house. As they segued into "Baba O'Reilly," the background changed to an American flag. Following "Behind Blue Eyes," they closed their set with "Won't Get Fooled Again"—easily read as a message to Al Qaeda—performing before a Union Jack flanked by two American flags, solidifying the special relationship between the two countries.

This theme of the conspicuous display of the American flag as a fashion statement of patriotism reached its peak during U2's halftime performance at Super Bowl XXXVI in early 2002, where Bono visibly displayed the American flag lining of his jacket (à la Roger Daltrey's Union Jack jacket circa 1968), and the band unfurled a giant scrim that listed the names of all the 9/11 victims. In keeping with the new pop reality, as artists rushed to show their support for a grieving nation, many seemed to retreat from the ideological positions on which their earlier reputations were built. The Who songs performed at the "Concert for New York City," which once threw down the gauntlet of intergenerational conflict, were resignified as antiterrorist anthems. The U2 at the Super Bowl was a very different band than the one whose defining moments included images of Bono carrying a white flag as he ranted against war on "Sunday, Bloody Sunday" in 1983. The post-9/11 McCartney related differently to the prospect of a long-term occupation of a foreign country than he did in 1972 when he protested the British occupation of Northern Ireland on "Give Ireland Back to the Irish."

Many artists also seemed to take unpredictable positions as spokespeople. Neil Young shocked his audience at the 2001 People for the American Way gala, at which he received a Spirit of Liberty Lifetime Achievement Award, when he endorsed administration policy by saying that "we're going to have to relinquish some of our freedoms for a short period of time."[2] Even Bruce Springsteen paid Bush an offhanded compliment when he told the *London Times* just before the release of *The Rising*: "The war in Afghanistan was handled well. It was deliberative, which I wasn't counting on. I expected a lot less from this administration."[3] Clearly, some of the biggest names in popular music—artists who would have been identified with an oppositional stance in a previous era—had adopted new positions in response to a new political reality.

COUNTRY MUSIC MATTERS

While rock has generally been associated with a loud, aggressive stance pitted in opposition to the status quo (despite the contradictions and ambiguities revealed in the preceding discussion), country music has always been coded as conservative and patriotic. So it was perhaps not surprising to see lyric content overwhelmingly supporting administration policy in post-9/11 country music. From the 9/11 attacks through the war in Afghanistan to the invasion of Iraq, popular country hits followed a rough trajectory from thoughtful reflection to conservative patriotism to strident fight songs.

On October 28, 2001—he remembers the exact date—Alan Jackson penned "Where Were You (When the World Stopped Turning)," which went straight to number one on the country singles chart and crossed over to the top thirty on the pop charts. "Where Were You" was a thoughtful rumination on the kinds of things people might have been doing when the Twin Towers were struck; it recalled the notion that most people remembered exactly what they were doing when John F. Kennedy was assassinated. Around the same time Aaron Tippin weighed in with "Where the Stars and Stripes and the Eagle Fly," which became the ninth most popular song of 2001. Lee Greenwood's "God Bless the USA"—which appeared on four different compilations by the end of 2001—came in at number six for the year. Both songs expressed pride in America and a willingness to pay a price to defend her freedom. It is remarkable that these songs found their way into the year-end top ten with only a couple of months of sales.

Greenwood actually had written his anthem in 1984; it became the title song on his 1990 album of the same name, during the buildup to the first Gulf War. At that time, Greenwood had turned to patriotism to bolster a flagging career. According to one biographer: "Though he tried to retain his audience through patriotic work during the 1991 Gulf War—even earning the Congressional Medal of Honor Society's Patriot Award and a Points of Light Foundation Award—he couldn't success-fully battle the onslaught of harder-edged, contemporary country artists that overtook country radio in the early '90s. By the middle of the decade, he was no longer charting singles."[4] The 9/11 attacks propelled "God Bless the USA" (and Greenwood) back into the upper reaches of the pop charts, and the war in Afghanistan provided the hit single with enough momentum to finish 2002 as the eleventh most popular song of that year as well.

In a similar way, Aaron Tippin began his career as a recording artist in 1991, releasing "You've Got to Stand for Something" from his debut album of the same name, in the wake of the first Gulf War. The song became a top-ten hit, and Tippin was invited to join Bob Hope's USO tour. A decade later, "Where the Stars and Stripes and the Eagle Fly" became a crossover hit that reached the pop top twenty. A number of other artists also recorded patriotic songs during the time frame of the first Gulf War. In 1990, Hank Williams, Jr. released "Don't Give Us a Reason," which told "old Saddam" that "you figured wrong." Billy Ray Cyrus contributed "Some Gave All" from the eponymous 1992 album.

If the sheer tragedy and disorientation of 9/11 produced a somewhat restrained and reflective patriotism in pop country, the rhetoric sur-rounding the war in Afghanistan and the increasing demonization of

Iraq as part of the "axis of evil" set a different tone. It was Toby Keith's "Courtesy of the Red, White and Blue (The Angry American)" from *Unleashed* (2002) that captured the new vengeful attitude more than any other song. With a number of platinum releases to his name, Keith was no stranger to stardom, but it was "Courtesy"—which warns anyone who messes with the "U.S. of A." that "We'll put a boot in your ass / It's the American way"—that made him a household name. On the strength of the hit single, *Unleashed* hit number one in 2002 and was certified double platinum by year's end.

In the countdown to the war in Iraq, Darryl Worley's "Have You Forgotten," went to the top of the country chart in five weeks, reminding listeners "about Bin Laden / Have you forgotten?"[5] Pat Garrett continued in this vein with "Saddam Stomp," which made an explicit connection between the Iraqi leader and Osama bin Laden. In fact, both songs provided Bush with a sorely needed, if symbolic, link between Iraq and bin Laden, which he was having great difficulty demonstrating in reality. These were followed by Clint Black's "I Raq and Roll," which warned the enemies of the United States to "be careful where you tread" and Lynyrd Skynyrd's "Red, White, and Blue," whose message was summed up by singer Johnny Van Zant as "love it or leave it," providing the group with its first hit in years.

The fact that many of these songs became year-end bestsellers suggested that they hit a nerve among large segments of the U.S. populace. Indeed, support for official U.S. foreign policy was very strong at the time.[6] The momentum created by these songs encouraged artists from other genres to get on board. R. Kelly contributed "A Soldier's Heart." Ray Stevens scored with a novelty track "Osama – Yo' Mama," which criticized bin Laden's mother for not raising him correctly (this was the same Ray Stevens who had a top-five hit with "Ahab, The Arab" in 1962). Neil Young weighed in with "Let's Roll," in honor of the passengers who reportedly fought the hijackers on Flight 93. This song presented his more liberal rock fans with something of a dilemma, as it trumpeted what had already become one of President Bush's (appropriated) classic one-liners. As critic John Metzger put it:

> Part of the problem with "Let's Roll" is its uncomfortable lyricism. While it pays tribute to those on ill-fated Flight 93 . . . it's also impossible not to take it as supportive of the current Administration and their poorly planned war-run-amuck. To be fair, at the time of the song's writing, America was in shock and was more willing to concede to its leaders' whims. But with lines like, "We're goin' after Satan / On the wings of a Dove," the song now stands as an odd

statement from someone like Young who long has rallied against war and unjust government policy. Then again, Young also spent a portion of the '80s speaking in support of Ronald Reagan.[7]

The fact that most of these songs delivered a conservative message was not, in itself, all that surprising. The vehemence with which the country music establishment rejected any alternative perspectives, however, reflected a new moment in the nation's political polarization.

Steve Earle was a case in point. As much a rocker as a country artist, Earle's songwriting is sharp and edgy, tending toward outlaw country, and his progressive political point of view has seldom won him any friends in Nashville. As concerned and confused as anyone about the events of 9/11, Earle included "John Walker's Blues"—about John Walker Lindh, the "American Taliban"—on the album *Jerusalem* (2002). On this song, Earle attempted to get inside Walker Lindh's head to explore from his point of view what might have led an American youth searching for truth in Islam to take up arms with the Taliban. While *Jerusalem* was a top-ten country album, which crossed over to pop, conservative commentators routinely branded Earle a traitor or denounced him for being sympathetic to one for attempting to humanize Lindh.[8]

The boycott of the Dixie Chicks was even more dramatic. The Dixie Chicks rose to superstardom on the strength of their 1998 multiplatinum debut major label release *Wide Open Space*. On *Home* (2002), the Chicks went deeper into their country roots with traditional instrumentation and few concessions to pop sensibilities. *Home* debuted at number one on the *Billboard* album charts and garnered not only Country Music Awards, but also American Music Awards, People's Choice Awards, and four Grammys. *Home* also included "Travelin' Soldier," a tender love song about a Vietnam-era casualty, which had been the group's only commentary on war and its consequences. Riding the popularity of their blockbuster album, the Chicks were selected to sing the national anthem at the 2003 Super Bowl. For a time it seemed as though they were the darlings of the whole country. But while on tour in London in March 2003, lead singer Natalie Maines told her audience: "We're ashamed the President of the United States is from Texas," an obvious reference to her dissatisfaction with his handling of the impending war in Iraq. Although she issued an apology to President Bush within days, calling her remarks "disrespectful," the Dixie Chicks were banned on some seventy-four country radio stations in the United States. The message was clear: it was not an option to criticize the president during a sensitive period of military engagement.[9]

Intended to silence the Chicks, this action instead emboldened them. Like many women in country, the Dixie Chicks were made of strong stuff, and they were no strangers to feminist or First Amendment values. At the very first show of the U.S. leg of their continuing tour, they addressed the controversy head-on with the performance of "Truth #2," a song about standing up for one's beliefs, during which they showed video footage of civil-rights and gay-rights events and pro-choice demonstrations, in conjunction with slogans like "freedom" and "truth" projected on the screen. Maines was outspoken in her defense of First Amendment rights even in a time of crisis, at one point telling her concert audience, "If you're here to boo, we welcome that, because we welcome freedom of speech."[10] Despite the country radio boycott, their sixty-two-date U.S. tour nearly sold out. Natalie Maines also held her own trading barbs with Toby Keith, whose "Courtesy of the Red White and Blue" she called "ignorant." The jousting reached its climax when Maines appeared on the Country Music Awards telecast wearing an "F.U.T.K." T-shirt.

CORPORATE RADIO STIFLES DISSENT

As pro-war anthems emerged as best-sellers in 2001 and 2002, protest and antiwar music remained underground and was seldom heard on mainstream radio. This absence of protest was notable, especially by the time of the war in Iraq. While the invasion of Afghanistan was generally applauded by the U.S. populace and widely supported abroad, nothing approaching a consensus existed at the advent of the Iraq War. World opinion was clearly opposed to a unilateral military action, and even in the United States the antiwar movement had established a significant national presence well before the war began. Many peace activists began to wonder aloud if protest music hadn't died.[11] In fact, there was plenty of protest music being produced; it simply wasn't being played on radio. The reasons behind this are complex and include a new level of consolidation in the radio industry in the wake of the 1996 Telecommunications Act, a period of suppression and self-censorship following the passage of the 2001 Patriot Act, and a new activist role for corporate radio deriving from a more conservative political climate and explicit ties to the Bush administration.

Many observers blamed the 1996 Telecommunications Act for constricting media offerings in general. The 1996 law, twelve years in the making, was the first major overhaul of the telecom landscape since the Communications Act of 1934. Often cited as a model of bipartisan cooperation, the legislation altered the telecom sector in ways that were not always beneficial to the consumer. The controversial Communications Decency Act, which was inserted as part of the legislation (and later declared unconstitutional by the Supreme Court), drew considerable attention away from one of the central provisions of the Act—the relaxation of the rules of ownership for media corporations. As a result, the concentration of media ownership within a handful of industry giants has increased significantly since the passage of this landmark bill.

When Ben Bagdikian wrote *The Media Monopoly* in 1983, he expressed concern that fifty corporations controlled most of the major mass-media outlets. By the 1990s, that number had shrunk to fewer than twenty and, as the new millennium began, it reached low single digits in the radio industry, with just four companies controlling 90 percent of the ad revenue.[12] In 2003, the FCC under the direction of Michael Powell, the son of Secretary of State Colin Powell, sought to relax the rules of ownership still further. It wasn't until hundreds of thousands of irate voters—and a list of organizations that included such a diversity of groups as the National Rifle Association, the Catholic Conference of Bishops, and the National Organization for Women—complained to their elected representatives, that Congress halted, even if temporarily, this headlong rush toward further media consolidation.

This level of concentration had serious implications for programming. Though there were about 30,000 CDs released in the United States in 2001, each of which contained on average more than a dozen songs, national radio hardly noticed. "In one recent week," reported *Rolling Stone* in August 2001, "the forty top modern-rock stations added a total of sixteen new songs, and the biggest forty-five Top Forty stations added a total of twenty."[13]

Clear Channel, the largest radio chain in the United States, was the poster corporation for these developments. In 1995, prior to the passage of the Telecom Act, Clear Channel owned forty-three radio stations. By the early 2000s it had acquired more than 1,200 stations in the United States, which took in more than $3 billion, or 20 percent of the industry dollar volume, in 2001; it had a lock on outdoor advertising, owning over 700,000 billboards; and it controlled 65 percent of the U.S. concert business, with a $1.1 billion gross from concert tours alone in 2002. In total, the corporation posted annual revenues in excess of $8 billion in 2002.[14] By this time the music industry was awash in stories of record companies decrying the difficulty of breaking new artists on the centrally programmed chain, and artists complaining that if they chose not to perform at a Clear Channel concert venue, they would pay the price in radio play.

Even without any political intent, then, it was clear that the "natural" commercial tendencies of corporate radio in the post-9/11 context played a major role in narrowing the range of cultural expression that might speak to topical issues of concern. Noting that popular hits like Crosby, Stills, Nash, and Young's "Ohio" had "played a crucial role in the national debate over the Vietnam War," Brent Staples argued in the *New York Times*, "A comparable song about George W. Bush's rush to war in Iraq would have no chance at all today. There are plenty of angry people, many with prime music-buying demographics. But independent radio stations that once would have played edgy, political music have been gobbled up by corporations that control hundreds of stations and have no wish to rock the boat."[15]

In the days immediately following the attacks of 9/11, for example, a program director at Clear Channel began to circulate among member stations a list of more than 150 "questionable" songs as potentially "inappropriate" for airplay.[16] Defended by Clear Channel as a simple act of sensitivity toward the victims' families, the list was denounced by its critics as an act of suppression and quickly took its place as part of a running battle pitting civil liberties and freedom of expression against the need for national unity and internal security. While the corporation reportedly never actually forbade any of its stations from playing a particular song, one thing was perfectly clear: given how centrally Clear Channel was organized and programmed, any list of songs to be avoided that was sent out from corporate headquarters was likely to be read as more than a suggestion.

The list included some obvious choices like Metallica's "Seek and Destroy" and AC/DC's "Shot Down in Flames" that could be credibly defended as inappropriate, and some not so obvious selections such as Carole King's "I Feel the Earth Move" and the Bangles' "Walk Like an Egyptian," whose transgressions appeared highly metaphorical at best and illusory at worst. The fact that the list also included "all Rage Against the Machine songs" further raised the specter of censorship, as this constituted the elimination of the entire body of work by a single group. Most surprising to many observers, John Lennon's "Imagine" was also included on the list, which made it all the more interesting that it was the song Neil Young chose to perform at *America: A Tribute to Heroes* the following week.

Clear Channel's choice of songs like "Imagine" said something about their particular approach. In the days and weeks following 9/11, all media outlets were concerned about what would be appropriate to play. An MTV spokesperson reported, "The music department started picking through the playlist in the library to figure out what we might add, what would be meaningful."[17] Most of the outlets that took this approach included "Imagine"—alongside other selections like Bob Marley's "One Love" and Prince's "When Doves Cry"—as songs that would provide solace and comfort in the midst of all the pain. In adopting a negative approach by choosing to eliminate a selection that most stations regarded positively, Clear Channel's practices could only be read as further reducing the diversity of voices in an era of already shrinking playlists.

Clear Channel also went on to adopt an activist posture that marked a new role for corporate radio. As the nation went to war against Iraq, grassroots peace activists organized numerous antiwar demonstrations around the country. Around the same time, a series of pro-administration events bearing the name "Rally for America" attracted up to 20,000 participants each in cities including Atlanta, Cleveland, San Antonio, and Cincinnati. At first, much like their antiwar counterparts, these rallies appeared to be organized from the ground up as spontaneous local events and were reported as such. It was later revealed that the rallies were organized and sponsored by Clear Channel, and at least two of them had been promoted on the company's Web site. "While labor unions and special interest groups have organized and hosted rallies for decades," wrote Tim Jones in the *Chicago Tribune,* where Clear Channel owned six radio stations, "the involvement of a big publicly regulated broadcasting company breaks new ground in public demonstrations." Added former Federal Communications Commissioner Glen Robinson, a law professor at the University of Virginia, "I can't say that this violates any of a broadcaster's obligations, but it sounds like borderline manufacturing of the news."[18]

It is not difficult to imagine that Clear Channel's support for administration policy might have been motivated by the fact that they had upcoming business before the FCC—business that would have allowed the radio giant to expand considerably, particularly into television. Furthermore, an even more troubling connection to the Bush family itself was also revealed. While a number of investigative reporters were connecting the dots between the Bush Administration and Middle East oil—not just between Vice President Cheney and the Halliburton Corporation, but between the Bush and bin Laden families as well—Paul Krugman, writing in the *New York Times,* also traced a direct connection from President Bush to Clear Channel:

> Experienced Bushologists let out a collective "Aha!" when Clear Channel was revealed to be behind the pro-war rallies, because the company's top management has a history with George W. Bush. The

vice chairman of Clear Channel is Tom Hicks. . . . When Mr. Bush was governor of Texas, Mr. Hicks was chairman of the University of Texas Investment Management Company, called Utimco, and Clear Channel's chairman, Lowry Mays, was on its board. Under Mr. Hicks, Utimco placed much of the university's endowment under the management of companies with strong Republican Party or Bush family ties. In 1998 Mr. Hicks purchased the Texas Rangers in a deal that made Mr. Bush a multimillionaire.[19]

It is, of course, always threatening to free expression when a public media company enjoys this degree of intimacy with any government agency, let alone the White House.

REAL PATRIOTS DON'T DISSENT

The restrictive, and at times partisan, practices of corporate radio were not the only reasons behind the lack of protest music on the national airwaves. Some observers felt that the passage of the Patriot Act had created a climate of intolerance for opposing viewpoints and caused many artists to censor themselves. Passed overwhelmingly by both houses of Congress one month after the 9/11 attacks, the Patriot Act created a Cabinet-level Department of Homeland Security and provided "enhanced surveillance" powers for police agencies, including so-called "sneak and peak" searches that allow police to enter and search a home or office without notifying the owner. It was revealed in a 2005 review of the Patriot Act that police had engaged in such searches 108 times in a twenty-two-month period. More important, the potential for abuse of civil liberties and the shroud of secrecy that had surrounded these practices clearly had a chilling effect on those who might otherwise have been inclined to express dissent.

Immediately following the passage of the Patriot Act, presidential strategist Karl Rove began meeting with leaders of the entertainment industry in a process that produced an uncommon consensus to close ranks around administration policy. Jack Valenti, then president of the Motion Picture Association of America, marveled at how the participating executives, "who are antagonists, who kill each other in the marketplace," produced "a circle of unity in that room, the likes of which I've never seen." Searching for a "new word" to describe this relationship with government, "one that encompasses the voluntary and patriotic nature of it," Bryce Zabel, chairman of the Academy of Television Arts and Sciences, exclaimed, "I think the new word is advocacy. We are now advocating America's message."[20] With homeland security as its prime directive, it was clear that tolerance for dissent was not on the agenda of the entertainment industry and that artists who chose to engage in it would be taking professional risks in doing so.

"We've seen dozens of acts quietly bury their edgier songs," complained Jeff Chang in 2002. "The Strokes pulled a song called 'New York Cops' from their album and Dave Matthews decided not to release 'When the World Ends' as a single."[21] When artists performed controversial protest material during this period, they often paid a price, even if in small, obscure ways. Bruce Springsteen was bold enough to perform "41 Shots" at one of his New York dates, about the N.Y.C. police shooting of unarmed Amadou Diallo, but it cost him his customary after-concert police escort to the airport. He chose not to include the controversial song on *The Rising*. On the tour supporting the release of *Riot Act*, Pearl Jam was accused of "impaling" a mask of the President on a microphone stand while performing "Bushleaguer" during an encore in Denver. Evidently spooked by subsequent calls for punitive action, they didn't play the song again for three weeks and removed it from the playlists of all but six of sixty scheduled tour dates. In 2003 Madonna reportedly withdrew a completed video for her "American Life" single because it portrayed her wearing army fatigues, tossing a grenade at a President Bush–like figure. Jethro Tull was banned from classic rocker WCHR-FM in New Jersey for complaining that drivers who hung American Flags from their cars and SUVs were confusing nationalism with patriotism. "As far as we're concerned," said program director and on-air personality Phil LoCascio, "this ban is forever."[22] In July 2004 Linda Ronstadt was banned from ever performing at the Aladdin Casino in Las Vegas after dedicating one of her songs to Michael Moore, as she had on every other date on her tour.

In such an unfriendly political climate and with the absence of radio play, many artists interested in protesting the war turned to the Internet, often posting protest songs as MP3s available for free download. A sampling of protest songs that were posted on the World Wide Web by major artists between Spring 2002 and Spring 2003 included the following:

Beastie Boys, "In a World Gone Mad"
Luka Bloom, "I Am Not at War with Anyone"
Billy Bragg, "The Price of Oil"
Chuck D, "A Twisted Sense of God"
Zack de la Rocha (w/DJ Shadow), "March of Death"
Nanci Griffith, "Big Blue Ball of War"
Mick Jones, "Why Do Men Fight"
Lenny Kravitz, "We Want Peace"

John McCutcheon, "We Know War"
John Mellencamp, "To Washington"
Meshell Ndegéocello, "Forgiveness & Love"
Leslie Nuchow, "An Eye for an Eye (Will Leave the Whole World Blind)"
R.E.M., "The Final Straw"
Spearhead, "Bomb the World"
Cat Stevens, "Peace Train"
System of a Down, "Boom!"

Because the Internet offered only limited possibilities for promoting such protest music, however, dissenting voices were often effectively silenced in the public sphere.

It is perhaps because of the pall that was cast over any meaningful dialogue about 9/11 that Bruce Springsteen's *The Rising*, released July 30, 2002, was greeted with such unbridled enthusiasm. Given Sony's promotional muscle and the return of the E-Street Band, a certain amount of gushing in the mainstream press was to be expected. What was more surprising was that the album was embraced, albeit with a few notable exceptions and some obligatory criticism, across the political spectrum from the *Socialist Worker* to *National Review*. To be sure, there was much to celebrate in *The Rising*. It avoided the jingoism and vengefulness of the most prominent 9/11 statements up to that date. And on songs like "Into the Fire," "You're Missing," and "Lonesome Day," Springsteen did what he does best: give voice to the voiceless, make everyday people his heroes, and try to build bridges that unite disparate people in their common humanity. At its best, *The Rising* is a sensitive, emotional engagement with the grief of 9/11 and a message of hope, all packaged in a rockin' good album. It is not, however, an overt political critique of 9/11 and its aftermath, and thus one can't help but wonder how much this contributed to its widespread acceptance.

The overwhelmingly positive reception of *The Rising* should not mask the fact that a multitude of statements about 9/11 were being made by popular musicians. Those that resonated with administration policy, like the conservative country anthems already examined, tended to get radio play. Those that were a bit edgier politically, like Steve Earle's "John Walker's Blues," were more likely to be met with harassment. Earle took on the politics of 9/11 even more directly on *Jerusalem*'s lead track, "Ashes to Ashes," where he reminds the listener that "every tower ever built tumbles, no matter how strong, no matter how tall." There were others as well. Released in the same time frame as *The Rising*, Sleater-Kinney's *One Beat* is brimming with anger and skepticism on cuts like "Far Away" and "Combat Rock," where Carrie Brownstein bellows, "Where is the protest song . . . dissent's not treason." A number of stalwarts continued to release antiwar material through the Iraq War. Just before the U.S. invasion, George Michael released a cover of Don McLean's "The Grave" after taking aim at British Prime Minister Tony Blair on "Shoot the Dog." Pearl Jam disparaged the president on "Bushleaguer," claiming "He's not a leader / He's a Texas leaguer." Public Enemy reinforced this notion on "Son of a Bush."

Throughout the post-9/11 period, the most radical anti-administration statements came from artists located in the more progressive sectors of punk and rap. Even before the United States invaded Afghanistan, Anti-Flag released "911 for Peace," whose chorus repeatedly shouts, "I don't wanna die, I don't wanna kill." NOFX addressed the Iraq War with "The Idiot Son of an Asshole," built simply around the endless repetition of the title's hook. Although rap had been roundly criticized for its violence, misogyny, and unabashed materialism throughout the 1990s and beyond, it was also the music that delivered the fullest, deepest, and most radical critique of U.S. foreign policy.

Special mention needs to be made of rap's relationship to the Twin Towers themselves and, therefore, to 9/11. As Murray Forman has astutely pointed out, "Following the 1993 terrorist bombing of the World Trade Center, MCs transformed the incident in their own unique manner into a potent metaphor that described the vulnerability of the city's urban infrastructures, commenting on the fallibility of those who possess authority and power."[23] The cover of Jeru the Damaja's *The Sun Rises in the East* (1994), for example, pictures the rapper hovering over the Manhattan financial district with the city skyline in flames and one of the WTC towers burned halfway to the ground. While Jeru the Damaja previewed the devastation of 9/11 visually, Dead Prez anticipated it in the lyrics of their 2000 release "Propaganda," when they rhymed: "Sign of the times, terrorism on the rise / Commercial airplanes, falling out the sky like flies."

This violent imagery inadvertently spilled over into the 9/11 era when the Oakland-based socialist rap group The Coup released *Party Music* in the summer of 2001. The original cover depicted the duo in front of the World Trade Center, with Boots Riley detonating bombs in both towers that looked frighteningly similar to photographs of the actual explosions of 9/11. Released more than two months before the Twin Towers were struck, The Coup defended their cover art as anticapitalist—not a statement about 9/11. Still, the group's label, 75Ark, quickly withdrew the cover. Oakland's fiercely political Paris picked up where The Coup had left off with the cover art on *Sonic Jihad* (2003), which depicts a speeding 747 about to crash into the White House. If The Coup's collision with 9/11 was an accident of history, Paris's cover was intentionally inflammatory. Controversial cover art was not the only thing these rappers had in common. Both also employed the infectious funk beats that had become a staple of West Coast rap to deliver their subversive messages. Between these two unabashedly political releases, there was a steady stream of pointed rap commentary throughout the post-9/11 period.

Somewhere between slam poet and dedicated hip-hop artist, Sage Francis released "Makeshift Patriot" in October 2001. The song, one of the first substantial responses to 9/11 in any genre, opens with a live audio track recorded by the artist at Ground Zero five days after the attacks. It leads to an extended rap set to a churchlike organ that captures all the horror ("Leaping lovers are making decisions to jump, while holding hands . . . to escape the brutal heat") and the contradictions ("We taught that dog to squat. How dare he do that shit in our own back yard!") of that fateful September day. He is clear about the outcome, however. "Freedom will be defended," he acknowledges, but quickly adds, "at the cost of civil liberties."

Some of rap's responses were more circumspect, manifesting their own internal tensions. Outkast's "The Whole World" presented a more vague, gut-level response to the initial attacks set to an up-tempo beat, as Big Boi moaned, "Lookin on the TV / Everything is looking Dismal." Talib Kweli expressed contradictory feelings toward police and other officials on "The Proud," accusing them one minute of killing "my people everyday" and admiring them the next for their selflessness at Ground Zero. On Wu Tang Clan's "Rules" Ghostface Killah, angry and confused over the bombings, showed respect toward Osama bin Laden with the line, "No disrespect, that's where I rest my head. I understand you gotta rest yours too nigga." But when he realizes that his people are dying as a result, he takes matters into his own hands: "Mr. Bush sit down, I'm in charge of this war."

As the war in Afghanistan began to segue into talk of invading Iraq with little in the way of hard evidence or concrete connections to justify it, some of the more outspoken political rappers took a more radical stance. Boston's Mr. Lif began "Home of the Brave" with a sample of a Kennedy speech that establishes thoughtful political protest as "the basis of all human morality." Then he tears into his subject, accusing Bush of stealing the presidency, asserting the complicity of the media, and going so far as to suggest that a war in the Middle East would amount to little more than a manipulation designed to divert people's attention from other pressing issues, such as a recession at home. Paris, who addressed the 1991 Gulf War with "Bush Killa," took this analysis to its logical conclusion on "What Would You Do," which was later included on the *Sonic Jihad* album. On this cut, Paris names Bush as the person who has the most to gain from a war in the Middle East and accuses the administration of creating an enemy to justify its actions: "It's plain to see / the oldest trick in the book is make an enemy / of phony evil now the government can do its dirt." On "Why" (2004), Jadakiss asked even more provocatively, "Why did Bush knock down the towers?"

There were hints of this dissatisfaction within the rap community among higher-profile artists as well. On "Rule" from *Stillmatic* (2002), Nas asked Bush to "call a truce, world peace, stop acting like savages." But these sentiments were overshadowed by the less important war between Nas and Jay-Z over rap supremacy in New York. Eminem included some critical verse in cuts like "Business" and "My Dad's Gone Crazy" on *The Eminem Show* (2002). The album's first video for "Without Me" featured the artist dressed as Osama bin Laden, doing the "running man" dance in a cave. On "Square Dance" he cautions young people about joining the war effort. For *Encore* (2004), Eminem (and Dr. Dre) produced a Spartan album with straightforward lyrics. On "Mosh" he unleashed a barrage of criticism, as he intoned "Fuck Bush, until they bring our troops home." Though these examples cannot be construed as the dominant message of rap and hip-hop in the first years following the attacks, they clearly establish the genre as the site of the most provocative political commentary in an otherwise timid and muted post-9/11 environment.

"TIME TO GET MAD"

By 2003, many musicians who were dissatisfied with this state of affairs began taking a more activist stance by joining forces with the broad-based Win Without War coalition, an organization that came together to prevent war in Iraq whose members included the NAACP, the National Council of Churches, Physicians for Social Responsibility and MoveOn, among others. Musicians United to Win Without War described itself as "a loose coalition of contemporary musicians who feel that in the rush to war by the Bush administration the voices of reason and debate have been trampled and ignored."[24] The group included the usual suspects, ranging from David Byrne and Sheryl Crowe to Ani DiFranco and Fugazi, as well as newcomers as diverse as Missy Elliot, Dave Matthews, and Bubba Sparxx. Other musicians, including Jackson Browne, Bonnie Raitt, and Michael Stipe, were also active but listed themselves as members of a sister organization, Artists United to Win Without War, which included mostly actors.

The momentum of their efforts brought together progressive voices across marketing categories as diverse as rock, rap, punk, and country. At MUWWW's founding press conference on February 27, 2003, Russell Simmons and Ben Chavis of the Hip Hop Summit Action Network gave the new group an additional shot in the arm by committing themselves, in the name of the hip-hop community, to joining the fledgling coalition. Rockers and rappers launched an energetic voter registration campaign, signing up nearly 100,000 new voters in a matter of weeks. MUWWW also convinced alt-country icons Emmy Lou Harris, Steve Earle, Rosanne Cash, and Lucinda Williams to sign their petition protesting the invasion of Iraq. By early 2004, a new group called the Music Row Democrats had formed in Nashville to organize a progressive political voice among country artists. Punks took a more aggressive stance. Under the leadership of Fat Mike from NOFX, they formed Punkvoter (www.punkvoter.com), dedicated to building a "united front in opposition to the dangerous, deadly, and destructive policies of George Bush, Jr." As Fat Mike told *The Nation*, "It's time to get mad."[25]

Although the invasion of Iraq proceeded without interruption, all this activity revealed considerable antiwar sentiment. Significantly, the partners in the Win Without War coalition were some of the same organizations and individuals protesting concentration in the mass media, the erosion of artists' and consumers' rights, and the globalization policies of the World Trade Organization. Attempting to pull these disparate strands of political activism into a united movement for social change, in November 2003, Billy Bragg launched the "Tell Us the Truth" Tour, which also featured Tom Morello now performing as the Nightwatchman, Steve Earle, Lester Chambers of the Chambers Brothers, and on some dates, rapper Boots Reilly of the Coup. The tour was sponsored by the AFL-CIO, Common Cause, The Future of Music Coalition, Free Press, and Morello's Axis of Justice. Other artists such as the Dixie Chicks, R.E.M., the Dave Matthews Band, Pearl Jam, James Taylor, John Mellencamp, and Bonnie Raitt joined the "Rock for Change Tour," mounted to support the Kerry/Edwards ticket in the 2004 presidential election. This electoral effort was perceived as sufficiently important that even Bruce Springsteen joined the tour, also endorsing the Democratic candidates (a first in his long career) in an op-ed piece for the *New York Times*.[26] The effort to defeat George Bush at the polls also yielded two *Rock Against Bush* compilation albums. While these developments represented a significant cross section of center-left U.S. political thought, they were not loud enough to drown out the chorus of nationalist anthems otherwise dominating American popular culture, or sufficiently compelling to voters to recapture the White House for the Democrats.

CONCLUSION

Amid a general public debate over the curtailing of civil liberties in the United States in the wake of 9/11, a less publicized struggle has also taken place involving the suppression and marginalization of voices resistant to dominant political ideologies, and this is nowhere more apparent than in the realm of popular music. Clearly, a variety of opinions have been expressed by popular musicians about the Bush administration and its war on terrorism. Given the changes in political climate and the corporate landscape of the culture industries, however, country anthems supporting military action as the appropriate response to the 9/11 attacks have overwhelmed more critical voices in rock and rap that challenged this course of action. Many of these rock and rap songs, released within the chart life of the country singles that domi-nated the national airwaves, could have contributed to a national debate on U.S. foreign policy. Instead, they received only the most limited exposure. One of the supreme ironies of the war on terrorism is that the freedoms the United States says it is fighting to protect have been among the first casualties of the war.

ACKNOWLEDGMENTS

Sections of this chapter appear in Reebee Garofalo, *Rockin' Out*, 3rd ed. (Prentice Hall, 2005). They are used with the permission of Prentice Hall. The material has been revised, reorganized, updated, and expanded for this volume. I am indebted to my research assistant, Andrew Ryan, for his help in conducting new research, particularly in the area of hip-hop.

NOTES

1. See Martin Cloonan, "Musical Responses to September 11th: From Conservative Patriotism to Radicalism," in *9/11—The World's All Out of Tune: Populäre Musik nach dem 11. September 2001*, ed. Dietrich Helms and Thomas Phleps (Bielefeld, Germany: Transcript Verlag, 2004), 14. This article is also permanently available online at the Freemuse Web site (http://freemuse.inforce.dk/graphics/Publications/PDF/cloonan11sept.pdf).

2. Carl Limbacher, "Pro-Bush Neil Young Shocks Leftists," newsmax.com, 13 December 2001, available at: http://www.freerepublic.com/focus/f-news/589986/posts.

3. "Brucie Bonus for Bush," *New Musical Express,* 29 July 2002, available at: http://www.nme.com/news/102502.htm

4. Tom Roland, "Lee Greenwood," *All Music Guide,* available at: http://www.allmusic.com/cg/amg.dll?p=amg&uid=CASS80310101206&sql=B3srz286c054a.

5. See Schmelz essay in this volume.

6. According to CBS polls, "Bush's highest job approval rating was in October 2001, when 90% approved of the job he was doing as president." See "Poll: Bush's Approval Sinking," 17 January 2004, available at: http://www.cbsnews.com/stories/2004/01/17/opinion/polls/main593849.shtml.

7. John Metzger, "Neil Young: Are You Passionate?" *The Music Box* 9(5), May 2002, available at: http://www.musicbox-online.com/ny-pass.html.

8. For instance, David Corn's "Capitol Games" blog on *The Nation*'s Web site reported on July 24, 2002: "First, Steve Gill, a conservative talk-show gabber in Nashville, denounced the song. Then Fox News Channel and *The New York Post* picked up the story. The Web site of the latter headlined its dispatch, 'Twisted Ballad Honors Tali-Rat' and claimed 'American Taliban fighter John Walker Lindh is glorified and called Jesus-like in a country-rock song . . . by maverick singer-songwriter Steve Earle.' Another Nashville DJ, Phil Valentine, called the song 'politically insane.' Gill declared, 'This puts [Earle] in the same category as Jane Fonda and John Walker and all those people who hate America.'" Available at: http://www.thenation.com/blogs/capitalgames?pid=84.

9. See Scherzinger essay in this volume for further analysis of the Dixie Chicks controversy and broadcast-media censorship.

10. Jenny Eliscu, "Chicks Triumph," *Rolling Stone,* 29 May 2003, 10.

11. See, for example, Jeff Chang, "Is Protest Music Dead?" AlterNet.org, 16 April 2002, available at http://www.alternet.org/story.html?StoryID=12880, as well as Joseph Schumacher, "Is Protest Music as Dead as Disco?" *Peace and Conflict Monitor,* 12 May 2003, available at http://www.monitor.upeace.org/innerpg.cfm?id_article=5.

12. Cynthia Cotts, "Telecom for Dummies," *Village Voice,* 5–11 September 2001. Available at http://www.villagevoice.com/news/0136,cotts,27860,6.html.

13. Greg Kot, "What's Wrong with Radio," *Rolling Stone,* 16 August 2001, 25.

14. Ray Waddell, "Touring Strong, But Some Numbers Cause Concern," *Billboard,* 28 December 2002, 77.

15. Brent Staples, "The Trouble With Corporate Radio: The Day the Protest Music Died," *New York Times,* 20 February 2003.

16. See also essays by Scherzinger and Pegley and Fast in this volume for more on the Clear Channel controversy.
17. "I Heard the News Today . . ." *Rolling Stone*, 25 October 2001, 32.
18. Tim Jones, "Media giant's rally sponsorship raises questions," *Chicago Tribune*, 19 March 2003.
19. Paul Krugman, "Channels of Influence," *New York Times*, 25 March 2003.
20. Mark Jurkowitz, "The Big Chill: One Casualty of the War on Terrorism Is America's Boisterous Discourse. Those Who Express Unpopular Opinions Do So at Their Peril. And There's No Telling How Long It Will Last." *Boston Globe*, 27 January, 2002, 10.
21. Chang, "Is Protest Music Dead?"
22. "N.J. Rock Station Won't Play Jethro Tull," *Associated Press*, 13 November, 2003, available at http://www.neilrogers.com/news/articles/2003111408.html.
23. Murray Forman, "Soundtrack to a Crisis: Music, Context, Discourse," *Television and New Media*, Vol. 3, No. 2, 2002, 194.
24. Posted on the MoveOn Web site: http://www.moveon.org/ musiciansunited/.
25. Kristin V. Jones, "Rocking the Hip Hop Vote," *The Nation*, 1 December, 2003, 8.
26. Bruce Springsteen, "Chords for Change," *New York Times*, 5 August, 2004.

2

"AMERICA: A TRIBUTE TO HEROES":

MUSIC, MOURNING, AND THE
UNIFIED AMERICAN COMMUNITY

Kip Pegley and Susan Fast

Music is prophesy . . . it makes audible the new world that will
gradually become visible, that will impose itself and regulate the
order of things; it is not only the image of things, but the transcending of the everyday, the herald of the future.

—**Jacques Attali (1985: 11)**

Certainly, how we conceive of ourselves determines how we conceive of others, and vice versa. If we conceive of ourselves as self-
identical, and we conceive of identity as opposed to difference,
and we conceive of anything or anyone outside of the boundaries
of ourselves as different, then we will conceive of anything different or outside of ourselves as a threat to our own identity. Identity
will be pitted against difference. Relations will be hostile.

—**Kelly Oliver (2001: 2–3)**

In the uncertain political and social climate that marked the immediate
aftermath of September 11, 2001, the significance and role of popular
music entered new and uncharted territory. On the one hand, the new
media landscape was marked by disturbing acts of censorship and
silencing, such as the infamous list of 156 songs a Clear Channel executive suggested removing from its 1,200 stations' playlists in the interest

of "sensitivity."[1] At the same time, music clearly took on a newfound importance in the public sphere for its ability to channel powerful emotions. Every large American media event following 9/11—including the World Series, the Super Bowl, the Olympics, the Academy Awards, and many others—featured musical performances that acknowledged the tragedy and paid tribute to the victims. Echoing these contradictions on a personal level, some artists chose to cancel tours altogether in the weeks and months that followed 9/11, while others opted to continue, altering their concerts by adding commentary and/or changing song lists to reflect new world concerns.

U2 was a case in point: fans (including the authors) lucky enough to attend the band's "Elevation Tour" prior to 9/11 were not only entertained but politicized vis-à-vis gun control and the NRA; the band also engaged in consciousness-raising around the international imbalance of wealth, particularly as it pertains to debt-laden Africa. Discrepancies between the first show we attended before the attacks (Buffalo, New York, May 31, 2001) and the second show after 9/11 (Hamilton, Ontario, October 13, 2001) included the abandonment of both of these agendas. Instead, the names of the 9/11 victims were scrolled on a screen. Moreover, a number of songs were omitted ("Mysterious Ways" and "Desire," among others) and replaced with an invitation to an enthusiastic fan to perform with them onstage. The link established between the band and the audience through the interaction of the young performer was a particularly poignant and symbolic union, a stripping away of the boundaries to which we are usually accustomed in stadium concerts (to say nothing of the new social and political "boundary making" since 9/11). This invitation to a male audience member replaced a cornerstone of previous U2 performances: Bono's practice of choosing a woman with whom to dance onstage. As such, the concert's traditional voyeuristic display of desire and romance (between just two people) was circumvented and a moment of connection between the band and an enthusiastic fan (representing all enthusiastic fans) was inserted. As moving as this performance was, however, perhaps the most poignant moment of the band's performance was at the end of "Sunday, Bloody Sunday": on the oversize screen the audience could see the silhouette of an audience member's hand forming the peace sign with Bono standing behind, draped in an American flag which he held tight and cradled, as if he meant to console the United States in the wake of the attacks. Moments later, the song gave way to applause and the screen faded to black, leaving behind a powerful, lingering, political image.

Moments like this in U2's concert, while significant and moving, were just that: moments. The most coherent performances of musical solidarity in response to the events of 9/11 were undoubtedly the series of benefit concerts that followed the attacks. This is not to suggest that these concerts shared a sense of uniformity: musical, gestural, and stylistic articulations differed, among other things, according to temporality, venue, and the intended audience (for instance, the families of the victims versus the N.Y.C. rescue personnel). Concerts held outside of the United States were also unsurprisingly differentiated: they were held in numerous languages, and proceeds benefited a range of recipients.

In this chapter we focus on "America: A Tribute to Heroes," the first post-9/11 American mass-mediated music event, aired on more than thirty-five broadcast cable TV networks and 8,000 radio stations in the United States (and internationally) on September 21, 2001. While this musical performance was described as a fund-raiser for aid relief, it accomplished much more: through the power of celebrity, music, and gesture, the concert attempted to forge a unified American community, wherein "appropriate" gendered and racialized behaviors were modeled. This celebrity-filled event was an opportune occasion for social modeling, for, as Raymond Durgnat reminds us, "stars are a reflection in which the public studies and adjusts its own image of itself" (1967: 137–8). Even when national conditions are stable, stars function in part to construct a notion of what people are "supposed" to be like, contributing in particular to the definition of social roles. "Stars represent typical ways of behaving, feeling and thinking in contemporary society," writes Richard Dyer, "ways that have been socially, culturally, [and] historically constructed" (1986: 17). It goes without saying that social modeling—which functions to reestablish key societal structures—became even more important after the disturbing and disorienting events of 9/11 and this concert was an important site for this process. Once the perception of an American community was established, particular political initiatives then were made explicit; this renewed sense of community subsequently reassured the home viewer of the strength and unity of the American people and the probability of their victory in the face of a likely—and, by the end of the concert—seemingly inevitable war.

We want at the outset to position ourselves as Canadians; accordingly, we come to the American-produced events and to the tragedy of 9/11 recognizing our particular outsider subject positions. The effects of this distance, at the least, will provide a different perspective on the music and events because we had access to Canadian and American media coverage of 9/11, the former of which was not available to most American viewers.[2] Barbie Zelizer and Stuart Allan have noted that some non-American journalism coverage of the events of 9/11 (particularly that of the BBC) offered important and unique insights not only into the events, but also into how events might be interpreted cross-culturally (2002: 13). We offer our critique in this same spirit.

"AMERICA: A TRIBUTE TO HEROES"

Before we heard the first note of the "Tribute to Heroes" benefit concert, the uniqueness of the event was already palpable: the program began with a quiet nighttime visual of New York foregrounding the Statue of Liberty; we were then relocated into a silent studio, the specific location of which was undisclosed for fear of further terrorist attacks. Although the performers were in secret locations—which the organizers wanted to remain secret—they identified the cities in which the performers were located, New York, Los Angeles, and London, by printing the name of the city in the corner of the screen as artists began to perform. This partial disclosure, of course, was empowering in that it invoked the significant cultural capital of these cities. Having established a concert tradition where the geographical location of a concert often becomes synonymous with the energy of the event itself ("Woodstock," "Newport," "Monterey"), citing even the names of the cities grounded this performance. The performers did not appear in a vacuum.

A silhouette began to perform. Already, we missed the busy sounds of New York, of an audience, and of the performer's introduction. Bruce Springsteen, the artist who gave us the vivid images of New Jersey and the streets of Philadelphia, launched into the story of his "city of ruins." The set was thin, including only Springsteen, his instruments (an acoustic guitar and harmonica), and seven backup singers. When the song ended—with the call to "rise up . . . rise up"—the camera panned back and to the right of the performance area to include another unidentified silhouette. We cut to a frontal midrange shot of this person, whom we now recognized to be Tom Hanks, standing alone in front of rows of cascading candles. This blending of the two spaces—featuring musical performance and spoken word—revealed the simplicity and seeming minimalism of the event. Hanks recounted the words of a handful of 9/11 heroes and invited us to call in with our pledges. The camera settled onto the next performer, Stevie Wonder, who was set to play.

That this concert began with Springsteen and Hanks is socially and, ultimately, ideologically significant: Springsteen speaks with a certain "authority" about "his" city, and Hanks has been represented over the years as an actor who, among other things, has been linked with narratives of American history and expansion (*Saving Private Ryan*, *Apollo 13*), and, on a personal level, he has demonstrated a commitment to bringing attention to the WWII Memorial. Hanks functioned here as a well-liked film celebrity who, unlike other figures associated with American expansion, such as Harrison Ford, lacks a sex-symbol status. It seems entirely appropriate, then, that Hanks served as the first speaker of this mournful, sorrow-filled event. The tribute was not about desire or celebrity; it was about people, community, and rebuilding America.

The notion of "celebrity" was frustrated in the tribute in order to foreground a unified community that included both the performers and the audience members at their TV sets. This was accomplished through a number of important means: the concert lacked a live audience and the familiar introductions to performers and speakers were noticeably absent throughout. Tom Hanks, in fact, made explicit reference to the common status of the speakers and performers: "Those of us here tonight are not heroes. We are not healers, nor protectors of this great nation. We are merely artists and entertainers here to raise spirits. . . ." Celebrities were often shown at the phone bank answering calls, reinforcing visually their new status as servers. Of course, they were still celebrities, which is why their presence at the phone banks was even noted. But even the efforts of organizing these celebrities were downplayed. As George Clooney stated several minutes later, "We have a phone bank here, and we wanted to show you a few of our friends that just showed up to answer the phones [and] take pledges." The suggestion that these celebrities just "showed up" was obviously an exaggeration, and Clooney's comments—successful or not—appeared intended to reassure somehow, to make the event seem more relaxed, even casual.

Despite the celebrities' repeated efforts to downplay their status, however, they were unable to undermine the effects of their power, for they could not control their image at the point of reception. The roles that these celebrities modeled for us can be examined across several axes; here we would like to point out just two. First, the modeling can be examined according to prescribed gender roles. Not surprisingly, female celebrities consistently told stories about hope; the safeguarding, nurturing, and protection of people; and the strength of the human spirit. Cameron Diaz related the story about first-grade teacher Shannon Greenfeld, who stayed behind with her class of frightened six-year olds: ". . . in the face of danger, in a time of chaos . . . Shannon Greenfeld and her colleagues gave their pupils a lesson in courage and kept them safe." Amy Brenneman and Calista Flockhart evoked the story of Anne Frank and her heartening diaries. George Clooney, meanwhile, told the story of Police Officer John Perry, who went to police headquarters to file his retirement papers on 9/11 and, on hearing the explosion of the first plane, decided to go to the site to help. He didn't return. "I don't think anyone would have blamed him if he had decided to stay behind that day," Clooney explained, "but he was a New York City policeman, he knew what he had to do and he did it." Similarly, Tom Cruise spoke about the heroism of Reverend Michael Judge, a fire department chaplain who arrived at Ground Zero before the towers fell. Judge knelt to administer last rites to a dying fireman then took off his helmet to lean closer. "He knew without a helmet he would be in danger, but it wasn't his job to be safe." Later, firefighters came and recovered his body and then went back to work; that, Cruise stated, is "what firefighters do." Such gendered positions (stories of nurturing, protective females told by women versus stories of active, heroic males recounted by male celebrities) were clear and unambiguous throughout the program.

While the content of these messages detailed highly gendered societal roles, it is also useful to examine how speakers were organized according to the construction of their personas vis-à-vis specific mass media. Figure 1.1 outlines the order of appearance in the *Tribute*: "F" represents a film star, "T" is a television personality, "A" is an athlete, and "C" is a stand-up comedian. Several celebrities' careers overlap two categories (George Clooney, for instance, first became well known in television before he moved to films). Their designation reflects the medium with which they were most well known at the time of airing, some of which include both television and film. (One exception is Jimmy Smits, who had moved from television into film, but, because he appeared in the "Tribute" with Dennis Franz, costar from *NYPD Blue,* he is identified here as a television actor.) Musical performances are italicized.

With only few exceptions, the chronological order reflects a general progression from film stars to television celebrities and back again. Important distinctions exist of course, between film stars and television celebrities. As John Langer points out, traditionally the film star has been separated out from our everyday lives and accordingly, we exit our daily routine to view a film that appears to us "larger than life" onscreen. In addition, we often do not know when the star will release another film until we see it advertised. They appear, as Langer writes, within the realm of "the spectacular, the inaccessible, the imaginary" (1981: 355). As P. David Marshall notes, the film star, unlike the television personality, appears less affected by economic concerns because the screen film is not structured around commercials, trailers, and other similar events. Without these capital-driven interruptions, Marshall argues, the film star's craft appears to have more integrity. As a result, the star—in relation to the television personality—maintains an "aura of distinction" (1997: 121).

Order of Appearance

Bruce Springsteen: "My City of Ruins"
Tom Hanks (F)
Stevie Wonder & Take 6: "Love's in Need of Love Today"
George Clooney (F)
U2: "Peace on Earth" [fragment]; "Walk On"
[Muslim Children's Message]
Will Smith and Mohammed Ali (F, A)
Faith Hill: "There Will Come a Day"
Kelsey Grammer (T)
Tom Petty and the Heartbreakers: "I Won't Back Down"
Jim Carrey (F)
Enrique Iglesias: "Hero"
[Video clips of friends and relatives of those who perished. Individuals tell stories
   and show pictures of their lost loved ones]
Neil Young: "Imagine"
Cameron Diaz (F)
Alicia Keys: "Someday We'll All Be Free"
Robin Williams (C/F)
Limp Bizkit and John Rzeznik: "Wish You Were Here"
Jimmy Smits and Dennis Franz (T)
Billy Joel: "New York State of Mind"
Amy Brenneman and Calista Flockhart (T)
Dixie Chicks: "I Believe in Love"
[Collage of video clips and still images taken on and after 9/11 to the soundtrack of
   U2's "One"]
Dave Matthews: "Everyday"
Conan O'Brien and Sarah Jessica Parker (T)
Wyclef Jean: "Redemption Song"
Tom Cruise (F)
Mariah Carey: "Hero"
Ray Romano (T)
Bon Jovi: "Livin' on a Prayer"
Lucy Liu (T/F)
Sheryl Crow: "Safe and Sound"
Sela Ward and Jane Kaczmarek (T)
Sting: "Fragile"
Julia Roberts (F)
Eddie Vedder: "Long Road"
Chris Rock (C/F)
[One minute of silence]
Paul Simon: "Bridge over Troubled Water"
Robert De Niro (F)
Celine Dion: "God Bless America"
Clint Eastwood (F)
Willie Nelson and celebrities/performers: "America the Beautiful"

Figure 1 "America: A Tribute to Heroes"

Television's personality system, meanwhile, is structured in opposition to that of film. As Langer states: "whereas stars are always playing 'parts' emphasizing their identity as 'stars' as much, perhaps even more than the characters they play, television personalities 'play' themselves . . . personalities are distinguished for their representativeness, their typicality, their 'will to ordinariness,' to be accepted, normalized, experienced as familiar" (1981: 355). Marshall echoes this idea, tracing this *familiarization* to a number of factors, including the "related family structure" under which the television is usually viewed, the serialization of television content, and the emphasis on the personal (1997: 131). One of the repercussions of this type of familiarity is that in television it is the characters that are highly memorable whereas the actors who portray them remain relatively anonymous. In other words, we may be more familiar with the star of *All in the Family* as Archie Bunker rather than Carroll O'Connor, whereas we are more inclined to remember a movie as a "John Wayne" film rather than the name of the particular character John Wayne played.

The television personality then, can contribute in particular ways toward encoding or reinforcing particular preferred meanings. Accordingly, in the "Tribute," Jimmy Smits and Dennis Franz spoke with a certain authority when they told of the bravery of police officer Jim Leahy, who gave "New York City a new reason to be proud." This message, appropriately, was conveyed before another New Yorker, Billy Joel, performed "New York State of Mind." Similarly, *Sex and the City's* Carrie Bradshaw (Sarah Jessica Parker) used her televisual authority when she spoke of how New Yorkers have bonded since 9/11. "There are no strangers here now," she explained. This statement has at least two possible readings. First, coming from a character who struggles to negotiate the emotionally tumultuous world of New York City, we are reassured: if Carrie Bradshaw can find meaningful bonds with strangers, so can we. Second, it may be important to note that this statement preceded Wyclef Jean's performance of Bob Marley's "Redemption Song." This reggae performance was embedded within a repertoire of pop songs, particularly ballads, rendering it the most musically isolated and marginalized performance of the evening. Parker's statement then may be read as an attempt to encourage the viewing audience to include the upcoming performers as part of the new community. If this was not enough to keep the viewers tuned, then it may not be coincidental that Tom Cruise, who at the time was arguably the world's most popular film star, broke the pattern of television personalities and spoke immediately following Wyclef Jean. His appearance, after all, was probably the safest bet of the night to bring many viewers *back* to their television sets.

Having pointed to just a few of the reasons for the placement of particular celebrities as well as their message content, we would now like to return to the first few performances of the concert to examine how particular ideologies were built sonically and visually from Bruce Springsteen's opening number to what might be considered the first significant politico-ideological break: Tom Petty's performance almost a half-hour later. This is followed by an analysis of the final, and most politically significant and explicit performances of the concert.

The image of a unified American community was built through a number of means, including the use of backup singers or the presence of instrumental or vocal choirs (Neil Young, for instance, was accompanied by a string ensemble in his rendition of John Lennon's "Imagine"). This metaphor for expanded community, however, was not always the result of simply adding more performers, but rather the addition of a choir with fewer than expected numbers of instrumentalists. As Robert Walser notes within the context of heavy metal music, "additional voices serve to enlarge the statements of the solo vocalist, enacting the approval or participation of the larger social world, or at least a segment of it" (1993: 45). Walser's observations also apply here: the numerous choruses (both vocal and instrumental) not only represent the extended community (including the viewing audience) but, importantly, *sanction* the soloist's sentiments.

Springsteen's opening performance emphasized community through the presence of background singers as well as the importance of the singer-songwriter (Springsteen, who was positioned in front of the singers, was the only instrumentalist, playing both acoustic guitar and harmonica). This was, however, a deceptive image: what was not shown was a musician playing the solid bass riff moving underneath the chords (this musician outlined the roots of the I–VI–IV–I chords followed by a descending stepwise movement from I down to IV). Both parts of this musical gesture contributed to a sense of rootedness and stability, ideal for the opening song. Yet, Springsteen did not play this line himself; either the performance was prerecorded or the performer simply was not visible. Instead, the nostalgic image of the solo singer-songwriter and his small choir was communicated, and the sparse image was poignant. His musical ability to speak for us was significant; indeed, his ability was presented as more powerful than it actually was.

This sonic stability was reinforced visually by an unchanging, dusky-blue background, broken by golden vertical streaks. At times these warm golden lights seemed like pillars; at other times, light from a sunrise (particularly behind the backup singers), fitting for the final call of the song's chorus for us to "rise up." It's a new day. This saturated golden color was significant for another reason: like red, orange, and lavender, it is what media scholars term an "advancing color." When given a dark value and intensity, these colors alter the viewing experience by making these objects appear closer to the camera (Boggs 1978: 176). In effect, it drew the studio and home viewing environments closer together.

This visual metaphor of community was strengthened by the physicality of the singers. While largely immobile, they moved their arms off camera from their sides (or in front of their bodies) to hold each others' hands, thus creating a human chain; by the song's conclusion, they had raised their clasped hands up together. Completing these gestures off camera enabled a gesture of solidarity and strength without outward motion, a point to which we will return momentarily. Finally, it is significant to the notion of "community" that there were no risers in this first performance: no one was elevated, and everyone was physically and symbolically located at "ground zero."

Springsteen's performance was followed by introductory words by Tom Hanks. The eclipse of instrumentalists continued in Stevie Wonder and Take 6's following performance of "Love's in Need of Love Today": Wonder appeared in front of the vocal group with most of the instrumentalists behind them. The view of these musicians largely was obstructed by Take 6, who formed a fairly dense human barrier in front of them. To the left of the singers was the only other fully observable musician, another keyboardist. The visible foregrounding of the two keyboardists with the singers was critical to creating a sense of gospel community. The performance was bathed in a receding blue and an adjacent, advancing color on the color wheel, lavender. The juxtaposition of these colors created a stained-glass effect, a midrange mixture of warmth and coolness.

George Clooney spoke next and was followed by U2, a band whose appearance differed in significant ways from the previous acts: U2's instrumentation was unobstructed and the band's deployment on stage resembled a concert format with guitarist The Edge at Bono's right (although not all of the instrumental parts were shown, including, for instance, the keyboard part). More noticeable, however, was the first usage of black-and-white film footage for the entire performance, and this starkness could be read in several ways: first, as Susan Fast has pointed out previously in relation to U2's *October* album cover, "black and white serves as a metaphor for simplicity, directness [and] honesty" (2000: 36). This aesthetic of course follows them as well in their videos; knowing fans of U2, then, might have read this lack of color as evidence of their ongoing commitment to stripping away artifice, returning us to the importance of music and the event rather than notions of celebrity.

To viewers unfamiliar with U2's pattern, however, this black-and-white footage, in relation to the preceding acts, could just as easily have been read in stark contradiction to the inviting, sometimes saturated colors of the American performers. Given that Bono addressed the viewing audience from their location ("Hello from London" he said), could this lack of color have been read as a metaphor for cultural outsiders?[3] Apparently, this use of black-and-white footage here was an aesthetic choice rather than one of necessity: Sting's performance from London later in the tribute was presented in color.

Within the context of this concert, U2 was visually not part of the same community established by Springsteen, Wonder, and Take 6. While they lacked community vis-à-vis color, however, they contributed to it through the inclusion of three background singers who were seen to the side of the stage. Before we leave this segment, we should point out that U2 and Sting were the only British performers in this concert: both sang of peace (U2 performed a fragment of "Peace on Earth" and Sting sang "Fragile"), and both are known by many beyond these specific performances for their nonviolent, activist agendas.[4]

Faith Hill followed U2; she was accompanied by instrumentalists and a gospel choir (comprised exclusively of African-American singers). Musically, the gospel style today denotes perhaps the most representative of black American musical traditions (Allen 1991: 4). The bodies were mobilized, choreographed, and unified, sharply contrasting with Springsteen's mostly white backup singers through expanded expressive gestures. Here, the gospel choir functioned to provide physical catharsis in a stereotypical way that white performers are not socially sanctioned to do. This echoes Samuel A. Floyd's observation that cross-culturally black dance tends to engage considerably more of the body than does dance stemming from white cultural traditions (2001: 118). Visually, then, the movement reinforced the music's unique black traditions, sharply contrasting with Springsteen's performance from the outset of the concert. The choir's large bodily expressions, which are derived from African cultural roots, link, as McClary and Walser observe, "the physical world with the spiritual, [and facilitate] the internalization and reenactment of *communal* beliefs" [emphasis added] (1994: 76). The notion of community—both among the performers and between performers and the viewing audience at home—is crucial here. Closeness and shared emotion were further emphasized by the lighting, which alternated between a blue, crimson, and the rich golden color again for the most advancing and warm combinations thus far. The instrumentation now was also more visible, although minimal, foregrounding keyboards (organ and piano) and percussion. Combined, the gospel style, the moving bodies, the lighting, and the visible instrumentation created visually and sonically the strongest gesture of (American) community, strength, and hope seen and heard thus far.

It is important here to bring attention back to the celebrity speaker: following Hill's performance we encountered the first appearance of a television personality. The speaker was Frasier, the psychiatrist played by Kelsey Grammer on the eponymous show, who lent his therapeutic touch to help us through our grieving, which then turned decidedly political. As he stated:

> In times like these we can find comfort and inspiration in the words of past American heroes, especially somebody like President John F. Kennedy who gave his life in service to this country. In *Profiles in Courage*, President Kennedy wrote: "A man does what he must in spite of personal consequences, in spite of obstacles and dangers and pressures and that is the basis of all human morality." And in his inaugural address, President Kennedy declared: "Let every nation know, whether it wishes us well or ill, that we shall pay any price, bear any burden, meet any hardship, support any friend, oppose any foe, in order to assure the survival and the success of liberty." That is the challenge President Kennedy put before us forty years ago, and now, confronted by evil, we must rise to the occasion. Please do your part.

This is a significant turning point in the tribute, for, rather than emphasize the power of community, television's favorite psychiatrist identified the unquestionable responsibility of the American nation-state to retaliate, even in the face of international isolation or adversity. Significantly, the song that followed was Tom Petty and the Heartbreakers' "I Won't Back Down." While the text needs little explanation, we would like to point out that the lighting for this performance included occasional oranges at the chorus, but was primarily dominated by cool—that is, receding—blues and greens. Moreover, the lighting featured triangular patterns significantly different from the stained-glass image seen earlier with Wonder and Take 6. Petty's lighting was much more like a concert performance than what we had seen thus far. Like U2, the instruments were visible, but now seen in vivid—albeit cool and isolating—color. Finally, this marked the first performance without a chorus. Apparently, America now stood alone.

The comedian-actor Jim Carrey was the next speaker; that a person known for his almost uncontrollable antics could now be solemn spoke to the seriousness of this event (this pattern was echoed later when Chris Rock, a comedian also known for his irreverent sense of humor, was the last personality to speak before the observation of one minute of silence). Carrey picked up where the performance left off, in the realm of the political: "Churchill taught us that courage is the first of human qualities, the quality which guarantees all others." He went on to speak of the courage of two men on 9/11, who, while descending the stairs in one of the towers, came upon a woman in a wheelchair and carried her down sixty-eight flights of stairs without even knowing her name. "To risk your life for a total stranger in need is not only courageous," Carrey added, "but divine. . . . In the face of that kind of selflessness we can no longer call each other strangers. That is brotherhood. That is America." This was an exceptional return to the work of forging American community, and an amazing segue to Enrique Iglesias's "Hero," to advancing lavenders and golden yellows, and yes, backup singers.

What we have tried to outline thus far are ways in which the individual sonic and visual features—from the use of choirs, lighting, and staging to the introductions by particular individuals—were arranged in such a way to evoke "preferred" viewer responses. Equally important, of course, was the final, and highly emotional image that would linger with us beyond the *Tribute's* conclusion. By the concert's end, the film stars replace the television celebrities, concluding with spoken text by Robert De Niro:

> Sixty years ago Franklin Delano Roosevelt spoke these words: "We look forward to a world founded upon four essential human freedoms. The first is freedom of speech and expression everywhere in the world. The second is freedom of every person to worship God in his own way everywhere in the world. The third is freedom from want everywhere in the world. The fourth is freedom from fear anywhere in the world."

De Niro's text, invoking the possibility of a call to action so that Americans can be free from fear, was followed by a musical introduction on soft strings which were quickly reduced to a single sustained high-register pitch; to this was added a single, repeated note on a piano. A female silhouette, bathed in white background light was gradually illuminated, revealing an "angelic" Celine Dion singing "God Bless America." Behind her was the largest gospel choir to appear in the concert that night. As the strings swelled to full orchestra and the choir sang with full dynamics, there were not one but two upward musical modulations, as if to indicate the height of American potential.

The final and perhaps most politically significant words were then provided by Clint Eastwood:

It was the twenty-first century's day of infamy. It was a day that will live in the annals of courage and patriotism. Tonight we have paid tribute to those who were lost and those who survived the fire and the fate that rained down upon them and the heroes at ground zero. We celebrate not only them, but all our fellow Americans, for the intended victims of this attack were not just on the planes and at the Pentagon and at the World Trade Center . . . the targets were not just the symbols of America, but they were the spirit of America and the intended victims were all 300 million of us. The terrorists foresaw a nation fearful, doubtful, ready to retreat. Oh, they left us wounded, but renewed in strength and we'll stand and we will not yield. The terrorists who wanted 300 victims instead are going to get 300 million heroes, 300 million Americans with broken hearts [and] unbreakable hopes for our country and our future. In the conflict that has come upon us, we are determined as our parents and our grandparents were before us to win through the ultimate triumph, so help us God. There is a song that cele-brates America and beckons to what we can become: "America, America, God shed His grace on thee, and crown thy good with brotherhood from sea to shining sea."

Here, Eastwood's filmic persona is second to none in preparing us for the upcoming nationalist project as *he* beckons the viewing audience to see what Americans "can become." As Richard Grenier pointed out long before 9/11: "Clint Eastwood, to judge by his films, has never had the slightest doubt as to the legitimacy of the use of force in the service of justice" (1991: 169). The star of *Dirty Harry, Magnum Force, The Enforcer,* and *Sudden Impact,* Eastwood goes beyond the call of duty in stopping social evils, performing "vigilante justice" as "a man alone in a corrupt world" (Grenier 1991: 183). Significantly, when he introduced the song ("There is a song that celebrates America . . .") the opening of "America the Beautiful" began behind Eastwood, marking the first time in the concert that an introducer's words became conflated with music, increasing the emotional potency of the message. Eastwood's voice—with its filmic aura of distinction—resonated on top of this symbolic song and served as a reminder of not only what the United States would be fighting for, but of the power of their forces to achieve their objective.

CONCLUSION

While the tribute attempted to pay homage, raise funds, and begin the collective mourning for the victims of 9/11, we have also pointed to other, less explicit effects of the event in social and political terms. Powerful metaphors of closeness, caring, protection, and community were established vis-à-vis instrumental choirs, songs inviting a once-powerful American city and people to rise again, and warm, advancing lighting schemes, all of which were designed to draw the American people together. Significantly, the bodies of African-Americans also denoted community and provided access to the physical release of powerful emotions (these bodies, however, were nested within the performance lineup: that the concert opened and concluded with largely immobile bodies of Euro-Americans points to the overall privileging of these more contained hegemonic expressions). Throughout, visual and social representations of closeness and community were eclipsed in timely fashion by the words of powerful political figures, including Kennedy and Churchill, evoked to communicate strength, leadership, and direction in the new nationalist project. We are united, and we will triumph, even if we go through this alone; in Petty's words, "We won't back down." Because "A Tribute to Heroes" was painfully close to the events of September 11, 2001, it was a significant, even pivotal moment where modeling of "appropriate" social norms could take place relatively unchallenged and unquestioned. Specifically, as we have argued here, it was a forum where gendered, racial and national images and agendas were carefully negotiated and quietly reinforced under the soft blanket of human tragedy.

REFERENCES

Allen, Ray. 1991. *Singing in the Spirit: African-American Sacred Quartets in New York City*. Philadelphia: University of Pennsylvania Press.

Attali, Jacques. 1985. *Noise: The Political Economy of Music*, trans. Brian Massumi. Minneapolis: University of Minnesota Press.

Boggs, Joseph. 1978. *The Art of Watching Films*. Menlo Park, CA: Benjamin/Cummings Publishing Company.

Durgnat, Raymond. 1967. *Films and Feelings*. London: Faber.

Dyer, Richard. 1986. *Heavenly Bodies: Film Stars and Society*. London: MacMillan Education.

Fast, Susan. 2000. "Music, Contexts, and Meaning in U2." In *Expression in Pop-Rock Music: A Collection of Critical and Analytical Essays*, edited by Walter Everett, 33–57. New York: Garland.

Floyd, Samuel A. 2001. "African American Dance and Music." In *African American Jazz and Rap: Social and Philosophical Examination of Black Expressive Behavior,* edited by James L. Conyers, Jr., 117–30. North Carolina and London: McFarland and Company.

Grenier, Richard. 1991. *Capturing the Culture: Film, Art and Politics.* Washington, D.C.: Ethics and Public Policy Center.

Langer, John. 1981. "Television's Personality System." Media, Culture and Society 4: 351–65.

Marshall, P. David. 1997. *Celebrity and Power: Fame in Contemporary Culture.* Minneapolis: University of Minnesota Press.

McClary, Susan, and Robert Walser. 1994. "Theorizing the Body in African-American Music." *Black Music Research Journal* 14(1): 75–84.

Oliver, Kelly. 2001. *Witnessing: Beyond Recognition.* Minneapolis: University of Minnesota Press.

Walser, Robert. 1993. *Running with the Devil: Power, Gender, and Madness in Heavy Metal Music.* Hanover and London: Wesleyan University Press.

Zelizer, Barbie, and Stuart Allan, eds. 2002. *Journalism after September 11.* London and New York: Routledge.

NOTES

1. The Clear Channel list of "banned" songs is discussed extensively by Garofalo and Scherzinger in this volume.
2. For more on differences between Canadian and American news coverage of 9/11, see Deaville's chapter in this volume.
3. One might be reminded of the use of black-and-white footage in Madonna's "Truth or Dare" here: the opening leg of the tour was in Japan during the rainy season, and the concerts were performed outdoors. This concert footage was in black-and-white and in the dub-over, Madonna expresses her disapproval: "I . . . was not in the mood for Eskimos and ice, and I think the only thing that kept me from slashing my wrists was the thought of coming back to America and doing the show it was meant to be." The next shot is of an indoor concert from the Joe Louis Arena, shown, of course, in color.
4. The U.K. was represented in the subsequent "Concert for New York City" in late October, but significantly, not by these performers. Instead, the roster included British invasion acts like The Who, and Mick Jagger and Keith Richards from the Rolling Stones, giving the event a considerably more assertive and oppositional energy.

3

THE SOUNDS OF AMERICAN AND CANADIAN TELEVISION NEWS AFTER 9/11:

ENTONING HORROR AND GRIEF, FEAR AND ANGER

James Deaville

The horrors of the attacks on the World Trade Center and Pentagon left indelible images in the minds of everyone who observed them on television. While the impact of the visual and verbal framing of the events in televised coverage has received significant scholarly attention, thus far researchers have largely ignored the music used to accompany those images.[1] To a certain extent, this exclusion is not surprising. The very invisibility (unhearability?) of music in media contexts, to consumers as well as researchers, is a significant part of its power to subliminally shape public opinion. The question then arises, how might television news music have had an impact upon viewers of network coverage of 9/11? And, perhaps more significantly, how did that music and its impact differ from network to network, from country to country?

In this essay, I offer a comparative study of televised newscast responses to the events of September 11 in the United States and Canada, reflecting upon the politics of news music in America while also putting them in a transnational (if specifically North American) perspective.[2] My analysis will focus on the 9/11 coverage presented by two leading twenty-four-hour news networks in their respective countries, CNN in the United States and CBC Newsworld in Canada. Foregrounding the role of music in this comparison adds a revealing dimension to the story of how networks attempt to tap into the personal narratives of audio-viewers, whether to reflect the mood of the country (and thus ensure market share) or to convince the audience of their particular take on the news.[3] As we shall see, while CNN communicated a message of "fear and anger" to American news consumers, Canadians received in their living rooms primarily sounds and images that invoked the horror and tragedy of the event. Without empirical evidence, it may be impossible to maintain with certainty that television news music directly influenced public opinion after 9/11. Nonetheless, it is hard to believe that economic and symbolic capital were significantly divorced from political considerations in the minds of American network executives, whose newscasts seemed to promulgate aggressive retaliation in the aftermath of the attacks, while their Canadian counterparts strove to put a human face on the tragedy.

THE POLITICS OF THE NEWS

The United States

Space does not permit an extended discussion of the politics of American network news since the Persian Gulf War of 1991, considered by many to be a milestone in the history of television news for the role it played in the rise of CNN, yet some consideration of the political context for television news music is essential for this study.[4] Much has been written about the so-called "CNN effect," whereby media coverage over the last decade and a half is said to drive foreign policy, yet the actual interrelationship between the two is often far more complex than indicated by the term.[5] Media critic Danny Schechter sees it more as a "mutually dependent relationship that exists between major media and politics, a nexus of power in which political leaders use media exposure to shape opinions and drive policy while media outlets use politicians to confer legitimation on their own power" (2004: 243–44). As entertainment values encroach on news programming in the United States, it becomes easier to manipulate public opinion with the news serving as, in Schechter's words, "a weapon of both mass distraction and misinformation" (ibid.).

The format of much American network and local newscasting reflects these trends. Within the half-hour format of the major network news programs at 6:30 p.m. EST, sound and visual bites have replaced in-depth reporting.[6] Around those "news bites" operates a system for framing items that both draws attention to them and contributes to their power. About this new format for the American news, Schechter writes, "It started with the Gulf War—the packaging of news, the graphics, the music, the classification of stories. . . . If you can get [a sedated public] hooked . . . you have a winner in terms of building audience."[7] The audio-viewer may not be aware of the sonorous and visual realms at work in a newscast, yet, as Nicholas Cook has shown in his study of televised commercials (1998), that very invisibility renders them all the more effective on a subliminal level.

And what messages do these elements communicate to the American public? While one would be taking Schechter's comments too literally to suggest that government officials and media executives openly conspire to influence opinion, there can be little doubt that their "mutually dependent relationship" has enabled each to tap into and shape the dominant American ideology of the time. Even before the advent of the so-called "War on Terrorism," Susan Carruthers convincingly argued that "[beginning in the Reagan administration], the mainstream media duplicated our own partial view [by] labeling specific acts and countries as terrorists . . . and through its reporting, actually built consensus for counter-terrorism measures" (2000: 193).

Canada

On first glance, the news as presented in local Canadian markets could easily be mistaken for U.S. local news, in format and content.[8] While some stylistic differences exist, the ubiquitous presence of commercials throughout Canadian news programming, including that of the Canadian Broadcasting Corporation, invites homologies with U.S. newscasts. As Gaëtan Tremblay succinctly states, "the design of the Canadian television system has been inspired by the British one, but its functioning and its content are largely influenced by the American television industry. . . . The CBC/SRC must combine revenues from advertising as well as government subsidies, which means that it is squeezed between a public and a commercial logic" (2004: 61). Indeed, Canadians themselves are accustomed to the format and production elements of American news—including the music—because of the border's proximity to large American television markets.

Differences are more evident at the national level, where Canadian network news is widely regarded as adopting a more international perspective and spending more time on individual news items.[9] Still, even the CBC regards itself as a private corporation rather than a public institution.[10] And music again reaches across the border, helping to create a North American community and market for news production elements, despite differing national regulatory agencies and policies for communications media.[11]

Thus, a comparison of American and Canadian television news responses to 9/11 will not necessarily reveal fundamental differences as the result of any varying technical approaches to the reporting of the tragic events. This is not to say that such differences did not exist, but that they are to be sought in the content rather than the framework of the news, which requires a review of Canadian public policy and private attitudes toward the United States. Political scientist Howard Cody perceives most Canadians as subscribing to a "continentalist" mindset, which contends that "Canada can keep a separate identity without distancing itself from American policies" (2003: 5). A more nationalist position among Canadians, Cody argues, presents their country as an "autonomous, peace-seeking middle power working globally through multilateral institutions" (p. 14). Still, political observers on both sides of the border regard North American integration as an inevitable process, even as the tired clichés of "longest undefended border" and "a special friendship" resound across the forty-ninth parallel.

Thus, it was in the sense of a "family member unjustly attacked" that Canada came to the support of the United States in the days after 9/11.[12] "Canadians," wrote political scientist Reg Whitaker in a later essay, "instinctively sympathized with Americans, shared their pain and anger" (2003: 252). As in the United States, both verbal outrage and acts of kindness immediately followed the attacks.[13] Canadian troops joined Americans in the ensuing war in Afghanistan, while the Canadian government reviewed its policies regarding terrorism and security, introducing a massive and hastily written Anti-Terrorism Act (Bill C-36) in Parliament just over one month after the attacks, similar to the timeline and passage of the Patriot Act in the U.S. Congress (Roach 2003: 8).

Still, a wide and varied debate sprang up in the Canadian press and on the airwaves regarding the appropriate response to September 11. Several noted Canadian voices sounded a cautionary note, with Thomas Homer-Dixon warning in the *Globe and Mail* against overreacting when it is necessary to find "the roots of this madness" and Alexa McDonough—leader of the most far-left standing national party, the National Democratic Party (NDP)—likewise looking for peaceful solutions to such "mindless violence."[14] A great deal of criticism was directed at the American media and their representation of the attacks. Dale Brazao noted in the *Toronto Star* on September 16, 2001, how "unlike so many U.S. outlets, especially CNN with its 'America's New War' graphic, CBC has offered many alternative points-of-view from the hawks of retaliation and revenge."[15] Canadian commentators and viewers appreciated what they regarded as the non-American coverage from their own network stations, which (among other things) involved, as John Doyle wrote in the *Globe and Mail* on September 17, not making "statements that only fanned the flames of knee-jerk blame."[16]

Yet as I have already suggested, Canadian and American coverage was not as differentiated in the first days after the attacks as the above-cited media observers might have wished. On September 13, John Doyle himself criticized the "voluminous and often confusing coverage across all the American and Canadian networks and all-news stations."[17] The distinctions became more significant and clear after the initial period of shock and confusion ended, giving way to each nation's reflections on its proper next steps and long-term responses. This transition was reflected in the U.S. media by the change in slogan for CNN's coverage at 9:00 a.m. on Friday, September 14, when the first days' graphic "America Under Attack" was replaced by "America's New War" (see Table 3.1 in this chapter's Appendix). The changes in news music in the days immediately after September 11, to which I shall now turn, were equally significant and illuminating.

MUSIC FOR THE NEWS

A multimillion-dollar industry is devoted to providing what might be called "disappearing yet convincing" music for the broadcast news media in North America. Normally, local television stations and even national networks do not possess the resources to support a composer on staff. Thus they turn to production companies that sell licensed packages of musical material, called "elements," for insertion at appropriate moments within a given newscast. Described briefly, the most popular such production elements in television news include:[18]

1) "Opens" and "closes," also known as "titles," which identify the newscast and which one can find in newscasts throughout the world.[19] Through fanfarelike themes in brass and strings over a driving beat, they create the impression of a dynamic newsroom, while at the same time establishing authority in the ears of the audio-viewer.

2) "Stingers" or "teases" are very brief musical and visual markers for an important news item. Occurring just before specific coverage begins, they serve the dual purpose of notifying the public about the importance of the reports to follow and, subliminally, helping to create an attitude within the viewership.[20]

3) "Beds," often also called "promo beds," provide framing and background music under voices and images.[21] Beds at the beginning of broadcasts often take the opening theme and loop several measures in the middle, so that a variable length is possible.

4) "Bumpers" are the musical lead-ins to and lead-outs from commercials, which, like stingers, create a mood for the news items
to which they refer.[22] In television news music, they have the
same effect as the act-ins and act-outs of network serials, since
they help mask transitions into and out of commercial breaks.
Bumpers within one newscast may widely differ, depending on
the topic of the referenced news item.

Thus standard signifying practices in this music industry have
created designations that describe either the placement of the music
(e.g., "opens") or its affect ("teases"), which foregrounds the role and
importance of music as, to use Cook's apt phrase, the "ultimate hidden
persuader" (2000: 122). Indeed, sound engineers working in the realm
of sound design strive for subliminal and thus "natural" effects upon
audio-viewers, in order that they buy into the particular message of
the medium being consumed. Lawrence Grossman, former president of
NBC News, put it even more succinctly with regard to the news music
of CNN and Fox: "The music on the cable channels . . . tells you what
to think."[23] The industry relies on musical signifying practices that are
readily understood and yet seem natural to the recipient. Such commercial uses of musical practices are nothing new, embodied, for example,
in the affectively organized anthologies of music for silent films from
the beginning of this century.[24]

Production companies of today fully subscribe to the idea of music
as bearer of explicit messages, as is evidenced by their own, often
disturbing, marketing rhetoric. Shelly Palmer Productions, Inc., of New
York City, for example, sells to radio and television stations news music
packages that are guaranteed to have an effect on listeners and viewers.
In the significantly named package "Brave New World," the production
elements are alternately described as "majestic," "hard-hitting," "jazz-
oriented," and "timeless," suggesting a full range of musical expression
and moods.[25] Designations like "Crime" and "Coping" make the signification of specific four-and-one-half-second cuts clear, musically
corresponding to our expectations from the descriptive titles.[26]

These examples prove that the networks have come to recognize for
their news broadcasts what television advertising agencies have long
known: music is unsurpassed in its ability to tap into the personal narratives of individual viewers and tie them into the diegesis. As Claudia
Gorbman observes in her landmark book *Unheard Melodies*, "Music
may act as a 'suturing' device . . . lessening awareness of the technological
nature of film discourse. Music gives a 'for-me-ness' to the soundtrack.
. . . [and] increases the spectator's susceptibility to suggestion" (1987: 5).

Put in slightly different terms, if music is an important component in the construction of personal narrative, and the newscast is geared to convince the viewer that its purpose coincides with his or her narrative ("following the stories that are important to YOU" or "keeping an eye on YOUR city"), then this can create a commonality so that the audio-viewer regards the music chosen for a particular production element as natural and his or her own choice.

These comments apply equally well to music produced for the Canadian broadcast news media. Like their counterparts in the United States, network and local television stations in Canada rely on standard news music practices to give shape to their newscasts (opens, stingers, beds, bumpers). Given the smaller market, Canadian news producers may even purchase music packages from American production companies, which helps foster cross-border connections between networks. One question that remains is to what extent this musical tapping into personal narrative can actually influence the audio-viewer of television news. Does television news music simply reinforce preexisting audience sentiments in hopes of increasing market share, or does it actually convince audio-viewers of a specific position on the news, exploiting a deeper nexus of ideology, semiotics, and public opinion? Comments by network executives make it clear that their strategy at the beginning of (and even before) the war in Iraq was to convince the American public that this was a "just" war, so that television news and its music took on the function of propaganda.[27] The same was true of the stingers and other production elements for the television news coverage of the Persian Gulf War. Such empirical evidence is lacking for television coverage of 9/11, however, both for the intentions of network executives and the actual impact of the production elements upon audio-viewers. Still, as already argued, the mainstream media—given its "mutually dependent relationship" with government—both reinscribed dominant American ideology about terrorism and "built consensus for counter-terrorism measures" (Carruthers 2000: 193). The American networks stood to benefit from openly advocating a pro-retaliation position. What is surprising is how quickly a network like CNN took up this call, with a musical theme that perfectly suited, and indeed worked to engender, an aggressive retaliatory politics.

THE SOUNDS OF TELEVISION NEWS MUSIC AFTER 9/11

At 16:02:40, September 11, 2001, CNN first presented its 9/11 graphic and image stinger, featuring footage of the second plane crashing into the World Trade Center under the words "America Under Attack" (without music, but with the sounds of the crash). The images were clearly intended to evoke feelings of shock, horror, and tragedy among the viewers. Ten hours later, at 2:00 a.m. on September 12, CNN added music to the package, and the *auricularity* of that particular music helped define a new affect.[28] In the music, we hear the sounds of military attack and tones of fear and anger introduced through the aggressive musical theme, which takes us beyond the here-and-now of the shocking, tragic video images. A whole sonic realm (which I will discuss in detail presently) worked with the visuals to produce their impact on the television audience. In the context of television, this political application of music, the "hidden persuader," is all the more powerful not only by virtue of the size of its audience, but also—when successful—because it "seems natural." Perceived "naturalness" is culturally determined, however, meaning that a given musical element is not the only, inevitable choice. Case in point: for news viewers in Canada, the music communicated a different perspective after the initial period of shock, not one of "fear and anger" but rather one of "tragedy."

Television networks in both countries were counting on the ability of music not only to sell their particular coverage of 9/11, but also as time went on to convey an attitude about that event, whereby American media empires seemed to be marching in lockstep with the administration's desire to foster a "climate of fear."[29] Music on CNN, for example, became a means for structuring and communicating its overriding message of fear and anger, most clearly manifested in the network's reuse of the same basic musical material for its unfolding crisis coverage from the early hours of September 12 through the bombing of Afghanistan on October 7. In contrast, though Canadian networks employed the same type of musical production elements in the days immediately following the attacks, as evidenced in CBC Newsworld coverage of unfolding events, they quickly abandoned the special format in their reporting on the war on terrorism.

United States

In his essay "Welcome to the Desert of the Real!" written on September 15, 2001, Slavoj Žižek speculated that the media (and Hollywood) had long been preparing the American public for just such a terrorist act as occurred the morning of September 11.[30] Borrowing from Morpheus's ironic greeting "welcome to the desert of the real" in the film *The Matrix* (a phrase originally inspired by Jean Baudrillard), Žižek noted how "the awareness that we live in an insulated artificial universe . . . generates the notion that some ominous agent is threatening us all the time with total destruction" (2002: 387). This is, of course, a frequently articulated point about American insularity and insecurity, but one that would be borne out anew—as if in response to Žižek's early questioning of "how the events will be symbolized, what their symbolic efficiency will be, what acts they will be evoked to justify" (p. 389)—in how U.S. television networks manipulated and exploited the continuous sense of threat and fear among the audio-viewing public during the hours, days, and weeks following 9/11. The following survey of CNN's developing coverage (presented in Table 3.1) and the gradual reintroduction of customary newscast elements between September 11 and 17 reveals how musical elements were also utilized in pursuit of this agenda.

As I have already noted, at 4:02 p.m. on September 11, CNN first presented the graphic it would use for the first four days of its coverage, "America Under Attack," adding music at 2:00 a.m. on the following day and thus giving audio-viewers their first full package of integrated 9/11 graphics, video, and music, as is typical of stingers for breaking events. It is important to linger for a moment over the musical theme introduced at this time, as it played a recurring role in CNN coverage of events stretching from 9/11 to the launch of the war in Afghanistan a month later. The composer of the theme is not known, but he or she was likely commissioned by CNN; the music does not appear to be archival, especially considering its appropriateness for the accompanying images. The essential musical ingredients include martial snare drums, a driving string part, and a concluding plagal cadence and bell sound, referencing the drums of attack and war, the urgent, leaping strings of action and danger, the unresolved cadence of open-ended conflict, and the bell of death and of a call to arms. I will henceforth call this theme "fear and anger" (Figure 3.1).

Given a lifetime of experiences with such music, audio-viewers could immediately sense from the theme, independent of any images used with it, that it fell within usual representations of military attack. This and the other network theme music for 9/11 thus served the dual purpose of reenacting the attack (evoking horror and fear in the news consumers) while simultaneously suggesting that we needed to respond (cultivating anger). The message embedded in this theme, I submit, is this: "Tragic as it may be, this was an attack on America that took place in your backyard. We should be afraid—it could happen again. Let us get the evildoers so they are punished and we make sure this does not happen again!"[31]

Media commentators are so unaccustomed to observing music that they actually misreported its use in American television newscasts after 9/11, forwarding the common (but erroneous) belief that the networks' coverage first focused primarily on the grievous results of the attack,

Figure 3.1 CNN Fear and Anger Theme, musical transcription.

and only later turned to thoughts of revenge. For example, MIT media specialist William Uricchio asserted that "by September 15, [CNN] news coverage carried the graphic 'America at War' accompanied by subdued martial theme music (an element conspicuously absent for the first two days or so)."[32] Close study of the video record of American network newscasts reveals this "conspicuous absence" as mere wishful thinking. From the start, the musical message was one of retribution for the attack, feeding from the climate of fear established well before 9/11, as Žižek and others have argued.

This is not to say that other musical tones and styles were lacking in television newscasting after September 11. A case in point is the "Adagio for Strings" by Samuel Barber, which was so ubiquitous in performance and in broadcasting that it became an unofficial "anthem" for 9/11.[33] Nevertheless, the "Adagio for Strings" and similarly doleful selections by Bach and others were not well suited for the purposes of news production elements, in great part because of the time they required "to say something." Indeed, reviewing the 9/11 stingers used by the major American networks reveals a uniformity of thematic materials that parallels similarities in graphics and other production elements: mournful music found its place among the diegetic sounds within news reports, but not as framing or structuring elements. In contrast, as we shall see, by significantly extending the stinger/promo bed at the beginning of its own newscasts (hereafter called "Special Open"), the Canadian network CBC Newsworld was able to work tones of sadness into its September 11 theme.

The introduction of the musical element in the CNN stinger at 2:00 a.m. on September 12 marked for the audio-viewing public an important orientation point. As the aforementioned production companies have demonstrated, most recently in the case of the war in Iraq, music is unsurpassed in creating impressions of reality and stability where they do not exist. In general, Uricchio posits that "the quick transformation of unpredictable live events into familiar narrative patterns . . . frames the event, establishing specific ways of thinking about the situation, together with an inclination towards narrative resolution."[34] In the case of the CNN musical theme, its recurrence for the next month under altered graphics and story lines reminded the American television news consumer that although the ongoing crisis may have entered new phases, "the desert of the real" remains a scary place until we exorcise those demons!

At 8:01 a.m. on September 12, CNN enhanced the normalizing process and heightened its authority by introducing for the first time its well-known station identification, "This is CNN," followed by an extended version of the "America Under Attack" stinger. Twelve hours later the network further increased its manipulation of the news through a 1' 20" promo bed, replete with the extended version of the 9/11 "fear and anger" theme and a modified graphic. This was the last stage in CNN's transformation of the chaos of early 9/11 into a regulated, controlling frame—the fact that the menacing music of "fear and anger" played over the various news items in the bed meant that all aspects of the crisis, including grief and mourning, would be subsumed under those elemental emotions. We were not allowed to grieve without experiencing hostility as well.

During the course of September 12, audio-viewers began to hear fragments of diegetic music, from the prayer vigil at the Senate, unidentified church services and even performances of street musicians (see Table 3.2 in the Appendix). Between 5:57:50 and 6:00:30 a.m. on September 12, CNN presented the public with one of several video montages in which music played a role, in this case, featuring images of the crashes, the collapses, smoke from the rubble, recovery attempts, grief-stricken searchers and volunteers, all over "Amazing Grace" as sung at the Rotunda the previous day. However, this and all of the other diegetic and nondiegetic music of mourning was broadcast at a "weak" point in the traditional news program, just before the hour. Often reserved for human-interest stories, the slot at the end of a newscast is the place for the "heart" in television newscasts, whereas the top of the hour brings the "real" news. Traditions in newscasting establish the hierarchy of items through the power and authority conveyed by relative position within the program. The message from the placement of items after 9/11 was direct: grieving must give way to action. Moreover,

CNN packaged and framed every aspect of the previous days' events like a music video. Editing took the place of spontaneity, affect replaced effect, and the best images of grieving were thus taken up into the "highlights" reel. In fact, CNN's pair of reporters for the live transmission of the prayer service from the National Cathedral at 11:00 a.m., September 14, sounded more like color commentators for a sporting event than observers of a dignified ceremony of national mourning.

These principles of editing, placement, and succession are best observed in the CNN newscast from 11:57:00 p.m. to 00:00:10 a.m. on September 14 (the network had already replaced the "America Under Attack" graphic with "America's New War" at 8:00 a.m. that morning). Here a video montage of grievous images over a performance of the song "Spirit of America" from the National Cathedral gives way at 11:59:40 to CNN's own expression of condolences (accompanied by a fragment from "God Bless America"), which yields in turn at 00:00:10 to the "fear and anger" stinger. The same progression is evident in the minutes before and after 8:00 p.m. that evening, moving from the music of candlelight vigils to that of the "fear and anger" stinger and promo bed. Promo bed comments like the following, spoken by Aaron Brown at 10:00:30 p.m. on September 14, could only reinforce the musical message: "Those who allegedly carried out the evil act are named, but more of them are said to be among us, ready to wreak more havoc."

The American networks all reintroduced commercial breaks into their newscasts on Sunday, September 16, as their programming also resumed its daily cycle. The return of commercials may have signaled the final stage in the restoration of normalcy on one level, but on another it enabled networks to do what they perhaps do best: use sound and image to sell their own product, their coverage of and take on the news. This meant bringing back the framing device of pre- and post-commercial bumpers that encouraged viewers to stay tuned and the commercial spots for a given network's coverage of the unfolding events. In the case of CNN, all of the traditional musical production elements—stingers, bumpers, promo beds—derived from the 9/11 fear and anger theme, which increased its presence even as those permitted (yet disempowered) echoes of mourning died away. The real news in the coming weeks consisted of a daily amalgam of reports about the aggressive hunt for the dehumanized non-Westerners behind 9/11 and about the potential new dangers lurking in our own backyard, whether Arab-Americans or biological/chemical agents. Let us take a closer look at the musical elements for the CNN hour-long evening newscast at 6:00 p.m., on a randomly selected day, September 24 (Table 3.2 in the Appendix). After the extended "fear and anger" stinger with promo bed at the beginning of the broadcast, which establishes the tone for the news and through its signification creates a link with the audio-viewer, we have five commercial breaks that also enable the theme to do its affective work as bumper before and after the break. Embedded within two of those breaks are advertisements for CNN's coverage of events, which exploit sound and image to sell the network's take on the unfolding events.

Thus when they tuned in to CNN on October 8, 2001, the day after military action in Afghanistan officially began, audio-viewers were well prepared for what greeted them: they had been hearing the musical call for such action for over a month, as CNN used the 9/11 theme music ("fear and anger") for the attack on Afghanistan. Again, it cannot be coincidental that CNN had created thematic material that could unproblematically bridge the stages of the crisis. Coupled with the theme's character, this continuity of musical material is one of the strongest arguments for suggesting that the network intended not only to reflect the mood of the country but also to have an impact on it.

Canada

Canadian networks also came up with musical themes for their coverage of the September 11 tragedy and its aftermath. For the purposes of this study, CBC Newsworld may well provide the best Canadian comparator with CNN, for it is a twenty-four-hour cable television news channel that, unlike the publicly funded CBC, receives its financial backing through commercial advertising and cable subscriber fees. CBC Newsworld shares a comparable venerability with CNN, to the extent that it is the third oldest such television service, after CNN in the United States and Sky News in the United Kingdom; CBC Newsworld began broadcasting in 1989. Like CNN (and other American and Canadian networks), it also provides titled news programs at key points of the day ("CBC News: Morning," for example), albeit in a more extended time slot. For CBC Newsworld, the prime-time national newscast is "The National," which airs at 9:00 p.m. and is anchored by Peter Mansbridge.

By 11:30 a.m. on September 11, CBC Newsworld was already using the graphic title "Attack on the U.S.A." Music did not yet play a role, with ongoing commentary over live video taking precedence. Unlike the American broadcasters, however, which relied on expert "talking heads," CBC Newsworld engaged in a dialogue with concerned citizens through call-ins, as MuchMusic was doing throughout the day.[35]

At 18:00 on that same day, CBC Newsworld initiated a media step that CNN would not undertake until early the following morning: it provided an extended musical theme to accompany video footage and a graphic title to identify its coverage of the unfolding story.[36] The editing and sound of the music suggest that the network was taking archival and new themes and revising them for the general need and specific video footage at hand. Indeed, over the following nine hours, CBC Newsworld carefully and constantly reworked the music (and images) for its top-of-the-hour theme, undoubtedly attempting to find the right tone for its 9/11 broadcasting. The result was a humanizing narrative, whereby the horrific spectacularity of the crashes gave way to the heart-wrenching human tragedy of the aftermath.

Like his or her CNN counterpart, the identity of the composer for the CBC Newsworld 9/11 music is unknown. In its first appearance, the CBC Newsworld theme falls into two parts, with separate cues. The first, in G minor, against the network's Special Report graphic, sounds very synthesized, with trumpet, bass, and percussion creating a "generic" solemn tone that could also be appropriate for an election-night special (Table 3.3 in the Appendix). There is no attempt to synchronize music and images and—significantly—this "canned" part of the theme does not return in later versions. After the initial voice-over ("This is a Special Report") ends, the second, longer part of the theme begins, in which aspects of the "CBC sound" vie with newly composed and edited musical materials, all accompanying powerful video footage of the two crashes and collapses (Figure 3.2).

Here synchronization is the rule. The trademark CBC cymbal swells or rolls (as also heard on "The National"), off the beat and yet synchronized with the images, must have been added in the editing room, suggesting that this section of the musical cue is archival as well. The sampled string sound is more sophisticated and convincing than the opening trumpet notes, and its driving, irregular rhythm—to all intents and purposes the "clave" rhythm—sustains the necessary sense of something dramatic happening.[37] Although the clave rhythm has associations with Latin American dance idioms and a certain tropicality and sensuality, here the syncopated rhythm gives a drive and intensity that may have simply arisen from the musical materials the composer had at hand to create those effects. For the sake of building in a melodic goal, the unnamed composer added a quick, rising minor third scalar figure at the end of the phrase, which repeats itself four times during the twenty-five-second theme. To enhance the drama, the music editor added cymbal rolls at key moments in the edited visual narrative: the first roll occurs just as the second jet collides with the building; the second is heard as the first tower collapses and smoke billows forth; and the third accompanies a scene of firefighters fleeing the fall of the

Key to "Graphic Hits" cues:

1. Splash cymbal synchronized with insert shot of plane approaching the South Tower.

2. Cymbal and gong swell synchronized to South Tower impact, with image tracking from left to right. Peak of swell (measure 3, beat 3) synchronized to explosion as insert image expands to full screen.

3. Bass drum and anvil synchronized to collapse of the North Tower as insert image expands downwards.

4. Cymbal and gong swell synchronized to continued footage of the North Tower collapse expanding downwards.

5. Bass drum, cymbal and vocal whoop synchronized with insert shot of dust cloud enveloping a New York street. Final cymbal swell synchronized with the approach of the cloud and the expansion of the insert image to full screen.

Figure 3.2 CBC Special Open Theme, musical transcription.

second tower. These sounds are not synchronized with the rest of the music and images, which creates a sense of unpredictability and disorder (the basis for later associations with madness), even as the cymbal rolls identify the coverage as that of CBC Newsworld. What is missing in all of this amalgam of music and images are the sounds of war: we lack the militance added by the snare drums, brass fanfares, and martial rhythms of American musical production elements after September 11. Rather, the theme bespeaks drama and concern, and does not easily lend itself to an interpretation as a call to arms.

Within traditions of television news music, the 18:00 production element on CBC Newsworld occupies an unusual niche. Too long for a customary newscast stinger, yet lacking the verbal narrative and invitation of the promo bed, the theme leads the audio-viewer through the day's events, from the horror to the grieving. For purposes of this study, this package of music and video will be called the "special open," with the music itself termed the "special open theme." This theme served as the basis for CBC Newsworld musical production elements for the rest of the week.

At midnight, the beginning of September 12, CBC Newsworld settled on a general format for the special open theme that would serve them far into the day, with some ongoing changes. The theme fell into two parts, the first accompanying new black-and-white video images against a heartbeat pulse, the second drawing upon the sights and sounds already audio-viewed at the 18:00 spot. The effect of the opening black-and-white section is to draw the audio-viewer into the human side of the tragedy, the absence of color creating a sense both of the documentary past and the postapocalyptic future, while the heartbeat reinforces the feeling of helplessness for the victims.

The point of transition to the second section is the appearance of the "Attack Upon the U.S.A." graphic in color. The clave-rhythm theme reappears with new images of the planes crashing and the buildings falling. It is clear that the editors now cut the film to the music: the preexisting music track remains unchanged, while the edits move the explosions to the beat. The cymbal swells continue to fall off the beat, but at a slightly later point in the sequence of images (the whole special open lasts over 40 seconds). The video footage still follows the sequence of events, from the initial crashes through the falling towers, but now new slow-motion images of suffering and grieving survivors follow, added undoubtedly as the footage became available to broadcasters. This human dimension is deepened by the introduction of the diegetic voices of horror when one of the towers collapsed. The editors return the audio-viewer to the larger drama at the end with another cymbal swell for final close-up video images of the collapse of Tower 5.

In this new version of the theme, the editors introduce the tubular bell to reinforce the beat (it is not given the same power of narrative emphasis that the cymbal swell possesses). Whereas the instrument has a certain set of significations for audio-viewers of CNN, in the case of CBC broadcasting, the public will recognize that sound as almost a trademark, a station identification for the network. Its alternation on the pitches of F and G also characterizes CBC practice, from its news broadcasts to comedic programs like "This Hour Has 22 Minutes."[38] The use of tubular bell may be a matter of CBC product "branding" or may reflect a preference by the composer under contract for the network's news music.

For the 1:00 a.m. presentation of the special open, the editors have again provided some revisions to that which came before. If the 12:00 a.m. version of the music included the greatest number of cymbal swells edited onto the music track, this one removed most of the percussion "punch-ups." The result is a gentler sounding, but also less dramatic, narrative.

The editors must have identified that problem with the 1:00 a.m. version; in the CBC Newsworld program an hour later at 2:05 a.m.—the same time as CNN's first use of music—the theme has several of the punches restored. It would appear that the desired balance was struck, for essentially the same version was used at 3:00 a.m. New in this version, however, is the greater reliance upon diegetic sounds, with a siren and more of the human voice added to the mix, so that the horrific and tragic aspects of the attacks are equally presented in the forty-second special open theme.

In the days following September 11, the editing of visual and musical elements continued, though CBC Newsworld did not depart from the basic musical theme that the public heard during the first night of coverage. At 12:00 noon on September 12, the special open presented primarily new images, although still following the rough chronological sequence of events on 9/11, with the addition of smoldering ruins at the end. The heartbeat at the beginning, the string "clave" melody with the rising minor third at the end, the cymbal swells timed to the footage of the crashes and collapses, the pitched tubular bells on F and G, the diegetic voices of horror: all of these elements are present, reinforcing the branding of the CBC Newsworld coverage.

CBC Newsworld reintroduced commercial breaks shortly after midnight on September 15. Advertising for the network's coverage of breaking news events enabled the CBC to transcend the limitations of functionality for music production elements. On September 17 at 19:25, for example, CBC Newsworld aired a thirty-second spot for its newscasting of breaking stories. Although the voice-over never mentions September 11, all of the video images are from that crisis. The sequence of one-second video bites seems almost random: the plane crashing into the second tower, the Statue of Liberty, George W. Bush, firefighters helping survivors, a damaged vehicle and flower near the site, walking firefighters, two helicopters, collapse of a tower, rescue efforts in the ruins, a candlelight vigil, a woman in prayer, the plane crashing into the second tower, fire hoses in action, firefighters at work, the smoldering ruins, a waving American flag, grieving observers, a distant shot of the wreckage, a close shot of the smoking first tower, and then a quick sequence of titles for the daily news programs offered by the network. It is important to note that these are not static video shots; rather, they involve quick pan-ins and -outs, shaky camera work, and the like, evoking the excitement of live coverage and the "happeningness" of amateur footage. The text: "CBC Newsworld, around the clock, 24 hours a day, seven days a week. Live. Responding immediately, on the scene, and on the air. Bringing you the latest when it happens, where it happens. Keeping you on top of the story. Watch CBC Newsworld, the best media coverage. We are Canada's news network." Against this we hear what is essentially a new, agitated percussion track with irregular accents, accompanied by a synthesized keyboard track that provides minimal melodic material. The sound is that of a tom-tom, which reaches a climax of rhythmic and dynamic excitement at the end of the spot, when the CBC Newsworld logo is revealed. Image, voice, and music are rhythmically coordinated, trying to convince us that the network's news coverage gives us what we want and need.

After the weekend of September 15–16, the CBC Newsworld 9/11 special open and its music disappeared from their news broadcasting, as did the other production elements specifically associated with the tragedy. The attacks and their aftermath still dominated the news, at least for the time being, but they were integrated into the framework of the traditional CBC newscast, with a return of the broadcast's standard titles theme and production music. 9/11 remained a matter for remembrance and concern, yet the next steps for the Canadians were not clearly articulated in the semiotics of television news. At least as far as CBC Newsworld was concerned, the events of 9/11 were a human tragedy and a call to vigilance, but not cause for single-minded coverage and thoughts of retaliation.[39] The rhetoric of a military response to the attacks did not have the same foothold in Canada, and thus the war in Afghanistan demanded a new set of production elements in October, when Canada decided to join the United States and its other allies.

CONCLUSIONS

As I have demonstrated through this analysis of selected media responses to September 11 on both sides of the forty-ninth parallel, different messages were being communicated by television networks in the United States and Canada through the potent medium of news music. In short, while the 9/11 theme and news music of CNN—at that time, the most widely watched American news provider—encouraged audiences' feelings of fear and anger, CBC Newsworld presented the Canadian audio-viewer with sounds evoking primarily the horror and tragedy of the event. Despite their common language and framework for reporting on the news, in the days after the attacks, CNN and CBC Newsworld revealed contrasting subject positions through distinct musical responses to 9/11, one seeming to encourage military retaliation, the other emphasizing the human tragedy of the events. In each case, the music served to brand its network's coverage of the attacks and their aftermath. While television news music alone may not have forced audio-viewers to adopt a specific response to the events of September 11, its power to participate in subliminal ideological persuasion among its consumers—as a medium that, in Lawrence Grossman's words, tells us "what to think"—cannot be denied (Engstrom 2003: 45). Ratings, affect, and effect were inseparable in this nexus of ideology, semiotics, and public opinion. Networks in both countries stood to benefit from openly advocating positions that fed from, reinforced, and ultimately helped shape the mood of each nation. As already argued, the mainstream media in the United States, operating in a "mutually dependent relationship" with the government, both reinscribed dominant American ideology about terrorism and "built consensus for counterterrorism measures," and this applies in particular to CNN (Carruthers 2000: 193). In contrast, CBC Newsworld showed no initial enthusiasm for taking military action, choosing to focus instead on the horror and tragedy of the events of September 11.[40] The music these networks used to accompany their voices and images performed its ideological role well: it was effective, yet natural and hidden. Welcome to the desert of the hyper-real.

APPENDIX

Table 3.1 Summary timeline (EST) for CNN news coverage, September 11–14

(Note: first use of repeated news music elements marked in bold; not all occurrences of "America Under Attack" stinger indicated)

September 11

07:49:50	CNN suspends commercial newscasting
16:02:40	**First use of graphic "America Under Attack"**
20:59:30	Images and sounds of senators singing "God Bless America"

September 12

02:00:00	**First use of graphic, video, and "fear and anger" theme for stinger**
05:00:00	**First use of musical station ID "This Is CNN"**
05:59:50	Organ music from an unspecified service
07:00:20	**First use of extended "America Under Attack" stinger**
08:01:20	Extended "America Under Attack" stinger
13:41:09	Bells and church choir
13:42:40	"God Bless America"
19:53:50	"Amazing Grace" from Senate prayer vigil
20:03:40	Altered, extended "America Under Attack" stinger
22:00:20	Altered, extended "America Under Attack" stinger (more fearful bells, percussion)
22:59:50	Street musicians playing "Taps"
23:01:00	**First use of extended "America Under Attack" stinger with promo bed**
23:56:00	Organ music, "My Country, 'Tis of Thee" from service in Paris
23:58:40	Music under comments from world

September 13

00:01:00	Short "America Under Attack" stinger
00:58:00	**First video montage using diegetic music**
01:00:30	Extended "America Under Attack" stinger
05:57:50	**First video montage using nondiegetic music** ("Amazing Grace" from Senate prayer vigil under images of first twenty-four hours)
06:00:30	Short "America Under Attack" stinger
06:59:00	Sounds and images of mourners

Table 3.1 (continued) Summary timeline (EST) for CNN news coverage, September 11–14

07:00:20	"This Is CNN" (hourly hereafter)
07:00:30	Extended "America Under Attack" stinger with promo bed
20:01:50	Extended "America Under Attack" stinger with promo bed
22:00:10	**First use of CNN "Our Thoughts and Prayers . . .," before extended "America Under Attack" stinger with promo bed**
	September 14
09:00:30	"Our Thoughts . . ."
09:00:50	**First use of new graphic "America's New War" with altered video, same music**
11:07:05	**Live coverage of dignitaries' arrival at Washington National Cathedral using diegetic music**
12:00:00–13:18:20	**Live coverage of prayer service from Washington National Cathedral using diegetic music**
17:59:40	Music of celebrating Palestinians
18:03:10	"Our Thoughts . . ."
19:02:40	"I'm Proud to Be an American" from live prayer vigil over video images
19:08:20	"This Is CNN," short "America's New War" stinger
19:59:50	Extended "America's New War" stinger with promo bed
20:59:50	Recorded excerpt from "The Battle Hymn of Republic" for orchestra from National Cathedral
21:00:10	*Larry King Live*: no music
21:59:00	Recorded excerpt from "America the Beautiful" for singer and guitar from National Cathedral
22:00:20	"Our Thoughts . . ."
22:00:30	Extended "America's New War" stinger with promo bed
23:57:00	Video montage of images from 9/11 and prayer service at National Cathedral, over "Spirit of America" from Cathedral service
23:59:40	"Our Thoughts . . ."
	September 15
00:00:10	Short "America's New War" stinger

Table 3.2 Timeline for CNN Evening News, 6:00 p.m. (EST) on September 24, 2001

18:00:00–18:01:10	Extended "fear and anger" stinger with promo bed
[...]	Unrelated coverage
18:17:40–18:18:00	"Fear and anger" bumper
18:18:00–18:20:30	Ads for Verisign, Centra, Hitachi, Brobeck, The Point, *Larry King Live*
18:20:40–18:20:50	"Fear and anger" bumper
[...]	Unrelated coverage
18:30:50–18:31:10	"Fear and anger" bumper
18:31:10–18:31:40	Ad for Monster.com
18:31:40–18:32:10	Ad for CNN "America's New War" coverage
18:32:10–18:33:10	Ads for Red Cross; Comcast
18:33:10–18:33:20	"This Is CNN"
18:33:20–18:33:40	"Fear and anger" bumper
[...]	Unrelated coverage
18:38:20–18:38:30	Short "fear and anger" bumper
18:38:30–18:41:00	Ads for Monster.com, Time/Life Jazz
18:41:00–18:41:10	Short "fear and anger" bumper
[...]	Unrelated coverage
18:47:20–18:47:40	"Fear and anger" bumper
18:47:40–18:50:10	Ads for Shell PSA, Qwest, Dell, Ad Council, Cigna
18:50:40–18:51:00	"Fear and anger" bumper
[...]	Unrelated coverage
18:55:10–18:55:30	"Fear and anger" bumper
18:55:30–18:56:00	Ad for Hitachi
18:56:00–18:56:20	Ad for CNN "America's New War" coverage
18:56:20–18:58:20	Ads for Bass Tire, Food Network, Slime, Toyota
18:58:20–18:58:30	"This Is CNN"
18:58:30–18:58:50	"Fear and anger" bumper
[...]	Unrelated coverage
18:59:50–19:00:00	Short "fear and anger" bumper

Table 3.3 CBC Newsworld "Stinger" for 6:00 pm (EST) Special Report, September 11, 2001

Time	Music	Dialogue	Video Images	Graphics
18:00:00–18:00:06	None	Voice of medic: "Any Suggestions? Should we set up here for medical alert?"	Firefighter, emergency vehicle, shaky camera, fade out	None
18:00:06–18:00:08	None	None	dark screen	None
18:00:08–18:00:16	G Minor, solemn theme (A) with synthesized trumpet, bass, and percussion	Announcer: "This is a CBC Special Report"	Fade in, none	"CBC News Special Report" over blue rotating globe and CBC logo
18:00:16	4x, last time cadential			

REFERENCES

Baum, Matthew A. 2002. "Sex, Lies, and War: How Soft News Brings Foreign Policy to the Inattentive Public." *American Political Science Review* 96 (1): 91–109.

Carruthers, Susan. 2000. *The Media at War.* New York: St. Martin's Press.

Chermak, Steven, Frankie Y. Bailey, and Michelle Brown, eds. 2003. *Media Representations of September 11.* Westport, CT: Praeger.

Chion, Michel. 1995. *Audio-Vision: Sound on Screen.* Translated by Claudia Gorbman. New York: Columbia University Press.

Chomsky, Noam. 2001. *9-11.* New York: Seven Stories Press.

Cody, Howard. 2003. "U.S.-Canada Trade, Defense, and Border Issues Since September 11: The View from Canada." In *Canadian-American Public Policy* 54 (September): 3–20.

Cook, Nicholas. 1998. "Introduction: Music and Meaning in the Commercials." In *Analysing Musical Multimedia*, 3–23. Oxford: Oxford University Press.

———. 2000. *Music: A Very Short Introduction*, 2nd ed. Oxford: Oxford University Press.

Deaville, James. 2006. "Selling the War in Iraq: Television News Music and the Shaping of American Public Opinion." In *Floodgates: Technologies, Cultural (Ex)Change and the Persistence of Place*, edited by Susan Ingram, Markus Reisenleitner, and Cornelia Szabó-Knotik, 25–35. Frankfurt: Peter Lang.

Denton, Jr., Robert E. 1993. *The Media and the Persian Gulf War.* New York: Praeger.

Engstrom, Nicholas. 2003. "The Soundtrack for War." *Columbia Journalism Review* 42(3): 45–47.

Gilboa, Eytan. 2002. "Global Communication and Foreign Policy." *Journal of Communication* 52(4): 731–48.

Gorbman, Claudia. 1987. *Unheard Melodies: Narrative Film Music.* Bloomington, IN: Indiana University Press.

Hoskins, Andrew. 2004. *Televising War: From Vietnam to Iraq.* New York: Continuum.

Jeffords, Susan. 1994. *Seen Through the Media: The Persian Gulf War.* New Brunswick, NJ: Rutgers University Press.

Perras, Lynne. 2002. "Close to Home: On Being Pro-Canadian and Pro-American." In *Canada and September 11: Impact and Response,* edited by Karim-Aly Kassam, George Melnyk, and Lynne Perras, 73–77. Calgary, Alberta: Detselig.

Rapee, Erno. 1925. *Encyclopedia of Music for Pictures.* New York: Belwyn.

Reynolds, Amy, and Brooke Barnett. 2003. "'America under Attack': CNN's Verbal and Visual Framing of September 11." In *Media Representations of September 11,* edited by Steven Chermak, Frankie Bailey, and Michelle Brown, 85–101. Westport, CT: Praeger.

Roach, Kent. 2003. *September 11: Consequences for Canada.* Montreal and Kingston: McGill-Queen's University Press.

Robinson, Piers. 2002. *The CNN Effect: The Myth of News Media, Foreign Policy and Intervention.* London: Routledge.

Schechter, Danny. 2004. "Slaying the Media Beast: The Media Channel as an Act of Personal Responsibility and Political Mission." In *International News in the Twenty-First Century,* edited by Chris Paterson and Anabelle Sreberry, 243–60. Eastleigh, UK: John Libbey.

Tremblay, Gaëtan. 2004. "Canadian Television." In *Contemporary World Television,* edited by John Sinclair, 61–63. Berkeley and Los Angeles: University of California Press.

Whitaker, Reg. 2003. "Keeping Up With the Neighbours? Canadian Responses to 9/11 in Historical and Comparative Context." *Osgoode Hall Law Journal* 41(2–3): 241–64.

Wittebols, James H. 1995. "News and the Institutional Perspective: Sources in Terror Stories." *Canadian Journal of Communication* [Online], 20(1). Available at: http://info.wlu.ca/~wwwpress/jrls/cjc/BackIssues/20.1/index.html.

Žižek, Slavoj. 2002. "Welcome to the Desert of the Real!" *South Atlantic Quarterly* 101(2): 385–89.

ACKNOWLEDGMENTS

My thanks extend first and foremost to the staff of the Vanderbilt Television News Archive, who enabled me to conduct onsite research into this topic during a visit in 2004. Melody Mostad and Cenk Enhos of Carleton University, Maxwell MacOdrum Library, provided invaluable assistance in searching their CBC Newsworld archival holdings. Without such archival collections of daily network newscasts and hourly coverage of breaking news stories like the war in Iraq, this type of investigative research would not be possible. Valuable comments have been contributed by Anahid Kassabian (Fordham University), Robyn Stilwell (Georgetown University), David Shumway (Carnegie Mellon University), Philip Tagg (Université de Montréal), and Michael Saffle (Virginia Tech), whom I thank for their generous assistance. Simon Wood merits special mention for his insightful observations about the CBC Newsworld coverage of September 11 and its aftermath.

NOTES

1. See in particular the collection *Media Representations of September 11,* edited by Steven Chermak, Frankie Y. Bailey, and Michelle Brown (2003). Though illuminating in many other ways, the volume as a whole is typically weak in its discussion of music and other audio aspects of broadcast media. For example, in an analysis of CNN's 9/11 coverage, Amy Reynolds and Brooke Barnett simply and unproblematically equate the verbal frame of the newscasts with their audio component (2003: 85–101).
2. The United States and Canada are arguably the two media markets that most significantly exploit music in televised news contexts, making a comparison of their news music particularly productive.
3. Michel Chion (1995) coined the term "audio-viewer" for the consumer of film and television, in order to foreground (or at least bring into balance) the sonic aspect of the media, which disappears through the traditional designations of "viewing" or "watching."
4. A number of studies about the news media and the Persian Gulf War have appeared, including Denton (1993), Jeffords (1994), and Hoskins (2004).
5. See especially Gilboa 2002 and Robinson 2002 for critical views on the "CNN effect."
6. All broadcast times in this essay are given according to Eastern Standard Time, even though the Vanderbilt Television News Archive indexes its holdings according to the local Central Standard Time.
7. Cited in Baum 2002: 105.
8. To date, there exists no comprehensive, comparative study of television news between Canada and the United States.
9. See Wittebols 1995.

10. For example, the CBC does not provide the general public with access to its archives unless a restrictive fee is paid, the same fee required of corporate users.
11. Tremblay (2004: 61–63) compares the regulatory agencies FCC and CRTC.
12. Lynne Perras uses this metaphor in her essay "Close to Home: On Being Pro-Canadian and Pro-American" (2002: 76). In a similar vein, the Canadian Department of Foreign Affairs and International Trade emphasized the "between friends" angle in a special issue of its quarterly journal *Canada World View* (Issue 14, Winter 2002), bearing the cover title "Compassion and Resolve: Canada's Response to the September 11 Terrorist Attacks."
13. It should be noted that some of the deceased were Canadians.
14. Both quoted in Roach 2003: 116–17.
15. Dale Brazao, "Unable to Look Away," *Toronto Star,* Entertainment, 16 September 2001.
16. John Doyle, "Television: Some Talking Heads Should Bite Their Tongues," *Globe and Mail,* 17 September 2001.
17. John Doyle, "Day After: Television: When 'Oh My God' Was All They Could Say," *Globe and Mail,* 13 September 2001.
18. These "definitions" might be better termed "descriptions," as no authoritative glossary of the industry exists. The descriptions are based upon my own observations of a variety of Web sites for television production element providers, though terms may well vary from one company to another.
19. Interestingly, "opens" from newscasts of other countries (visual and sonic elements) are often presented in North American reporting about the contents of those foreign newscasts—this practice must establish a certain authenticity for the North American representation of the "exotic Other." That music integrally contributes to the establishment of identity here bespeaks its effectiveness as "hidden persuader" (Cook 2000: 122).
20. Probably the best-known "stinger" is associated with CNN's coverage of the Persian Gulf War: a timpani roll that decrescendos against a visual of a tank that quickly comes into focus. The very simplicity of the music creates a believable enemy, whom we vanquish with an authentic cadence.
21. The "promo bed" serves the practical purpose of introducing the leading news items for a broadcast, thus functioning as a hook for the audio-viewer. As always, the prominent role for music in the promo bed adds to the pitch made to convince the audio-viewer that this is the newscast that coincides with his/her personal narrative.
22. Bumpers do not figure in continuous, commercial-free newscasting after a crisis, such as the attacks of 9/11, although networks might use bumpers before and after advertising for their own coverage of the crisis.
23. Quoted in Engstrom 2003: 45.

24. Among the most noted such collections is Erno Rapee's *Encyclopedia of Music for Pictures* (1925), which is a compendium of hundreds of suggestions for musical cues, drawn from the classical and light-classical repertoires and arranged by mood and location.

25. See http://www.shellypalmer.com/pages/bnw.htm.

26. Shelly Palmer Productions offers, for example, three different themes described as "Crime," each with eight varying orchestrations according to the time of day and type of newscast. They also can provide the enterprising station with two "Coping" themes, this time with seven variants for each.

27. See the author's essay "Selling the War in Iraq: Television News Music and the Shaping of American Public Opinion" (2006) for an exposé of the motives behind the networks' musical choices in covering the war's launch in March 2003.

28. I would like to propose the introduction of the terms "auricular" and "auricularity" to provide the sonorous equivalent of "spectacle" and "spectacularity." Up to now, we have had to rely on words from the visual realm to talk about overwhelming musical or sonic experiences.

29. Among the many sources that use the phrase "climate of fear" in discussing Bush administration domestic policy, see in particular Chomsky 2001.

30. Dated September 15th, 2001, Žižek's essay was later published in *South Atlantic Quarterly* (Spring 2002), the version from which quotes in the present chapter are drawn. The work was later revised and expanded as part of Žižek's book of the same title (London: Verso, 2002).

31. Obviously, this represents a personal reading of the media message broadcast to its consumers.

32. William Uricchio, "Television Conventions," contained in the "Intersections" subpage of the Web site Re-constructions, available at http://web.mit.edu/cms/reconstructions/interpretations/tvconventions.html.

33. See Tregear in this volume.

34. Uricchio, "Television Conventions."

35. Uricchio, "Television Conventions."

36. Even though this theme serves the purpose of a stinger, it is too extended and elaborate to justify calling it that. Also, it would be called upon to function as a promo bed, so that a more general designation is appropriate.

37. The "clave" rhythm is a two-measure pattern in 4/4 time, in which the second note occurs off-the-beat and the other values largely fall on unaccented beats; it is widely used in popular music and several versions exist.

38. A product of CBC television and Alliance Atlantis, *This Hour Has 22 Minutes* is a comedy series that features political satire in a series of sketches, news parodies, and editorials.

39. As mentioned above, the Canadian government enacted a set of
    security measures after September 11 that arose both from requests of
    the American administration and from the potential danger of similar
    terrorist attacks on Canadian soil.
40. From my perspective, this take on the events seems to have been shared
    by other Canadian news networks, though a more conclusive assertion
    would of course require closer examination of their taped broadcasts
    from that time period.

4

MODELS OF CHARITY AND SPIRIT:

BRUCE SPRINGSTEEN, 9/11, AND THE WAR ON TERROR

Bryan Garman

In August 2004 Bruce Springsteen published his first-ever editorial, titled "Chords of Change," in the *New York Times.* "A nation's artists and musicians have a particular place in its social and political life," he wrote. "Over the years I've tried to think long and hard about what it means to be an American. . . . I've tried to write songs that speak to our pride and criticize our failures."[1] In the editorial and on both *The Rising* and *Devils and Dust*, his first two albums after 9/11, Springsteen reflected upon the events of that day and their aftermath, and, along with a great number of other poets and songwriters in the United States and abroad, strove to wring meaning from the ashes. In so doing, Springsteen embraced the responsibility that Wendell Berry ascribed to all poets: to address and give historical depth to the moral and political issues of the day, "remind[ing] poet and reader alike of things they have read and heard" by recalling "past voices into presence" (1990: 88–89). Since 9/11, Springsteen has invoked through song an American history steeped in religious principles in an attempt to celebrate those who lost and risked their lives, help the nation grieve, and imbue the event with the moral imperative to ensure that the fallen did not die in vain. Drawing on the nation's (and his own) predominantly Christian heritage, he has comforted and called his listeners to action with familiar biblical imagery and historical references, stripped these references of their dogmatic elements, and summoned his audiences to embrace a humanistic spiritualism. In the process, he has countered politicians and other popular musicians who have framed the ongoing "war on terror" in vengeful, jingoistic terms.

In this essay, I examine selections from Springsteen's post-9/11 work as well as a number of his recent public pronouncements, situating them within the spectrum of American reactions to the attacks and interpreting them through the lens of the Christian tradition to which they so frequently allude. I argue that the spiritual, rather than dogmatic, approach to religion that suffuses Springsteen's works points the way toward a path of redemption and reconciliation that starkly contrasts with the religious and political rhetoric adopted by the Bush administration.

SITUATING SPRINGSTEEN WITHIN THE POLITICS OF FEAR, FAME, AND FAITH

Many Americans, predictably and perhaps understandably, responded to the attacks on the World Trade Center and the Pentagon with a mix of fear, national pride, and anger. No event in the living memory of the country had prepared them for dealing with a violent act of that scale on American soil, and the horrific scenes that unfolded on national television, the ghastly and recurring images of the Twin Towers crumbling, and the harrowing reports of men and women leaping to their deaths etched the day's events deeply into the collective national consciousness. When President Bush visited "Ground Zero" in New York three days later, his words comforted Americans of diverse political stripes. "I can hear you," Bush said to the exhausted rescue workers searching through the rubble. "The rest of the world hears you. And the people who knocked these buildings down will hear all of us soon."[2] Thoughts of self-defense, if not outright revenge, were on the minds of many Americans, and Bush's rhetoric found a receptive audience.

Indeed, those thought to have ties to Al Qaeda heard early and often from U.S. military forces, who were deployed to Afghanistan less than a month after the attacks. Successful in initially dislodging the Taliban regime, they were less so in their attempt to pin down Osama bin Laden. When the apparent architect of 9/11 proved elusive, the Bush administration shifted its focus (and that of the American public) to Iraq, where Saddam Hussein had allegedly stockpiled weapons of mass destruction. Beginning with an air campaign launched in March 2003, designed to "shock and awe" the Iraqis, in both rhetoric and deed "Operation Iraqi Freedom" relied from the outset on violence, lethal force, and a self-assuredness bordering on arrogance. "Overall, our plans are on track," reported General Richard Myers, Chairman of the Joint Chiefs of Staff, early in the war. "We are degrading Iraqi forces, particularly the Republican Guard, by air. . . . And we will engage them with the weight of our combat power at a time and place of our choosing."[3] The U.S. military, Myers and the Bush administration assured the nation, was in firm control; decisive victory was a matter of choosing the timing, after which the weapons of mass destruction would be found. At this writing, more than three years after the invasion, the reality has not corresponded to the rhetoric.

As others note in this volume, a similar language of revenge and retributive justice quickly made its way into American country and other popular music in the weeks and months following the attacks.[4] To cite the most unambiguous example, Toby Keith's career-making 2002 hit "Courtesy of the Red, White & Blue (The Angry American)" asserts that many men and women had died to preserve American "peace" and freedom, and suggests that those who threw this "sucker punch" will be repaid in kind with a "boot in [their] ass / It's the American way." Keith was one of dozens of artists to assert their patriotism and support for the "war on terror" in similar terms.

Bruce Springsteen's 2002 album *The Rising* provided a stark contrast to jingoistic sentiments such as Keith's, offering a far more measured response to the recent national tragedy. At a time when many Americans were voicing mistrust and even animosity toward Muslims, and amid a tremendous upsurge of public references to the Judeo-Christian tradition, Springsteen invoked familiar Christian imagery to comfort his audience, presenting Christian symbols in a manner that eschewed fundamentalism.

Of course, as scholars of cultural studies are quick to remind us, Springsteen's work, along with that of all popular musicians, is produced within complex commercial networks and distributed to diverse audiences whose individual interpretations are shaped by countless factors, many of them idiosyncratic and unknowable.[5] Springsteen's work and career in particular serve as rich case studies for exploring the politics of popular culture: for decades, his songs have been claimed by politicians and fans holding a variety of political perspectives. And given the topics that the album addressed, the charged emotional and political context in which it was released, the historical complexity of the critical response to Springsteen's work, and the then-ebbing state of his popularity, *The Rising* was bound to be open to a variety of interpretations.

The album's release was accompanied by the most intense and focused media campaign for a Springsteen album since *Born in the U.S.A.*

catapulted him to mythic status in 1984. As early as 1975, Springsteen had won the hearts of critics with *Born to Run*, but *Born in the U.S.A.* gave him unprecedented commercial success (over 18 million in sales) and exposure, particularly when Ronald Reagan claimed Springsteen as a fellow traveler during a campaign speech for the 1984 presidential election.[6] The singer would seem to be an unlikely spokesman for the Republican president: the narrator of "Born in the U.S.A.," the album's rousing title track, was a down-and-out, unemployed Vietnam veteran, and the lyrics of this song and "My Hometown," a ballad about a jobless family man, did not easily lend themselves to the conservative social and military policies of the Reagan presidency. As I have argued elsewhere, however, Springsteen's macho image, elusive lyrics, fist-pumping rock-and-roll delivery, and use of the American flag and working-class iconography on the album and in the stadium tour that supported it, obfuscated his political intentions.[7] Following the Reagan episode, he self-consciously sought to clarify his politics, making a public and purposeful move to the left that continued into the 1990s. He recorded a concert version of Edwin Starr's "War" for his *Live 1975–1985* album and introduced the song with a monologue in which he referred to Vietnam as a "bad war" and warned his listeners that "blind faith in your leaders, or in anything, can get you killed." He proclaimed an affinity for Woody Guthrie, the leftist folksinger who espoused pro-labor and antiracist politics. He headlined a 1988 world tour that celebrated the Declaration of Human Rights. And in a long profile published in *The New York Times Magazine*, he criticized the platforms of both Bob Dole and Bill Clinton for not adequately supporting working families in the 1996 presidential election.[8]

Musically, Springsteen's political affiliations were less consistently expressed. In the eighteen years between *Born in the U.S.A.* and *The Rising*, Springsteen produced four albums of original work (excluding *Tracks*, a four-disc compendium of unreleased material), none of which rivaled the commercial success of the Reagan years. *Tunnel of Love* (1987) was a critically acclaimed, introspective album about relationships that did not engage overt political themes. *Human Touch* and *Lucky Town*, both released in 1992, were largely critical failures, and contained some of the most vapid, apolitical work of his career. With the 1995 album *The Ghost of Tom Joad*, however, Springsteen returned to folk music and the leftist inspiration of John Steinbeck and Woody Guthrie; the title track, for example, mocked the "new world order" that George H. W. Bush had predicted would be created by the 1991 Gulf War. A pair of singles recorded for feature films also signaled Springsteen's reengagement with liberal political causes. "Streets of

Philadelphia," written for Jonathan Demme's *Philadelphia*, a film about a gay man dying of AIDS, returned Springsteen to the popular airwaves and earned him an Academy Award. A year later, he wrote the title song for Tim Robbins's politically charged film about the death penalty, *Dead Man Walking*.

Consequently, by the time Springsteen cut *The Rising* in early 2002, his leftist credentials were well established; his position in the market, however, was not at its peak. Seeking to recapture his glory days, Columbia Records unleashed a media blitz that advertised *The Rising* as Springsteen's "first studio album with the E Street Band since *Born in the U.S.A.*" and touted its 9/11 content.[9] Meanwhile, *Time* and *Rolling Stone* ran cover stories lauding the album and the artist. In the *Time* article, Josh Tyrangiel drew attention to Springsteen's personal involvement with the families of victims of the attacks, reverently describing how Springsteen, moved by a number of obituaries that identified deceased 9/11 victims as his fans, personally called surviving family members to express his sympathy and support.[10] Likewise, the *Rolling Stone* article burnished his image as the people's, if not the nation's, poet; Mark Binelli and Rob Sheffield related Springsteen's account of the inspiration for *The Rising*, significantly adding to the heroic mythology that surrounded the album:

> Springsteen still remembers the moment that he realized he needed to make this album. It was a few days after September 11th, and he was leaving the beach. A man drove by, rolled his window down and yelled, "We need ya!" Then he rolled his window up and kept going. "And I thought, 'Well, I've probably been a part of this guy's life for a while,'" Springsteen says. "And people wanna see other people they know, they wanna be around things they're familiar with. So he may need me right about now. That made sense, like, 'Oh, I have a job to do.' Our band, hopefully, we were built to be there when the chips are down. That was part of the idea of the band, to provide support."[11]

Critics were quick to echo the mythologizing tone of these stories. In a review of a show from *The Rising* tour written for the *Washington Post*, David Segal offered heartfelt thanks to Springsteen: "Lordy, lordy, we needed that," he wrote. "We needed Bruce Springsteen even more than we thought, and we thought we needed him a lot."[12]

Cast as a rock-and-roll poet being called to serve the public, the normally private, television-shy Springsteen accepted a flurry of invitations for televised appearances. He performed and was interviewed on NBC's *Today Show*, appeared on CBS's *Late Night with David Letterman*, performed on NBC's *Saturday Night Live*, was interviewed on ABC's *Nightline*, and, near the end of the tour, allowed portions of a pre-recorded concert performance to be aired in prime time. Critics greeted the new album with great enthusiasm. Kurt Loder of MTV and *Rolling Stone* observed that Springsteen's "most resonant works stand as milestones in the lives of millions of fans. Even for him, though, *The Rising*, with its bold thematic concentration and penetrating emotional focus, is a singular achievement. I can't think of another album in which such an abundance of great songs might be said to be the least of its achievements."[13]

At the same time, in an echo of *Born in the U.S.A.*'s reception during the Reagan era, some listeners read *The Rising* as an endorsement of Bush administration politics. In the album's opening track, for instance, "Lonesome Day," Springsteen's narrator could be interpreted to be advocating military retaliation for the 9/11 attacks: "House is on fire, vipers in the grass / A little revenge and this, too, shall pass / This, too, shall pass / I'm gonna pray / Right now all I got's this lonesome day." The potentially aggressive meaning of such lyrics was underscored in the *Time* article, where Springsteen concurred with what seemed to be the prevailing American sentiment: "I think the invasion in Afghanistan was handled very, very smoothly."[14] The ambiguous lyrics combined with such comments led journalist Jonathan O'Brien to lament that Springsteen had lined "himself up squarely with the hawks to support the Bush family's war on terrorism."[15] O'Brien and others implied that Springsteen's leftism had been swept away in the general flood of post-9/11 patriotism. But after the United States turned its focus from Afghanistan to Iraq, and after the rationale for the invasion of Iraq—Saddam Hussein's active WMD program—proved chimerical, Springsteen once again found himself needing to clarify his political orientation, something he ultimately accomplished by publicly criticizing the war and supporting John Kerry in the 2004 presidential campaign.

SPIRITS ABOVE AND BEHIND: A READING OF CHRISTIAN THEMES IN SPRINGSTEEN'S POST-9/11 WORKS

The marketing blitz and Springsteen's apparent support of military operations in Afghanistan certainly made it difficult, at least in the months after *The Rising*'s release in August 2002, to see the album and the artist as anything but supportive of U.S. foreign policy. Moreover, Springsteen's ample use of Christian imagery in *The Rising* (discussed in detail below) would seem on the surface to complement the rhetoric of faith and Christianity that marked President Bush's declarations about the war.[16] Nevertheless, a careful consideration of the lyrics and Springsteen's performances reveals subtle but important nuances that departed dramatically from Bush's Christian rhetoric. Avoiding both dogma and certainty, *The Rising* complicates fundamentalist interpretations of Christianity, provides a space for critical reflection, and seeks to forge connections between different faith traditions.

For instance, given the moment in which he wrote *The Rising*, Springsteen's careful, emotional depiction of a Muslim suicide bomber in "Paradise" ("In the crowded marketplace / I drift from face to face / I hold my breath and close my eyes [x2] / And I wait for Paradise") strikes me as both provocative and courageous. So, too, does "Worlds Apart," where he sings of "Allah's blessed rain" and describes the travails of two lovers struggling to ford the chasm of faith, tradition, and geography that separates them. The music and vocals of Pakistani *qawwali* singer Ashid Ali Khan blend uneasily with Springsteen's, signifying a real tension that might, with time and patience, be resolved into harmony. A Sufi tradition that has "developed its own poetry and music as an essential means for devotional expression and the attainment of religious ecstasy," *qawwali* points toward a sublime state that feels as desirable, and unreachable, as the utopia about which Springsteen's song narrator dreams.[17] His collaboration with Khan exemplifies a tactic that Springsteen deploys several times in *The Rising*: he strips religious traditions of dogma to celebrate the spiritual essence that binds them together. Another example of this practice, the opening verse of "Mary's Place," suggests an unprecedented ecumenicalism by referring to Buddha, the prophet Muhammad and "eleven angels of mercy" from Christianity.[18] In doing so, Springsteen poetically merges Buddhist, Islamic, and Christian references into a preamble for celebration, a call for a new holy trinity, and a holy spirit that would carry the lost to eternity.

This cross-cultural, interfaith sense of the spirit is, in the end, what guides Springsteen's work. He is less interested in theology than in spirituality, in creed than in deed. The distinction recalls the Dalai Lama's contention, in his *Ethics for the New Millennium*, that while ritual and doctrine serve important purposes, we should be primarily "concerned with those qualities of the human spirit—such as love and compassion, patience, tolerance, forgiveness, contentment, a sense of responsibility, a sense of harmony—which bring happiness to both self and others"; religion, the Dalai Lama observes, "is something we can perhaps do without. What we cannot do without are these basic spiritual qualities" (1999: 22). Springsteen's songs and public pronouncements identify a comparable set of "basic spiritual qualities." For even as his work commemorates the lost, it urges Americans to extend the charity of spirit demonstrated in New York and Washington, D.C., following 9/11 to the nation and the world. Without a rebirth of the spirit, Springsteen suggests, Americans would be unable to appreciate fully the sacrifice of those who died, would be unlikely to understand the roots of terrorism, and would be unable to break free of the economic and racial injustices that have long plagued the country. As *The Rising* tour drew to a close, Springsteen began to argue that a sea change of heart and spirit, not simply a change of administration in the 2004 presidential election, was necessary to create a more charitable and just world.

Springsteen's initial effort to commemorate 9/11 came ten days after the attacks, when he opened the entertainment industry's telethon for victims, "America—A Tribute to Heroes."[19] With an acoustic guitar, harmonica, and background singers, a somber Springsteen introduced "My City of Ruins" as a "prayer for our fallen brothers and sisters." The song had been written prior to 9/11; Springsteen performed it during his 2000 tour, and its lyrics originally referred to the dilapidated state of his former stomping grounds, Asbury Park, New Jersey. But this hymn of urban decay took on new meaning in his televised performance. The first major popular artist to address the nation after the attacks, Springsteen ascended the pulpit and assumed the role of eulogist and minister: his lyrics, the grain of his voice, the lighting and staging converged to create an image designed to assuage grief and provide hope by imagining and enacting through song and performance a model of charity and community.

In the context of "Tribute to Heroes," the acoustic arrangement of "My City of Ruins" is both reverent and comforting. When Springsteen has something important to say, he frequently reaches for the acoustic guitar and harmonica, tools of the trade that invoke the populist morality of Woody Guthrie and Bob Dylan. The music is spare, but in the chorus, the musical history that would be amplified in the studio version of the song is already discernible. In the opening chords, Springsteen evokes the melody and vocal harmonies of "The Weight," a legendary song recorded by The Band, the roots rock-and-roll group that first earned its fame by backing Dylan. In this song about a weary traveler, three members of The Band—Levon Helm, Rick Danko, and Richard Manuel—sing the infectious, uplifting chorus: "Take a load off, Fanny / Take a load for free / Take a load off Fanny / And put the load right on me." In "My City of Ruins," Springsteen seemed similarly willing to bear the burden of grief. His grim facial expressions and the solemn glance skyward that comes near the end of the performance broadcast an image of both anguish and a shaken faith. And if the bluesy guitar from the album version of "My City of Ruins" and the soulful saxophone solo featured on the *Live in Barcelona* concert video are not yet audible, the sacred sounds of African-American gospel already resonate here. The song begins as a prayer, perhaps as a dirge, but the combination of musical traditions it assembles, the musical memories that it evokes, place 9/11 in a context of struggle and triumph, faith and hope. Springsteen's music proclaims that the country will overcome.

The textual references to community and spirituality in "My City of Ruins" complement and deepen its musical affect. In a broad sense, the song's lyrics speak of communal disintegration, and imply that an ethos of caring must be resurrected to rebind it. In the "Tribute to Heroes" performance, Springsteen specifically reckons with the collective grief and confusion that afflicted the nation in the days following the attacks. "There's a blood red circle / On the cold dark ground / And the rain is falling down," begins the anguished voice. "The church door's thrown open / I can hear the organ's song / but the congregation's gone / My city of ruins." The reference to the lost congregation could have a variety of meanings: Springsteen's own lapsed Catholicism, the secularization of America, the actual destruction of congregations in New York that took place on 9/11. But in this moment of national soul-searching, I want to argue that it also points toward a network of historical religious references, and that exploring those references adds depth to the reception of the song and the album.

To begin, the lines quoted above evoke colonial New England congregations presided over by the likes of John Winthrop. With their focus on predestination, Puritans such as Winthrop often offered narrow visions of community that excluded those who were not among the chosen, but nevertheless enacted among themselves a palpable model of brotherhood and charity, marked by a communal ethos of caring. "We must entertain each other in brotherly affection; we must be willing to abridge ourselves of our superfluities, for the supply of others' necessities," Winthrop advised in his landmark sermon of 1630, "Model of Christian Charity." "We must delight in each other, make other's condition our own, rejoice together, mourn together, labor and suffer together."[20] The collective well-being of the community was of utmost importance to Winthrop; Massachusetts Bay would "be as a city upon a hill," and if the colony failed, so too would the possibility to live in the spirit of charity he envisioned.

The Bay, of course, prospered more than Winthrop could have imagined. And as the ports busied and fortunes grew at the end of the seventeenth century, the communal ethos waned. The Puritans nevertheless bequeathed an ideal of caring for one's neighbor that had a deep and lasting impact on the country's cultural and political history. It was precisely this ideal that allowed their descendents to hear the "sweet bells of mercy" that toll in Springsteen's post-9/11 landscape:

Now the sweet bells of mercy

Drift through the evening trees

Young men on the corner

Like scattered leaves

. . .

My city of ruins.

If the unfaithful did not tend to their brothers and sisters in Asbury Park, the song's original referent, those citizens on the smoky streets of New York certainly did. The indifference that enables dehumanization and poverty, that normally permits us to turn away from the "young men on the corner / like scattered leaves"—a line that after the attacks acquired further meaning, evoking the bodies that were in fact scattered outside of the World Trade Center—was replaced by a culture of caring for the remainder of the autumn of 2001. Indeed, in both New York and Washington, D.C., people cared for one another in the streets and for the families of the lost with great and unprecedented reverence.

The reference to men as scattered leaves also points to a familiar inspiration in Springsteen's work: the songs of Woody Guthrie. In Guthrie's poignant ballad "Deportee (Plane Wreck at Los Gatos)," a longtime favorite of Springsteen's, migrant Mexican farm workers die in a plane crash and remain anonymous and unmourned in a news report about the disaster; they "fall like dry leaves and rot on my topsoil" and are "called by no name except deportees."[21] In its pre-9/11 context, the allusion to scattered leaves recalled the largely Latino agricultural laborers and exploitative economic system about which Guthrie sang (and which, judging by current debates over immigration, remain an ongoing concern). More generally, in its original performance context, the nod to Guthrie had served to draw attention to the continued economic and racial inequalities of post-industrial America, demonstrating that charitable models had not been successfully followed. In the aftermath of the 9/11 attacks, however, Springsteen's channeling of Guthrie resonated with the new revelation that Americans could—if only temporarily, and within nationalist limits—look beyond race and class and see the bonds of their common humanity, overcoming the physical "city of ruins" that lay before them.

If prejudice and the trauma of 9/11 had conspired to create lost souls, as the third verse of Springsteen's song would now seem to intimate, there was hope to begin again, to "rise up" not in retribution, but to resurrect a promise of community. And so it is that "with these hands," Springsteen prays not for revenge, but for "strength" and for "love." It is worth noting that in this invocation, Springsteen prays not for the nation, but for "this world," a visionary act that departs from the jingoistic rhetoric of both the American president and Toby Keith. In the "Tribute to Heroes" and other performances in the months after 9/11, Springsteen presented himself as a poet invoking a history of values, a history of the spirit, to transform suffering into a community of faith and charity. The mourning had begun, hope had been restored, and through the assembling of diverse musical traditions, through the singing of the background choir, the lost congregation was invited to come home and live in peace.

Springsteen built upon "Ruins" and these Christian references in his most lyrical and metaphoric commemoration of 9/11, the title track "The Rising." When considered in the context of the album—particularly in relation to "Into the Fire" and "Nothing Man," elegies for those who risked and lost their lives—"The Rising" can be read as a claim that individual and sacrificial acts of courage are squandered without a spiritual and political reawakening. "May your strength give us strength / May your faith give us faith / May your hope give us hope / May your love give us love," he sings of the selfless men and women of "Into the Fire." Invoking Paul's letters to Corinthians—"There are in the end three things that last: faith, hope and love, and the greatest of these is love"[22]—Springsteen's narrator seeks the strength to turn faith, hope, and love into a fitting tribute that will inspire the living, casting this cataclysmic moment in American history in the charitable terms of Winthrop's Puritan ethic of community.

Weaving together these influences and wearing, if not bearing, "the cross of his calling," the narrator of "The Rising" casts the disaster of 9/11 in Christian terms that speak to possibilities of spiritual resurrection and, perhaps, political change. Struggling to "make [his] way through the darkness," the narrator finds himself in unfamiliar territory, feeling only "this chain that binds" him to responsibility, carrying the weight of a "sixty pound stone," a symbol for the work he must do to move his audience from the depths of darkness to a "sky of blessed life." Springsteen's live performance of the song on October 16, 2002, which opens the *Live in Barcelona* DVD and on which I base this analysis, underscores its deeply spiritual nature. As Springsteen launches the song and the concert, he stands at the microphone bathed in soft light, a lone ray of hope shining behind him, palms opened outward as if he is laying healing hands on the audience. As a synthesizer undulates slowly toward full-scale rock and roll, he beseeches his audience: "Come on up for the rising / Come on up, lay your hands in mine." Those who doubt the transformative power of rock and roll are encouraged to place their trust in Springsteen, who promises to carry them to higher ground.

By the time he unleashes the E Street Band, Springsteen is mining the Gospels for imagery, inspiration, and good news. In particular, Christ's agony in the garden on the night before his crucifixion serves as a touchstone. Prior to being arrested, Jesus retreats with his disciples to the Garden of Gethsemane, where he asks God to reconsider his fate. As the disciples drift off to sleep, Jesus, according to popular interpretations, watches the sins of humanity pass before his eyes in apocalyptic fashion. Despite his plea to "let the cup of suffering pass," the son ultimately accepts the burden of responsibility from the father and agrees to give his life to redeem others.[23] Alluding to this moment, Springsteen draws parallels between Christ and the selfless heroes of 9/11, who similarly risked their lives. As the narrator of "The Rising" witnesses his own apocalyptic phantasm of lost "spirits" and "faces," he asks, standing before God, that the "precious blood" of the victims and heroes "forever bind" him to the spirit in which their lives were sacrificed and to the compassion they awakened.

Springsteen's narrator expresses hope, however, that their blood will do more than create communion between past and present; it also has the power to serve as a new covenant for the future. In the fourth verse, the tempo slows in anticipation of another prayer, setting the stage for a final congregational chorus of "li-li-li"s, which, along with the band's impassioned performance, signals redemption and resurrection. "I see you Mary in the garden," begins the meditation, at which point Springsteen, like a pulpit preacher healing those who have strayed, stands variously with arms outstretched at his side or overhead, his palms open to the crowd.

In the garden of a thousand sighs

There's holy pictures of our children

Dancin' in a sky filled with light

May I feel your arms around me

May I feel your blood mix with mine

A dream of life comes to me

Like a catfish dancin' on the end of the line

The verse rings with a multiplicity of meanings, many triggered by Christian references. Here is Mary in the Garden of Eden, examining the pictures of the future, contemplating the lost innocence of the most mythical, Edenic of nations, one that erected its bulwark on the agrarian tradition. Here is Christ's mother standing in Gethsemane, reckoning with her son's suffering, struggling with his death and contemplating his resurrection. And here is Mary in heaven, at Mary's place, standing in the light-filled sky, looking over those who have died and those orphans who have been left behind.

The figure of Mary has long played a prominent role in Springsteen's cast of characters, particularly in such classics as "Thunder Road" and "The River." Since her introduction on *Greetings from Asbury Park, NJ* (1973), fans have watched Mary come of age in his songs. Now, in "The Rising," Springsteen's Mary tries to sort out the meaning of tragedy, the connection between past, present, and future. Whether the reference is sacred or secular, Mary's presence comforts, like the simple nostalgia that is conjured up by the catfish dancing on the fishing line. Meanwhile, the photographs of children suggest a hopeful future. So, too, does Springsteen's laying of hands on the audience in the Barcelona performance—he seems to transmit his passion and hope directly to the crowd.

This prayer of loss moves quickly and inexorably toward hope for the future. The "blackness and sorrow," "memory and shadow," and "glory and sadness" are ultimately transformed into a "sky of fullness, sky of blessed life." In Springsteen's symbolic world, life is always more powerful than death, love than hate, joy than sorrow. And with the allusion to "blessed life," Springsteen recalls the beatitudes, the essential teachings that Christ delivered in the Sermon on the Mount, teachings that embody the world that Winthrop, the Dalai Lama, Springsteen, and Guthrie imagine: "blessed are the poor in spirit, the mournful, the meek, the seekers of righteousness, the merciful, the pure in heart, the peacemakers, the persecuted and the reviled" (Matthew 5: 3–12). Members of this blessed community, Christ contended, would be the "light of the world"; like "a city set upon a hill [they] cannot be hidden" (Matthew 5: 14). In "The Rising," Springsteen's music acts as a balm, but it also can be heard to invoke the past in an attempt to redeem history, to unearth the fabled city. Out of chaos and struggle, he seems to be saying, the nation can be born again.

SAVING SOULS:
SPRINGSTEEN AND AMERICAN POLITICS
IN THE POST-9/11 WORLD

In his *New York Times* op-ed piece, Springsteen argued that the opportunity for moral and spiritual renewal opened by 9/11 was subsequently lost as the U.S. military response strayed from its original purpose and other national policies contributed to longstanding patterns of socioeconomic injustice. "In the aftermath of 9/11, I felt the country's unity. I don't remember anything quite like it," he wrote in "Chords of Change." "I had hoped that the seriousness of the times would bring forth strength, humility and wisdom in our leaders. Instead, we dived headlong into an unnecessary war in Iraq, offering up the lives of our young men and women. . . . We ran record deficits. . . . We granted tax cuts to the richest one percent . . . increasing the division of wealth that threatens to destroy our social contract with one another and render mute the promise of 'one nation indivisible.'"[24] The social covenant, insofar as it ever existed, was not renewed. Death begat not life but more death; unity led not to further freedom but to a more concentrated distribution of wealth; love did not bring peace, but was transformed into the hatred of Abu Ghraib. "It is through the truthful exercising of our best human qualities . . . that we come to life in God's eyes," Springsteen continued. "It is how our soul, as a nation and as individuals, is revealed." To turn the political and spiritual tide, to save souls, Springsteen announced that he would headline the "Vote for Change Tour," an affiliation of musicians who sought to unseat Bush and elect John Kerry to the presidency. This endorsement marked an important turning point for Springsteen. It not only reversed what had initially seemed to be his endorsement of the Bush administration's "war on terror"; it was also the first time that Springsteen took an explicitly partisan position in a presidential election.

While the Bush administration sought to bring terrorists to justice and the media represented terror in terms of Islamic fundamentalism, Springsteen offered his listeners a nondogmatic spiritual humanism and compelled audiences toward an examination of their conscience. "Devils and Dust," released on an album of the same name nine months after Springsteen published "Chords of Change," translated his op-ed into poetry:

> Now every woman and every man
> They want to take a righteous stand
> Find the love that God wills
> And the faith that He commands
> I've got my finger on the trigger
> And tonight faith just ain't enough
> When I look inside my heart
> There's just devils and dust

Well I've got God on my side
And I'm just trying to survive
What if what you do to survive
Kills the things you love
Fear's a dangerous thing
It can turn your heart black you can trust
It'll take your God filled soul
Fill it with devils and dust

Here, God is presented in universal terms that warn against moral arrogance and extreme ideologies that promote hate, whether they are followed in the name of Christianity or Islam. In doing so, he suggests, as the Quaker educator Parker Palmer writes, that "all the great spiritual traditions, when you boil them down, are saying one simple thing: BE NOT AFRAID! They don't say you *can't* have fear . . . but they say you don't have to *be* your fears, and you don't have to create a world in which those fears dominate the conditions of many, many people."[25] If the charitable model that Springsteen imagined had any hope of becoming real, Americans would need to find novel and imaginative ways to make it possible. "Without a global revolution in the sphere of human consciousness," writes Palmer, "nothing will change for the better in the sphere of our being as humans." Change, Palmer argues, requires a recognition that "matter . . . is not the fundamental factor in the movement of history. Spirit is. Consciousness is. Human awareness is. Thought is. Spirituality is. Those are the deep sources of freedom and power with which people have been able to move boulders and create change."

Since 9/11, Springsteen has carefully tended to his listeners' individual and collective spiritual selves. His interpretations of our national consciousness frequently explore a poverty of spirit and reckon with our inability to transcend deeply held prejudices, ideologies, and interests, which in many cases allow us to dehumanize one another. This spiritual poverty speaks both to human limitations and national failures, of which the Iraq war and the U.S. government's response to Hurricane Katrina in September 2005 are painful recent examples. Time and again, Springsteen reveals that this poverty of spirit results from ordinary struggles not so much between good and evil, but between spirit and flesh, love and hate, hope and fear. Such tensions are as omnipresent in daily life as they are on *The Rising* and *Devils and Dust*, and the ways in which many Americans have negotiated such polarities, the choices they have made and have allowed others to make for them, have shaped the nation's response to terrorism and tragedy. It is difficult to export models of charity abroad when they have not yet been successfully built at home. But Springsteen keeps the faith. In his remembrance of 9/11 and of history, he reminds Americans of their country's flawed but potentially liberating religious past, of their lapsed but potentially redemptive spiritual selves.

REFERENCES

Berry, Wendell. 1990. *What Are People For? Essays by Wendell Berry.* New York: Northpoint Press.

Dalai Lama. 1999. *Ethics for the New Millennium: His Holiness the Dalai Lama.* New York: Berkley Publishing Group.

Garman, Bryan. 2000. *A Race of Singers: Whitman's Working-Class Hero from Guthrie to Springsteen.* Chapel Hill: University of North Carolina Press.

Lenzerini, Federico. 2005. "Intercultural Dialogue in Springsteen's Poetry." Paper presented at "Glory Days: A Bruce Springsteen Symposium," Monmouth, New Jersey, September 9–11.

Lipsitz, George. 1990. *Time Passages: Collective Memory and American Popular Culture.* Minneapolis: University of Minnesota Press.

Qureshi, Regula. 1972. "Indo-Muslim Religious Music, an Overview." *Asian Music* 3(2): 15–22.

———. 1995 [1986]. *Sufi Music of India and Pakistan: Sound, Context and Meaning in Qawwali.* Chicago and London: University of Chicago Press.

DISCOGRAPHY

America: A Tribute to Heroes [DVD]. 2001. Directed by Beth McCarthy-Miller and Joel Gallen. Wea/Warner Brothers.

Keith, Toby. 2002. *Unleashed.* Dreamworks Nashville.

Springsteen, Bruce. 1973. *Greetings from Asbury Park, N.J.* Columbia.

———. 1975. *Born to Run.* Columbia.

———. 1984. *Born in the U.S.A.* Columbia.

———. 1986. *Live/1975–1985.* Columbia.

———. 1992. *Lucky Town.* Columbia.

———. 1992. *Human Touch.* Columbia.

———. 1995. *The Ghost of Tom Joad.* Columbia.

———. 1998. *Tracks.* Columbia.

———. 2002. *The Rising.* Columbia.

———. 2003. *Live in Barcelona* [DVD]. Performed by Bruce Springsteen and the E Street Band. Columbia Music Video.

———. 2005. *Devils & Dust.* Columbia.

The Band. 1976. *The Best of the Band.* Capitol.

ACKNOWLEDGMENTS

NOTES

1. Bruce Springsteen, "Chords of Change," *New York Times*, 5 August 2004, late ed.
2. Robert McFadden, "Bush Leads Prayer, Visits Aid Crews; Congress Backs Use of Armed Force," *New York Times*, 15 September 2001, late ed.
3. See transcript of Department of Defense News Briefing conducted by Secretary of Defense Donald Rumsfeld and General Richard B. Myers, 28 March 2003, available at: http://www.defenselink.mil/transcripts/2003/t03282003_t0328sd.html.
4. See in particular the essays by Garofalo and, in reference to country music, Schmelz.
5. In this vast web of intricacies and inconsistencies, argues George Lipsitz, "it is impossible to say whether any one combination of sounds or set of images or groupings of words innately express one political opinion" (1990: 13).

6. At a speech in Hammonton, New Jersey, Reagan said that "America's future rests in a thousand dreams inside your hearts. It rests in the message of hope in songs so many young Americans admire: New Jersey's own Bruce Springsteen. And helping you make those dreams come true is what this job of mine is all about." Quoted in Garman 2000: 213.

7. For an extended discussion of Springsteen's politics, see Garman 2000: 204–52.

8. Nicholas Dawidoff, "The Pop Populist," *New York Times Magazine*, 26 January 1997, 26–33, 64, 69, 72, 77.

9. The quotation comes from a sticker affixed to the outside of the CD case of *The Rising*.

10. Josh Tyrangiel, "Bruce Rising," *Time*, 5 August 2002, 52.

11. Mark Binelli and Rob Sheffield, "Bruce Springsteen's American Gospel," *Rolling Stone*, 22 August 2002, 62.

12. David Segal, "Thanks, Boss; Bruce Springsteen Rises to the Occasion at MCI Center," *Washington Post*, 12 August 2002.

13. Kurt Loder, "The Rising," *Rolling Stone*, 22 August 2002, 81.

14. Tyrangiel, "Bruce Rising," 52.

15. Jonathan O'Brien, "Springsteen: The Rising Fall of the Boss," *Sunday Business Post Online*, 11 August 2002, available at http://archives.tcm.ie/businesspost/2002/08/11/story359132628.asp.

16. Bush's use of faith is not merely dogmatic. As Ron Suskind has argued, Bush's "faith-based presidency" is based on a "with-us-or-against-us model" that devalues empiricism and critical thinking, in part because these are the very things that undermine faith. Indeed, Suskind contends, it was faith, not data, that ultimately led Bush to decide to invade Iraq. As he considered the appropriate course of action, Bush explained, "I was praying for strength to do the Lord's will. . . . I'm surely not going to justify the war based upon God. Understand that. Nevertheless, in my case, I pray to be as good a messenger of his will as possible." Furthermore, on at least two occasions, Bush publicly referred to the "war on terror" as a "crusade," and, according to former Reagan policy adviser and columnist Bruce Bartlett, has run his presidency on a "Messianic idea of what God has told him to do. . . . This is why George W. Bush is so clear-eyed about Al Qaeda and the Islamic fundamentalist enemy. He believes you have to kill them all. They can't be persuaded that they're extremists, driven by a dark vision. He understands them, because he's just like them." See Ron Suskind, "Without a Doubt," *New York Times* Magazine, 17 October 2004.

17. Quote taken from Qureshi 1972: 20; for more detailed information on Sufi *qawwali*, see Qureshi's landmark study *Sufi Music of India and Pakistan* (1995).

18. I am indebted here to Federico Lenzerini's paper "Intercultural Dialogue in Springsteen's Poetry" (2005).

19. For more on the "America: A Tribute to Heroes" benefit, see essays by Garofalo and by Pegley and Fast in this volume.
20. All quotes from John Winthrop's 1630 sermon "A Model of Christian Charity," available at http://religiousfreedom.lib.virginia.edu/sacred/ charity.html, with an introduction by John Beardsley.
21. For further discussion of Springsteen's use of "Deportee," see Garman 2000: 241–42.
22. 1 Corinthians 13, *New American Bible.*
23. See Matthew 26: 36–46; Mark 14: 32–42; Luke 22: 39–46.
24. Springsteen, "Chords of Change."
25. This and all ensuing quotes from Parker Palmer, "Leading from Within," a talk delivered to the Meridian Street United Methodist Church in Indiana, 23 March 1990. Author's collection, formerly posted at http://www. teacherformation.org/html/rr/index.cfm. For a revision of this work, see (http://www.couragerenewal.org/?q=resources/writings/leading).

5

DOUBLE VOICES OF
MUSICAL CENSORSHIP AFTER 9/11

Martin Scherzinger

In April 2003, shortly after the outbreak of war between the United States and Iraq, the Hollywood actor and activist Tim Robbins reported on a case of post-9/11 censorship: "A famous middle-aged rock-and-roller called me last week to thank me for speaking out against the war, only to go on to tell me that he could not speak himself because he fears repercussions from Clear Channel. 'They promote our concert appearances,' he said. 'They own most of the stations that play our music. I can't come out against this war.'"[1] This description of censorship in our times has two striking features. First, the restriction felt by the musician is not the result of a public body of censors (with links, say, to the State); and second, the artist is not receiving the direct attentions of a censor (who overtly supervises his/her public pronouncements). Thus we find two common ideas associated with censorship challenged: (1) that censorship properly belongs to the public domain; and (2) that the public operation of regulation and control is properly framed by a legal principle, which directly sanctions censored activities. That is, the apparatus of regulation must be publicly recognized; its field of operation officially authorized.[2] A state ban on the exposure of women's breasts on public television, for example, would count as an uncontroversial case of (principled?) censorship. In this restricted sense of the term—censorship construed as a legally sanctioned public ban—the attacks of September 11, 2001, did not result in any new censorship of music in the United States.

Yet the case Tim Robbins cited draws attention to a different kind of censoring body, which issues a different kind of constraint. Here the artist exhibits a kind of pathological watchfulness, involuntarily incorporating a censor-figure into his/her interior, acting out an imagined quiescence. In Danilo Kiš's view, this kind of introverted censorship is more powerful than the overt kind: "[It] means reading your own text with the eyes of another person, a situation where you become your own judge, stricter and more suspicious than anyone else" (1986: 45). For Kiš, this kind of censor-as-alter ego cannot be defeated, for its prohibitionary/inhibitionary power is all-consuming. The very anonymity of Robbins's "famous middle-aged rock-and-roller" registers this crude power. Even in the relatively unrestricted environment of the blogosphere the name of the artist remains concealed. Is Robbins telling the truth? If so, the often-used argument that artists actively seek controversy by pushing the limits of social acceptability—to nurture anti-establishment credibility, for instance—is obviously not applicable here. Instead the musician's act of silence testifies to a policed self: silent and invisible to the public, silenced by an internalized and invisible censor. In Kiš's terms, this could amount to one of the worst kinds of censorship, for the censoring subject is itself censored and thus kept from public scrutiny.

It is prudent nonetheless to exercise caution in defining a mode of nontraditional censorship (invisible, anonymous, interiorized), for the voice of the invisible censor must be weighed against the necessary internalized resistances without which artists cannot create. The belief in direct speech, authentic expression, unfettered creativity, and so on, strikes us as naive today. In a context of poststructuralist textual production, for example, we no longer isolate what Mikhail Bakhtin calls "direct, unrefracted, unconditional authorial discourse" without a degree of skepticism. According to Bakhtin, a kind of hidden dialogic discourse is a *general* condition of speech; "every thought, feeling, experience must be refracted through the medium of someone else's discourse, someone else's style, someone else's manner" (1984: 202). The "someone else" to which Bakhtin's analysis points is not only a persecutory figure of the censor, but, being its condition of possibility, also the irreducible set of restrictions placed on all utterances by their addressees. The shift from the figure of the restraining censor to that of the productive artistic obstacle requires but the slightest tilting of logical angle.

In *Discipline and Punish*, Michel Foucault argues against the very concept of "censorship" as a diagnostic perspective on society: "We must cease once and for all to describe the effects of power in negative terms: it 'excludes,' it 'represses,' it 'censors,' it 'abstracts,' it 'masks,' it 'conceals.' In fact, power produces; it produces reality; it produces domains of objects and rituals of truth. The individual and the knowledge that may be gained of him belong to this production" (1979: 194). Far from functioning as an impediment to subjectivity and knowledge formation, internalized forms of surveillance (by "eyes that must see without being seen") are, in Foucault's analysis, the very discipline that constructs and constitutes subjectivity along with attendant forms of knowledge (p. 171). The role of punishment in society ("directed above all at others, at all the potentially guilty"), for example, is to shape discourse among individuals, thereby producing homogenous effects of power (p. 108). In short, the "anxious awareness of being observed" is the necessary impediment that makes possible the normative individual (p. 202).

The idea that internalized obstacles are a necessary condition for normative behavior underlines many theories of art-making as well. In the Freudian paradigm, sublimation itself lays at the heart of all artistic production. The self, for Freud, is not a unity but multiply divided. Artists are people who can negotiate the inner tensions of these multiple selves and manage their antagonistic drives more or less successfully. Importantly, in Freud's account, the process of artistic production involves not only satisfying but also occasionally *denying* the demands of these inner drives. The internal process of selecting, organizing, and assigning value to artistic material constitutes a field of aesthetic and political judgments without which there can be no artwork. Furthermore, when music is mediated by the interests of a sponsoring corporation responsible for its dissemination, an additional field of judgments weighs upon its content. But the question of whether styling, advertising, engineering, and marketing strategies of the sponsoring body constitute a *restrictive* or a *productive* intervention in the artistic process is hotly contested and open to debate. Cases on both sides of the debate abound: Prince, for example, has at times claimed the former, while Nigel Kennedy, for example, has suggested the latter. The point is that, far from representing straightforward sites of censorship, these mediating layers are overdetermined. A business executive's decision about music's styling may compromise an artistic vision, for example, but in doing so it may also multiply the product's dissemination. It is a question of assessing how the harms and benefits, from the point of view of both artists and listeners, weigh up against one another. One might call these the *double voices* of musical censorship.

At the same time, it is important to distinguish between the artist's various internalized constraints; to disentangle those intimate censor-figures that intrude and persecute from those that facilitate and inspire.

Drawing on Freud, the South African novelist J. M. Coetzee invites us to consider the dual (and dueling) aspects of this kind of internalized censor-twin in terms of a figure-of-the-father and a figure-of-the-beloved:

> Imagine . . . a project in writing that is, at heart, a transaction with some such figure of the beloved, that tries to please her (but that also tries continually though surreptitiously to revise and create her as the-one-who-will-be-pleased); and imagine what will happen if into this transaction is introduced in a massive and undeniable way another figure-of-the-reader, the dark-suited, bald-headed censor, with his pursed lips and his red pen and his irritability and his censoriousness—the censor, in fact, as parodic version of the figure-of-the-father (1996: 38).

While the courted figure (the beloved) in Coetzee's scenario proffers restrictive hurdles that are the match of those imposed by the censorious figure (the father), the latter are unwanted and destructive: "Working under censorship," writes Coetzee, "is like being intimate with someone who does not love you, with whom you want no intimacy, but who presses himself against you" (1996: 38). Nonetheless, the opposite ends of the censor-twin often remain closely aligned; the beloved often interwoven with (if only as a constituent inversion of) the oppressive father—an inner tension that can be plausibly mapped onto current theories of popular music. According to Tyler Cowen, for example, rock and roll emerged as a pro-individualist cultural rebellion against State control; its seductions, one might say, gaining traction from its denunciations (1998: 178).

This essay offers a brief typology of music's restricting circumstances in a particular historical moment: the post-9/11 United States. The cases presented below do not represent an exhaustive list of effectively censored music in these times; nor do they present a consistent theory of censorship. Also, while the argument takes a special interest in the *intrusive* side of music's inevitable mediating layers, with particular reference to new sites and forms of censorship following the terrorist attacks in September 2001, it will not lose sight of the paradoxical nature of musical censorship—its double voices—in assessing its scope and authority. The essay begins by discussing some cases of relatively overt censorship, with a particular focus on the removal of existing songs from various important broadcasting channels (or the placing of prohibitive obstacles before them in such contexts).[3] Following this general discussion, the essay will examine the removal of music by the Dixie Chicks from many radio stations in 2003 in more detail. The second set of cases explored in this essay present a more subtle form of censorship: the *voluntary* removal of musical products or cancellation of events out of forbearance or sensitivity in the context of a current political sentiment. In particular, the essay will examine the Boston Symphony Orchestra's cancellation of a performance of choruses from John Adams's *The Death of Klinghoffer*. As it is with the very definition of censorship, gauging such exercises of control over music's circulation is a vexing task: perhaps these amount to a more insidious form of censorship than the public banning of music; on the other hand, and equally plausibly, perhaps these do not constitute censorship at all. Here the analysis necessarily shrinks from the question of whether the decision to withdraw music from public circulation is willful or enforced, or some blending of the two. In any of these cases, the act of withdrawal registers the limits of American toleration at a particular historical moment and thus functions as an ideological gauge. These limits, in turn, mark the conditioning grounds for internalized censorship.

The underlying justification for this essay is the contention that it is the silent and invisible acquiescence of the cautious and compromised artist that ultimately registers the extent of genuine political power. That which cannot be sung needs most to be spoken about.

QUESTIONABLE SONG LYRICS, UNPATRIOTIC POLITICS?

After September 11, 2001, cases of silencing musical dissent emerged in various quarters. Martin Cloonan has reported that in September 2001 the group Rage Against the Machine (RATM) had its message boards closed on its official Web site after their ISP provider received repeated calls from agents of the federal government. According to Cloonan, these boards, which were used for political and social discussion among fans, were deemed to contain "anti-American sentiments" by "the Secret Services."[4] Other musicians whose views conflicted with official government opinion often felt pressured to rescind them. Moby apologized for questioning the competence of the CIA and FBI—agencies that existed, in his view, to protect Americans from atrocities like the attacks on the World Trade Center. Likewise, Kevin Richardson of the Backstreet Boys expressed regret because of a question he asked in a Toronto interview: "What has our government done to provoke this action that we don't know about?"[5] The record label 75 Ark pressured the political hip-hop group The Coup to change the cover design for their album *Party Music*. The original cover, which depicted the two rappers standing in front of an exploding World Trade Center in New York was "intended as a metaphor for the effect music can have on a corrupt system."[6] The design was replaced post-9/11 with a photograph of a hand holding a full martini glass from which flames emerge. In November 2001, the Boston Symphony Orchestra canceled four performances of choruses from John Adams's *The Death of Klinghoffer* because they allegedly portrayed a Palestinian point of view. The orchestra released a statement describing the decision in terms of sensitivity in the context of "the current mood of its audiences in the aftermath of the terrorist attacks."[7] Following composer Karlheinz Stockhausen's ill-considered description of the September 2001 attacks as "the greatest artwork in the cosmos," the student-run new music group Ossia at the Eastman School of Music was required by the school's administration, which feared a controversial backlash, to cancel a performance of Stockhausen's *Stimmung* scheduled for December 2001 in New York City. Arguably, these were isolated decisions about appropriate programming taken at an individual and local level. Considered together, however, these various events can be seen to point to a gravitational force, instantiated in multiple and diverse forms, that exerts censoring pressure in sync with government values in a time of political crisis.

Most notoriously, Clear Channel Radio, owner of over 1,200 stations in the United States, issued a "don't play" list of 156 songs days after September 11, 2001, in deference to the national mood of mourning.[8] Deemed "lyrically questionable," the choices on the list ranged from reasonable to absurd. The exercise of restraint in airing songs seems understandable in some cases—Drowning Pool's "Bodies," with the refrain "Let the bodies hit the floor," eerily evokes traumatic images following the attacks on the World Trade Center, for example—but it seems dubious in most cases. It takes an exaggerated literalism, for example, to deem songs like Steve Miller's "Jet Airliner," the Red Hot Chili Peppers' "Aeroplane" (a mode of transport transformed into a deadly weapon?) or The Beatles' "Ob-La-Di, Ob-La-Da" (an acronym for Osama bin Laden?) lyrically questionable. More disturbingly, however, Cat Stevens's "Peace Train" or "Morning Has Broken," The Doors' "The End," Black Sabbath's "War Pigs," and John Lennon's "Imagine" (which ironically became an anthem of post-9/11 mourning in various quarters), seem motivated less by the content of the lyrics than by the religious beliefs, antiwar stances, or political persuasions of the musicians themselves.[9] *All* songs by the left-wing Rage Against the Machine, for example, were placed on the Clear Channel list.

Radio, argues Michael C. Zalot, became the medium of choice in the months following September 11, 2001, when it came to providing comfort to communities across America. Listeners, writes Zalot, "turned to local rock, pop and country stations for a sense of community, in a virtual public space that television did not provide" (2002: 34).

Given the overall slant of Clear Channel's don't-play list, one might conclude that, its historical aspirations to anti-establishment irreverence notwithstanding, rock music on these stations came to serve as a natural conduit for ideological control at a critical historical moment. In the words of Murray Forman: "The conscription of music can be approached through what Middleton . . . identified as a theory of articulative process whereby music and musical meanings are rechanneled in a manner that reproduces the hegemonic structure and, *pace* Gramsci, reaffirms the prevailing social order of domination and subordination" (2002: 194).

Taken as a whole, the Clear Channel list is heavily skewed against musical expressions on the left of the political spectrum.[10] And yet, the politics of the list may be more bewildering than coherent. For example, the list contains some anomalies, such as Neil Diamond's rousing pro-America song "America" and Don McLean's anthemlike "American Pie." Perhaps Clear Channel was trying to prevent an overly nationalist social backlash as much as a critical one. On the other hand, these two songs may still fit the ideological bill. The lyrics of Don McLean's "American Pie" are notoriously elusive; the title of the song is rumored to refer to the plane in which Buddy Holly, The Big Bopper, and Ritchie Valens were killed.[11] The song's widespread appeal notwithstanding then, "American Pie" may have risked reverberating ominously in the context of terrorist attacks using airplanes. Likewise, instead of noticing the open celebration of core American values (presented in lines like "freedom's light burning warm") in Neil Diamond's "America," Clear Channel's senior executives may have heard something more disturbing. Perhaps the triumphal refrain at the end of Neil Diamond's song "They're coming to America" (from "everywhere around the world") takes on menacing overtones in the context of an attack by non-Americans orchestrated from within the country's borders. Finally, as J. M. Coetzee observes, agents of censorship do not as a rule acknowledge their own censoring activities. Even in police states authorities tend to avoid the word "censorship."[12] Clear Channel's denials thus follow a well-worn historical pattern of sidestepping accusations of censorship.

A similar list of undesirable songs, with a similar refutation from the censoring agent, appeared in March 2003 following the outbreak of war between the United States and Iraq. The broadcast standards department of MTV Europe issued a memo recommending that music videos with images of "war, soldiers, war planes, bombs, missiles, riots and social unrest, executions" and "other obviously sensitive material" not be aired in Europe.[13] Examples of offensive videos listed in the memo included System of a Down's "BOOM!" (described by Mark Sunderland of MTV as an "anti-war video containing facts and figures about, amongst other things, the projected casualties in the war in Iraq"); Aerosmith's "Don't Want to Miss a Thing" ("contains footage from the film 'Armageddon'"); Manic Street Preachers' "So Why So Sad" ("contains footage of soldiers being killed and man throwing a hand grenade"); Passengers/U2's "Miss Sarajevo" ("contains missiles, guns and buildings being blown up"); Bon Jovi's "This Ain't a Love Song" ("contains war scenes and victims in distress"); Iggy Pop's "Corruption" ("contains wars, riots, guns and captions 'we love guns' and 'we love rifles'"); Paul Hardcastle's "19" ("contains war footage"); Radiohead's "Lucky" ("contains war footage including injured children"); Billy Idol's "Hot in the City" ("contains an atomic explosion"); Armand van Helden's "Koochy" ("contains an atomic explosion and ships being blown up"); and Trick Daddy's "Thug Holiday" ("contains soldiers being killed at war").

Videos containing words associated with war ("bomb," "missile," etc.) were also not to be shown by MTV Europe. The memo identifies Outkast's "B.O.B (Bombs over Baghdad)," Megadeth's "Holy Wars," Gavin Friday's "You, Me and World War Three," and Radiohead's (nonexistent!) "Invasion," as songs whose titles "may offend." All songs by the Atlanta-based B-52's were to be avoided.[14] As justification for its recommendations, the memo refers to the programming code of the Independent Television Commission (ITC), which regulates commercial television in Britain. Although the memo cites the code's obligation "not to broadcast material which offends against good taste or is offensive to public feeling," it does not rely on or cite the examples provided by the code. (The code itself does not mention images of or references to war.) As a result of the memo, System of a Down's "BOOM!" was not shown in Europe.[15] The video, which was directed by documentary filmmaker Michael Moore, begins with the words: "On February 15, 2003, ten million people in over 600 cities around the world participated in the largest demonstration in the history of the world. Because we choose peace over war, we were there too." According to System of a Down's Web site, "The video 'BOOM!' is a life-affirming video that rallies people to visualize, and then create, the world they want to live in. 'BOOM!' looks to empower people with the knowledge that war is ultimately their choice, not the media's nor the government's." The video presents footage from antiwar demonstrations in cities across the globe, quotations from various protestors that become song lyrics, war imagery, and a satirical cartoon animation of George W. Bush, Tony Blair, Saddam Hussein, and Osama bin Laden flying over cities on missiles. Headlines of various newspapers appear as subtitles beneath the flow of images: "Halliburton wins contract to rebuild Iraqi oilfields,"

"Iraqi oil reserves worth $4 trillion," "War to cost U.S. $70 Billion," "Pentagon orders 77,000 body bags," and so on.[16] As it was with Clear Channel, MTV denied enacting a ban on songs mentioned in the list; MTV spokesman Graham James explained that "the leaked document was never intended to be implemented."[17] This denial notwithstanding, the song was conspicuously absent from MTV's European playlists.

GRASSROOTS FLAK OR CORPORATE CENSORSHIP?

In March 2003 dozens of radio stations, including prominent stations owned by Clear Channel Communications, all fifty country stations owned by Cumulus Broadcasting, and all stations owned by the Cox Radio chain, removed the country musicians the Dixie Chicks from their playlists (Rohr 2004: 74). The blacklist followed a comment made by Natalie Maines, lead singer of the Dixie Chicks, at a concert on March 10, 2003, in a London nightclub: "Just to let you know, we're ashamed the president of the United States is from Texas."[18] At the time of the comment the Dixie Chicks quintuple-platinum album *Home* featured two massive radio hits. "Landslide" (written by Stevie Nicks) was number one on the adult contemporary chart and "Travelin' Soldier" was number nine on the country chart. In the days following the comment, however, various public actions were taken against the band. In Kansas City, Missouri, a "chicken toss" took place, at which Dixie Chicks CDs and tapes were tossed into the trash (Nuzum 2004: 156). Likewise, KRMD-FM, part of Cumulus Media, organized and sponsored a CD-smashing rally in Louisiana.[19] In an effort to lure Dixie Chicks fans away from Dixie Chicks concerts, some protestors organized alternative concerts offering free entry to Dixie Chicks concert ticket-holders. The South Carolina State House passed a resolution requesting that the Dixie Chicks apologize directly to South Carolinians and also that the band should feel obliged to offer a free concert for military families and troops.[20] Two DJs, Dave Moore and Jeff Singer, at KKCS in Colorado Springs were suspended for playing a Dixie Chicks song.[21] Jerry Grant, the manager of KKCS, explained the station's ultimatum in stark terms: "I gave them an alternative: stop it now and they'll be on suspension, or they can continue playing them and when they come out of the studio, they won't have a job."[22] It should be noted that at the time of the Dixie Chicks blacklist Clear Channel also used its considerable market power to garner support for the U.S. invasion of Iraq. On March 15, for example, Clear Channel's WGST sponsored a pro-military rally in Atlanta attended by 25,000 people.

In defense of its censorious actions, radio executives at Clear Channel and Cumulus Broadcasting claimed that the measures responded to grassroots initiatives taken by local listening audiences.[23] Far from meting out censorship, the removal of the Dixie Chicks from radio playlists, according to these defenses, reflected conservative social pressure on these stations. Such pressure, which Frederick Schauer would call *censure* (or private censorship), cannot properly be conflated with public censorship, as it does not reflect a legally sanctioned restriction on freedom of speech (1982). In short, the censoring actions of a privately owned media company cannot properly amount to the stifling of free expression; rather, the media company arguably asserts *its* free expression in these contexts. Gabriel Rossman interprets the Dixie Chicks controversy as a case of censure ("flak" from aggrieved citizens). The blacklist, he maintains, was a measure of a "vengeful audience to whose wishes corporations responded with varying degrees of haste" (2004: 76). Using radio airplay data from *Radio and Records*, a trade magazine for the radio industry that uses airplay charts and other data tables, Rossman effectively demonstrates the power of the citizenry to pressure radio corporations to remove unwanted artists from the airwaves: "Rather than corporate interests punishing dissent and imposing conservative values on the citizenry, in this instance [the Dixie Chicks blacklist] citizens imposed conservatism and punitiveness on corporations" (p. 76).

Rossman determines the extent of social pressure on radio stations by way of various "independent variables": the first set of variables measures the percentage of electoral support for George W. Bush in 2000 and the percentage of the population in active military duty; the second set of variables measures the degree of support for military action in Iraq in August and September 2002 and a question designed to measure tolerance for free speech: "Suppose [an] admitted Communist wanted to make a speech in your community. Should he be allowed to speak, or not?" (p. 71). Rossman's variables accurately predict a greater decline in Dixie Chicks airplay in markets (1) that showed larger electoral support for G. W. Bush; (2) with more active-duty military personnel in their communities; (3) whose citizens supported the war; and (4) were relatively less tolerant of free speech. These findings resonate with Rossman's descriptions of country music, which he associates with "pastoral white America and its values, such as independence, patriotism, and religion" (p. 68). Furthermore, Rossman demonstrates that blacklists were as prevalent, or more prevalent even, among independent radio stations as they were for large chains; and that blacklists were more prevalent on country stations than they were on adult contemporary stations, which "skew [more] female" (p. 75).

Although he makes one reference to "angry phone calls" that apparently "flooded" a Nashville radio station (p. 62), Rossman does not offer an ethnographic account of either the extent to which, or the mechanism by which, the citizenry actually exerted pressure on the radio stations. For example, the Colorado-based radio station KKCS, where the DJs Dave Moore and Jeff Singer were suspended for playing the Dixie Chicks, did receive "flak" from its listeners, but it was less one-sided than Rossman's model would imply. According to the Associated Press, "The station has received a couple of hundred calls and 75 percent favored playing the music."[24] Instead of offering ethnographic evidence, Rossman's variables for registering right-wing political sentiment are measured abstractly and assumed cleanly to map onto playlist decline. Neither do the variables directly address issues pertaining to the Dixie Chicks, music, or culture. Instead they are framed in terms of politics pure and simple (support for Bush, support for the war, etc.). Furthermore, the variables measuring conservative sentiment are qualitatively different from the variable measuring tolerance for dissent. The former are closely linked to contemporary political contexts (the profile of the Bush vote, the current number of military personnel, etc.), while the latter invokes as a yardstick an entirely different historical era (Cold War attitudes toward communism). For Rossman, intolerance for communism counts as a "reasonable proxy for attitudes towards repression of this kind" (2004: 73). The problem is that a *word* like "communist" (like the word "liberal") routinely registers instant hostility among Americans. Eric Alterman argues that, while many Americans distance themselves from an appellation like "liberal," for example, polls show that most Americans generally espouse liberal positions.[25] To bring the question of tolerance into the qualitatively similar contemporary arena as the questions about support for conservatism thus requires a less inflammatory reference point than "communism." Take the question, "Suppose a mother who lost her child in the Iraq war wanted to make a speech criticizing war in your community. Should she be allowed to speak or not?" This less provocative, but more relevant, question would unlikely produce the same profile of abstract figures required to yield the relative intolerance, which in turn stands in for grassroots pressure in Rossman's account.

While grassroots flak probably played some role in the formation of the blacklists, Rossman's account fails to reckon with the complicating details of media ownership and its relation to organized political movements. For example, in congressional hearings held on July 8, 2003,

Simon Renshaw, representing the company that manages the Dixie Chicks, disclosed that members of his office had received death threats, which, according to evidence presented to congress, were orchestrated by "right-wing political" groups (Holland 2003). If Renshaw is correct, the conservative flak registered by Cumulus media may have reflected less the broad "grassroots" censure to which Rossman points than that of a highly organized, aggressive and vocal minority.[26] Although it is impossible to settle the question decisively, Renshaw's assessment would tally with the actual calls made to KKCS in conservative Colorado Springs, where three-quarters of all callers favored *continuing* airplay of Dixie Chicks songs.[27] It is easier to settle the question about who gave the actual orders to take the Dixie Chicks off the air. Facing questions from John McCain and Barbara Boxer, Lewis W. Dickey Jr., CEO of Cumulus, conceded that *he* had ordered Cumulus stations to remove the Dixie Chicks and that local station managers "fell in line" with the corporate decision.[28] In response to Dickey's appeal to grassroots pressure ("a groundswell, a hue and a cry from listeners"), Boxer argued, that this is "what happens when you have a diversity of views, discourse." For Boxer, "A hue and a cry is a beautiful noise. It's the sound of freedom" (Holland 2003). McCain argued that, because it came from corporate headquarters, the order was "a strong argument that First Amendment erosion is in progress" (ibid.). At the very least, the corporate directive disconcerts the idea that the ban was merely the result of local grassroots sentiment.

Although his argument attempts to debunk the notion that corporate ownership influences media content, Rossman leaves out certain facts about the large corporations involved in the Dixie Chicks blacklists. Rossman does not mention, for example, that Clear Channel increasingly controls the music reported in the industry trade magazine *Radio and Records,* on which his figures rely.[29] In 2001, *Radio and Records* decreased (from 200 to 140 markets) the number of stations reporting their weekly playlists to the magazine.[30] Only seven Clear Channel stations lost their reporting status. Moreover, *Radio and Records* uses the Clear Channel–owned system *Mediabase* to verify the accuracy of reporting. More generally speaking, if it were true that Clear Channel stations were entirely responsive to local political sentiment one might reasonably expect stations in markets like Atlanta to organize (and sponsor?) pro-war rallies, which they did, and stations in markets like New York to organize antiwar rallies, which they did not.[31] Rossman ignores Clear Channel's uneven responsiveness to local political sentiment in different parts of the nation. The narrow focus on country stations in conservative markets obscures Clear Channel's tendency to nurture conservative sentiment and downplay progressive sentiment in all markets.

Censorship and restrictions on artistic expressions can be as effective when they are imposed within a highly concentrated market place as when they are imposed directly by the federal government. The distinction between the public and private becomes especially porous when the censoring media corporation has close links to government. The circle of mutual assistance between corporations and government (via campaign contributions, and the like, which in turn assure tax breaks, subsidies, and corporate leverage over the political process) can streamline these interests—a condition exacerbated by increased corporate consolidation of the media. The bond between the owners of Clear Channel and the Bush administration, for example, extends beyond the rationally predictable logic of mutual support. The Vice Chair of Clear Channel, Tom Hicks, is a member of the Bush Pioneer Club for elite and generous donors. Paul Krugman, writing in the *New York Times*, reported, "When Mr. Bush was governor of Texas, Mr. Hicks was chairman of the University of Texas Investment Management Company, called Utimco, and Clear Channel's chairman, Lowry Mays (a personal friend of former President Bush), was on its board. Under Mr. Hicks, Utimco placed much of the university's endowment under the management of companies with strong Republican Party and Bush family ties. In 1998 Mr. Hicks purchased the Texas Rangers in a deal that made Mr. Bush a multimillionaire."[32]

One of the companies benefiting from the University of Texas's tilted investments, mentioned in connection with Tom Hicks of Clear Channel above, is the Carlyle Group, a global private equity firm with George Bush Sr. on its payroll. The Carlyle Group's primary focus is on the aerospace and military defense industries, though they have expanded these areas to include industries such as telecommunications and media.[33] While it is impossible to establish the exact connections between government interests as they interface with military investments and the content of media broadcasting, it is reasonable to predict that this alliance of agendas could become integrated in practice. Perhaps this alliance explains why Clear Channel radio stations air cultural expressions reflecting the party line and censor cultural expressions dissenting from it. Aside from the banning of the Dixie Chicks and the sponsorship of pro-war rallies, it should not come as a surprise, for instance, that Clear Channel radio stations gave little airplay in 2003 to antiwar songs by musicians like Lenny Kravitz and Michael Stipe of R.E.M.; nor should it come as a surprise that Clear Channel concert promoters threatened to remove Ani DiFranco from the stage in March 2003 in New Jersey if she permitted antiwar representatives to speak; nor should it come as a surprise that the company syndicates talk-radio hosts like the extreme Republican conservative Rush Limbaugh and the radical homophobe Dr. Laura Schlessinger; nor should it come as a surprise that Clear Channel refused to display Project Billboard's image critical of the war in Iraq with the words "Democracy is Best Taught by Example, Not by War" in New York City in July 2004; nor should it come as a surprise that Clear Channel fired Community Affairs Director Davey D from KMEL/San Francisco, a hip-hop journalist known for his presentation of controversial issues and personalities on October 1, 2001; and so on (Kim et al. 2002: 201).

Clear Channel's meteoric rise to prominence cannot be underestimated. Clear Channel owns and operates radio stations and businesses in over sixty countries across Europe, Asia, Africa, South America, New Zealand, and Australia. In August 2001, NIPP (*Nobody in Particular Presents*), a small independent promotions firm that handles local concerts of Pearl Jam and Beastie Boys, filed an antitrust suit in the Federal Court in Denver, Colorado. NIPP charged the company with using monopolistic, predatory, and anticompetitive business practices. According to NIPP, Clear Channel coerces artists to use their promotional outlets, and practically thwarts attempts by independents to buy advertisements on Clear Channel stations.[34] Clear Channel owns the country's largest concert promoter (SFX Entertainment, recently renamed Clear Channel Entertainment), over a hundred concert venues, numerous radio research companies, trade magazines, syndicated programming, and an airplay monitoring system. In May 2003 Clear Channel introduced a venture that will sell live music on CD within a few minutes of a concert's conclusion, thereby cannibalizing sales of official CD releases it does not control.[35] This development reflects an intracorporate struggle, which explains why some of the loudest voices against media centralization come from within the music business. Thus the emergence of Clear Channel is another episode in a long battle between record companies and broadcast companies that goes back to the 1920s. When it must bring itself into line with the imperatives and interests of such highly concentrated, unaccountable economic power, musical censorship occurs less visibly than if it were inscribed in law, with artists second-guessing the wishes of industry executives. Under these conditions, the musician can become cautious and compromised, seeking to balance his/her artistic vision with a duty to serve the ideological demands and political interests of industry executives and their advertisers, which, in turn, articulate with the highest forms of political authority and power.

And yet, since corporations are private entities, the First Amendment does not strictly apply to their censoring ambitions. J. M. Coetzee states the problem thus: "When censure is not only expressed but acted upon by bodies that hold an effective monopoly on particular media of expression (via, for instance, distribution or retail networks), freedom of expression may be stifled as effectively as under outright legal ban. On the other hand, monopoly holders can argue that in exercising censure they are simply asserting their own freedom of expression rather than stifling anyone else's" (1996: 235). The question is: Does radio have a public dimension that transcends its private ownership? The 1934 Communications Act established radio as a public resource managed according to a model of "trusteeship" by the federal government. Broadcasters receive a free slice of the radio spectrum in exchange for serving the "public interest, convenience and necessity." The act also included provisions to promote diversity and localism.[36] As a public resource, radio stations, according to this legislation, have public obligations.[37] To this extent, even though it expands the strict definition of censorship, acts of corporate censorship, especially when they are taken at the highest levels, approximate blunt modes of legal censorship. Today's censoring agents may not be tied directly to the state, but their scope and authority is its match.

PRUDENT FORBEARANCE OR COMPROMISED SELF-CENSORSHIP?

One feature of overt censorship is that it can work out inconsistently in practice, often spawning a backlash. A paradoxical logic seems to launch itself against the censoring agent, as if the object of its censoring attention contained some hidden and prohibited authenticity, something the censor cannot afford to tolerate. As Joseph Jacobs, an editor of *Aesop*, writes, "A tyrant cannot take notice of a fable without putting on the cap that fits."[38] Newly endowed as a cipher of buried truth, the suppressed cultural item then receives more attention than it might if it circulated freely, and the censoring body, descended in esteem, is set up as an object of ridicule and contempt. The banning of the Dixie Chicks is a case in point, producing an array of scornful commentary, jokes, blogs, and cartoons that regard the censor with derision. One well-known example of this ridicule was the end of Michael Moore's acceptance speech on receiving the 2003 Oscar for best feature documentary: "Shame on you, Mr. Bush, shame on you. And any time you've got the Pope and the Dixie Chicks against you, your time is up. Thank

106 • Martin Scherzinger

you very much." More seriously, the backlash against the ban on the Dixie Chicks reverberated at a Senate Commerce Committee Meeting on July 8, 2003, where it was regarded as a case of censorship at a chain level, and thus contributed to an argument against deregulation of media ownership rules.[39] Overt censorship, one might say, often meets its match.

But another kind of censorship, more covert and voluntary, seems to elude this paradoxical logic to some extent. It is as if the relationship between action and reaction exists on an inverse continuum. In diametric contrast to overt censorship, self-censorship, in its purest form, remains wholly outside the grasp and logic of public reception. Cases of musical censorship after 9/11 often lie in-between these two extremes. The controversy surrounding the decision by the Boston Symphony Orchestra to drop four performances of choruses from John Adams's *The Death of Klinghoffer* is a case in point. Adams's opera depicts the hijacking of the cruise ship *Achille Lauro* in 1985 by Palestinians. During the opera one of the ship's passengers, Leon Klinghoffer, is killed by the hijackers. On the one hand, by withdrawing performances, the orchestra risks yielding to a censoring reflex that diverts culture from its proper task. According to at least one dominant strain in theories of art (in the West), unreflective censoriousness flies in the face of art's historical mission to challenge and contest, open perspectives, test limits.[40] In his critique of the Boston Symphony Orchestra, Anthony Tommasini demonstrates an allegiance to this view of art: "[H]ow patronizing for the orchestra's directors to presume what audiences will or will not find offensive. Of course, art can provide solace and comfort. Yet art can also incense and challenge us, make us squirm, make us think."[41] Thus, the liberal argument goes, the act of banning challenging work deflates (and thereby paradoxically also inflates) the work's actual social valences and relevance. "The Boston symphony missed an opportunity to present an acutely relevant work," Tomassini writes; "Mr. Adams and his co-creators tried [to help us understand why so many Muslims hate us]." In the composer's view, too, the work, while "upsetting" to some, offers "the sad solace of truth." Instead of being "too soft on the terrorists," then, the envelope-pushing *Klinghoffer* is aligned here with the long-term interest of the nation. This position reflects the liberal ideal that the free circulation of challenging ideas is a measure of a free and progressive society, or perhaps even a *positive* feature of such a society. In Jeremy Waldron's words, "If . . . widespread moral distress is detectable in the community, then far from being a legitimate ground for interference, it is a positive and healthy sign that the processes of ethical confrontation . . . are actually taking place" (1987: 417).[42] Under this reading, then, *Klinghoffer*'s confrontational stance should be welcomed in a free society.

The liberal stance often supports its position with reference to the so-called "slippery slope" argument, which claims that it is near impossible to devise a principle separating offensive from nonoffensive art. Instead of elaborating a standard that might arbitrate the offensiveness of art's content, the liberal position accepts tolerance for free speech as an overarching value. As a solution to the problem of offensive work, liberalism offers *choice* to the consumer of art: as one is free to make art, one is free to not pay attention to it. Reactions to Richard Taruskin's *defense* of the decision by the Boston Symphony Orchestra to cancel its scheduled performances of the *Klinghoffer* choruses testify to the tensions inherent to the liberal position outlined above.[43] Taruskin's argument (about which more below) is in favor of the cancellation on grounds of sensitivity and forbearance in a time of national crisis. On the one hand, readers unsympathetic to Taruskin's view pointed out art's challenging social role, as well as the consumer's freedom to avoid it. For example, Jeffrey Shallot writes: "Richard Taruskin sees the Boston Symphony's decision to not perform the 'Klinghoffer' choruses as admirable 'self control.' . . . Self-censorship is a force that decreases art's diversity and homogenizes art's response to life's difficulties. . . . Self-control is needed, but it is the self-control of the audience, not the artist. If one thinks that one would be offended by attending 'Klinghoffer,' the option is simply to not attend the symphony that night."[44] Dramatizing the paradox of "deflation/inflation," no less than the problem of the "slippery slope," on the other hand, readers sympathetic with Taruskin's view quickly stretched the implications of his argument to cover additional cases of art they found offensive. One reader wrote, "Richard Taruskin's statement that 'there is no need to shove Wagner in the faces of Holocaust survivors' can logically be extended to: there is no need to shove offensive images into the faces of New Yorkers who are required to pay for the images—as the Brooklyn Museum did when it displayed the Virgin surrounded by pornographic images."[45] The reader is here referring to Chris Ofili's work *The Virgin Mary*, which was exhibited at the Brooklyn Museum of Art two years earlier under the rubric "Sensation: Young British Artists from the Saatchi Collection" (1999). *The Virgin Mary*, which uses elephant dung and pornographic images to depict the Virgin Mary, caused a controversy that involved the mayor of New York, who threatened to remove funding from the museum on account of the work's purported moral offensiveness. In sync with the paradoxical logic of censorship, however, the mayor's threats quickly spawned massive attendance and protests.

On the other hand, when the choice to remove an artwork from public display or performance lies with the *producer* (or, perhaps by extension, the sponsor), the problem can become more vexing. As Taruskin argues in the context of the *Klinghoffer* case in Boston, an internally imposed expurgatory action must be distinguished from an externally imposed one:

> Where should control come from? Unless we are willing to trust the Taliban, it has to come from within. What is called for is self-control. That is what the Boston Symphony laudably exercised; and I hope that musicians who play to Israeli audiences will resume exercising it. There is no need to shove Wagner in the faces of Holocaust survivors in Israel and no need to torment people stunned by previously unimaginable horrors with offensive "challenges" like "The Death of Klinghoffer."[46]

Taruskin plausibly suggests that the public has a right to defend itself from work that is considered offensive. Thus the work's offensiveness in this account supersedes the liberal tolerance for an artistic challenge. Taruskin nonetheless shies away from dismissing altogether the liberal aversion to censorship. This kind of argument hinges on the idea that art, and music in particular, can be harmful in certain contexts (which raises the question about the nature of this harm), and that control can be self-imposed (which raises the question of the self/social body that does the imposing).

Let me deal with these two ideas in turn. On the former point, Taruskin frames the crux of his argument with ethnographic and historical evidence of music's dangers in various quarters. While he mentions four "Western" examples (Plato's resistance to the effects of rhythm and harmony on the soul, medieval suspicions of music's sensuous power over the body, the Nazi rejection of art that was not close to the spirit of the people, and the Soviet resistance to formalism), it is the banning of music by the Taliban, then in power in Afghanistan, that holds pride of place in Taruskin's argument. The article begins as if in a conversation—"And on top of everything else, the Taliban hate music too. . . . After taking power in 1996, the Islamic fundamentalists who ruled most of Afghanistan undertook search-and-destroy missions in which musical instruments and cassette players were seized and burned in public pyres"—and ends with an argumentative punch line: "In the wake of Sept. 11, we might want, finally, to get beyond sentimental complacency about art. Art is not blameless. Art can inflict harm. The Taliban know that. It's about time we learned." The Taliban seem to play an odd role here. On the one hand, they are casually offered as a self-evident example of unacceptable intolerance in the non-West ("Musicians caught in the act were beaten with their instruments and imprisoned for as many as 40 days") and, on the other, offered as a serious alternative to complacent, perhaps even repressive, tolerance in the West ("[*Klinghoffer*] express[es] a reprehensible contempt for the real-life victims of its imagined 'men of ideals,' all too easily transferable to the victims who perished on Sept. 11"). The contradictory use of the Taliban *does*, however, point toward a consistency of argument, one that acknowledges the logical proximity of all censoring/expurgatory activity. By surrendering an aspect of the pure liberal position (its unqualified embrace of free speech), that is, Taruskin acknowledges that his argument shifts to the ballpark of Plato, St. Augustine, John of Salisbury, Joseph Goebbels, Andrei Zhdanov, and the Taliban. Yet these are the "utopians, puritans and totalitarians" most prominently associated with outright censorship, and with whom Taruskin does not identify. While he agrees that art can be harmful, what distinguishes Taruskin's attitude toward that harm from the attitude of these outright censors is the aspect of (public) *volition*. It is in this respect, it seems, that "we" are not "willing to trust the Taliban."[47]

What is the nature of the harm caused by art? Is it truly injurious or simply offensive? Is it a genuine assault or a groundless aversion? And on whom is this harm inflicted? Is it a class of people or a whole society? Does society's right to protect itself from harm (to safeguard its core values, for example) surpass the rights of the individual? Taruskin does not tackle these questions directly, but he does offer a moral argument, which draws on a competing value held by Western society in the extended sense, to show that music, and *Klinghoffer* in particular, does indeed inflict harm.

> If terrorism—specifically, the commission or advocacy of deliberate acts of deadly violence directed randomly at the innocent—is to be defeated, world public opinion has to be turned decisively against it. The only way to do that is to focus resolutely on the acts rather than their claimed (or conjectured) motivation, as crimes. This means no longer romanticizing terrorists as Robin Hoods and no longer idealizing their deeds as rough poetic justice. If we indulge such notions when we happen to agree or sympathize with the aims, then we have forfeited the moral ground from which any such acts can be convincingly condemned.[48]

Here we can identify the harm Taruskin has in mind. By indulging *Klinghoffer*'s challenge we threaten to lose our *moral* bearings.[49] Morality, in this view, is associated with fortitude and conviction about particular deeds (in contrast, say, to an ethics of foundational empathy as elaborated by Emmanuel Levinas, Jacques Derrida, and others), and the belief that thinking about or listening to some kinds of art and music can erode this conviction.

The advantage of this moral mindset lies in not doubting itself; the disadvantage lies in not being able to afford to doubt itself. Thus Taruskin must freeze the dichotomy between *act* and *motivation* when it comes to terrorism (the defeat of which can be achieved only via resolute focus on the former and absolute negation of the latter). When it comes to acts of self-imposed censorship, in contrast, Taruskin's frozen dichotomy reverses itself; here the focus is resolutely on the motivations of the censoring community and concomitantly all consideration of the resulting acts is suspended. As long as the community (out of "sensitivity," "forbearance," "mutual respect," etc.) decides to censor its own cultural productions, the act is legitimate. It is noteworthy, for an argument that is doubtlessly confident that certain acts transcend all possible motivating ideas (as in the case of terrorism), that certain motivating ideas (such as sensitivity and forbearance) can sufficiently transcend their resulting acts. As a result, Taruskin cannot register complexity in either case; he can neither afford to entertain a motivation, however appalling and misguided, behind the terrorist attacks in New York City, nor can he afford to register an affront, however slight, on another fundamental value held by liberal Western democracy as a result of the Boston Symphony Orchestra's censorious act. The difference between the position that opens to such complexity and the position that does not is not, as it is often construed, the difference between relativism and fundamentalism. Consider Tomassini's solution to the challenge facing the Boston Symphony Orchestra: "The Boston Symphony missed an opportunity to present an acutely relevant work. It might have sponsored preconcert panels, bringing Middle East historians together with Mr. Adams, Ms. Goodman, and the director Peter Sellars, who was involved with this opera from its inception."[50] Although Tomassini and Taruskin share the same basic horror of terrorism and distaste for censorship, Tomassini calls for more information about what lies behind the attacks in New York City, and Taruskin calls for less; concomitantly Tomassini favors fewer acts of self-censorship, and Taruskin favors more. Far from reflecting a fundamental difference in moral values, then, these writers offer different views about what is actually required to reduce terrorism in America, on the one hand, and censorship in America, on the other.

The second key idea in Taruskin's argument about music's dangers as they intersect with the dangers of censorship is that of *volition*. Voluntary control over cultural production, it seems, is acceptable; it does not count as censorship. The question arises, What is the character and size of the social unit that can coherently (sincerely?) act on its own volition? Can it extend beyond a single person? A like-minded community of concern, perhaps? If so, how is this like-mindedness ascertained? Can like-mindedness extend to an entire society? A nation? How does this emphasis on volition reckon with conflicts of interest within the group? Again, Taruskin does not tackle these questions directly. And yet the very difference between Taruskin and Tomassini (as well as David Wiegand, columnist for the *San Francisco Chronicle*, and Mark Swed, music critic at the *Los Angeles Times*, among others) registers such conflicting interests. In Barbara Boxer's lexicon, this is the "beautiful noise" of a free country. Moreover, while it is difficult to ascertain the exact details of it, the case of the Boston Symphony Orchestra seems equally embattled. On the one hand, Tommasini reports that a member of the Tanglewood Festival Chorus, scheduled to sing the choruses in Boston, had been personally connected to the tragedy of September 11, 2001.[51] Other members of the chorus were therefore reluctant to perform the work. On the other hand, not everyone was in agreement with the decision to cancel. The composer, for example, disagreed with the reasons given for the cancellation:

> I do think that symphonies and opera companies are very skittish in this country, and I'm sorry that they are, because it confirms the distressing image of symphony-goers as fragile and easily frightened. That's really a shame, because I want to think of symphonic concerts as every bit as challenging as going to MOCA or to see "Angels in America."[52]

Taruskin's emphasis on volition seems unobjectionable if one does not factor into its conditioning ground conflicts of this sort, which are especially vexing in the context of terrorist attacks that were met with widespread bewilderment after 9/11. Once conflicts are accepted as routine, the power relations between members of the community become relevant. How is consensus reached? Should the audience be factored into this consensus? Who holds positions of authority along the path to consensus? Should power relations be taken into account here? Is there a restraint on the use of coercion, for example? If so, how is coercion to be identified? Once again, the questions proliferate.

To consolidate his case, Taruskin might show, first, that the Boston Symphony Orchestra acted in the real interests of the community and, second, that the harms flowing from a performance of *Klinghoffer* outweigh whatever benefits may be claimed for it. This act of moral vigilance involves the paradoxical task of identifying (inventing?) both the interests promoted by the removal of the work and the community that is deemed too vulnerable to experience the opera. The argument should also demonstrate why to experience the harm is to suffer the harm, and finally, why the outright withdrawal, instead of a counter-representation, is not the appropriate action to take. Intuitive appeals to "forbearance" and "sensitivity" need to be assessed against these criteria lest they descend into unqualified prejudice. Nonetheless, Taruskin's insistence on voluntary behavior *does* avert the problems that accrue to officially sanctioned censorship backed by the force of law. Unlike the "utopian" protagonists of his argument, Taruskin's position, in theory at least, opens up to the possibility of this line of questioning and analysis from members of the community in whose interests he claims to act.

AFTERWORD

As is evident from these examples, it is practically impossible to present a characterization of musical censorship after 9/11 at a general level. Instead, the examples discussed in this essay provide an entryway into various debates: the play of productive artistic restrictions against censorious ones, the role of art and freedom of speech in society, the nature of art's social benefits and ills, the nature of appropriate action in the face of artistic transgressions, the question of individual rights as against the rights of a collective, and so on. Of particular interest in this field of competing interests is the tension between the institution of censorship, on the one hand, and the aspirations of art, on the other. According to John Milton, the professional censor should be "above the common measure, both studious, learned and judicious." For Milton, the problem is "there cannot be a more tedious and unpleasing journey-work . . . than to be made the perpetual reader of unchosen books. . . . Seeing therefore those who now possess the employment . . . wish themselves well rid of it, and that no man of worth . . . is ever likely to succeed them . . . we may easily foresee what kind of licensers we are to expect hereafter, either ignorant, imperious, and remiss, or basely pecuniary" (1968: 88). Milton suggests that those willing to act as censors are, practically by definition, not suited to the task. If art's social role is to test the limits of social conventions and laws, which is to say to probe their fault lines and weaknesses, the ideal artist places a high premium on individual expression and treats prejudgments with suspicion. Thus, the ideal artist's mindset is in direct contrast to the necessarily bureaucratic, foreclosing and judgmental mindset of the ideal censor. While some acts of censorship seem warranted (desirable even) in certain circumstances, these fundamentally opposed interests, should—when it comes to assigning power to the censor—give us pause.

It is not always clear in the examples examined in this essay whether censoring power has been exercised over music. Yet, after 9/11 signs of musical constraint abound. Madonna, for example, withdrew her anti-war video "American Life," "out of sensitivity and respect to the armed forces," in March 2003.[53] The video presents images of Muslim children in the context of an escalating frenzy of war imagery: weapons exploding, missiles launching, fighter planes on the wing, bombs dropping, buildings burning, mushroom clouds blooming, and so on. The song's antiwar message is dramatized by the peace sign in the upper corner of the screen. On the one hand, Madonna's withdrawal of the video from the American public appears to be a clear case of "voluntary abstinence" in the context of war between the United States and Iraq; and yet, on the other hand, it resonates with the cautious attitude of the effectively muzzled musician to whose plight Tim Robbins alerts us. Either way, the withdrawal of the video—as it is with all the cases discussed in this paper (the withdrawal of songs from various radio stations, the cancellation or obstruction of musical performances, etc.)—registers the limits of artistic expression in the post-9/11 moment. In this (negative) sense we can discern how the behavior of cultural commodities in a particular political climate discloses the political standards of our times. The question is whether these signs of ideological limits produce a climate of self-constraint that diverts art from free expression, which, according to the liberal position, is a precondition for art's proper task, or not. When censoring activity assumes significance in the inner life of the musician alone, it is no longer open to public scrutiny or debate. It then risks violently descending into the anxious silence of Foucault's "panopticism"; inducing a "state of conscious and permanent visibility," which, as unverifiable, assures "the automatic functioning" of non-individualized power (1979: 201).

ACKNOWLEDGMENTS

I would like to thank Richard Leppert for his helpful input regarding this essay. I am also grateful to the Princeton University Society of Fellows for supporting my research on this topic.

REFERENCES

Bakhtin, Mikhail. 1984. *Problems of Dostoevksy's Poetics.* Edited and translated by Caryl Emerson. Manchester: Manchester University Press.

Cloonan, Martin. 2004a. "What Is Music Censorship? Towards a Better Understanding of the Term." In *Shoot the Singer! Music Censorship Today*, edited by Marie Korpe, 3–5. London and New York: Zed Books.

———. 2004b. "Musical Responses to September 11th: From Conservative Patriotism to Radicalism." In *9/11—The World's All Out of Tune. Populäre Musik nach dem 11. September 2001*, edited by Dietrich Helms and Thomas Phleps, 11–32. Bielefeld, Germany: Transcript Verlag.

Coetzee, J. M. 1996. *Giving Offense: Essays on Censorship*. Chicago and London: The University of Chicago Press.

Cowen, Tyler. 1998. *In Praise of Commercial Culture*. Cambridge, MA, and London: Harvard University Press.

Forman, Murray. 2002. "Soundtrack to a Crisis: Music, Context, Discourse." *Television and New Media* 3(2): 191–204, 194.

Foucault, Michel. 1979. *Discipline & Punish: The Birth of the Prison*. Translated by Alan Sheridan. New York: Vintage.

Holland, Bill. 2003. "Radio Under Fire: Chicks Ban Comes Back to Haunt Chain." *Billboard Magazine*, 19 June 2003.

Kim, Jee, Jeremy Glick, Shaffy Moed, Luis Sanchez, Beka Economopoulos, and Walida Imarisha, eds. 2002. *Another World Is Possible: Conversations in a Time of Terror*. New Orleans: Subway and Elevated Press.

Kis, Danilo. 1986. "Censorship/Self-Censorship." *Index on Censorship* 15(1): 43–45.

Milton, John. 1968. *Areopagitica*. Edited by J. C. Suffolk. London: University Tutorial Press.

Nuzum, Eric. 2004. "Crash into me, baby: America's implicit music censorship since 11 September." In *Shoot the Singer! Music Censorship Today*, edited by Marie Korpe, 149–59. London and New York: Zed Books.

Patterson, Annabel. 1991. *Fables of Power*. Durham: Duke University Press.

Phleps, Thomas. 2004. "9/11 und die Folgen in der Popmusik 1. Ton-Spuren." In *9/11—The World's All Out of Tune. Populäre Musik nach dem 11. September 2001*, edited by Dietrich Helms and Thomas Phleps, 57–66. Bielefeld, Germany: Transcript Verlag.

Rohr, Christiane. 2004. "Musiker Unter Druck: Zensorische Massnahmen im Irakkrieg." In *9/11—The World's All Out of Tune. Populäre Musik nach dem 11. September 2001*, edited by Dietrich Helms and Thomas Phleps, 67–79. Bielefeld, Germany: Transcript Verlag.

Rossman, Gabriel. 2004. "Elites, Masses, and the Media Blacklists: The Dixie Chicks Controversy." *Social Forces* 83(1): 61–79.

Schauer, Frederick. 1982. *Free Speech: A Philosophical Inquiry*. New York: Cambridge University Press.

Scherzinger, Martin. 2005. "Music, Corporate Power, and Unending War." *Cultural Critique* 60 (Spring): 23–67.

Scherzinger, Martin, and Stephen Smith. Forthcoming. "From Blatant to Latent Protest (and Back Again): On the Politics of Theatrical Spectacle in Madonna's 'American Life.'" *Popular Music.*

Waldron, Jeremy. 1987. "Mill and the Value of Moral Distress," *Political Studies* 35: 410–23.

Zalot, Michael C. 2002. "Turning Away from the Television Tape Loop: Characterizing Some Local Rock, Pop and Country Music Radio Stations Responses to the September 11, 2001, Terrorist Attacks." *New Jersey Journal of Communication* 10(1): 26–48.

NOTES

1. Cited in "Tim Robbins' Speech (Part 2)," posted on http://moby.com/index2.html, April 21, 2003.
2. Addressing music specifically, Martin Cloonan registers a similar starting point toward a definition of censorship: "For many commentators censorship has to be systematic. It has to be part of a deliberate process, often at the behest of government or its agencies" (2004a: 4).
3. Another case of censorship might emerge when obstructions are placed before possible musical events. Unlike the restriction or outright suppression of music, such censorship involves prior constraint—forbidding what can take place musically. In the fall of 2004 the Zimbabwean mbira player Forward Kwenda and the American-Muslim singer Yusuf Islam (Cat Stevens), for example, were denied entry into the United States, the latter "on national security grounds" (according to Transportation Security Administration officials). These cases register the heightened vigilance toward immigration movements in a time of national crisis. While probably no less harmful a form of censorship today, this essay will not concern itself with such cases of interference.
4. Quoted in Cloonan 2004: 14. It is likely that the surveillance of RATM's Web site, and the subsequent phone calls to its ISP provider, originated in a branch of American intelligence forces other than the Secret Service, which is primarily charged with protecting the U.S. president. Regardless of the exact source of the calls, to date the RATM message board remains closed.
5. Moby and Kevin Richardson incidents reported in Kim et al. 2002: 120.
6. Quoted in the Pitchfork Media online review, where the original and revised CD covers also remain posted: http://www.pitchforkmedia.com/record-reviews/c/coup/party-music.shtml. For more on The Coup's *Party Music,* see Garofalo in this volume as well as Nuzum 2004: 150–51.
7. Tommasini, Anthony. "John Adams, Banned in Boston," *New York Times,* 25 November 2001.

8. It is not clear whether the list was actually enforced. On September 20, Pam Taylor, a Clear Channel spokesman, stated that the list was a fake (see Phleps 2004: 60). As the story gained attention in the media, Clear Channel also released a press statement, which denied the banning of songs from its radio stations and affirmed Clear Channel's commitment to the First Amendment and freedom of speech (for a full citation of the Clear Channel statement, see Nuzum 2004: 158–59). Nonetheless, Clear Channel did not deny the existence of the list in its official statement, even as it did call on each program director and general manager to "take the pulse of his or her market to determine if play lists should be altered" (cited in Nuzum 2004: 158). Eric Nuzum reports that the list had the practical effects of a ban when it came to the actual content of programming on Clear Channel stations: "While many Clear Channel programmers were quoted in the media as saying that they did not follow the suggestions of the e-mail, many times more said that they did indeed remove songs from the broadcast because of the list or its suggested use of restraint" (2004: 151–52). Martin Cloonan points out that at least one radio station did not play any music on the list (2004b: 16).
9. As it is with another song on the Clear Channel list, Simon & Garfunkel's "Bridge over Troubled Waters," it is ironic that Lennon's "Imagine" was heavily requested on classic radio stations in the United States in the months following the World Trade Center attacks (Cloonan 2004b: 21).
10. It is not surprising, in this regard, that the highly vocal right-wing blogosphere did not come down against the Clear Channel list.
11. See http://www.rareexception.com/Garden/American.php
12. On the wide-reaching system of official censorship in the Republic of South Africa under apartheid, for instance, Coetzee writes: "Called in official parlance not censorship but 'publications control' (censorship was a word it preferred to censor from public discourse about itself), it sought to control the dissemination of signs in whatever form" (1996: 34).
13. See Neil Strauss, "The Pop Life: MTV is Wary of Videos on War," *New York Times,* March 26, 2003. The contents of the memo can also be found on http://board.unearthed.org/viewtopic.php?t=1738.
14. Fred Schneider of the B-52's was baffled by MTV Europe's ban: "I guess MTV doesn't have a research department, because from Day 1 we've said in interviews that our name is a slang term for the bouffant hairdo Kate and Cindy used to wear—nothing to do with the bombers" (ibid.)
15. Although it did appear on MTV in the United States, the band's singer Serj Tankian points out that the video was not being shown on the music-video network MuchMusic USA either (ibid.).
16. On the official System of a Down Web site, Michael Moore provided sources for every claim made in the video. See also Rohr 2004: 71–2.

17. The *San Francisco Chronicle* reported James as saying: "There is absolutely no MTV policy anywhere in the world banning war-related music videos. . . . The memo was only a recommendation from a staffer and was not and will not be implemented. It was ludicrous. In the U.S. and everywhere, all voices have been and will continue to be heard on MTV." From Joe Garofoli, "Artists React to Tale of Intimidation," *San Francisco Chronicle*, 5 April 2003.

18. Betty Clarke, "Pop—The Dixie Chicks—Shepherd's Bush Empire London," *The Guardian*, 12 March 2003.

19. Stephen Marshall, "Prime Time Payola," *In These Times*, 5 May 2003, 23–24. See also Paul Krugman, "Channels of Influence," *New York Times*, 25 March 2003.

20. NBC News, March 19, 2003. Available at http://www.nbc4.tv/news/2051323/detail.html.

21. Alisa Solomon, "The Big Chill," *The Nation*, 2 June 2003, 17–22.

22. Associated Press, May 6, 2003. Available at http://www.polarity1.com/pcrr50.html.

23. See, for example, remarks about the "groundswell, a hue and cry from listeners" made by Lewis W. Dickey Jr., CEO of Atlanta-based Cumulus Broadcasting in Bill Holland's "Radio under Fire: Chicks Ban Comes Back to Haunt Chain" (2003; see http://www.recordingartistscoalition.com/press.php?content_id=27705). Executives at Clear Channel advanced the same basic defense of its actions: their radio stations, it was claimed, were buckling under grassroots pressure.

24. Associated Press. May 6, 2003. See http://www.polarity1.com/pcrr50.html.

25. Alterman writes: "In a May [2005] survey published by the Pew Research Center for the People and the Press, 65 percent of respondents said they favor providing health insurance to all Americans, even if it means raising taxes, and 86 percent said they favor raising the minimum wage. Seventy-seven percent said they believe the country 'should do whatever it takes to protect the environment.' A September Gallup Poll finds that 59 percent consider the Iraq War a mistake and 63 percent agree that U.S. forces should be partially or completely withdrawn [from Iraq]." From Alterman's "Corrupt, Incompetent & Off Center," *The Nation*, 7 November 2005, p. 12.

26. The claim that conservative flak did not represent a majority of the citizenry does not in itself undermine the legitimacy of the politicized minority. Jean Hardisty and Deepak Bhargava describe the success of the right-wing rise to power at the turn of the century in terms of astute political mobilization: "Conservatives focused on building powerful mass-based institutions that could provide muscle for the conservative agenda, such as the National Rifle Association, the Moral Majority, the American Family Association and, later, Focus on the Family, Concerned Women for America and the Christian Coalition of America" (Jean

Hardisty and Deepak Bhargava, "Wrong about the Right," *The Nation,* 7 November 2005, 23). Many of these groups actively pressure the culture industry to conform to a conservative agenda.

27. By most accounts, the issue was more contested than Rossman's analysis would imply. On March 19, 2003, NBC news, for example, reported: "'A lot of people were calling up saying they were never going to listen to the Dixie Chicks again,' B93-FM radio personality 'Some Guy Named Tias' told WYFF News 4's Todd Gladfelter, 'A lot were saying they have the right to say whatever they want to say'" (see http://www.nbc4.tv/news/2051323/detail.html). WYFF is based in Greenville, South Carolina.

28. Ibid.

29. Using different databases, Michael Moore reported opposite sales figures for the Dixie Chicks on April 7, 2003: "This week, after all the attacks, their album is still at #1 on the *Billboard* country charts and, according to *Entertainment Weekly,* on the pop charts during all the brouhaha, they ROSE from #6 to #4" (See http://www.globalaware.org/noticeboard/mm_dixie.html).

30. Eric Boehlert, "More Waves in the Radio Business," Salon.com, August 6, 2001 (http://dir.salon.com/ent/music/feature/2001/08/06/radio_records/index.html).

31. Rossman's argument is strikingly consistent with arguments advanced in corporate headquarters at Clear Channel. Executives at Clear Channel, for example, insisted that the Atlanta rally on March 15, as well as other sponsored rallies organized by Clear Channel's talk show host Glenn Beck, were a reflection of audience sentiment. Clear Channel spokeswoman Lisa Dollinger said, "Any rallies that our stations have been a part of have been of their own initiative and in response to the expressed desires of their listeners and communities," while Beck maintained these were simply "grassroots" rallies (See Tim Jones, "Media Giant's Rally Sponsorship Raises Questions," *Chicago Tribune,* 19 March 2003). Yet the *New York Times* reports that of the eighteen "Rally for America!" events held across the country during the month of March, thirteen were cosponsored and actively promoted by local Clear Channel stations (See John Schwartz and Geraldine Fabrikant. "War Puts Radio Giant on the Defensive," *New York Times,* 31 March 2003, Business Section).

32. Paul Krugman, "Channels of Influence," *New York Times,* 25 March 2003.

33. For a critical appraisal of the Carlyle Group, see http://www.takeback-themedia.com/radiogaga.html; for a company statement, see www.carlylegroup.com/funds.htm.

34. Eric Boehlert, "Suit: Clear Channel is an Illegal Monopoly," Salon.com, 8 August 2001 (http://dir.salon.com/ent/clear_channel/2001/08/08/antitrust/index.html).

35. Mirapaul, Matthew. "Concert CDs Sold on the Spot by Radio Giant," *New York Times,* 5 May 2003.

36. In 1996, Congress passed the Telecommunications Act to replace the 1934 law. The principal aim of the 1996 law was to deregulate all communication industries. As a result, Clear Channel grew from owning just forty to over twelve hundred radio stations in the first nine years after the law's revision.

37. The arguments by business executives claiming "grassroots pressure" as the cause of the Dixie Chicks blacklist backhandedly testify to the public obligations of radio. Similarly, the arguments claiming increased "diversity" on the consolidated airwaves (often with reference to the concept-metaphor of "formats") equally acknowledge these obligations. For example, David F. Poltrack, Executive Vice President, Research and Planning at CBS, indicates that the public is served by deregulation because of the sheer increase in television channels in the last decade. Similarly, Dennis Swanson, Executive Vice President and Chief Operating Officer of Viacom Television Stations Group, maintains that media consolidation has increased the actual number of minutes of programming devoted to local news (see remarks made by Poltrack and Swanson at the Forum on Media Ownership Rules held at Columbia University on January 16, 2003, webcast of proceedings available on http://www.law.columbia.edu). For a critique of these arguments, see Scherzinger 2005.

38. Quoted in Patterson 1991: 17.

39. See http://commerce.senate.gov/hearings/testimony.cfm?id=831&wit_id=2340 and Holland 2003.

40. J. M. Coetzee offers historical reasons for the hostility between governmental authority and writing, especially in the context of the disseminative power afforded by printing. "Hostility between the two sides, which soon became settled and institutional, was exacerbated by the tendency of artists from the late eighteenth century onward to assume it as their social role, and sometimes indeed as their vocation and destiny, to test limits (that is to say, the weak points) of thought and feeling, of representation, of the law, and of opposition itself, in ways that those in power were bound to find uncomfortable and even offensive" (1996: 9). This hostility is considerably intensified in the context of vast new technologies of dissemination today.

41. Anthony Tommasini, "John Adams, Banned in Boston," New York Times, 25 November 2001. All following quotes by Tommasini are drawn from this article.

42. Waldron's position echoes what Barbara Boxer calls a "beautiful noise."

43. Richard Taruskin, "Music's Dangers and the Case for Control," New York Times, 9 December 2001.

44. Jeffery Shallit, "Music's Dangers: Whose Self-Control?" New York Times, 23 December 2001.

45. Michael Trombetta, "Music's Dangers; Brooklyn Too," New York Times, 23 December 2001.

46. Taruskin, "Music's Dangers," 2001. All following quotes by Taruskin are drawn from this article.
47. Taruskin differs from Plato, St. Augustine, and John of Salisbury (but less so from Goebbels and Zhdanov) in another important respect as well: Where Plato, Augustine, and John tend to emphasize the purely musical aspects of music (its harmonies, rhythms, polyphonies, etc.), Taruskin is more interested in its hermeneutic aspects (the political, possibly anti-Semitic, dimensions of Adams's opera, etc.). Taruskin does attempt to transfer the argument to the music itself ("The libretto commits many notorious breaches of evenhandedness, but the greatest one is to be found in Mr. Adams's music"), but this argument rests on an analogy; a cryptographic association between the musical language accompanying the words of Jesus in the *St. Matthew Passion* and that accompanying the Palestinians in *Klinghoffer*. Taruskin does not question the musical aspects of the "Bachian aureole" as such (with its "effects of limitless expanse in time or space," etc.), but rather the composer's choice of protagonists with which such sublimity is associated.
48. Taruskin's attempt to identify the harm embodied by Klinghoffer is erratic, often creating the conditions of the argument's undermining. On (*Los Angeles Times* music critic) Mark Swed's upholding of the post 9/11 relevance of the opera, for example, Taruskin writes: "But whence this quaintly macho impulse to despise comfort (women's work?) and even deny it haughtily to sufferers? And whence the idea of seeking answers and understanding in an opera peopled by wholly fictional terrorists and semifictionalized victims, rather than in more relevant sources of information?" In an apparently feminist gesture, Taruskin here paradoxically feminizes an apparently masculinist pose, and then rhetorically insists that not canceling the performance denies comfort to sufferers. The problem with this construal lies less with the exaggerated claim about suffering (surely only the removal of a musical performance could deny anyone anything), and more with the diminished claim about art's relevance, which undermines the very impulse that launches Taruskin's critique. If the opera is as "fictional" (and thus futile to the cause of "understanding") as claimed, why is it construed as harmful enough to warrant withdrawal?
49. On whether this loss leads to tacit acceptance of terrorist acts Taruskin's text is silent.
50. Tommasini, "John Adams," 2003.
51. Ibid.
52. Mark Swed, "'Klinghoffer': Too Hot to Handle?" *Los Angeles Times,* 20 November 2001.

53. For an extended analysis of Madonna's video in the context of impending war, see Scherzinger and Smith's "From Blatant to Latent Protest (and Back Again): On the Politics of Theatrical Spectacle in Madonna's 'American Life,'" forthcoming in *Popular Music*.

6

"HAVE YOU FORGOTTEN?":

DARRYL WORLEY AND THE MUSICAL POLITICS OF OPERATION IRAQI FREEDOM

Peter J. Schmelz

The unfolding of the unforeseen was everything. Turned wrong way round, the relentless unforeseen was what we schoolchildren studied as "History," harmless history, where everything unexpected in its own time is chronicled on the page as inevitable. The terror of the unforeseen is what the science of history hides, turning a disaster into an epic.

—Philip Roth, *The Plot Against America*[1]

In the grip of an inexorable forward lurch into the next war—the blame for which could be endlessly debated, endlessly fine-tuned—we stumbled into a future there had not been time even to anticipate.

—Geoffrey O'Brien, "Is It All Just a Dream?"[2]

Music that makes you think they're singing about you.

—Radio motto of WQNY 103.7 FM, "Q-Country," Ithaca, NY[3]

After 9/11, country music more than any other genre captured and channeled the mood of the American public. From the outset, songs like Alan Jackson's "Where Were You (When the World Stopped Turning)?", premiered in November 2001, indicated the degree to which country music would become integral to the public remembrance of September 11, and to the responses at each stage in the subsequent "war on terror."[4] As the U.S. government "inexorably lurched forward" in response to the 9/11 attacks, to borrow Geoffrey O'Brien's apt phrase for the march to war, country musicians kept pace. Following the Bush administration's invasion of Afghanistan, country music applauded the move, perhaps most prominently in Toby Keith's song of rage, "Courtesy of the Red, White, and Blue (The Angry American)," released in late May 2002 and directed at the Taliban. During the protracted buildup to the invasion of Iraq, from late 2002 until March 19, 2003, the role of country musicians and country music in American political discourse became still more pronounced. Even as other prominent popular musicians, especially in rock and hip-hop, began organizing against the impending war, country music took the lead in promoting the invasion, particularly Darryl Worley's song of enraged remembrance, "Have You Forgotten?"[5]

Worley's song, in fact, became the "hit" of the early Iraq War, broadcast widely on radio and television. In this essay, I argue that "Have You Forgotten?" offers a crucial perspective on this recent period of American history, documenting how the meanings of the song—and even the song itself—changed as the United States prepared for war and eventually invaded Iraq. Indeed, when future historians attempt to comprehend the popular support of (and the many justifications for) the launch of the Iraq War, they would do no better than to look at the changing reception of Worley's song, as there is arguably no richer cultural artifact of that moment. Cecilia Tichi writes that "country music . . . enables us to see vital parts of the national identity that otherwise are hidden, obscured, overshadowed, blacked out in painful self-censorship" (1994: 18). While I would argue that all music does this, from "popular" to "classical," from country to hip-hop, in this particular instance Worley's song does amplify a "vital part of the national identity" at a vital moment in that nation's history, even as its details today are slowly being effaced by memory's failings and obscured by the self-justifications of actors along the entire political spectrum.[6]

As an active participant in public debates over the war in Iraq, Worley's hit invites a number of questions regarding music's role as a political agent, and its ability not only to subvert but also to support dominant political actions and ideologies. As we shall see, Worley's song illustrates how music can both reflect and affect events, embodying sentiment and instigating action. Many writers have surveyed the country music produced during the major American conflicts of the twentieth century, and particularly the country hits of the Vietnam era, but no one has investigated both the words and music of a specific song and traced its reception and participation in an ongoing cultural dialogue.[7] As John Street has argued in a recent discussion of popular music and politics, "a more productive route [to understanding the relationship of politics and music] lies in seeing how particular songs or performances engage with particular political moments and issues. This is not to return to the music as the expression of a time or era, but rather to its role in shaping and focusing experience."[8] What Street neglects to point out is that few scholars have examined the specific ways in which popular music often supports dominant ideological trends rather than offering an idealized locus for resistance, the preferred object of interest for pop music scholars.[9] Beyond its immediate topical value, then, Worley's "Have You Forgotten?" acts as an ideal case study for exploring country music's audience and country music's possible meanings, as well as broader questions of signification and representation in popular music.

THE GENESIS OF A COUNTRY MUSIC ANTHEM

"Have You Forgotten?" fits within a long trajectory of wartime odes in American country music. Most country songs written or performed during World War II, the Korean War, and Vietnam were of the "mother and home" or "girl I left behind" variety, as Jens Lund dubs them.[10] During World War II, there were, of course, some that attempted to motivate direct action against the enemy, such as "Remember Pearl Harbor," "There's a Star Spangled Banner Waving Somewhere," "We're Gonna Have to Slap the Dirty Little Jap (And Uncle Sam's the Guy Who Can Do It)," and the Gene Autry-inspired recruiting song, "I'll Trade My Horse and Saddle for a Pair of Wings."[11] These, however prominent, were the exceptions.

The Vietnam War also had its share of "girl I left behind" songs, but those aimed at convincing listeners of the necessity of the cause took on a higher profile. While the most famous of these, Staff Sergeant Barry Sadler's "Ballad of the Green Berets," recalls the general patriotism heard in pro-war songs of previous conflicts, a significant number of the country songs that supported the Vietnam War responded, either directly or implicitly, to the burgeoning antiwar movement at home.[12] Examples are abundant; a typical example is Tom T. Hall's "Hello Vietnam," which reached no. 1 in 1965 in Johnny Wright's rendition:

That fires we don't put out will bigger burn.

We must save freedom now at any cost.

Or some day our own freedom may be lost.

Another is Dave Dudley's recording of Tom T. Hall's "What We're Fighting For," also from 1965:

You tell me there are people marching in our streets,

The signs they carry say we don't fight for peace.

There's not a soldier in this foreign land who likes this war.

~~Oh, Mama, tell them what we're fighting for.~~[13]

Other examples include Stonewall Jackson's "The Minute Men Are Turning in Their Graves" (1966, written by Harlan Howard) and Autry Inman's "The Ballad of Two Brothers" (one a patriotic soldier, the other a protestor; 1968, written by Bobby Braddock, Buddy Killen, and Curly Putman).[14]

Twenty years later, country music again took the lead during Operation Desert Storm (the "First" Iraq War) in 1991, with Lee Greenwood's "God Bless the U.S.A." ("I'm proud to be an American / Where at least I know I'm free") as the leading candidate for that brief war's most ubiquitous anthem. Its only competition, Aaron Tippin's "You've Got to Stand for Something" and Waylon Jennings's "The Eagle," also came from the country music world. In contrast to the context-specific songs of the Vietnam era, all three of these songs were patriotic only in a general sense; none referred directly to the current conflict.[15] The generic message of Greenwood's song in particular allowed it to be resuscitated in the wake of 9/11 and again for the 2003 war in Iraq. As Charles Passy observed in late 2001, "Perhaps the key element . . . behind the song's ["God Bless the U.S.A."] repeated resurrection . . . is Greenwood's reference to an unnamed enemy. To quote the lyrics: 'I thank my lucky stars to be living here today 'cause the flag still stands for freedom, and they can't take that away.' On Sept. 11, America found a new 'they'—and Greenwood's song seemed more relevant than ever."[16]

Despite the popularity of Greenwood's "God Bless the U.S.A.," Worley's "Have You Forgotten?" serves as a better representative of its cultural/historical moment precisely because of its specificity and singularity. Thanks to the brevity of the 2003 war in Iraq—or at least its "major combat operations"—"Have You Forgotten?" had little competition on the airwaves during the conflict's peak. Furthermore, the song enjoyed greater success than any of its Vietnam-era precursors at a time when country music had gained a much wider audience.[17] Nonetheless, as Worley's opening lines reveal, "Have You Forgotten?" is clearly indebted to songs like Hall's "What We're Fighting For":

I hear people saying we don't need this war.

I say there's some things worth fighting for . . .

They say we don't realize the mess we're getting in.

Before you start your preaching,

Let me ask you this my friend: Have you forgotten?

These lines set the hortatory tone from the outset, as they coerce the listener to become part of the (American) collective. "Have You Forgotten?" was hawked by DreamWorks Records Nashville as "A song you'll always remember about an event we can never forget," another conflation of "you" and "we," in which the individual reader can only gain entry into the group by listening to (and purchasing) Worley's anthem. Worley's song performed the same function as the ubiquitous bumper stickers proclaiming "Support Our Troops" that sprouted on cars in the fall of 2004 in the lead-up to that year's presidential election, reminders of the more spontaneous proliferation of flags fluttering from car windows in the fall of 2001 after the September 11 attacks.[18] Unlike Jackson's narrative persona in "Where Were You?" Worley's did not want to hear your response; he assumed that you had forgotten and was trying to assail your guilty conscience. Like World War II posters commemorating Pearl Harbor, the song could plausibly have been called "Remember September 11!" (Toby Keith's, on the other hand, would have been its partner: "Avenge September 11!")[19] By framing his title as a question, Worley achieved better sales; apparently guilt works better than a command.

In the first verse of Worley's song the addressee is unclear: What people were "preaching" to him? Though there had been large protests in October 2002 and January 2003 (only a week after Worley's first public performances of his song), the biggest day of protesting against the war came well after the song was written, on Saturday, February 15, 2003, when millions of protestors took to the streets in cities across the United States and across the globe.[20] But Worley's opening targets might have been more imagined than real, straw men conjured by the insecurities of the soldiers he met in Afghanistan as a USO (United Service Organization) performer over the Christmas 2002 holiday (from December 18–24, 2002).[21] Here chronology becomes important, for the creation and reception of Worley's song and its video are best read in counterpoint with the political and military actions of late 2002 and early 2003 (see Appendix 1). According to Worley's Web site:

> I literally had soldiers come up to me and say, "You know, we're over here fighting for you and your family, and we need for you to go back home and fight for us." And I knew exactly what they meant. It became a mission to me, a duty to come back here and do something to honor them. I didn't even think the song would get recorded—I just had something to say.[22]

Other versions of the story had Worley responding to disparaging remarks that he overheard once he returned.[23] Worley's visit itself became incorporated into the music and lyrics in the song's third verse when he sings: "I've been there with the soldiers / Who've gone away to war," effectively erasing the distinction between the singer and the narrative persona of the song. This "authenticity" and, to use a term coined by country music scholar Jimmie Rogers (1989), the "sincerity contract" it forged with its audience, was a primary aspect of the song's advertising, video, and, ultimately, successful reception.[24] Worley's "authentic" support for the troops was underscored by his own well-established "authentic" country credentials. As one writer enthused, he was a Tennessee native with a "drawl thick enough to insulate a house," who already had a no. 1 hit under his belt for "I Miss My Friend" in 2002.[25]

"Have You Forgotten?" was premiered during Worley's four performances at the Grand Ole Opry on January 11 and 12, 2003. Worley described the mood:

> At the first Friday-night show, they started applauding in the middle of the song. It startled me so much that I forgot a line. Every performance of it that weekend got ridiculous ovations. On the televised Grand Ole Opry show, on Saturday night, people actually stood up at the beginning of the song and remained standing throughout the whole performance. They cheered and cheered and cheered. I'd never seen anything like it. It really got ahold of my heart.[26]

Each evening he received standing ovations for the song.[27] Soon MP3 files of the song were circulating on the Internet.[28] The overwhelming public response led Worley's label to "rush" a recording of the song, although the studio version was not officially released until late February 2003; it debuted at no. 41 on the "Hot Country Singles & Tracks" in *Billboard* the week of March 8.[29] Worley told a later interviewer, "We [Worley and cowriter Wynn Varble] didn't think it would be a radio single. . . . We knew it had the potential for some controversy, and we wrote it pretty in-your-face. I said to Wynn, 'Let's not write this like we're even think-ing about radio. If it sits on the shelf like those other 1,500 songs in my publishing company, so be it.'"[30]

The Grand Ole Opry version of the song is important, as the differ-ences between it and the studio version reveal the changing perception of the justification for the invasion of Iraq. The primary differences are instrumental and structural, the live performance naturally lacking the polish of the studio recording, and featuring a stripped-down ensemble minus the prominent fiddle heard on the later recording. The audience on the live recording is also as prominent as Worley's account suggests, with considerable applause that begins during the second line of the first verse and continues throughout the song. The applause is loudest during the pauses following choruses, but it also swells at important lyrics like that in the second chorus: "Have you forgotten / When those towers fell?" or the mention of Osama bin Laden at the end of the same stanza. The live version is also approximately twenty seconds longer (4:20 as opposed to 4:00), including a repeat of the final chorus not in the studio recording.

The most significant difference from a sociopolitical standpoint is a slight change in the choruses between the Opry performances and the studio recording of "Have You Forgotten?" This is where chronology becomes particularly important, because between January 11, 2003, and the release of the song late the following month, several important events occurred. First, President Bush delivered his State of the Union Address, in which he expanded on the prominent theme of his 2002 State of the Union Address. In that earlier speech, Bush had famously singled out Iran, South Korea, and Iraq as the "axis of evil," and ominously warned that these states posed "a grave and growing danger."[31] The connection between the 9/11 attacks, Al Qaeda, and Iraq implicit in the 2002 speech was made explicit a year later:

> With nuclear arms or a full arsenal of chemical and biological weapons, Saddam Hussein could resume his ambitions of con-quest in the Middle East and create deadly havoc in that region. And this Congress and the American people must recognize another threat. Evidence from intelligence sources, secret com-munications, and statements by people now in custody reveal that Saddam Hussein aids and protects terrorists, including members of al Qaeda. Secretly, and without fingerprints, he could provide one of his hidden weapons to terrorists, or help them develop their own.

The link between Hussein and Al Qaeda was underscored in a terrifying scenario painted by Bush:

> Before September the 11th, many in the world believed that Saddam Hussein could be contained. But chemical agents, lethal viruses and shadowy terrorist networks are not easily contained. Imagine those 19 hijackers with other weapons and other plans— this time armed by Saddam Hussein.[32] It would take one vial, one canister, one crate slipped into this country to bring a day of horror like none we have ever known. We will do everything in our power to make sure that that day never comes.

Bush ended by giving Hussein an ultimatum to disarm, announcing:

> And tonight I have a message for the brave and oppressed people of Iraq: Your enemy is not surrounding your country—your enemy is ruling your country. And the day he and his regime are removed from power will be the day of your liberation.

Though the President and his administration had been putting this message across in public venues since his September 12, 2002, address before the U.N. General Assembly,[33] the State of the Union provided a very public, more immediate backdrop for both the initial reception and the rewriting and recording of Worley's song, which premiered only seventeen days earlier and was already circulating widely in bootleg form.[34]

In addition to Bush's State of the Union Address, on February 5, 2003, Secretary of State Colin Powell also addressed the U.N. Security Council regarding Iraq's weapons of mass destruction, again making connections between Iraq and Al Qaeda. Powell stated:

> What I want to bring to your attention today is the potentially much more sinister nexus between Iraq and the al-Qaida [sic] terrorist network, a nexus that combines classic terrorist organizations and modern methods of murder. Iraq today harbors a deadly terrorist network headed by Abu Musab al-Zarqawi, an associate and collaborator of Usama [sic] bin Laden and his al-Qaida lieutenants. . . . Iraqi officials deny accusations of ties with al-Qaida. These denials are simply not credible. Last year, an al-Qaida associate bragged that the situation in Iraq was "good," that Baghdad could be transited quickly.[35]

Against this drumbeat to war, peace protestors took to the streets all over the world on February 15, while Worley continued to plug his newly released song, appearing on March 1 on the *Today Show* via satellite from the Grand Ole Opry.

This political environment directly affected the recording and video for "Have You Forgotten?" and set the stage for its swift rise up the charts. The most significant change was the revision of the second chorus. At the Opry performance, choruses ended with either "And you say we shouldn't worry 'bout bin Laden" or "Don't you tell me not to worry 'bout bin Laden." By the time of the studio recording, the second chorus had been rewritten to end with "And we vowed to get the ones behind bin Laden."[36] This seemingly minor change represents a major shift in emphasis. Before Bush's State of the Union, Worley's song argued implicitly for the country to go after a specific person (bin Laden); now, in seeking to "get the ones behind bin Laden," Worley's studio recording buttressed administration arguments by advocating action against a different target, which in this context could only be presumed to be the Hussein regime in Iraq.[37] The confusion of the early post-9/11 period, the confusion of Alan Jackson's "singer of simple songs" from his "Where Were You (When the World Stopped Turning)?" who could not "tell you the difference in Iraq and Iran," had been resolved. According to reporter Jim Farber, "Worley has come under fire for [his] lines, which draw a direct link involving Osama, 9/11 and Saddam Hussein. While at first the singer denies that his words make that controversial connection, he adds, 'the real deal is that Saddam supports international terrorism. We've known that for years. That's enough of a connection for me.'"[38]

The video representation of Worley's song further underscored this message, as it used the traditional narrative technique of country music and country video to create a deliberate visual "plot" that lent a sense of inevitability to the calls for war propounded by the lyrics and the music.[39] In fact, Worley's video portrayed the opening of hostilities before they had actually occurred. The visual representation of "Have You Forgotten?" is crucial, because for most Americans, and for most of the world, 9/11 was a visual event witnessed live on television. Worley's masochistic—"I can take it"—second verse invokes the visual aspect of the events and the specific trauma they inflicted on viewers, while implying that repeated exposure to TV-mediated images of 9/11 is necessary to keep the country focused on its new antiterror mission:

They took all the footage off my T.V.

Said it's too disturbing for you and me.

It'll just breed anger, that's what the experts say.

If it was up to me I'd show it every day.[40]

Despite arguing for increasing the 9/11 footage, such images are infrequent in the video, which begins not with shots from 9/11, but with a standard music video (and especially country music video) trope: images of the singer and his band hard at work in the recording studio. Only during the second verse do any 9/11-related images appear. From the outset, then, the video follows a straightforward performance format with the musicians foregrounded; they will be the touch points, the mediators, for the "plot" that follows.

As the resolutely midtempo tune begins, ushered in by the prominent glissando slide guitar on the upbeat, announcing its genre from the get-go, the first image we see is of Worley and his microphone silhouetted against the brightly lit orange soundproofing of the studio walls. The second shot is of a guitar on its stand and other studio equipment (speakers, cables), which cuts in turn to a grainy, Super 8 (or faux Super 8) scan of a pile of photos of posed smiling soldiers scattered on top of the mixing board. Then we see the guitar again, Worley's profile, the slide guitar player, and the drummer, before returning to a shadowy front view of Worley singing the first lines of the song: "I hear people saying we don't need this war."

At this point the first topical footage is shown as the video cuts to film of protestors, initially with their backs to the camera and walking away from us, a visual underscoring of their cowardice. In succeeding shots, the placards they are holding read "No Iraq War," among other things. Incidentally, this footage appears to be taken from the protests across the United States on February 15, 2003, well after Worley had penned his lines about "preaching" protestors. Since the original late 2002/early 2003 authoring of "Have You Forgotten?" both Worley and his opponents had become more hardened, and more vocal, in their positions.

These opening shots set the tone for what follows: alternating shots of the musicians, Worley writing the words to the song, and footage that matches the content of the lyrics. The sterile surroundings of the studio set off the images of protest, images of Lower Manhattan after the collapse of the World Trade Center, and images of soldiers going off to war. The inevitability of the upcoming war is underscored by this visual movement from protest to destruction to mobilization, and the routine studio musician shots put the more provocative and painful images in stark relief.

As the preceding summary suggests, the images intensify with each verse. The first verse concentrates on the protestors, followed by shots of Worley and, presumably, his cowriter Wynn Varble looking over the photos from the USO tour in Afghanistan and penning the song. The second verse contains footage from Lower Manhattan after the World

Trade Center collapse. The images here are all quick and fragmentary, allusive rather than explicit, as Worley attempts to negotiate between his own second verse's call for repeatedly viewing the towers fall and the danger of offending his viewers' sensibilities in the process.[41] Therefore, this segment of the video is also very brief, and after the "tasteful" (Worley's word) glimpse of the immediate physical destruction of 9/11, the second chorus visually returns to the song's theme of remembrance, focusing on the immediate emotional aftermath: images of people grieving over the makeshift memorials of that tragic day.

The video moves from protest as denial in the first verse, to remembrance in the second, to necessary action in the bridge, as if Worley and his director are leading the viewer step-by-step through the grieving process. The action of the bridge's lyrics is prefigured by the footage accompanying the guitar solo that follows the second chorus, in which Worley is shown performing for U.S. soldiers in Afghanistan, and a phalanx of soldiers marches grimly toward the camera with an American flag held high. Next, during this abbreviated "third verse," we see shots of soldiers going off to war, images of husbands tearfully bidding farewell to their wives (or girlfriends or fiancées), and fathers waving goodbye to their weeping children. This is the ultimate consequence of the song's central message: these soldiers are getting ready to go off to the war that Worley is supporting as just and necessary in his song. In fact, as we watch the video, we actually see them going off to war. This is one of the most powerful, and manipulative, moments in the video; we voyeuristically observe as the wives and children watch their husbands and fathers leave, as these "real" people enact what Worley proclaims needs to happen.

The emotional weight of the visual images during the bridge/third verse is underscored by the accompanying music and lyrics. During this entire climactic section Worley revisits his trip to Afghanistan and reinforces his own "authentic" voice. He has been with the soldiers and is conveying a message for them; he is channeling their emotions and sentiments in this song. To convey this musically, Worley and his band settle on overt word painting, a military tattoo on the snare drum, which commences after the guitar solo and builds through the end of the bridge before leading into the third chorus. Here the shots of the departing soldiers are followed by the musical climax. The chorus's opening "forgotten" is followed by a *tutti* downbeat—illustrated literally in the video by a shot of the drummer hitting the crash cymbal—followed by a slide guitar glissando ("Have You Forgotten?"—crash—glissando). Coming after the military images of the bridge, the glissando suggests a rocket attack or a missile shot, the countrified sounds of war.[42]

The images in the video for the third chorus return to remembrance, "all the people killed" evoked by the lyrics. We again see shots of the impromptu memorials that appeared throughout Lower Manhattan the evening of September 11, along with shots from the candlelight vigils held in the days after the attacks. The camera focuses on a succession of phrases imprinted on the placards at these events: "Lenny U will always be our hero!," "Don't give up," "I still ♥ New York." As these lines suggest, the shots in this final chorus become increasingly more explicit. Worley asks, "Have you forgotten about our Pentagon?" And before there can be a response, the video cuts immediately to a shot of the damaged building, followed by a woman crying, bowing her head as she clutches a girl to her. The grief is now made as explicit as possible to amplify the necessity of the forced separations we observed in the previous verse. Given this manipulative shot sequence, the final 9/11 image of the video is predictable: the previously unseen World Trade Center, as it was before the attacks, on a bright, clear day. This is the only time a full view of the towers appears in the video.

It is easy to see and hear why the song and its video were such a success; despite some clunky, and frankly embarrassing, lyrics (e.g., "And her people blown away"), Worley and Varble constructed an evocative and infectious song. Simple yet memorable lyrics and a tuneful, easily sung melody contribute to its effectiveness. Worley's lyrical delivery is conversational, with certain lines containing fewer syllables than expected—such as "worth fighting for" in the first verse—creating an impression of being casually uttered. The music in the studio version is well honed (if not overly so), with the climax of the bridge and third chorus providing a cathartic release for the anger and resentment that the song had been calling forth in the first two verses and choruses.

The video offers a different interpretation of the verbal images of the song, but it is arguably more powerful still, taking the visual traces from the original disaster and coupling them with the song's lyrical cues to craft an imagined documentary of a future war. Only in the video does the future sacrifice of the soldiers become explicit and ineluctable. In an interview with *Billboard* published after the war had started but obviously conducted before war was declared, Worley announced his own belief in the inevitability of the conflict, "I personally believe that George W. Bush is doing his best to try to protect the American people. I hope the conflict in Iraq can be resolved in a peaceful manner, but under the present conditions I would support a war against Iraq."[43] Despite his statement in "Have You Forgotten?" that the United States was "just out looking for a fight," he told another reporter, "I'm not a war-loving person. . . . I stand behind our president on this issue, for this war. I pray every day that we'll avoid this conflict, but I just see Hussein playing games and buying time."[44] Worley might have been trying to support the troops, but he was also sending them forth into combat, even before the nation did.

THE ANTHEM OF THE WAR

The story of Worley's song and its video is nonetheless more complicated than that of a song that marshaled support for the war. The song's message and its intended audience shifted once more after war was declared. By the week ending on Saturday, March 15, 2003, its second week on the charts, "Have You Forgotten?" had climbed to no. 22, and also debuted at no. 50 on the *Billboard Hot 100*, the highest debut by a country single played only on the radio since *Billboard* had begun counting nonretail recordings. Most significant was the fact that Worley's airplay was coming almost exclusively from country music stations, which were responsible for 99.9 percent of his "spins" (though this is not as limited an audience as it might initially seem, given the breadth and depth of country music's popularity at the time).[45] Furthermore, Worley's was the "fastest-rising single" on the country charts since Alan Jackson's "Where Were You (When the World Stopped Turning)?" which had reached no. 6 in *Billboard* during its third week on the charts, the week of December 8, 2001.[46] Worley's video kept up with the single, and in the same week the single reached no. 22, the video for "Have You Forgotten?" had reached no. 15 on CMT.[47]

These dates are important, as they align with the launch of the war itself: on Monday, March 17, President Bush delivered his ultimatum to Saddam Hussein, and two days later the United States invaded (early Thursday morning, March 20, Baghdad time). At the end of that week, March 22, the song's third week on the charts, the single moved to no. 9, and had become the most-requested song for many of the nation's country radio stations, as well as on Country Music Television (CMT) and Great American Country (GAC).[48] As Johnny Gray, the music director of Atlanta stations WKHX and WYAY, told *Billboard*, "It's one of the biggest records we've had in the last three years. . . . It speaks to a lot of people who aren't speaking up right now."[49]

By the end of the first week of the war, CMT was putting its full muscle behind the war, creating shows especially for soldiers and their families like "CMT Military Messages" and hawking war-related songs both past and present, dubbed "Music of American Spirit," including

Lee Greenwood's "God Bless the U.S.A.," Johnny Cash's "Ragged Old Flag," and Aaron Tippin's "Where the Stars and Stripes and the Eagle Fly."[50] During the week ending March 23, 2003 (the first week of the war), Worley's was the ninth-most-played video on CMT (the Dixie Chicks were at no. 7 with "Travelin' Soldier," despite the furor erupting over their comments in London two weeks earlier, and Toby Keith held at no. 21 with "Courtesy of the Red, White & Blue," ten months after the song's release).[51]

The popularity of the song even led DreamWorks Records Nashville to release Worley's next album early, on April 15 instead of the originally planned May 20, 2003.[52] As Melinda Newman noted in *Billboard* on April 5, the key difference between "Have You Forgotten?" and the most popular antiwar songs from the same period, the Beastie Boys' "In a World Gone Mad," System of a Down's "Boom!," Zach de la Rocha and DJ Shadow's "March of Death," and OutKast's "B.O.B. (Bombs over Baghdad)," was that Worley's song was the only one being promoted on radio by a major label: "For whatever reason, the raft of artists releasing antiwar songs, including John Mellencamp, R.E.M., Beastie Boys, and Lenny Kravitz—all of whom have major-label deals—have opted to release their tunes via the Web instead of having them worked by their labels' promo departments. And, so far, radio has only given them scant airplay, if any."[53] DreamWorks knew it had a hit on its hands and pushed the song as much as it could, with patriotic packaging and a selection of Worley's previous hits to round out the *Have You Forgotten?* album. The antiwar figures chose (or were forced to choose) a less mainstream, more populist approach and released their music only on the Internet. Of course, *Billboard*'s conventional airplay statistics cannot measure the full distribution of those songs or their impact, but according to standard measures of success in the music business, they failed utterly.[54]

According to the more elusive standards of political success, the antiwar songs also languished as the lack of mainstream distribution limited their effectiveness as political propaganda.[55] Of course, as David Hajdu argues, this failure could reflect a lack of an audience for such songs at that time, rather then the mode of their distribution:

> In the absence of a significant antiwar movement through which [protest] music could be employed, contemporary protest songs have purpose but not function. Pete Seeger used to say, "It's not how good a song is that matters, it's how much good a song does." What good is the most impassioned challenge to the Iraq war on its own, in the face of public indifference?[56]

Worley's success demonstrates that, taken as a whole, the record-buying public was hardly indifferent to the war. To the contrary, his consumers lined up behind the Bush administration and, as Worley's first lines encouraged, came out strongly against the protestors.

"Have You Forgotten?" reached No. 1 on the *Billboard* charts on the week ending April 5, the second week of the war, and it stayed there for six weeks, more than two weeks after Bush declared the end of "major combat operations" in Iraq on May 1. During this remarkable run, Worley's song, and its video, played a more complex role than simple cheerleading for the Bush administration and the soldiers—though on April 16 Worley literally played that role in a Pentagon victory concert, introduced by Secretary of Defense Donald Rumsfeld himself.[57] Judging by record sales and video and airplay statistics, "Have You Forgotten?" served to assuage any lingering doubts about the war among its listeners, as its main impact came after the initiation of hostilities. The song's eventual target was thus no longer limited to the protestors that Worley took issue with in its first lines, but any average American who still harbored doubts about the war, and who might still be reluctant to see American troops put in harm's way again. Worley's video had sent the soldiers off to war, and now they were actually engaged in combat. The time for doubts had passed, or had you forgotten?

Predictably, though, the song became a favorite of those who had never had doubts, and especially the families of military servicemen—the target audience of "CMT Military Messages"—who were glad to hear Worley deride those against the war. More generally, "Have You Forgotten?" now served as a nationalist symbol, purchased by patriotic Americans to signal solidarity with the war's cause. Playing and listening to "Have You Forgotten?" showed that "you" had not forgotten. It advertised support for the war and the soldiers, alongside the numerous American flags and yellow ribbons also for sale on store racks. Worley's song thus lived up to the worst fears of those thinkers who regard mainstream popular music as commercially and ideologically compromised.

Commerce undeniably played a crucial role, giving Worley more visibility than, for instance, the musicians protesting the war on the Internet. Yet DreamWorks only capitalized on a connection that had already been made. The song was already creating a "buzz" when DreamWorks chose to release the single, and the single was already nearing the top of the charts when they decided to release the album early. To view "Have You Forgotten?" only as a compromised commodity risks missing the specific manner in which it constructed its ideological message, and the content of that message. Worley was a thinking cultural actor who channeled and further fueled emotions experienced by a large number of Americans.

Importantly, even as "Have You Forgotten?" signaled patriotism and attempted to quell dissent as the country went to war, it also continued to reinforce administration claims tying the Iraq campaign with the 9/11 attacks and Osama bin Laden. Immediately after 9/11, only 3 percent of Americans thought that Iraq or Saddam Hussein were linked to the attacks. By January of 2003, according to a Knight-Ridder poll, 44 percent thought that "most" or "some" of the 9/11 hijackers were from Iraq, a figure repeated in mid-March 2003 on the eve of the war, when a New York Times/CBS poll showed that 45 percent of Americans believed that Saddam Hussein was "personally involved" with the 9/11 attacks.[58] Though there is no way to measure the direct influence of Worley's song on public opinion, given its ubiquity on the airwaves it certainly played a noteworthy role in the media environment that caused that percentage to rise to 69 percent by early August 2003.[59] As Chris Hedges writes in his powerful indictment of militarism, *War Is a Force That Gives Us Meaning*: "The use of a nation's cultural resources to back up the war effort is essential to mask the contradictions and lies that mount over time in the drive to sustain war" (2002: 63).

CONCLUSION

Country music scholars Jimmie N. Rogers and Stephen A. Smith resist the idea that easy generalizations can be made about the political inclinations of country music artists and country music audiences, arguing against the prevailing view that "Merle Haggard's 'Okie from Muskogee' is the quintessential political statement of country music" (1999: 113).[60] While they offer a salutary reminder of the political complexity of country music fans, singers, and song themes, they miss country's increasingly visible links with conservative politics, a trend already apparent at the time of their writing, and one that Worley and other country musicians have done much to reinforce in recent years, particularly after 9/11, the Iraq War, and the 2004 Presidential election. Rogers and Smith's statistical study also fails to account for the popularity, and hence prestige, accorded certain songs over others; their model does not explain how a song like "Have You Forgotten?" could have reached number one for six weeks in April and May 2003.[61] While the diversity of country music as a whole certainly argues against any single political constituency, songs like "Okie from Muskogee" and "Have You Forgotten?" demand special consideration by virtue of their very popularity.

In denying a singular political ideology in country music, Rogers and Smith (among others) also downplay the perceived nationalist tenor of the genre. They argue that:

> A few [country] songs support our national government, some (especially the songs expressing regional preferences) find satisfaction with particular political environments, and a few will support a political or governmental unit if it is attacked by outside forces. However, the primary emphasis is once again on the individual's exasperation with constraints levied by those outside the primary group (1999: 119).

They conclude that country music listeners are "anarchists," or more mildly "libertarians." Country music from the post-9/11 period, however, and specifically Worley's war hit and its reception, forces us to qualify these labels, at the least.[62] Arguing for a distinction between "mainstream" and "hard" country, for instance, Barbara Ching writes that "while mainstream country does occasionally articulate controversial themes, more often it can be heard as a toe-tapping form of assent to the status quo" (2001: 6). Even this distinction does not go far enough in assessing country's politics in the post-9/11 environment, however. As I hope to have shown in this essay, Worley's song goes well beyond merely "assenting" to the "status quo." Indeed, in the post-9/11 world, many country musicians have become active advocates of both a politicized form of remembrance and, in Keith's and Worley's cases, direct action in support of administration goals.

That country music might take this path should not come as a surprise. The dominant political ideology of the genre today, and the relationship between its current conservative cast and the changing American political landscape, has been apparent since the early 1990s. As journalist Bruce Feiler proposed in 1998:

> Just as rock 'n' roll foreshadowed many of the changes in gender and race relations that followed in the sixties, country music in the nineties—with its themes of family and renewal—became the clearest reflection of many of the conservative ideals that were just beginning to surface in American life. In short, country music, once the voice of a distinct minority in America—working-class Southerners—had become the voice of the new American majority: middle-class suburbanites (1998: 38).

Though Rogers and Smith would certainly find fault with these generalizations, they offer a provocative incentive for further examinations of the political and class roles of country music in the post-Bush

v. Gore era, the era of "red" states and "blue" states.[63] This is not meant as an indictment of country music or its many listeners, but rather as a reminder that in the realm of popular music, powerful "official" voices deserve as much scrutiny as the "resistant" voices on the margins, if not more so. After all, exploring how popular music—or any music—supports dominant ideologies also offers insights into how it may resist them.

The opening epigraphs to this essay encapsulate the instigation and motivation for the composition and reception of Worley's "Have You Forgotten?" In the face of the uncertain future after the September 11 attacks, when each successive day brought new trauma, from anthrax attacks to repeated terror alerts, from mobilization for one and then multiple wars, country music offered solace. Country musicians were, as WQNY put it, "singing about you." Worley's song and its video prodded the conscience of its audience, asking listeners if they had "forgotten" 9/11, even as the government's contradictory rhetoric urged them to "go about their business." In its bravado, nationalist tone, and cajoling reminders of the traumatic past, it synthesized the public sentiments of early 2003, urging action and reassuring listeners of the righteousness of that action once it was initiated. Thanks to the "sincerity" of "Have You Forgotten?"—its "authentic" inspiration, evocative lyrics and heartfelt performance, buttressed by the inevitability of the plot conveyed by its video's "authentic" images (together with DreamWorks' marketing prowess)—the Iraq War had its anthem.

APPENDIX I:
TIMELINE FOR IRAQ WAR AND "HAVE YOU FORGOTTEN?"

Bold items indicate those events directly related to Worley's song

September 12, 2002	President Bush addresses the U.N. regarding Iraq threat.
October 10	U.S. Congress approves Joint Resolution to authorize use of military force against Iraq (H.J.Res. 114).
October 27	Marches protesting potential war in Iraq held in Washington, D.C. and San Francisco.
November 8	U. N. Security Council adopts resolution 1441, giving Iraq "a final opportunity to comply with its disarmament obligations under relevant resolutions of the Council."
December 18–24	**Worley in Afghanistan as USO performer.**
January 11–12, 2003	**Worley premieres "Have You Forgotten?" at the Grand Ole Opry. It begins to circulate via the Internet.**
January 18	National March Against the War held in Washington, D.C., and San Francisco, as well as Portland, Oregon, and Tampa, Florida.

January 28	President Bush's third State of the Union Address.
February 5	Secretary of State Colin Powell addresses the U.N. Security Council regarding Iraq's weapons of mass destruction.
February 7	United States Terror Alert level raised to "Orange" ("high"); citizens advised to purchase duct tape and plastic sheeting in preparation for chemical or biological weapons attack. The level was lowered to "Yellow" ("elevated") on February 27.
February 15	Coordinated protests against the war held in cities across the U.S. and around the world.
February 24	United States, Great Britain, and Spain introduce a new resolution before the U.N. Security Council calling for military action against Iraq; despite intensive lobbying it is never approved.
February 26	"Virtual march" protesting war organized by MoveOn.org.
March 8	**"Have You Forgotten?" debuts at no. 41 on Billboard Hot Country Singles & Tracks, and the video receives its world premiere on CMT (the single was released in late February, first appearing on some charts the week of February 26).**
March 15	**"Have You Forgotten?" at no. 22 on *Billboard* Hot Country Singles; also debuts at no. 50 on the Billboard Hot 100.**
March 16	United States, Great Britain, and Spain give the United Nations one day to vote on resolution authorizing force against Iraq.
March 17	President Bush declares Saddam Hussein must leave Iraq within forty-eight hours.
March 18	U.S. Terror Alert level again raised to "Orange"; comprehensive domestic security plan dubbed "Operation Liberty Shield" implemented.
March 19	President Bush addresses the nation, announcing the beginning of hostilities with Iraq.
March 22–23	**"Have You Forgotten?" at no. 9 in *Billboard*; "Many country stations report that it is their most-requested song." Video for "Have You Forgotten?" at no. 9 on CMT.**
March 29–30	**"Have You Forgotten?" at no. 2 in *Billboard*; Video at no. 1 on CMT. (On MTV, rapper 50 Cent's "In Da Club" is at no. 1.)**
April 5–6	**"Have You Forgotten?" reaches no. 1 in *Billboard*; it will stay at no. 1 until the week ending May 24. Worley's video now at no. 6 on CMT.**
April 7	**Worley performs "Have You Forgotten?" at the CMT Annual "Flameworthy Music Awards," receiving a standing ovation.**
April 9	The fall of Baghdad; U.S. Marines help Iraqis topple statue of Saddam Hussein in central Baghdad's Firdos Square; Worley receives the 2003 USO Merit Award in Washington, D.C.

April 12–13	Worley's song still at no. 1 in *Billboard*. It sets a new record "for most detections in a single week" (6, 366 "spins"). Video at no. 9 on CMT.
April 15	*Have You Forgotten?* album is released.
April 16	Worley plays concert at the Pentagon, introduced by Secretary of Defense Rumsfeld.
April 26–27	"Despite reports of diminished combat in Iraq" the song was still at no. 1 in *Billboard*, though it dropped slightly in its number of plays. It had now been no. 1 for four weeks. Video at no. 3 on CMT.
May 3	*Have You Forgotten?* album debuts at no. 1 on the *Billboard* Top Country Albums chart and at no. 4 on the Billboard 200. By this point, "Have You Forgotten?" the single had been at no. 1 on the Hot Country Singles & Tracks chart for five weeks.
May 1	Bush declares an end to "Major Combat Operations" in Iraq from the deck of the aircraft carrier U.S.S. Abraham Lincoln.
May 24	After seven weeks at no. 1 and 11 weeks on the chart, "Have You Forgotten?" falls to no. 3 in *Billboard*. It will gradually descend in rank until it leaves the chart on July 26, 2003 (after 20 weeks on the chart), replaced by Worley's slowly rising new song, "Tennessee River Run" (then at no. 43 after three weeks, it will eventually reach no. 31).
May 31	*Have You Forgotten?* album falls to no. 2 after 4 weeks at no. 1. It will begin a slow descent that keeps it in the top 25 until the week of September 13, 2003; it will stay on the chart until November 15, when it exits after twenty-eight weeks.
June 21	Worley's album is certified Gold (500,000 units) for May 2003.

ACKNOWLEDGMENTS

The majority of this essay was written in late 2004 and early 2005, with final substantive revisions added at the end of 2005. Accordingly, it does not take into account the many subsequent and relevant musical and political events, including Worley's label switch from DreamWorks Records Nashville (since May 2004 part of UMG Nashville) to 903 Music and his recent Iraq-related song "I Just Came Back From a War" (on his 2006 album *Here and Now*). My thanks to J.S.L., Michael Long, and the editors of this volume for their invaluable help with this project.

Lyrics to "Have You Forgotten?" reproduced with the kind permission of Anita Hogin, International Artist Management.

REFERENCES

Andsager, Julie L., and Kimberly Roe. 1999. "Country Music Video in Country's Year of the Woman." *Journal of Communication* 49(1): 69–82.

Balliger, Robin. 1999. "Politics." In *Key Terms in Popular Music and Culture*, edited by Bruce Horner and Thomas Swiss, 57–70. Malden, MA, and Oxford: Blackwell Publishers.

Barnet, Richard D., Bruce Nemerov, and Mayo R. Taylor, eds. 2004. *The Story Behind the Song: 150 Songs That Chronicle the 20th Century*. Westport and London: Greenwood Press.

Bennett, Tony. 1993. *Rock and Popular Music: Politics, Policies, and Institutions*. London and New York: Routledge.

Brackett, David. 2001. "Banjos, Biopics, and Compilation Scores: The Movies Go Country." *American Music* 19(3): 247–90.

Buckley, John. 1993. "Country Music and American Values." In *All That Glitters: Country Music in America*, edited by George E. Lewis, 198–207. Bowling Green, Ohio: Bowling Green State University Popular Press.

Ching, Barbara. 2001. *Wrong's What I Do Best: Hard Country Music and Contemporary Culture*. New York and Oxford: Oxford University Press.

Cusic, Don. 2002. "Politics and Country Music, 1963–1974." In *Country Music Annual 2002*, edited by Charles K. Wolfe and James E. Akenson, 161–85. Lexington, KY: University Press of Kentucky.

Dimaggio, Paul, Richard Peterson, and Jack Esco Jr. 1972. "Country Music: Ballad of the Silent Majority." In *The Sounds of Social Change: Studies in Popular Culture*, edited by R. Serge Denisoff and Richard Peterson, 38–55. Chicago: Rand McNally and Company.

Eyerman, Ron, and Andrew Jamison. 1998. *Music and Social Movements: Mobilizing Traditions in the Twentieth Century*. Cambridge: Cambridge University Press.

Feiler, Bruce. 1998. *Dreaming Out Loud: Garth Brooks, Wynonna Judd, Wade Hayes and the Changing Face of Nashville*. New York: Avon Books.

Fenster, Mark. 1993. "Genre and Form: The Development of the Country Music Video." In *Sound and Vision: The Music Video Reader*, edited by Simon Frith, Andrew Goodwin, and Lawrence Grossberg, 109–28. London and New York: Routledge.

Fox, Aaron. 1992. "The Jukebox of Desire: Narratives of Loss and Desire in the Discourse of Country Music." *Popular Music* 11(1): 53–72.

———. 2005. "'Alternative' to What?: *O Brother*, September 11, and the Politics of Country Music." In *Country Music Goes to War*, edited by Charles K. Wolfe and James K. Akenson, 164–91. Lexington, KY: University Press of Kentucky.

Garofalo, Reebee, ed. 1992. *Rockin' the Boat: Mass Music & Mass Movements*. Boston: South End Press.

Goodwin, Andrew. 1992. *Dancing in the Distraction Factory: Music Television and Popular Culture*. Minneapolis: University of Minnesota Press.

———. 1993. "Fatal Distractions: MTV Meets Postmodern Theory." In *Sound and Vision: The Music Video Reader*, edited by Simon Frith, Andrew Goodwin, and Lawrence Grossberg, 45–66. London and New York: Routledge.

Hedges, Chris. 2002. *War Is a Force That Gives Us Meaning*. New York: Public Affairs.

Hill, Trent. 2002. "Why Isn't Country Music 'Youth' Culture?" In *Rock Over the Edge: Transformations in Popular Music Culture*, edited by Roger Beebe, Denise Fulbrook, and Ben Saunders, 161–90. Durham and London: Duke University Press.

Horstman, Dorothy. 1966. *Sing Your Heart Out, Country Boy*, 3rd edition. Nashville, Tennessee: Country Music Foundation Press.

Jensen, Joli. 1998. *The Nashville Sound: Authenticity, Commercialization, and Country Music*. Nashville: Vanderbilt University Press.

Johnston Wadsworth, Anne, and Lynda Lee Kaid. 1990. "Political Themes and Images in Music Videos." In *Politics in Familiar Contexts: Projecting Politics Through Popular Media*, edited by Robert L. Savage and Dan Nimmo, 159–70. Norwood, NJ: Ablex Publishing Company.

Kaplan, E. Ann. 1987. *Rocking Around the Clock*. New York and London: Routledge.

Lipsitz, George. 1994. *Dangerous Crossroads: Popular Music, Postmodernism, and the Poetics of Place*. London and New York: Verso.

Lund, Jens. 1972. "Country Music Goes to War: Songs for the Red-Blooded American." *Popular Music and Society* 1(4): 210–30.

Malone, Bill. 2002. *Country Music U.S.A.* 2nd edition. Austin: University of Texas Press.

McLaurin, Melton A. 1992. "Songs of the South: The Changing Image of the South in Country Music." In *You Wrote My Life: Lyrical Themes in Country Music*, edited by Melton A. McLaurin and Richard A. Peterson, 15–34. Langhorne, PA: Gordon and Breach Scientific Publishers.

National Commission on Terrorist Attacks Upon the United States. 2004. *The 9/11 Commission Report*. New York and London: W. W. Norton and Company.

Peterson, Richard A. 1997. *Creating Country Music: Fabricating Authenticity*. Chicago and London: University of Chicago Press.

Pratt, Ray. 1990. *Rhythm and Resistance: Explorations in the Political Uses of Popular Music*. New York: Praeger.

Rogers, Jimmie N. 1989. *The Country Music Message: Revisited*. Fayetteville and London: University of Arkansas Press.

Rogers, Jimmie N., and Stephen A. Smith. 1999. "Popular Populism: Political Messages in Country Music Lyrics." In *Mass Politics: The Politics of Mass Culture*, edited by Daniel M. Shea, 111–21. New York: St. Martins Press.

———. 1993. "Country Music and Organized Religion." In *All That Glitters: Country Music in America*, edited by George E. Lewis, 270–84. Bowling Green, Ohio: Bowling Green State University Popular Press.

———. 1990. "Political Culture and the Rhetoric of Country Music: A Revisionist Interpretation." In *Politics in Familiar Contexts: Projecting Politics Through Popular Media*, edited by Robert L. Savage and Dan Nimmo, 185–98. Norwood, NJ: Ablex Publishing Company.

Roth, Philip. 2004. *The Plot Against America*. Boston and New York: Houghton Mifflin Company.

Rudder, Randy. 2005. "In Whose Name: Country Artists Speak out on Gulf War II." In *Country Music Goes to War*, edited by Charles K. Wolfe and James K. Akenson, 208–26. Lexington, KY: University Press of Kentucky.

Sample, Tex. 1996. *White Soul: Country Music, the Church, and Working Americans*. Nashville: Abingdon Press.

Sakolsky, Ron, and Fred Wei-han Ho, eds. 1995. *Sounding Off!: Music as Subversion/ Resistance/ Revolution*. Brooklyn, NY: Autonomedia.

Scheurer, Timothy E. 1991. *Born in the U.S.A.: The Myth of America in Popular Music from Colonial Times to the Present*. Jackson and London: University Press of Mississippi.

Shreffler, Anne C. 2000. "The Myth of Empirical Historiography: Response to Joseph N. Straus." *Musical Quarterly* 84(1): 30–40.

Sifry, Micah L., and Christopher Cerf, eds. 2003. *The Iraq War Reader: History, Documents, Opinions*. New York and London: Touchstone.

Straus, Joseph N. 1999. "The Myth of Serial 'Tyranny' in the 1950s and 1960s." *Musical Quarterly* 83(3): 301–43.

Street, John. 2001. "Rock, Pop, and Politics." In *The Cambridge Companion to Pop and Rock*, edited by Simon Frith, Will Straw, and John Street, 243–55. Cambridge and New York: Cambridge University Press.

Tichi, Cecilia. 1994. *High Lonesome: The American Culture of Country Music*. Chapel Hill and London: The University of North Carolina Press.

Vernallis, Carol. 2004. *Experiencing Music Video: Aesthetics and Cultural Context*. New York: Columbia University Press.

Willman, Chris. 2005. *Rednecks & Bluenecks: The Politics of Country Music*. New York and London: The New Press.

Wolfe, Charles K., and James K. Akenson, eds. 2005. *Country Music Goes to War*. Lexington, KY: University Press of Kentucky.

NOTES

1. Roth 2004: 113–14.
2. Geoffrey O'Brien, "Is It All Just a Dream?" [Review of Michael Moore, *Fahrenheit 9/11*], *New York Review of Books* 51, no. 13 (12 August 2004).
3. Heard on the air during early 2005. The current motto is: "This Is Your Country!" See the station Web site: http://www.qcountry1037.com.
4. Randy Travis was the first country singer out of the gate with a song called "America Will Always Stand," reportedly written two days after the September 11 attacks. Other country singers quickly revamped or

dusted off old hits, as with Charlie Daniels's retooling of his 1980 song "In America," or the return of Lee Greenwood's seemingly ubiquitous "God Bless the U.S.A." Others plugged recent recordings, such as Billy Ray Cyrus's "We the People" and "Some Gave All" (Brian Mansfield, "Country Stars Show Stripes With Songs of National Unity," *USA Today*, 9 October 2001). Jackson's song was first heard at the 35th annual Country Music Association (CMA) Awards, a collective highpoint for country patriotism. From the CMA Web site: http://www.cmaawards.com/2004/history/history.asp?yr'00&title'2000s (inoperative link, originally accessed January 31, 2004).

5. Commentators noted that country songs were becoming more aggressive than their rock counterparts. See Dave Ferman, "Country Music Waves the Flag: It's Like No Other Genre For Rallying Fans During Wartime," *Fort Worth Star-Telegram*, 19 April 2003, and Neil Strauss, "MTV Is Wary of Videos on War," *New York Times*, 26 March 2003. Or, as conservative commentator Stanley Kurtz (speaking of the war in Afghanistan) announced in *National Review*, "I went looking for the war on MTV and couldn't find it" (Stanley Kurtz, "Love Your Country," *National Review*, vol. 54, no. 19, 14 October 2002). Country singer bad-boy Steve Earle was one of the exceptions. With songs like "John Walker's Blues" about the so-called "American Taliban," John Walker Lindh (on Earle's 2002 *Jerusalem* album released by Artemis records), he quickly set himself against the Bush Administration.

6. For a representative sampling of opinions both for and against the war, see Sifry and Cerf 2003.

7. Of this literature, see the following, for example: Dimaggio et al. 1972; Lund 1972; McLaurin 1992; Buckley 1993 (especially 201, "Patriotism"); Horstman 1996 (esp. 266–86, "Songs of War and Patriotism"); Cusic 2002; Malone 2002; Wolfe and Akenson 2005; and, from a different perspective, Rogers and Smith 1999; Barnet et al. 2004; and Willman 2005 (esp. 141–56).

8. Street 2001: 249. This sentiment is echoed in Robin Balliger's essay on "Politics" in *Key Terms in Popular Music and Culture* (1999: 57–70).

9. Most research on popular music and politics has looked at rock or pop and focused on how music resists; see the following, for example: Pratt 1990; Lipsitz 1994; Scheurer 1991; Eyerman and Jamison 1998; and Garofalo 1992. A more extreme example ("We hereby 'sound off!' in an oppression-detonating explosion of pain, anger, love and joy") is found in Sakolsky and Wei-han Ho 1995 (quote on p. 9). See also the essays in Bennett 1993; Balliger's aforementioned "Politics"; and John Street's "Rock, Pop and Politics" (2001), which includes a good, albeit brief, list of other works on the topic.

10. Lund 1972: 213. See also the various essays on country music during World War II and the Korean War in Wolfe and Akenson's edited volume *Country Music Goes to War* (2005).

11. The first three songs cited here are from Lund 1972: 212. The fourth comes from Gene Autry's WWII repertoire; it was written by Dick Reinhart and sung by Jimmie Dean, Eddie Dean, and Johnny Bond on the 26 July 1942 "Melody Ranch Radio Show," during which Gene Autry was sworn into the United States Army Air Forces. A recording of the complete show is available on *Gene Autry: The Cowboy Is a Patriot: Original Broadcast Recordings from World War II* (Varèse Sarabande 302 066 408 2, 2002). See also Cusic 2005: 48–50.

12. Another well-known Vietnam-era country song, Merle Haggard's 1968 "Okie from Muskogee," did indirectly attack members of the peace movement—"We don't burn no draft cards down on main street"—but in so doing offered only implicit endorsement of the war.

13. The lyrics are cited in Lund 1972: 214–17; see also Malone 2002: 304.

14. Lund also mentions Bill Anderson's "Where Have All Our Heroes Gone?," Ernest Tubb's "It's America (Love It or Leave It)," and Haggard's "The Fightin' Side of Me" (2002: 223). See also Willman 2005: 141–48.

15. See Richard Harrington, "Country Music Goes to War," *The Washington Post,* 30 January 1991. Greenwood wrote his song in September 1983 after the Soviet downing of Korean Airlines (KAL) flight 007, though he reportedly "always wanted to write a song to honor the veterans of the Vietnam War." In 1985 it won CMA's Song of the Year award, and the song's reputation was cemented by its prominence during the 1991 Gulf War and its adoption in 1992 as George H. W. Bush's presidential campaign song. On 12 December 2005 Greenwood's Web site proclaimed: "If any doubt existed of Greenwood's 'forever imprint' on America, it was dispelled in 2003—the 20 year anniversary of its release—when 'God Bless the USA' was voted online by Americans [on America Online] as the 'most recognizable patriotic song' in the nation. The song that Lee Greenwood wrote bested competition that included 'God Bless America' and the 'National Anthem' as a modern national anthem of the common man" (http://www.leegreenwood.com/?p=bio; this quotation no longer appears on the site).

16. Charles Passy, "'God Bless the U.S.A.' Has Blessed Lee Greenwood," *Pittsburgh Post-Gazette,* 23 December 2001.

17. Garth Brooks is usually credited with fueling the rise of country during the early 1990s. By 1993, 42 percent of Americans were tuning in to country radio stations, double that from ten years previously, making it the leading radio format in the U.S. (Feiler 1998: 37). See also Monroe 2002: 420–21, and Willman 2005: 5–6.

18. These stickers themselves inspired another country song, Chely Wright's "Bumper of My S.U.V." The first verse tells of a hostile reaction the narrator encountered to her Marines bumper sticker, ironically pitting an icon of suburban domesticity—the minivan—against an icon of suburban escapist fantasy—the SUV: "I've got a bright red sticker on the back of my car/Says: "United States Marines."/And yesterday a lady in a mini-van/Held up her middle finger at me./Does she think she knows what I stand for/Or the things that I believe?/Just by looking at a sticker for the U.S. Marines/On the bumper of my S.U.V." This song revels in the nostalgia for an imagined, utopian past so rampant in contemporary country music. The nostalgia of Wright's music, echoed by the glorified military actions of her family members (grandfather, father, and brother) in the lyrics, meshes nicely with the nostalgia for the wilderness and the frontier that SUV marketing and advertising so effectively exploits. See also Willman 2005: 133–39.

19. These posters ("Avenge December 7" and "Remember Dec. 7th!") are available online through the Northwestern University Library World War II Poster Collection: http://www.library.northwestern.edu/govinfo/collections/wwii-posters/index.html. The Vietnam era was also one of commands and not questions: stickers proclaimed, "America: Love It or Leave It!"

20. See Robert D. McFadden, "From New York to Melbourne, Cries for Peace," *New York Times,* 16 February 2003; Alan Cowell, "1.5 Million Demonstrators in Cities Across Europe Oppose a War With Iraq," *New York Times,* 16 February 2003; and Dean E. Murphy, "On Day of Their Own, Thousands Rally in San Francisco," *New York Times,* 17 February 2003.

21. E-mail to the author from USO, February 10, 2005.

22. This excerpt was on Worley's Web site (http://darrylworley.dreamworks-nashville.com/bio.HTM) on August 8, 2004, but by December 2, 2004, it had been revised to read: "After overhearing a conversation about the Afghan War, he quickly wrote and recorded the topical 'Have You Forgotten?'" Worley reported to CNN.com that his USO trip "was probably the best thing I'd ever done" (Curtis Ross, "Musicians Sound Off," *The Tampa Tribune,* "Friday Extra!" March 22, 2003).

23. This is apparent in the revision of his biography on the DreamWorks Web site mentioned above, but Worley also told Chuck Yarborough of the Cleveland *Plain Dealer* that "We went during the Christmas holidays. I came back home to a lot of things like people saying things that just didn't sit well with me." See Chuck Yarborough, "Singer Turns a Scientific Eye to the Art of Country Music," *Plain Dealer* (Cleveland, Ohio), 21 February 2003 (Yarborough's title refers to Worley's degrees in biology and chemistry from the University of North Alabama, and

his prior ownership of a chemical-supply business). According to one source, Worley heard the critical remarks while exercising in a gym after his return from Afghanistan (Willman 2005: 123–24).

24. "Authenticity" has, of course, been a central, and fruitful, focus of research in country music scholarship. For good recent examples see Peterson 1997 and Jensen 1998. Aaron Fox (1992) offers a more theoretical and provocative deconstruction of the representations and schisms in country music and, by extension, all popular songs (see especially his page 69).

25. Yarborough, "Singer Turns a Scientific Eye." See also Peterson 1997: 218–19.

26. Quote on Worley's Web site (http://darrylworley.dreamworksnashville.com/bio.HTM; inoperative link, originally accessed August 4, 2004).

27. Dan DeLuca, "Songs of Protest from Both Sides Now," *Philadelphia Inquirer,* 12 March 2003.

28. Despite reportage to the contrary, according to my correspondence with the Grand Ole Opry, "The performance was never posted on our Web site, although you may be referring to the archived Opry shows on WSMonline.com" (personal communication with OpryInquiries@gaylordhotels.com, 14 July 2005). Regardless of the source, it is unclear which evening's performance was put into circulation. See also Phyllis Stark, "Nashville Scene," *Billboard,* 10 May 2003.

29. It was reportedly the "highest debut since Shania Twain's 'I'm Gonna Getcha Good!' entered at no. 24 in the Oct. 19, 2002 issue" (Silvo Pietroluongo, Minal Patel, and Wade Jessen, "Singles Minded," *Billboard,* 8 March 2003, 63). See also Brian Mansfield, "Country Anthem Plays a Drumbeat for War," *USA Today,* 26 February 2003.

30. Phyllis Stark, "Nashville Scene," *Billboard,* 10 May 2003, 36.

31. The full text of President Bush's 29 January 2002 State of the Union Address is available at: http://www.whitehouse.gov/news/releases/2002/01/20020129-11.html.

32. The qualifier, "this time," slipped unnoticed by most Americans, who continued to believe that Hussein had armed the 9/11 hijackers in the first place. See references below.

33. In his speech before the U.N. General Assembly in September 2002, Bush did not explicitly juxtapose Saddam Hussein and the 9/11 attacks or Al Qaeda as he did in the 2003 State of the Union address. Instead, he spoke of a broader threat "that terrorists will find a shortcut to their mad ambitions when an outlaw regime supplies them with the technologies to kill on a massive scale. In one place—in one regime—we find all these dangers, in their most lethal and aggressive forms, exactly the kind of aggressive threat the United Nations was born to

confront." The regime, of course, was Hussein's in Iraq. The full text of the September 2002 U.N. speech is available at: http://www.white-house.gov/news/releases/2002/09/20020912-1.html.

34. The full text of the 2003 State of the Union Address is available at: http://www.whitehouse.gov/news/releases/2003/01/20030128-19.html. During the second half of 2005 (and the final revisions of this essay), this speech—and the general U.S. rationale for waging war with Iraq—came under renewed scrutiny, fueled by documents like the British "Downing Street Memo" and its claims that the Bush administration "fixed" (or, more colloquially, "sexed up") its intelligence. Related to this were the false allegations regarding Iraq's acquisition of uranium from Niger, and the associated scandal over the outing of CIA agent Valerie Plame Wilson. Of course, these debates are not the topic of the current essay, concerned as it is with events as they were known or alleged in 2002–2003. For a general survey of the Downing Street Memo and a recounting of the road to war from mid-2002 to early 2003 at it appeared from the vantage of mid-2005, see Mark Danner, "The Secret Way to War," *New York Review of Books* 52, no. 10 (9 June 2005).

35. These are the preferred State Department transliterations. The full text and exhibits from this presentation are available on the United States Department of State Web site: http://www.state.gov/secretary/former/powell/remarks/2003/17300.htm.

36. Though it is possible that this was the line that Worley forgot at the Grand Ole Opry, it seems more likely that he was referring to the beginning of the second verse, where he needed to forcibly start the line above the wild applause and cheering that followed the first chorus. As a result it sounds as though he is entering prematurely, unsure of where to begin.

37. For an apologist reading of Worley's intentions in writing "Have You Forgotten?," see Rudder 2005: 218–19. Rudder calls Worley "country's most misunderstood artist" of the time, and claims that he (Worley) was "censored" as a result of the song.

38. Jim Farber, "Patriot Worley's Sales Don't Flag," *Daily News* (New York), 15 April 2003.

39. The video was produced by Robin Rucker and directed by Shaun Silva. Its narrative style is typical of country music videos, developed in opposition to what Mark Fenster has argued is the "more disjointed, fragmented narratives of pop/rock videos" (1993: 115). Beyond Fenster's work, few subsequent studies of country music videos have been written, though David Brackett (2001) has looked at country music in films such as *Five Easy Pieces, The Last Picture Show, Urban Cowboy,* and other films and "biopics," and Julie Andsager and Kimberly Roe (1999) conducted a statistical survey of female artists and characters in country videos. For an essay that considers the relationship between music videos and politics, however loosely defined (categorizing videos

as "'War' Videos," "Peace Videos," and "American Values Videos"), see Johnston and Kaid 1990, especially pp. 166–69. Scholarly attention to music video overall has lagged since its heyday in the early 1990s, when discussing music video and MTV in relationship to postmodernism was a recurring topic, including its champions (Kaplan 1987) and its detractors (Goodwin 1992; 1993). Finally, for a more recent study on music videos, see Vernallis 2004.

40. The "experts" Worley refers to undoubtedly included the National Center for Post-Traumatic Stress Disorder (PTSD). On 28 September 2001, this organization posted on its Web site a "fact-sheet" titled "How the Community May Be Affected by Media Coverage of the Terrorist Attack," authored by Jessica Hamblen, Ph.D. (http://www.ncptsd. org/facts/disasters/fs_media_disaster.html; inoperative link). Similar information from groups like the Veterans Administration was also circulating in the aftermath of the 9/11 attacks.

41. Though the source of this footage is not identified on the "Have You Forgotten?" DVD, many of the shots appear to be from French filmmakers Jules and Gedeon Naudet's documentary *9/11*, originally broadcast uninterrupted on CBS on 10 March 2002. See Worley's commentary to the DVD of "Have You Forgotten?" (DreamWorks DVD B0001209-09, 2003), and Jules and Gedeon Naudet, *9/11* (Paramount, 2002).

42. The Grand Ole Opry performance was different: two measures of buildup linked the end of the bridge with the third chorus, driven by the crescendoing bass drum pedal on the downbeats.

43. Carla Hay, "Acts Line up On Both Sides of War Debate," *Billboard,* 22 March 2003.

44. DeLuca, "Songs of Protest From Both Sides Now."

45. Silvio Pietroluongo, Minal Patel, and Wade Jessen, "Singles Minded," *Billboard,* 15 March 2003. For statistics about country's audience, see also note 17.

46. Silvio Pietroluongo, Minal Patel, and Wade Jessen, "Singles Minded," *Billboard,* 22 March 2003.

47. "Video Monitor," *Billboard,* 29 March 2003.

48. Hay, "Acts Line up On Both Sides of War Debate"; see also Susanne Ault, Ed Christman, Dana Hall, et al., "Impact of Iraq War Will Hit Touring Sector Hardest," *Billboard,* 29 March 2003.

49. Hay, "Acts Line up On Both Sides of War Debate."

50. This information is from CMT's Web site, http://www.cmt.com/shop/feat/american.spirit.artists.cdshop.jhtml (inoperative link, originally accessed April 17, 2003).

51. "Video Monitor," *Billboard,* 5 April 2003. The Dixie Chicks would later fall lower in the charts because of lead singer Natalie Maines's March 10 statement that she was "ashamed the president of the United States is from Texas" (see Phyllis Stark, "Dixie Chicks Comments Spark Country

Radio Boycotts," *Billboard,* 29 March 2003, 7). Most writers on country music after 9/11 have focused on this controversy (Willman 2005: 1–54; and Rudder 2005).

52. A portion of the proceeds from the album were also apparently to be donated "to the families of American soldiers," though as of March 22, the exact percentage or other details remained to be decided (Hay, "Acts Line up On Both Sides of War Debate").

53. Newman continued to muse, somewhat disingenuously: "I don't know why these songs aren't getting play, it could be because they aren't any good, it could be because of their stance, or it could be for various other reasons. However, if all dissenting voices are silenced through economic pressures, corporate blacklisting, or political persuasion, we risk the very real danger of having the freedoms promised by the Founding Fathers exist in theory only" (Melinda Newman, "The Beat," *Billboard,* 5 April 2003). David Hajdu also mentioned "conspiracy theorists in the music trades," who feared that Clear Channel, the nation's largest owner of radio stations and a corporation with connections to the Bush administration, was intentionally preventing antiwar songs from getting airplay (David Hajdu, "Where Has 'Where Have All the Flowers Gone?' Gone?" *New Republic,* 28 June 2004, 33). For more on issues of music censorship post-9/11, see the Garofalo and Scherzinger essays in this volume, as well as Rudder 2005: 212–14. Finally, for a more positive view of the Internet marketing of protest music, see Larry Kratz, "Notes of Conflict: Internet Fuels Boom of Songs About U.S. Involvement in Iraq," *Boston Herald,* 2 April 2003, and DeLuca, "Songs of Protest from Both Sides Now."

54. Country singer Clint Black's "I Raq and Roll" (pronounced "I rock and roll") was an exception. It made the charts despite being available only through his Web site (http://www.clintblack.com). See "Patriotism Lifts Pro-War Songs; Chicks Suffer" in *Billboard,* 5 April 2003.

55. Groups on the left evidently realized the limited political effectiveness of Internet-only distribution; the following year, in the months preceding the 2004 presidential election, they instead released a number of anti-Bush CD compilations, including *Rock Against Bush* (Fat Wreck Chords, 2004), and *Future Soundtrack for America* (Barsuk Records, 2004), produced in conjunction with the progressive political organization MoveOn.org.

56. Hajdu provides a useful critique of the protest songs of the Iraq War, singling out OutKast's "Bombs Over Baghdad," Public Enemy's "Son of a Bush," and the Beastie Boys' "In a World Gone Mad" as the best of what he saw as a rather undistinguished sampling. Hajdu, "Where Has 'Where Have All the Flowers Gone?' Gone?"

57. Rumsfeld told the audience, "I mentioned that I was going to come over here and be with Darryl Worley . . . and the president said, 'Well, I know who that is. I'm a country music fan.'" Reported in Conor O'Clery,

"Chicks Learn How Patriotism Is Fastest Way to Climb the Country Music Charts," *The Irish Times*, 19 April 2003. On June 13, 2005, Worley continued his relationship with the Bush administration and the U.S. government by performing at the Senate Spouses Luncheon in Washington, D.C., also attended by First Lady Laura Bush (http://www.darrylworley.com/index.htm?inc=news&nws_id=5592; inoperative link, originally accessed 15 July 2005).

58. Reported in Linda Feldmann, "The Impact of Bush Linking 9/11 and Iraq," *The Christian Science Monitor*, 14 March 2003.

59. This figure is from a *Washington Post* poll conducted on August 7–11 and published the week of September 6, 2003 (Dana Milbank and Claudia Deane, "Hussein Link to 9/11 Lingers in Many Minds," *The Washington Post*, September 6, 2003). Vice President Cheney himself persisted in linking the two, most publicly on NBC's "Meet the Press" on September 14, 2003, asserting: "We learn more and more that there was a relationship between Iraq and Al Qaeda that stretched back through most of the decade of the '90s, . . . that it involved training, for example, on [biological and chemical weapons], that Al Qaeda sent personnel to Baghdad to get trained on the systems" (Anne E. Kornblut and Bryan Bender, "Cheney Link of Iraq, 9/11 Challenged," *The Boston Globe*, September 16, 2003). On the same show Cheney also declared, "If we're successful in Iraq . . . then we will have struck a major blow right at the heart of the base, if you will, the geographic base of the terrorists who had us under assault now for many years, but most especially on 9/11" (Walter Pincus and Dana Milbank, "Al Qaeda-Hussein Link is Dismissed," *Washington Post*, June 17, 2004). On September 18, 2003, President Bush distanced himself from such claims: "We have no evidence that Saddam Hussein was involved with the 11 September attacks" (quoted in "Bush Rejects Saddam 9/11 Link," http://news.bbc.co.uk/1/hi/world/americas/3118262.stm). In its final report, the 9/11 Commission declared, "We have seen no evidence that these [possible contacts between Iraqi officials and bin Laden or his aides in 1999] or the earlier contacts ever developed into a collaborative operational relationship. Nor have we seen evidence indicating that Iraq cooperated with al Qaeda in developing or carrying out any attacks against the United States" (2004: 66). Yet, as Pincus and Milbank reported, Cheney again said in a speech on June 14, 2004, two days before the commission announced its findings about the claims, that Saddam Hussein "had long-established ties with al Qaeda" (Pincus and Milbank, "Al Qaeda-Hussein Link").

60. Rogers and Smith have taken the same tack with the place of religion in country music (1993: 270–84), but they are not alone in their argument. In his very personal *White Soul: Country Music, the Church, and Working Americans*, Tex Sample also refutes those who see "Okie from Muskogee" as a "flag-waving, authoritarian, super-patriotic, reactionary

song" (1996: 124–25). See also Malone 2002: 319, 372–74, on "Okie from Muskogee"; and Trent Hill's "Why Isn't Country Music 'Youth' Culture?" (2002: 161–90, esp. 162–63).

61. For a recent example of the same problem in the world of "art music" scholarship, see Joseph Straus's "The Myth of Serial 'Tyranny' in the 1950s and 1960s" in *Musical Quarterly* (1999), and Anne Shreffler's response (2000).

62. Sample agrees with Rogers and Smith: "I contend that the best reading of the politics of country music as it is used by working people is as a form of resistance [against 'the system'] and as a traditional populist anarchism." As this sentence suggests, Sample's argument is marred by the vagueness of his terms, including "working people," "resistance," "the system," and "traditional populist anarchism" (Sample 1996: 130, 118).

63. For a compelling start to this project see Aaron A. Fox's "'Alternative' to What?: *O Brother*, September 11, and the Politics of Country Music" (2005). A broader journalistic foray into this territory is contained in Willman 2005.

7

FOR *ALLE MENSCHEN?*

CLASSICAL MUSIC AND REMEMBRANCE AFTER 9/11

Peter Tregear

At a time when the Western classical music canon seems to be of ever-diminishing importance in our cultural economy, at a time when the cultural capital once bestowed by such "high-brow" music has been largely usurped, as John Seabrook might put it, by "no-brow" music, it is curious that there yet remain circumstances when we seem irresistibly drawn to this venerable repertoire.[1] Just such a circumstance was the commemoration of the anniversary of the attacks in America on September 11, 2001. To take a handful of examples: at exactly a year to the moment when the first hijacked plane hit the north tower of the World Trade Center, the former mayor of New York, Rudolph Giuliani, stood within the footprint of the destroyed Twin Towers and began a recitation of the names of the 2,801 known victims to the accompaniment of the Sarabande from J. S. Bach's Suite for Unaccompanied Cello in C Minor (BWV 1011), performed in situ by Yo-Yo Ma. Meanwhile, a "Rolling Requiem" had already been underway for some hours, for which around two hundred choirs in some twenty-eight countries sang Mozart's *Requiem Mass,* cued to begin according to the time zone of their respective host nations.[2] And just over a week later, the New York Philharmonic launched a series of commemorative concerts with a performance of Beethoven's Ninth Symphony alongside a new commission by John Adams, which had been composed to accompany it and which would later win a Pulitzer Prize, entitled *On the Transmigration of Souls.*[3] To be sure, as indeed other essays in this book testify, such commemorative programming forms only a small part of the musical record that related directly to the aftermath of the events on 9/11, but the official status and particular prominence of the events mentioned above makes their choice of music worthy of particular comment.

At first glance, the pairing of such music with a public commemoration of loss might seem to be both uncontrived and uncontroversial, reflecting as much the life-affirming capacity that we continue to bestow upon this art as the desire to make our public rituals approach the condition of popular cinema and its ubiquitous soundtrack. But like the application of a soundtrack, this pairing is also, however, a fictionalizing one. Music above all the arts is by its very nature radically removed from the events it might be chosen to accompany. It cannot of itself create some kind of aesthetic simulacrum of an event in the way that, say, monumental sculpture or painting can. Instead, the function of music in such circumstances seems to lie precisely in its presumed otherworldliness, in the qualities such as nobility, or theological gravitas, that we imagine it can bestow. Moreover, because it avoids a direct, mimetic, relationship with historical events, commemorative music can easily appear coy when confronted with the ever-suspicious gaze of the historical imagination. The problematic aesthetic ontology of much classical music, in particular, the fact that it by and large does not attempt to imitate everyday concepts or things and cannot be reduced to any unambiguous assertion of fact or feeling, has traditionally granted this music an exemption from direct political interrogation; certainly it offers a critic no straightforward or well-worn pathway to trace from a performance of a musical work to its political repercussions.

Such difficulties, however, are precisely what makes this music at the same time supremely able to lend a sense of transcendence, of sublime consolation, to a particular occasion that might otherwise eschew it. The perceived otherworldly sanctity that surrounds such music can thus serve to help inhibit an open discussion as to the meaning of the historical events that it accompanies. The use of this music, therefore, remains undeniably a political act worthy of interrogation, notwithstanding both the magnitude and depth of grief that it might be seen to help to articulate or console, and the broader interpretative difficulties that we might face in trying to examine it. The challenge remains, as Judith Butler exhorts, to consider "how the norm governing who will be a grievable human is circumscribed and produced in these acts of permissible and celebrated public grieving, how they sometimes operate in tandem with a prohibition of the public grieving of others' lives, and how this differential allocation of grief serves the derealizing aims of military violence" (2004: 37).

* * *

How might Western classical music therefore reflect or reinforce the political import of these acts of commemoration after 9/11? Not least given the wider historical context of the events, a particularly useful starting point can be found within the more worldly discourse of musical nationalism, one where we have been more inclined to acknowledge the political role of music, and trace that role in more straightforwardly functional terms. Typically, studies of musical nationalism demonstrate how musical artifacts help to define a sense of collective identity through a mixture of stylistic inclusions and exclusions. Ultimately, however, it is not the substance of the music per se, but the associations we bring to it that matters. Nationalist music, therefore, does not need to have specific nationalist signifiers, such as quotations of folk music or poetic allusions to a nation's landscape or history or literature. As the German music historian Carl Dahlhaus notes, key to modern ideas of nationhood was the idea of the "spirit of the people," which was considered to be the basis of the "truly fundamental, creative, and stimulating element in art as in other human activities" (1980: 81). A general recognition of great art created in a nation's midst, in and of itself, was enough to signify the greatness of a nation.

Similarly, Benedict Anderson's now well-established idea of nationalism as the projection of an "imagined community" reminds us that there is, in any event, little, if anything, essential about a nation's conception of self. Anderson considers nationalism to be at base an incantation that serves to transform "fatality into continuity, contingency into meaning," a way of avoiding the sense of loss that has accompanied the rise of the modern, industrialized, secular, nation state (1991: 11). Such formative social acts represent an effort, as Butler states, "to overcome an impressionability and violability that are ineradicable dimensions of human dependency and sociality" (2004: xiv). So it was that at precisely the moment that the modern nation-state demonstrated its renewed vulnerability in the post–Cold War world, the U.S. response after 9/11 was to reassert its inalienable sovereignty and correspondingly distance itself from more subtle principles of collective identity founded in international institutions, international norms, and international law.[4] So, too, the acts of commemoration, whether it be the sudden appearance of the Stars and Stripes in suburban front lawns after 9/11, or the character of the commemorative events held a year later at "Ground Zero" seemed designed, at least in part, to drive home that 9/11 was not to become just a sacred day, but a sacred American day, notwithstanding the multinational occupancy of the World Trade Center buildings, the fact that they claimed to house a *world* trade center, or indeed the early attempts at forging a united international response to the tragedy.[5]

Beyond the expected performances of the national anthem and other patriotic songs, however, what was surprising about the music for these events was the relative absence of music that might more directly evoke, or reflect on, the particular time and place of the events being commemorated. An explanation lies, I think, in a peculiar consonance between the "magic" of nationalism, its ability to act as a suture on what might otherwise be a fractious, contingent, social reality, and the typical reception of this kind of classical music in our culture more generally. I wish to suggest that a key concept of nineteenth-century German musical nationalism has particular relevance. Simply put, it is the idea that such music can represent at the same time both an exemplary cultural expression of the German people *and* a universal style, against which all other Western art-music traditions are to be defined and judged.

The potential for this otherwise contradictory formulation to buttress an idea of nationhood was well understood in Germany at the time. For instance, in his essay *Betrachtungen eines Unpolitischen* (Reflections of a Nonpolitical Man, 1918), Thomas Mann gives forceful expression to a view that was in fact commonplace, that the universal qualities of greatness expressed through German music were one and the same time the supreme expression of a uniquely German character. While it was (and still is) commonly said that German music is "without accent"—its principle virtue residing in its ability to transmit otherworldly qualities such as inwardness, transcendence, and sublimity—these qualities also became part of the narrative of German national identity, itself thought to reside principally in the realm of the nominal, fundamentally removed from the parochialism and vicissitudes of everyday life. No wonder that Nietzsche, himself intoxicated by the German musical canon, could come to think that the German nation was "purely a metaphysical conception," and as such "unique in the history of the world."[6]

Brahms's *Ein Deutsches Requiem* (A German Requiem), itself one of the large-scale choral works that were programmed in concerts across America on and around September 11, 2002, is an apposite historical example of this merging of transcendent musical and nationalist discourses.[7] Brahms himself compiled the text, which he freely chose from the German Bible, without reference to any specific liturgical service or rite in order to emphasize the universality of its message of comfort and consolation. Later in life he also commented that he would have liked to change the word "German" to "Human" in the title. Arguably, however, Brahms was at the very least unwittingly dissembling, for it was precisely its claim to universal greatness that made his *Requiem* a supremely German work. What was not conveyed as German by means of the title most certainly was through his compositional technique, especially his virtuosic evocations of the contrapuntal style of J. S. Bach. Bach, after all, was the composer whom the historian Johann Nicolaus Forkel had exhorted the German nation in 1802 to be "proud . . . but at the same time, be worthy of him!" (1920: 152). Bach's music was thought to be a universally supreme example of musical craftsmanship, and it was this belief allied to music's privileged position in relation to the other arts, its avoidance of the social and symbolic materiality of representational art forms, which best enabled it to signify that equally mysterious "authentic communion" that was thought to lie at the heart of the concept of Germanness itself (McClary 1988: xv). *Ein Deutsches Requiem* therefore exemplifies a politics of the unpolitical common to German musical thought as a whole, where the idea of national identity became the privileged-yet-covert fellow traveler of the German canon of art music.[8] Thus, Mann asserts without irony that "German humanity basically resists politicization . . . in fact, the political element is missing in the German concept of *Bildung* (culture)" (1956: 103). It would be more accurate to say, of course, that the political element becomes *Bildung*, claiming for itself the characteristic philosophical conception of the German musical artwork. To take a more recent example, James Hepokoski has suggested that the insistence in much more recent German musicology on the "autonomy of nineteenth-century German music had the effect of helping to normalize (and thereby defuse) contemporary West Germany's relationship to a problematic past" (1991: 225). For Mann, it was only after witnessing the rise of German fascism that he was able to discern the aggressive political corollary that had accompanied the shared pretense of music and national identity claiming for themselves transcendent universality. German musical hegemony had, he came to realize, acted as an aid to German political hegemony.

Without wishing at all to suggest any crude parallels between the dismal course of German history in the mid-twentieth century and recent American history, it is nevertheless possible to discern a functional similarity between the claim to universal validity of canonical German classical music and aspects of contemporary American national self-awareness. The latter is often defined in terms that are similarly universal in their reach, such as "democracy," "rule of law," "free marketplace," and "individualism." These are invoked as quintessentially American, in contrast to more traditional restrictive nationalist discourses based on ethnicity, religion, language, and geography.[9] From this has arisen the otherwise rather contradictory idea of American nationalism as a type of "postnationalism." Postnationalism in this sense, though, simply means a form of nationalism where the demarcations of traditional nation-state no longer apply, and instead the nation is defined in terms of a sublime communion of shared ideals (Habermas 1996). It is not of itself an idea singular to America. When, for instance, Salman Rushdie was asked on a visit to India what it meant to call this particular "crowd of separate national histories, conflicting cultures, and warring faiths, a nation," he replied that "it's by the lack of definition that you know it's you."[10] What at first seems like a contradictory answer points, though, to the sort of transcendent, seemingly unknowable, claim to communal authenticity that typically arises in postnationalist discourse. It is precisely the vagueness, the irreducibility, of such a concept of nationhood that makes it so powerful. I would suggest that performances of German classical music, as artifacts deemed to be of similarly irreducible value, are therefore particularly susceptible to reinforcing such narratives in so far as they are also received as transcending the specificity of their own historical origin while at the same time bringing credit upon the historical moment that brings them forth—whether as new compositions or, as here, performances. That is, in the case of commemorative concerts after 9/11, precisely because they are held to reinforce what is universally good about Western culture, they can also bolster what is good about being, in this case, American.

We could also consider in this context the one work by an American composer that did commonly appear on commemorative programs: Samuel Barber's *Adagio for Strings*. It is worth noting that the work, Barber's own arrangement of the second movement of his String Quartet in B minor, was roundly criticized at the time of its first performances in 1938 for its stylistic conservatism and, by extension, for not being identifiably American. Indeed, technically speaking, the work is wedded to the German classical music tradition. Despite (or because?) of this, it has nevertheless subsequently become associated with great public occasions in the U.S.; it was played at the funerals of Franklin Delano Roosevelt, Albert Einstein, and most famously, John F. Kennedy, among others.[11] Arguably, it is precisely the evocation of this apparently supra-national tradition of great music and its elevation of a particular mood into a register of sublime universality that helps explain its attractiveness for these occasions.[12]

The susceptibility of contemporary American culture to such mélanges of aesthetic production with expressions of national consciousness has for some time been a favorite target for criticism in what John Carlos Rowe has described as the "New American Studies" (2000; 2002). Likewise the now-not-quite-so-New Musicology would claim to draw out the contradictions inherent in any assertion that a musical work might somehow stand outside its particular cultural and social setting. Or one might simply wish to argue, as the New York architecture critic Herbert Muschamp did recently with regard to designs for a new war memorial in Washington, that we "do not honor history by seeking to transcend it."[13] Yet criticism along such lines of the music that accompanied the commemorations in September 2002 has not been forthcoming. Instead, the wish to transcend history was arguably precisely what this music was chosen to address. Certainly, this was what John Adams had in mind when he composed his work in memory of 9/11, *On the Transmigration of Souls*. In an interview with John Rockwell before the first performance, he spoke of his task as a composer in terms of creating "something out of time, the way great art ought to," to invoke the "power of art to transcend the moment."[14]

Without offering up a detailed taxonomy of the compositional style he employs, it is nevertheless possible to hear in this work how the minimalist-informed musical language that underpins the work helps to place the subject matter and the particular musical references in the work into a dehistoricized aesthetic frame. The chorus's text is assembled from phrases on the missing-persons notices and memorials that were posted around the ruins of the World Trade Center, alongside a mixture of factual descriptions and public expressions of love and grief. A prerecorded tape provides not just a background of city noise to this recitation, but also provides additional voices (including Adams's own) reading a selection from the list of the names of the dead. As Michael Kimmelman notes, however, a "world that does not seem to agree about anything can settle on the names of the dead. Lists of names promise closure, a conflict-averse path to catharsis in an age of instant gratification and short attention spans."[15] Moreover, the resulting textual amalgam does not provide an overall narrative course for the work; rather, the slowly shifting collage gives it the character of a ritual incantation. So, too, the music takes historically evocative material and ritualizes it by subjecting it to a musical discourse of transcendence. Mournful tones from an offstage solo trumpet, recalling Charles Ives's *Unanswered Question*, merge with numerous allusions to American popular musical idioms. The repetitive scales, harmonies, and rhythms reference similar gestures in American pop music and jazz (if not also evoking Umberto Eco's idea in *Travels in Hyperreality* [1983] of America as culture of vaunted excess). The chorus's repeated exhortation to "remember," for instance, shares more than a passing resemblance to the same exhortation in Dean Pitchford and Michael Gore's title song to the musical *Fame*, and the use of recorded street noises throughout the work recalls at the very least the sampling techniques of hip-hop. But all such contexts are forgotten (or perhaps here forgiven?) in the face of the transfiguring aesthetic power of Adams's underlying technique of slow, ritualistic repetition. We are thus not asked by the composer to contemplate the music's own contingencies, as we are not asked either to contemplate the historical contingencies surrounding the event it seeks to commemorate. As Andrew Clements, music critic for the U.K. *Guardian* mused, this is out of character for the composer. So many of Adams's scores had until that time "made a point of taking unexpected perspectives on traditional forms: on grand opera in *Nixon in China*, the symphony in *Harmonielehre*, the oratorio in *El Niño*. One might have expected a similar obliqueness of approach in *Transmigration*, a measure of emotional distancing and some clear-eyed political perspective. What we get, however, is much less convincing . . . the acerbic orchestral writing that could undercut the sentimentality never materializes."[16]

Adams seems to acknowledge the radical neutrality that he sought for his composition in his description of the work as a simply a "memory space." But this seems inadequate as an explanation, let alone a defense. As Peter Novick has written, "memory simplifies; sees events from a single, committed perspective; is impatient with ambiguities of any kind; reduces events to mythic archetypes. Historical consciousness, by its nature, focuses on the *historicity* of events—that they took place then and not now, that they grew out of circumstances different from those that now obtain. Memory by contrast, has no sense of the passage of time; it denies the 'pastness' of its objects and insists on their continuing presence" (1999: 4). One might posit that in certain respects neo-minimalist music like Adams' is especially susceptible to such a reception. If so, once again it can be compared to the canon of nineteenth-century German classical music, a stature to which this music in any case arguably aspires. The music is received both as something essentially American and yet of universal validity at the same time. Indeed, recent studies of musical minimalism by Edward Strickland (1993) and Robert Schwartz (1996) support this idea in acknowledging that, by the use of radically pared-down musical material, and by avoiding traditional formal narrative design, minimalist-inspired music can, like its sculptural counterpart, somehow avoid sociohistorical enquiry.[17] Thus empowered with these magical properties, such music joins with minimalist architecture and sculpture in becoming the presumptive style for commemorative art, providing what Michael Kimmelman calls "the sculptural language of the memorial sublime."[18]

Perhaps this context also helps us to understand Adams's claim in the press release for the first performance of his work by the New York

Philharmonic Orchestra, paired with Beethoven's Ninth Symphony, that "[c]learly, whatever this piece may be, it needs to be in the spirit of those very words of Schiller that will be heard later in the evening— that we are all united by a common bond of humanity. That seems to be a *fundamental assumption of the American artistic experience* as well, whether it be in the words of Whitman, or the music of Ives, and I intend to take my cue from the models they have already set forth [my emphasis]."[19]

It is instructive in this context to examine in some detail the use of Beethoven's Ninth Symphony as the companion piece to Adams's work. The Ninth, of course, has one of the more convoluted and awkward reception histories of any piece of classical music. From its first performance the work has been propelled into the center of a pantheon of masterworks that, among other things, helped prop up the idea of the German nation in its various post-Napoleonic guises. To this end the ideas contained in Schiller's Ode, the lines about *"Alle Menschen werden Brüder,"* and so on, were something of a gift, enabling the work to be at once the handmaiden of both left- and right-wing ideologues right into in the twentieth century. As I have argued elsewhere, Beethoven's vision of Schiller's joy, however, remains particular and ideological even as it claims for itself universal import.[20] An examination of the use of the Ninth Symphony as a political device, as traced by Buch and Brusniak (1998), Dennis (1996), and others, provides compelling evidence for this assertion. And yet, notwithstanding the violently disparate uses to which the work has been put, the belief in the work's transcendent, universal reach has never been seriously questioned.

The most potent source for this kernel of stable meaning derives principally from Beethoven's adaptation of Schiller's "An die Freude," and the vision of universal fraternity, of community reconciled with individualism that it appears to bestow upon the finale. In setting several verses of the Ode, it seems, Beethoven provided the listener with what seems to be an authoritative and compelling guide to the interpretation of the music. As opposed to the musical score, we can presume to *know* definitively what the Ode is about, and through that, we can come to know what the whole Symphony is about. Hence in 2001 the director of the "Proms" Festival in London, scheduling a concert four days after 9/11, presumably had fewer qualms about performing the choral finale of this work as a stand-alone movement than he might have had with truncating other canonical works. The finale is presumably thought to possess the core substance of the whole symphony, one that does not require the playing out of some grand, purely musical, design in order to be grasped.

But, we might counter, is not the Ode, as a text, especially liable to deconstruction? In fact, it seems that once again, the presumed transcendental reach of the subject matter results in a distinct lack of critical interpretations of it. Here, both Beethoven's avoidance of the specific political import of the Ode, especially as conveyed in its original version from 1785, and the peculiar quality of the music of the finale is crucial. In the original version of the Ode, for instance, Schiller praised the power of joy to efface class distinctions, but the version from 1803 that Beethoven adapts expresses a much more indirect, idealistic vision of joy, no doubt in part because by this time both Schiller and Beethoven had taken fright at the excesses of the French Revolution and the rise of Napoleon Bonaparte.[21] Thus

Deine Zauber binden wieder

Was der Mode Schwert geteilt

Bettler werden Fürstenbrüder

Wo dein sanfter Flügel weilt

[Your magic reunites

What the sword of custom has divided

Beggars become royal brothers

Where your gentle wings tarry]

becomes . . .

Deine Zauber binden wieder

Was die Mode streng geteilt

Alle Menschen werden Brüder

Wo dein sanfter Flügel weilt.

[Your magic reunites

What strict custom has divided

All people become brothers

Where your gentle wings tarry]

In addition, the schema of the poem lends itself to this idealized, dehistoricized, vision of joy in that its very imagery moves from the finite to the infinite, from personal friendship to the mass of humanity, from earthly existence to the Supreme Being beyond the stars (Nisbet 2000: 81).

Elevated from *Realpolitik* to *Idealpolitik*, the vision thus becomes open to all manner of what might otherwise be thought of as incongruous appropriations, whether Nazi party rallies or memorials to terrorist acts.

Furthermore, the very immediacy of the "Ode to Joy" theme, the "divinely sweet, pure and innocent human melody" as Wagner described it in his famous essay on Beethoven of 1870, in its own way helps to divert our attention from the contingencies of the text insofar as the tune seems complete in itself without words—indeed, it is presented in full four times before we hear a single word of Schiller's Ode.[22] Ironically, Adorno once praised the apparent lack of themes typical of Beethoven's other music with the exclamation that "[e]verywhere in his music is inscribed the injunction: 'O Freunde, nicht diese Töne,' (Oh friends, not these tones!)" for it is precisely when these words appear in the Ninth that the most famous of his tunes appears (1998: 51). We might best think of the text as a vehicle for the music rather than the other way around, suggesting perhaps that the meaning of the Ode itself is also to be understood as approaching the condition of the purely musical, that is, above historically contingent interpretation. In effect, setting aside that they are also usually performed in the original German, the actual words of the Ode have become insignificant. We "hear" only the sublime sentiment of joy and universal fraternity that they are presumed to exude through the unfolding of Beethoven's melody. Just such a sublimation was noted by Nietzsche as early as 1871:

> That Schiller's poem "Ode to Joy" should be absolutely incongruous with the dithyrambic world-redeeming jubilation of this music, and that it should even be submerged like pale moonlight by this sea of flames, who can deprive me of this totally certain feeling? And who would dispute my affirmation that this feeling finds its cry of expression, when hearing this music, only because the music had deprived us of every capacity for images and words, and because we hear almost nothing of Schiller's poem?[23]

Another particular aspect of Beethoven's musical setting of the Ode which one might have expected to cause us to pause for thought when appropriated for a post–September 11 commemoration concert is the presence of the *Alla marcia* [*Alla turka*] section. Are we not here explicitly drawn away from notions of universal fraternity into the infamous East/West cultural paradigm that politicians since September 11 have been at pains to avoid? It is true that the musicologist Lawrence Kramer, for one, has argued that the inclusion of this passage indicates the composer's intent of portraying brotherly love as extending even to those who might represent the antithesis of European culture, the Ottoman Turk (1995). His argument relies, however, on a highly nuanced reading of the early-nineteenth-century German reception of Classical myth. The use of the Turk as a paradigm of the oriental Other remains a more convincing one, if only because it seems more obvious both for early-nineteenth-century Vienna and for today. There is, in fact, some tantalizing evidence to suggest that Beethoven's own intention was indeed to suggest an association far less universal. The nineteenth-century German music historian Gustav Nottebohm made a note in his transcriptions from the sketches for the Ninth that the Turkish music was originally intended for the words that conclude verse two of the Ode: "*Und wer's nie gekonnt, der stehle Weinend sich aus diesem Bund*" ["and who cannot share in our joy shall steal away in tears from this union"] (1887: 186). That is, at the point where we are informed that those unlucky or unsociable enough not to share in the ecstatic vision of universal fraternity shall "steal weeping away." Theodor Adorno considers this moment in the Ode to represent the moment where the text reveals to itself an essential truth of such totalizing visions, to wit: that any vision of universality implies the violent subjugation of those unable or unwilling to share in it, or, given its original historical context, that *égalité* and the Reign of Terror are dialectically dependent upon each other.[24] Schiller's vision, he concludes, is

> . . . at once totalitarian and particular. What happens to the unloved or those incapable of love in the name of the idea in these lines unmasks that idea, as does the affirmative force with which Beethoven's music hammers it home (Adorno 1998: 212).

Or, as George W. Bush (in)famously declared in a speech on 6 November 2001: "You are either with us or against us."

There are also other musical cues we might use to support this rather less universal, fraternal, reading of the finale, not least in the fact that the original "Turkish" topic has survived as a more generic military one and thus retains at least the possibility of a menacing undertone.[25] And the remarkable fugue that follows the *Alla marcia* passage could be heard not so much to signify, as Leo Treitler and others have argued, that "a sonata procedure is in progress," but rather, with reference to the literal meaning of "fugue," that some kind of battle or conflict is underway.[26] This effect is heightened not just by the fact that the last lines of text heard in the chorus at this point are "*Freudig, wie ein Held zum Siegen*" ("Joyful, as a hero to victory") but also that the music moves suddenly from a martial-like rhythmic insistence to a passage of rhythmic flux, a technique that Beethoven incidentally also uses for similar visceral effect in *Wellingtons Sieg.*[27] The harmonic movement from tonal chaos to diatonic affirmation in the fugal section is also reminiscent of the overture to *Die Ruinen von Athen,* where a similar tonal movement is used to evoke the broad theme of the play for which it was written, the triumph of Enlightenment Europe over the Infidel. When combined with the affirmative "hammering" that follows, the rush toward an ecstatic outpouring of sound makes the Finale a rather uncomfortable expression of the idea of universal joy indeed.

Whatever the case, at the very least the retention of lines like *"wer's nie gekonnt, der stehle Weinend sich aus diesem Bund"* in the later revision of the Ode make it quite explicit that Schiller's joy is universal in import only if one signs up to a very particular vision of universality.[28] To that extent, the Ode reflects rather well the contradictory values at the heart of any claim to subsume universal values with national identity, and aspects of American nationalism after 9/11 in particular; America claims for itself ideals that are aspired to by the rest of humanity, including freedom, liberty, and democracy, but at the same time America has a right to pursue policies to preserve its national sovereignty at the expense of others. Beethoven's Ninth Symphony, which became one of the most-performed commemorative works after 9/11, is complicit in this contradictory projection of universality and particularity. Commemorating an event using such music therefore becomes a contingent and political act at the very moment it claims transcendence, and thus can rightly be interpreted as a commentary on the politics of the event itself.

* * *

A political critique of the use of such music for commemorative occasions after 9/11 might therefore note that the catastrophe of that day has been characterized as an all-out attack on "civilization," on "liberty," indeed on precisely those mythic community values that have been projected through American minimalist and postminimalist music or Beethoven's setting of Schiller's *Ode,* or Western classical music more generally. Such a critique might also note that the 9/11 attacks can nevertheless be viewed as a consequence of specific alliances and actions, without inferring moral justification or excuse. The use of music that claims for itself a transcendent, apolitical realm of meaning for commemorative purposes helps to elevate the audience safely into the first line of interpretation, a realm of meaning safely channeled away from the "corruption" proffered by a more contingent understanding of events. As Adorno warns, works like the Ninth Symphony "exert a mesmerizing influence; the power they have by virtue of their structure is translated into power over people. After Beethoven, art's power of suggestion, originally borrowed from society, has rebounded on to society and become propagandistic and ideological" (1984: 347).

Must music therefore remain silent on such occasions? Curiously, one suggestion to the contrary comes from the world of literature, and no less an author as Thomas Mann. In his late novel *Doktor Faustus*, the imaginary composer Adrian Leverkühn decides that his last composition, the *Dr. Fausti Weheklag [Lamentation of Dr. Faustus]*, which he composes in response to the death of a beloved child and which he completes as the Nazis seize power in Germany, will, as he eloquently puts it, "take back" the Ninth Symphony. The work, as it is meticulously described in the novel, is literally a negation of the Ninth, ending with an "Ode to Sorrow." For this extreme lament, nothing will do but the "speaking unspokenness given to music alone"; here, "the final despair achieves a voice," but one that permits "no consolation, appeasement, transfiguration" (1996: 490–91). But this work exists only in the mind of its author. We, however, seem to prefer art not to be so brazen in its attempt to reflect the inconsolability of loss. As Richard Taruskin suggested in his defense of the Boston Symphony Orchestra's decision to cancel scheduled performances of choruses from John Adams's *The Death of Klinghoffer* shortly after September 11, 2001, "Why shouldn't people be spared reminders of recent personal pain when they attend a concert?" Preempting the argument that Adams's music in this instance tries not so much to comfort as to make the audience think more critically about labels such as "terrorist," Taruskin questions why we should ever seek understanding in a work of art, which by necessity fictionalizes reality, rather than "more relevant sources of information."[29] But surely a kind of fictionalization is precisely what the performing of music that aims simply to comfort also achieves, only in a much less politically overt (and thus surely much more problematic) fashion. It is a pity, therefore, that Taruskin here fails to follow his own injunction, penned in 1989, to seek after historically informed musical knowledge: "Works of music are created by the time-bound for the time-bound, and we cannot decide that we, or the works we study, are outside history" (1989: 157). Indeed, when using art commemoratively the challenge of both artists and critics alike should be not simply to help us remember epochal events and their impact upon us, but also to enable the much more difficult task of reflecting critically both on that past and ourselves.

Maybe it was thinking along such lines that caused one commentator on English public radio to suggest that the *Missa Solemnis* would have been a much better work of Beethoven's to have been performed for such an occasion. It is a curious thought, but maybe the very aspect of the *Missa Solemnis* that so troubled a critic as insightful as Adorno, its retreat into an archaic religious form, would become here its critical moment; not least given some of the historical and religious background to the events on 9/11.[30] This is not just because it would undeniably *not* be a work that could easily claim universal import, but also because of the curious shape of the music itself. As Adorno noted, the work lacks the developmental paradigm, the dialectical contrasts, of Beethoven's symphonic works, at the same time that it also lacks truly memorable themes. Thus the conclusions of the various movements of the Mass seem curiously enigmatic; "because no path has been traveled, no resistance of the particular overcome, the trace of arbitrariness is transferred to the whole" (1998: 150). With all that in mind, what better way to end such a performance than with the cries of "*Dona nobis pacem*" [Lord, grant us peace], which Beethoven set to the distant rumble of trumpets, as if to acknowledge that our cries for freedom from strife become more often than not a prelude to war. Indeed, Adorno believed, this movement thereby takes on something of the burden of suffering that the "Crucifixus" setting has in Bach's Mass in B minor (1998: 148).

To be sure, however, there is no neat solution to the problem of how art can adequately respond to the conflicting claims of truth and consolation when it is used commemoratively. We must instead accept from the outset that both the work of art and the historical memory to which it is applied are always imagined, contingent, truths. As Walter Benjamin famously, and starkly, wrote: "[t]here is no document of civilization which is not at the same time a document of barbarism" (1969: 256). We cannot escape the fact that even our most cherished ideals, our most idealized works of art, remain forever tainted, for better or worse, by that mess of contingencies and compromises we call the "real world." In any event, it may be that Adams's *On the Transmigration of Souls*, at least, will not be able to avoid this kind of analysis, particularly when performed outside America. Unlike the Ninth Symphony, which was not composed to commemorate any occasion in particular, *On the Transmigration of Souls* is unable to claim for itself the kind of rarefied status that has helped make the Ninth so adaptable to a variety of contexts, and so tricky to critique. As demonstrated by the decidedly mixed reviews of Adams's work at its U.K. premiere in 2003, the very specificity of its text, assembled as noted above from phrases on missing-persons notices and memorials that were posted around the ruins of the World Trade Center, has led to accusations of mawkishness and sentimentality.[31] Here, outside of the United States, the text seemed as much a culturally specific response to particular tragedy as a musically mediated communion with all human suffering. Such an awareness is, however, no bad thing. 9/11 is commonly claimed to be an event of epochal significance in shaping the political imagination of a new century. If so, both the event itself and the way we commemorate it must remain unashamedly the subjects of our critical attention.

REFERENCES

Adorno, Theodor. 1984. *Aesthetic Theory*. Translated by C. Lenhardt. London: Routledge & Kegan Paul.

———. 1998. *Beethoven: The Philosophy of Music*. Edited by Rolf Tiedemann, translated by Edmund Jephcott. Cambridge: Polity.

Anderson, Benedict. 1991. *Imagined Communities: Reflections on the Origin and Spread of Nationalism*. London: Verso.

Applegate, Celia. 1992. "What Is German Music? Reflections on the Role of Art in the Creation of the Nation." *German Studies Review* 15: 21–32.

Benjamin, Walter. 1969. "Theses on the Philosophy of History." In *Illuminations*, edited by Hannah Arendt, translated by Harry Zohn, 253–64. New York: Schocken Books.

Bodnar, John. 1992. *Remaking America: Public Memory, Commemoration and Patriotism in the Twentieth Century*. Princeton: Princeton University Press.

Buch, Esteban, and Friedhelm Brusniak. 1998. "Schiller und die Musik." In *Schiller-Handbuch*, edited by Helmut Koopmann, 179–181. Stuttgart: Alfred Kröner.

Buch, Esteban. 1999. *La Neuvième de Beethoven: Une histoire politique*. Paris: Gallimard.

Buck-Morss, Susan. 2000. *Dreamworld and Catastrophe: The Passing of Mass Utopia in East and West*. Cambridge, MA: MIT Press.

Burke, Edmund. 2001. *Reflections on the Revolution in France*. Edited by J.C.D. Clark. Stanford, CA: Stanford University Press.

Butler, Judith. 2004. *Precarious Life: The Powers of Mourning and Violence*. London; Verso.

Dahlhaus, Carl. 1980. "Nationalism and Music." In *Between Romanticism and Modernism*, translated by Mary Whittall, 79–101. Berkeley: University of California Press.

Dennis, David. 1996. *Beethoven in German Politics 1870–1989*. New Haven: Yale University Press.

Eco, Umberto. 1983. *Travels in Hyperreality*. Translated by William Weaver. San Diego: Harcourt Brace Jovanovich.

Foerster-Nietzsche, Elizabeth, ed. 1922. *The Nietzsche-Wagner Correspondence*. Translated by Elizabeth Foerster-Nietzsche. London: Duckworth.

Forkel, Johann Nicolaus. 1920 [1802]. *Über Johann Sebastian Bachs Leben, Kunst und Kunstwerke*. Translated by Charles Sanford Terry. London: Constable.

Habermas, Jürgen. 1996. "The European Nation-State—Its Achievements and Its Limits: On the Past and Future of Sovereignty and Citizenship." In *Mapping the Nation*, edited by Gopal Balakrishnan, 281–94. London: Verso.

Hepokoski, James. 1991. "The Dahlhaus Project and its Extra-Musicological Sources." *Nineteenth-Century Music* 14: 221–46.

Heyman, Barbara B. 1992. *Samuel Barber: The Composer and His Music.* New York: Oxford University Press.

Johnson, Julian. 2002. *Who Needs Classical Music?: Cultural Choice and Musical Value.* Oxford: Oxford University Press.

Kramer, Lawrence. 1995. "The Strange Case of Beethoven's *Corolian*: Romantic Aesthetics, Modern Subjectivity, and the Cult of Shakespeare." *Musical Quarterly* 79: 256–80.

Kropfinger, Kraus. 1991. *Wagner und Beethoven: Richard Wagner's Reception of Beethoven*, trans. Peter Palmer. Cambridge: Cambridge University Press.

Liebert, Georges. 2004. *Nietzsche and Music.* Chicago: Chicago University Press.

Lieven, Anatol. 2004. *America Right or Wrong: An Anatomy of American Nationalism.* Oxford: Oxford University Press.

Mann, Thomas. 1956 [1918]. *Betrachtungen eines Unpolitischen.* Frankfurt am Main: Stockholmer Ausgabe.

———. *Doctor Faustus.* London: Minerva, 1996.

McClary, Susan. 1988. "The Undoing of Opera: Towards a Feminist Criticism of Music." Foreword to *Opera, or the Undoing of Women*, by Catherine Clément, translated by Betsy Wing. Minneapolis: University of Minnesota Press.

Nisbet, H. B. 2000. "Friedrich Schiller, 'An die Freude': A Reappraisal." In *Landmarks in German Poetry*, edited by Peter Hutchinson, 73–96. Oxford: Peter Lang.

Nottebohm, Gustav. 1887. "Skizzen zur neunten Symphonie." In *Zweite Beethoveniana: nachgelassene Aufsätze*, 157–92. Leipzig: J. Rieter-Biedermann.

Novick, Peter. 1999. *The Holocaust in American Life.* Boston: Houghton Mifflin, 1999.

Pei, Minixin. 2003. "The Paradoxes of American Nationalism." *Foreign Policy* (May/June): 30–38.

Rowe, John Carlos, ed. 2000. *Post-Nationalist American Studies.* Berkeley: University of California Press, 2000.

———. 2002. *The New American Studies.* Minnesota: University of Minnesota Press.

Saunders, Ernst. 1964. "Form and Content in the Finale of Beethoven's Ninth Symphony." *Musical Quarterly* 50: 59–76.

Schultheis, Alexandra W. 2001. "Postcolonial Lack and Aesthetic Promise in *The Moor's Last Sigh*." *Twentieth Century Literature* 47: 569–97.

Schwartz, K. Robert. 1996. *Minimalists.* London: Phaidon Press.

Seabrook, John. 2001. *Nobrow: The Culture of Marketing, the Marketing of Culture.* New York: Vintage.

Seidel, Wilhelm. 1994. "9. Symphonie d-Moll Op. 125." In *Beethoven: Interpretation seiner Werke*, v. 2, edited by Albrecht Riethmüller, Carl Dahlhaus, and Alexander L. Ringer. Laaber: Laaber-Verlag.

Solie, Ruth. 1993. "Introduction: On 'Difference.'" In *Musicology and Difference: Gender and Sexuality in Music Scholarship,* edited by Ruth Solie, 1–22. Berkeley: University of California Press.

Strickland, Edward. 1993. *Minimalism: Origins.* Bloomington: Indiana University Press.

Taruskin, Richard. 1989. "Reply to Brown and Dempster." *Journal of Music Theory* 33: 157–63.

Tregear, Peter. 2003. "The Ninth after 9/11." *Beethoven Forum* 10: 221–32.

Treitler, Leo. 1980. "History, Criticism, and Beethoven's Ninth Symphony." *Nineteenth-Century Music* 3: 193–210.

Vaget, Hans Rudolf. 2002. "Nationalism and Universal: Thomas Mann and the Paradox of 'German' Music." In *Music and German National Identity*, edited by Celia Applegate and Pamela Potter, 155–77. Chicago: University of Chicago Press.

Van den Toorn, Pieter C. 1995. *Music, Politics and the Academy.* Berkeley: University of California Press.

Will, Richard. 2002. *The Character Symphony in the Age of Haydn and Beethoven.* Cambridge: Cambridge University Press.

Wolfe, Alan. 2003. "The Difference Between Criticism and Hatred: Anti-American Studies." *The New Republic* (10 February): 25–32.

Žižek, Slavoj. 2002. *Welcome to the Desert of the Real.* London: Verso.

NOTES

1. The phrase "no-brow" comes from the title of Seabrook's recent book (2001); for a recent response to this perception of devaluation of classical music, see Johnson 2002.

2. See the online archives at http://www.rollingrequiem.org and http://www.symphony.org/911. The performance of Mozart's *Requiem* in New York was undertaken by The Juilliard Choral Union and Juilliard Orchestra.

3. This program was performed at Avery Fisher Hall, New York, on September 19, 20, 21, and 24, 2002.

4. For a recent critical examination of the new American nationalism, see Lieven 2004.

5. We might note that "ground zero," once a term with general application, now seems to have resolved into a singular meaning, reinforcing this particular catastrophe's claim to unique status in the pantheon of human calamities.

6. Quoted in Foerster-Nietzsche 1922: 143.

7. A performance of excerpts, for instance, was broadcast by the Cleveland Orchestra.

8. One could make a useful comparison here with the case of Edmund Burke and the relationship between his aesthetics of the sublime, and his post–French Revolution political conservatism, as famously described in his *Reflections on the Revolution in France* (2001).

9. For more on this point, see Pei 2003: 30–38.

10. Quoted in Schultheis 2001: 569.

11. For more on the American performance history of Barber's *Adagio*, see Heyman 1992: 170–73.

12. It is arguably this very aspect of the music that jars in Oliver Stone's Vietnam War film *Platoon* (1987): the attempt to visualize the immediacy and insane violence of war sits awkwardly with the music's elevation of the opening battle sequence as a kind of requiem for all war.

13. Herbert Muschamp, "New War Memorial Is Shrine to Sentiment," *New York Times*, 7 June 2001.

14. Quoted in John Rockwell, "Challenge of the Unthinkable: John Adams Delivers a Commissioned Work on 9/11," *New York Times*, 17 September 2002.

15. Michael Kimmelman, "Finding Comfort in the Safety of Names," *New York Times*, 31 August 2003.

16. Andrew Clements, "BBCSO/Adams." *Guardian* (U.K.), 29 July 2003.

17. I am also indebted here to Chris Willis and his unpublished essay on "Minimalism as American Nationalism."

18. Kimmelman, "Finding Comfort in the Safety of Names."

19. New York Philharmonic Press Release, 12 February 2002.

20. See the author's "The Ninth after 9/11" (2003). What follows is drawn in part from this essay.

21. For more on this shift, see Nisbet 2000: 90.

22. Quoted in Kropfinger 1991: 97.

23. Translated and cited in Liebert's *Nietzsche and Music* 2004: 91.

24. Note, for instance, the declaration by the Jacobin Committee of Public Safety at the outset of the Terror that "When the French people has manifested its will, everyone who is opposed to it is outside the sovereignty; everyone outside the sovereignty is an enemy. . . . Between the people and its enemies, there is nothing in common but the sword." Quoted in Buck-Morss 2000: 11.

25. See Seidel 1994: 268.

26. Quote taken from Treitler 1980: 198; see also Saunders 1964: 59–76.

27. See Will 2002: 194–96.

28. See Tregear 2003. Slavoj Žižek makes a more general point along similar lines in arguing that benefits of late capitalism fundamentally "cannot be universalised," and that the obscene truth underpinning a discourse of universal human rights is "the Wall separating those covered by the umbrella of Human Rights and those excluded from its protective cover" (2002: 149–50).

174 • Peter Tregear

29. Richard Taruskin, "Music's Dangers and the Case for Control," *New York Times,* 9 December 2001.
30. Curiously, this critical potential seems to have been avoided by the "Rolling Requiem" project. However, concert performances of the *Requiem* Mass, whether by Mozart, or Faure, or Lloyd Webber and the like, have, it appears, long since divorced themselves from any liturgical associations, and seem rather to have become poetic meditations on mortality per se. Settings of the ordinary of the mass, on the other hand, seem less able to relinquish their religious specificity.
31. The first U.K. performance was given on 27 July 2003 by the BBC Symphony Orchestra, conducted by the composer, in Royal Albert Hall, London.

Part Two:
Music and 9/11 Beyond the United States

8

TERROR IN AN ANDEAN KEY:

PEASANT COSMOPOLITANS INTERPRET 9/11

Jonathan Ritter

To be injured means that one has the chance to reflect upon injury, to find out the mechanisms of its distribution, to find out who else suffers from permeable borders, unexpected violence, dispossession, and fear, and in what ways. . . . [T]he dislocation from First World privilege, however temporary, offers a chance to start to imagine a world in which that violence might be minimized, in which an inevitable interdependency becomes acknowledged as the basis for global political community.

—Judith Butler (2004: xii–xiii)

In mid-February 2002, several hundred people ascended to the Waswantu Plateau in the southern Peruvian Andes to celebrate and compete in an annual song contest that marks the height of carnival festivities in the region. Festooned in wide-brimmed hats laden with fresh-cut flowers and wearing the broad *pullera* skirts and wool ponchos typical of *campesino* (peasant) dress in the area, competing groups regaled the assembled crowd and judges throughout the day with newly composed songs that ranged, in usual carnival fashion, from the bawdy to the biting, the raunchy to the reflective. Late in the day, one such group, the "Falcons of Mt. Wamaqo," entered the ring of rocks marking the performance area and offered its final round entry, a song entitled "Osama bin Laden" (Figure 8.1):[1]

Figure 8.1 The Falcons of Mt. Wamaqo perform "Osama bin Laden," February 10, 2002 (Photo by Jonathan Ritter).

Estados Unidos masiñallataqsi	Fellow people of the United States
Estados Unidos nacionllañataqsi	Citizens of the United States
Maskarawañas lluqsimun	Have come out with masks on [i.e., "with an attitude"]
Challay barbasapata tarimusun nispa	"We will find that bearded one," they say
Chayman qinañataqsi Osama bin Laden	The reason is that Osama bin Laden
Habas ukuyllataña mandaykullasqaku	Has sent fava bean farts [i.e., explosives]
Estados nacionman	to the States
Tayta Dios ninchikpa kastigunmi nispa	"It is our God's punishment," they say,
kachay kullasqaku	he let loose
Once de septiembre wata dos mil unutas	September 11, 2001
Once de septiembre wata dos mil unutas	September 11, 2001
Llapa apurunapas waqastillan purisqa	All those wealthy people walked along crying
chayllay llakillawan	with that tragedy
Manas puñuyllapas chayallasqallachu	They found no rest,
llapa gringotaqa	all those gringos
Manas churillantapas qunqarqullasqañas	Unable to forget their children,
chayllay vidapiqa	that's how life was

Social commentary, political critique, absurd humor, and tragic pathos are frequent (if incongruous) companions in carnival and carnivalesque performances in Peru, and "Osama bin Laden" fit well within this tradition, prompting scattered applause and nods of approval from the audience, punctuated by bemused laughter at its fart joke. Indeed, for a contest determined in large part by thematic novelty, the Falcons' performance was somewhat *too* typical: amid perennial condemnations of traitorous lovers and government corruption, 9/11 was one of the most popular themes of the day, taken up by a third of all competing groups. If the audience response was not all that the Falcons had hoped for, it appeared that had less to do with any deficiency in their performance than with the fact that the crowd had already heard it all before.

What are we to make of a song—let alone many songs—about 9/11 performed by rural peasants in a remote corner of the Andes? Where to start the process of cultural translation and ethnographic interpretation of a performance whose subject is, several years after that fateful day, so intimately familiar to people all over the world and yet, in this context, so seemingly out of place, so strange and foreign? When I have played the video of "Osama bin Laden" for diverse North American audiences over the last few years, reactions almost invariably have begun with astonishment at the song's very existence, followed by puzzlement at its unknown references and its rhetorical mixture of sympathy, humor, and critique. In a world reduced to a "clash of civilizations," some have wanted to know, which one does this song belong to? Are they with us or against us?

The sheer unexpectedness of Andean songs about 9/11, and their inability to fit within what Joan Didion has critically called the "fixed ideas" of American political life after 9/11 (2003), reveals a paradox at the heart of contemporary debates over globalization that I wish to take as a starting point for this essay. In spite of the celebratory discourse of a "flat world" of universal access and information promoted by globalization's cheerleaders (e.g., Friedman 2005), "Osama bin Laden" highlights the continued disparities and disjunctures of global communications today, exposing the relative insularity and univocality of mass media discourses from which many people (particularly in the West, but also elsewhere) obtain their information about the world, as well as their tendency to exclude or marginalize divergent voices. Speaking as a U.S. citizen, 9/11 songs by Peruvian peasants appear surprising for one of the same reasons the 9/11 attacks themselves did: We are not used to hearing back from our Others.

The Falcons of Mt. Wamaqo have clearly heard from, and about, us. Yet, paradoxically, they and their fellow performers provide a forceful reminder that the ever-deepening penetration of mass media into local lives everywhere does not, *ipso facto*, eliminate or arguably even significantly diminish the diversity of voices and perspectives in the world. Indeed, contrary to popular expectations of gradual global homogenization, what Alan Lomax gloomily referred to years ago as "cultural grey-out" (1968: 4–5), global phenomena—from popular music to 9/11—continue to be reread and reinterpreted by people through the lenses of decidedly local cultural practices, a process some have come to refer to as "glocalization."[2] In celebrating the resistant and polyphonic potential of this sort of reinterpretation, I do not deny the very real issues of economic, political, and military power at work in the globalizing world. Judging by world events since 9/11, power clearly still counts. However, an emphasis on the "incorrigibly plural" nature of how people make sense of that world opens the possibility of interrogating these issues from alternate perspectives,[3] ones that question the assumptions and presumed natural or inevitable character of Western hegemony, and highlight the agency of subaltern peoples to interpret and reimagine the world that we all inhabit.

The events of September 11 and their aftermath pose a tremendous and critically important challenge for comprehending these local/global fissures. As Eric Hershberg and Kevin Moore note in their introduction to an edited volume on the topic, perspectives on 9/11 have "everything to do with where one sits—politically and geographically" (2002: 3), and are rarely reducible to the bifurcated, "with us or against us" mentality of both the Bush administration and much of the U.S. media immediately after 9/11.[4] If one person's "terrorist" is another's "freedom fighter," as the new common wisdom holds, the difference between the two often lies as much in the layers of local history and cultural signification that give meaning to such terms as it does in opposing political allegiances.[5] My point here is not to justify or explain away violent attacks on civilian populations in the name of a radical cultural or historical relativism, but rather, as Luis Rubio has argued with reference to other readings of 9/11, "to analyze the nature of those responses and explore their meaning" (2002: 61). Put simply: As terrorism has globalized, how is understanding it being localized?

Latin America offers a compelling case in point. Rarely considered a party to the current "war on terror," decades of political violence in the region, fueled by guerrilla movements, drug trafficking, and paramilitary death squads, have nonetheless given its residents a deep and varied understanding of "terrorism" and its relationship with U.S. foreign policy. From the wars that devastated Central America in the 1980s to the ongoing "war on drugs" in Colombia and elsewhere in the Andes, the contested meanings of terms like "terrorist" have long been subject to public debate in the streets, songs, and opinion pages of the region. Even the date itself, September 11, already carried a powerful set of associations prior to 2001, marking the day a U.S.-backed military coup deposed the socialist government of Salvador Allende in Chile in 1973, installing Augusto Pinochet as dictator and ushering in a period of violent repression against supporters of the former government (Valdivia 2003). In Peru, as I will explore in this essay, local understandings of "terrorism" after 9/11 were filtered through the experience of nearly two decades of political violence in their own country that had come to an inconclusive end just a few years before. Consequently, while official government responses to 9/11 throughout Latin America (including that of Fidel Castro's Cuba) were unanimous in initially offering sympathy and support to the United States, private sentiments varied widely, with many people viewing the attacks as the inevitable outcome of a long history of U.S. interventionism and support for brutal and/or corrupt regimes all over the globe, including beyond its southern border.[6]

If not enough attention has been paid to the diversity and complexity of international perspectives on the meanings of 9/11, even less has been said about the role of music and other forms of performative culture in expressing them. As explored in many of the essays in this volume, musical responses to the attacks soon emerged both within the United States and in many places throughout the world, as performers and audiences drew upon music's emotional and expressive potential, and the liminal space of performance itself, to make sense of the events and offer possible frameworks for their interpretation. Though various forms of popular music have clearly played an important role in this regard, and consequently have received the bulk of scholarly attention,[7] anecdotal evidence suggests that many forms of traditional music performed for more narrowly circumscribed groups—from shadow-puppet theater in Indonesia to carnival songs in highland Peru—have also fulfilled this function.[8] If we are to be serious about examining the various ways in which the events of 9/11 have been understood, these sites of interpretation also deserve our consideration.

Ethnomusicology brings an important disciplinary perspective to the music(s) of 9/11, not least because it is the field where these sorts of links between "world music" and cultural meaning have typically been studied. More important, ethnomusicology's emphasis on interpersonal, long-term ethnographic research as a primary research methodology offers a crucial route into exploring these cultural texts and the ways in which they are embedded and understood within real people's lives.

As Marina Roseman has argued, musical ethnography's "attentiveness toward individual and social constructions of reality" can, ideally, be "held in productive engagement with recognition of the brute consequences of state and global intrusions on local lives" (2000: 132). This "productive engagement," I believe, is precisely what is called for in approaching the kind of local/global issues raised by 9/11 and the "brute consequences of state and global intrusions" of which it is both cause and effect. Indeed, if our purpose is to uncover the local knowledge inherent in musical performances with regard to 9/11, ethnography is, to my way of thinking, quite possibly the *only* way of approaching the task.[9]

Returning to the Peruvian 9/11 songs, then, this essay seeks to demystify the reasons for their existence and convey, if only in part, some of the deeper and less obvious meanings that they held for the audience on the Waswantu Plateau that day in 2002. Drawing on nearly two years of field research in Ayacucho's Fajardo Province before and after that date, I begin with an overview of how terror and violence emerged as salient themes in carnival musical practices in the region long before 9/11, as a result of the "dirty war" fought there between Maoist guerrillas and the Peruvian state from 1980 through the mid-1990s. I contend that carnival song contests, called *concursos*, created an important forum for protest and political commentary in the midst of that war, one in which local residents attempted to make sense of the violence that surrounded them, and in which they continue to engage with questions of memory, politics, and their place in the world today. Finally, I return to Ayacuchan musical reactions to the events of September 11, exploring how these more recent songs have been shaped and mediated by their creators' prior experiences with terror and violence. The implicit, and at times explicit, invocation of that local history within the 9/11 songs constitutes, in my eyes at least, a powerful and generous statement of empathy and a desire for mutual understanding, sentiments that have had all too fleeting a presence in the post-9/11 world.

TERROR AND CARNIVAL IN THE FAJARDO PROVINCE

In May of 1980, a relatively obscure Maoist splinter of the Peruvian Communist Party, known as *Sendero Luminoso*, or the "Shining Path," declared war on the Peruvian state. Led by Abimael Guzmán, a charismatic philosophy professor at the state university in the city of Ayacucho, Sendero envisioned itself as the vanguard of a new worldwide communist revolution. Rigidly doctrinaire, it dismissed all other existing communist movements and governments as "revisionists" (including post-Mao China), and planned a long-term war to topple the Peruvian state by, following Maoist dogma, "surrounding the cities from the countryside." Launching their armed struggle at a moment when the country was savoring the end of twelve years of military dictatorship, and when even the other revolutionary Marxist parties in Peru were embracing electoral democracy, *Sendero* was dismissed by most political observers as a marginal movement of disaffected intellectuals in a remote province, marching against the tides of Peruvian history (Gorriti 1999).

That characterization proved catastrophically incorrect, with consequences that have been the source of much anguish and soul-searching in the country ever since. Within a few years, the guerrillas had succeeded in significantly expanding their base in the countryside, periodically dynamiting the electric towers serving the nation's cities and ruthlessly assassinating anyone opposed to their vision of a Maoist utopia. In response, the Peruvian government launched a counterinsurgency campaign in Ayacucho in late 1982 that quickly ranked as one of the hemisphere's most bloody and repressive, a considerable and tragic feat in the midst of Latin America's so-called "lost decade." For most of the Quechua-speaking peasantry, who quickly grew disillusioned with the Shining Path and its penchant for violence but remained equally distrustful of the military and its indiscriminate scorched earth policies (the "terrorism" of one virtually indistinguishable from the "tactics" of the other), the 1980s became known as the *manchay tiempo*, the "time of fear." When the war finally subsided after Guzman's capture in 1992 and *Sendero*'s gradual demobilization in following years, the statistics were staggering: 70,000 people killed or forcibly "disappeared," most of them indigenous peasants and civilians; hundreds of thousands internally displaced within the country; and the democratic system the guerrillas fought so hard to overthrow preemptively usurped by an autocratic president, Alberto Fujimori, who used the terrorist threat to consolidate his own hold on power for over a decade.[10]

Carnival songs in Ayacucho played an important role in the war, the social liberty afforded by the celebration of carnival offering one of the few public spaces for people to protest the atrocities being committed against them. This was especially true in the communities of the eastern Fajardo province, in central Ayacucho, where residents had been holding formalized song contests called *concursos* during carnival since the mid-1970s. This was a unique circumstance, and one that bears some elaboration here. Fajardo is home to a distinctive genre of carnival music known as *pumpin* (pronounced "poom-PEEN"), played on twelve-string guitars tuned to a high register and featuring female vocalists who sing in the high, strident style typical of many indigenous communities throughout the Andes. Originally the project of a young anthropology student in Ayacucho interested in the "folklore" of his native village, the first *concurso*, held atop the Waswantu Plateau in 1976, aimed to reinvigorate and legitimize a waning tradition of intercommunal musical competition in this genre during carnival.[11] Events took an unexpected turn when the *concursos* were infiltrated and radicalized several years later by Shining Path organizers, who saw them as a useful propaganda vehicle in preparing the region for armed struggle. Within a few years, largely as a result of this influence, social and political commentary was a mainstay of virtually all songs at the contests, even among groups not affiliated with the guerrillas. As one musician then in his teens recalled to me in an interview much later, *pumpin* made a "180-degree turn" at that time, away from themes of "love, agriculture, and the daily-goings on of peasant life," and towards songs with a "direct message."[12]

The radical moment in *pumpin* ended in late 1982, when the Peruvian government finally responded to the growing crisis in the highlands by declaring much of the Ayacucho department, including the Fajardo province, under a state of emergency. The army's campaign of terror, in which all rural residents were presumed terrorists, quickly emptied the region as people were forcibly "disappeared," murdered outright, or fled to the growing shantytowns surrounding Ayacucho and Lima. Citing security concerns, both the military and the Shining Path at this point forbade large public gatherings in areas under their control, which dealt a major blow not only to the popular carnival *concursos*, but also religious practices in the region, which centered on the celebration of numerous annual Catholic fiestas.

The forum for social commentary and political protest opened by the *concursos* was not closed so easily, however, particularly in a social and political environment where other forms of speech were so tightly controlled. In 1984, *pumpin* was resurrected in the rapidly expanding Fajardino migrant/refugee community in Lima, where residents who had fled the violence in the highlands organized a new *concurso* during the carnival season; within a few years contests were also being held in Ayacucho and, eventually, even back in the Fajardo Province. In place of the revolutionary rhetoric of the Shining Path, or the agrarian concerns of the past, *pumpin* composers and performers turned their attention in the mid-1980s to commemorating those lost in the violence and protesting the excesses of the Peruvian military (or their political enablers). In this body of "testimonial music," as it became known, a new vocabulary of metaphors and tropes related to the violence emerged that eventually gained a wide acceptance, repeated year after year by different performers as a shorthand for collective experiences of grief and mourning; prominent phrases in these songs included *yawar waqay*, "to cry blood," *yawar mayu*, "a river of blood," *llakipi tarikun*, "to be found in sadness," references to "beloved children" that go missing, and more. As one songwriter in Ayacucho put it to me in reference to *mestizo* versions of the testimonial repertoire, "music was the only place we could talk about the terrible things happening in our lives."[13]

In the 1990s, as the violence slowly abated in the province, *pumpin* composers continued to commemorate the losses of the war, but also began turning their attention to broader issues. The experience of refugee flight and migrant life in the capital cities of Ayacucho and Lima, together with the growing availability of satellite television in the province, and even the long-term presence in the region of international human rights groups and development agencies, was reflected in an increasingly global worldview on the part of local residents. Even as many people continued to wake up in adobe homes and work the land with technology literally dating to the days of the Incas, they returned home at night to watch Venezuelan *telenovelas* and stand in line at the village phone to talk to their children and cousins in Ayacucho, Lima, and even Florida. Consequently, in addition to now-commonplace songs about the shortcomings of the Peruvian government and the receding atrocities of the war, contest songs appeared in the late 1990s dedicated to topics as varied as the El Niño weather pattern, monsoon flooding in India, and the U.S. bombing of Iraq (in 1998). *Pumpin*, to borrow the memorable phrase of a Yoruba musician, had become a "very modern tradition" (Waterman 1990).

In the year 2000, when I first arrived in the Fajardo province to begin fieldwork for my dissertation, *pumpin concursos* remained the most important forum in the region for presenting and debating issues of public importance, including national and international political topics, and they remained the site par excellence for public remembrance of the years of violence. Given this context, the presentation of songs about 9/11 seemed not only not surprising, but almost inevitable.

THE SONGS OF "11-S"

In mid-January 2002, I returned to Peru after an absence of six months to find that recent events had pushed death and political violence once again into the national limelight. Just two weeks before my arrival, a massive fire ripped through five blocks of Lima's central market, known as Mesa Redonda, leaving 291 people dead and more than a thousand critically injured. The circumstances of the fire, accidentally set off in an area dominated by unlicensed street vendors (*ambulantes*) selling cheap fireworks for New Year's festivities, spurred an intense public debate over the lax regulation of the country's informal economy. While some blamed the *ambulantes* for carelessly igniting the fire (or the police for allowing them to congregate with what amounted to giant explosives in the tightly packed market), others argued that the vendors were the fire's most tragic victims: working-class entrepreneurs forced to work in the "gray market" to survive in the country's otherwise dismal economy, whose bodies and businesses were the first to be incinerated when the inferno erupted.[14] Discussions of the Mesa Redonda fire thus became as much a referendum on how to address the structural violence of Peru's endemic poverty as an elegy for the lives lost there.[15]

The overt political violence of the Shining Path era was also once again making headlines. In June 2001, interim president Valentín Paniagua announced the formation of a Truth and Reconciliation Commission (CVR, in its Spanish acronym) to revisit the violence of 1980 to 2000 and offer suggestions for its redress.[16] This commission had just begun its highly publicized work, and the change in the public discourse regarding the years of violence was palpable in comparison to how it had been just a few months before. In the place of former president Fujimori's frequent declarations of having "defeated terrorism," and a culture of silence otherwise surrounding the events of the dirty war in much of the public sphere, grieving *campesina* women from Ayacucho were now being shown and interviewed on national television, as the clandestine graves holding the remains of their husbands and children were located and exhumed by forensic teams from the CVR.

Further adding to this stew of emotions, my return to Peru came just four months after 9/11, and the local media environment remained saturated with coverage of "11-S," as it was referred to there, and its aftermath. Much of this coverage focused on New York, where five Peruvian citizens had died in the collapse of the World Trade Center, and where the substantial Peruvian community living in nearby Paterson, New Jersey, provided a local angle for the story on Peruvian television. Public opinion about the attacks, as expressed to me personally in conversations with friends and acquaintances, as well as gleaned from the print and broadcast media, was overwhelmingly sympathetic to the United States at that point, at least in reference to the victims of the attacks. The war in Afghanistan was somewhat more controversial, and it is perhaps telling in that regard that not a single Latin American country, including Peru, had committed troops to the war effort.

Leaving metropolitan Lima for the highlands later that month, conversations about these broad issues took on a personal hue as I reconnected with old friends in the city of Ayacucho and the rural Fajardo province. The topic of 9/11 and its aftermath dominated my interactions with virtually everyone. "Did I live close to the towers?" some wanted to know. "Had I been scared?" "Did I lose any friends or family in the attacks?" "What did I think of the government's response?" One friend in Ayacucho ruefully joked that I seemed to be taking back the worst of Peru with me each time I returned to the United States—first tainted elections (i.e., Bush v. Gore 2000), now terrorist attacks. This last comment, though offered in jest, brought into the open the role-reversal that was taking place in this barrage of questions about *my* presumed experience with terrorism. I had spent much of the previous year and a half asking similar questions of the very people now querying me, interviewing them about their lives during the Shining Path conflict. There was, of course, no equivalence between my "experience" of 9/11, seated quite safely before a television in Los Angeles, and their experience of a brutal war that devastated their communities and families for more than a decade, and I did my best to communicate that. Still, we pondered together the strange ways of the world that had led me to do research on political violence and terror in their country, only to find myself two years later answering questions about how it had come to pass in my own. I was the one "localizing" the understanding of terrorism in their eyes.

The personal, intersubjective space of empathy opened in these conversations extended to my first, unexpected encounter with that year's carnival songs. Composers and performing groups jealously guard their new compositions each year prior to the competitions, in order to prevent others from stealing their musical and topical ideas, and as a consequence I had not yet heard any of the new songs for 2002. Just days before the first contest, I was invited to join a prominent *pumpin* group, Voces de Colca ("The Voices of Colca"), as a guitarist, and was thus given a sneak preview of their new compositions when we met to rehearse.[17] As we tuned up our guitars that evening in the director's house in Ayacucho, we chatted about plans for carnival, gossip about people in the community, and inevitably, what I had been doing on September 11. This proved a fitting segue into rehearsing their first song, still untitled at that point, which I recorded. The following is an excerpt from that recording:[18]

Yuyarillasun tragediata	We remember the tragedy
Hermanullay paisanullay Fajardo masillay	Brother, countryman, fellow Fajardino
Yuyarillasun desgraciata	We remember the misfortune
Hermanullay paisanullay Peruano masillay	Brother, countryman, fellow Peruvian
Chunka hukniyuq septiembreta	On September 11th
hatun llaqta waqallata	the great country cried
Kuyasqallam wawallankuna	When its beloved children
wañullaptim chinkallaptim	died and disappeared

Spoken:

Asi es, Jonathan. Imaynaraq karqanki kay punchaw . . .

Spoken:

That's it, Jonathan. How you must have been (felt) on that day . . .

Sung:

Chaypachallachum munduruna	For that reason, people of this world
Hermanullay paisanullay Fajardo masillay	Brother, countryman, fellow Fajardino
Chaypachallachum munduruna	For that reason, people of this world
Hermanullay paisanullay Peruano masillay	Brother, countryman, fellowman of Peru
Todo poderoso nacionkuna	The all-powerful nations
Bin Ladenpa kausallampi	for fault of bin Laden
Afghanistan llaqtallata	Are killing and disappearing
wañuchichkan chinkachichkan	the people of Afghanistan

Llaqtanchikpipas Perupipas	It's the same here in our Peru
Hermanullay paisanullay Fajardo masillay	Brother, countryman, fellow Fajardino
Llaqtanchikpipas Perupipas	It's the same here in our Peru
Hermanullay paisanullay Peruano masillay	Brother, countryman, fellowman of Peru
Mesa Redonda nillasqampi	In Mesa Redonda
achka runa wañukuychkan	many people died
Lliuchachallan Peruanukuna	All Peruvians
yawarllata waqallanchik	we are crying tears of blood

As the song ended, I was immediately struck by the relative complexity and sophistication of its portrayal of world events, at once sympathetic to American victims of the September 11 attacks while also protesting the ensuing war in Afghanistan and making an explicit comparison to the suffering of people in Peru due to the Mesa Redonda fire. In fact, throughout all eight verses the song makes a powerful plea to "brothers, countrymen, and fellowmen of Fajardo"—a common, consensus-building trope in *pumpin* songs—to identify with any and all victims of violence, registering a corresponding protest against its perpetrators, be they bin Laden or "all-powerful nations." The spoken interjection between verses by Donatilda, a veteran singer whose teenage daughters were the only other vocalists that night, brought that identification to a personal level, that of her relationship with me. Her vocal inflection at the end of the statement signified empathy, a shared sense of sorrow and, reflecting our prior conversation, a rumination on how I had coped with the events of that day.

Listening to the recording later that night and transcribing the lyrics, I began to sense the deeper ways in which local experiences and understandings of terror were being mapped onto the song's reading of September 11. Most prominently, the frequent use of the verb *chinkay*, "to disappear"—not an obvious choice in this context—recalled the very potent local associations of the word with the Peruvian army practice of abducting and killing individuals and henceforth denying any knowledge of their detainment. More than simply a poignant and poetic reference to the vanished bodies of those who perished in the World Trade Center or those who were dying in Afghanistan, the use of the word "disappeared," in addition to phrases like "crying tears of blood," made an implicit connection between these events and how terrorism had been experienced (and sung about) in Ayacucho. Furthermore, the song contains numerous textual echoes of one of its composer's most famous works written a decade earlier, "El Desaparecido" ("The Disappeared One"), which follows a mother's tragic search for her missing "beloved child" who has been "disappeared" by the army. Many songwriters recycle material from year to year for practical reasons, but in this case the re-use made an intertextual reference to a well-known song that protested the impunity of murderers during the years of violence in Ayacucho—a reference that local residents surely would not miss.

Still, the circumstances surrounding the creation of this song were unique with regard to its subject matter. It was composed by a long-time *pumpin* promoter and lawyer residing in the city of Ayacucho, a member of the regional *mestizo* elite with decidedly urbane tastes and substantial access to the international media. Long associated with the more politicized, "testimonial" faction of *pumpin* songwriters, he had also been briefly imprisoned and threatened with torture by the military during the dirty war. Perhaps most significant, at the time of the 9/11 attacks, his eldest daughter was living and working in New York City, giving him a deeply personal and emotional interest in those events. As we prepared to perform at the song competitions, I wondered if others in the province without his personal connection to 9/11 would share his perspective, and if so, be compelled to write songs about it.

The answer, as the song contests the following weekend showed, was a resounding yes. In addition to numerous songs about the incipient work of the Truth Commission, the collapse of the Fujimori regime the previous year, and the usual host of songs about traitorous lovers and *campesino* life, five of the fifteen groups that participated in the Waswantu *concurso* performed songs related to the September 11 attacks.[19] All were relatively similar in tone and content to "Bin Laden," offering sympathy to the victims of the attacks, condemning the war in Afghanistan, and drawing on metaphors and verbal tropes developed first in songs referencing their own experience of terror in the 1980s and 1990s. Several, like "Bin Laden," also compared the sense of loss in the United States to that felt in Peru after the Mesa Redonda fire. Though similar in these broad strokes, there were also subtle differences between some of the songs that indicate opinions regarding 9/11 were not monolithic in the region. To show the range of these perspectives, I will focus my comments and analysis here on the two songs that contrasted most sharply: the elegiac "Waqay Vida Llaki Vida" ("Life of Sadness, Life of Tears"), performed by the group Santa Rosa of Huancaraylla; and the protest-oriented "Tragedia en Norteamerica" ("Tragedy in North America") by the New Voices of Huancapi.

Of all the 9/11 *pumpin* songs, "Waqay Vida Llaki Vida" is focused most closely on drawing a sympathetic comparison between the suffering caused by 9/11 and that of the Mesa Redonda fire, emphasizing the tragic aspects of shared loss and grief. It begins:

Hermanullay paisanullay	My brothers, my countrymen,
yuyallachkanchikmi	we remember
Hermanullay paisanullay	My brothers, my countrymen,
rikullarqanchikmi	we have seen
Enterullay continente Americanapi	In the entire American continent
Waqay vida llaki vida pasakullasqanta	A life of sadness and tears has been passing
Chayllay iskay jatun wasi	Those two towers
wichiykullasqanta	have fallen
Waranqantin runamasinchik	Thousands of people
chinkaykullasqanta	have disappeared

Chaynallataqsi hermanullay	In the same manner, my brothers
Lima capitalpi	in the capital of Lima
Chaynallataqsi paisanullay	In the same manner, my countryman
Mesa Redondapi	in Mesa Redonda
Waqay vida llaki vida pasarqukullasqa	A life of sadness and tears has been passing
Hermanullanchik paisanullanchik	Our brothers, our countrymen
ninapi chinkarquptin	have disappeared in the fire
Waqay vida llaki vida pasarqukullasqa	A life of sadness and tears has been passing
Hermanullanchik paisanullanchik	Our brothers, our countrymen
ninapi chinkarquptin	have disappeared in the fire
Yantallachum paqpallachum	As if they were firewood
kallanmankukarqa	or *cabuya*[20]
Ninallapa chawpillanpi	In the midst of the fire,
uchpa yanankupaq	they were reduced to ashes
Enterullay centro Limas	All of the center of Lima
wichqakuykullasqa	was closed
Wawallankuta churillankuta	While boys and girls
maskaspankuriptin	searched in vain
Mamallankuta taytallankuta	Looking for their parents
manaña tarispa	they could not find them

The sympathy extended to 9/11 victims and their survivors is couched here, as with "Bin Laden," in inclusive, collective language, addressing "*my* brothers" and "*my* countrymen" of the "*entire* American continent" (my emphasis), and thus drawing victims of both disasters into the same metaphoric community. Driving home the comparison, an identical phrase ("a life of tears and sadness has been passing") is used to describe each event, and the verses for each are connected by an explicit verbal equation, *chaynallataqsi* (roughly, "in the same manner"). Avoiding explanation of the causes behind either tragedy, and the attendant political positioning that would entail, "Waqay Vida" offers the simple message that all victims of such disasters merit mourning in equal measure.

The ghosts of the dirty war are largely implicit in "Waqay Vida," contained once again in the recycling of well-known phrases and symbols from earlier songs. In addition to some that have already been discussed, such as the use of the verb *chinkay* ("to disappear"), the depiction in the third verse of people being "reduced to ashes" "as if they were firewood" is striking. Though certainly an accurate description of what happened in the Mesa Redonda fire, the phrase also draws on language used just two years earlier at the contest by this same group. In "Julio Arotoma," Santa Rosa's 2000 song dedicated to the memory of their group's founder (and relative of several current members), who was captured and disappeared by the Peruvian military in 1991, the song's protagonist repeatedly asks where he might be, guessing that his body may have been buried or "perhaps like firewood, reduced to ashes" ("*yanta qinachuch uchpayarunki*"). Though this textual echo of the group's earlier composition doubtless escaped many in the crowd, and may or may not have been intentional on the part of the composers, the theory that the army cremated the bodies of people that it disappeared is widespread enough in Ayacucho that evoking the horror of bodies "reduced to ashes" likely evinced responses among many listeners that went beyond a reflection on the Mesa Redonda fire.

The *fuga,* or final, concluding verse of "Waqay Vida" contains the only hint at political commentary in the song, asking from a first person perspective:

Avionllay avion de guerra	Little plane, war plane
Kutirimuspa apakullaway	Turn around, take me back
Vueltarimuspay pusakullaway	Turn around and return
Manasa mamallay kanchu	I no longer have my mother
Manasa taytallay kanchu	I no longer have my father
Maypiraq churiy nispa ninampaq	Who will say, "Where is my son?"
Maypiraq waway nispa ninampaq	Who will say, "Where is my daughter?"

Whose "war plane" is referred to here is left an open question. Presumably, the reference is either to the hijacked planes of 9/11 or American military planes in Afghanistan, though the lack of specificity is suggestive. Regardless, the antiwar message is self-evident: the plane must turn around, go back in time, and stop the violence before the song's protagonist is orphaned. If earlier songs about the dirty war are to be any judge, the breaking of parent/child bonds by death or disappearance was seen as one of the greatest horrors of political violence and terrorism in Ayacucho, and its evocation here is certainly poignant and powerful. Similarly, the use of the first-person at the end of this verse again blurs the boundary between "their" and "our" experience of political violence, projecting an imagined community of victims of terrorism in which the sentiments of one orphaned by 9/11 are interchangeable with those of the young *campesina* women, also survivors of political violence, literally giving them voice in this performance.

In contrast to "Waqay Vida" and its focus on empathy and shared grief, "Tragedy in North America," performed by Nuevas Voces de Huancapi ("New Voices of Huancapi"), presents the most pointed political critique of both bin Laden and the U.S. reaction to the attacks. Written by a couple from the town of Huancapi known for their politicized and at times controversial songwriting, the first verses of "Tragedy" describe the 9/11 events in simple and noncommittal terms, noting the Bush administration's hasty reaction and hinting that the decision to go to war in Afghanistan was ill-considered. The song then offers a fictional monologue by Osama bin Laden, ostensibly in response to George Bush, in which bin Laden's language recalls the Maoist rhetoric of Abimael Guzmán far more than it does bin Laden's own presumed religious fundamentalism:

Bin Ladenñataq contestamunsi	Bin Laden answered:
Kayllay liderman igualawaqchu nispa	"Are you my match as a leader?" he said
Chinkarusaqmi wañurusaqmi	"I will disappear, I will die
llapan burguesta chinkarachispay nispa	'disappearing' all the bourgeoisie" he said
Wañurasaqmi chinkarusaqmi	"I will die, I will disappear
capitalistata chinkarachispay ninsi	'disappearing' all the capitalists"

The mapping of Guzman's persona onto that of Bin Laden implicitly suggests a critical stance toward the latter—Guzman is widely reviled in Fajardo today, and the Shining Path has been bluntly criticized in earlier songs by this very group—which is made explicit in the final verses:

Umaykiya barbasapa	What's in your head, bearded one?
Sunquykiya chawar barba	What's in your heart, stringy beard?
Wawakunas waqallachkan mikuymanta	Children cry from lack of food
Runamasikis wañullachkan yarqaymanta	Your people are dying of hunger
Huk nacionman ayqiruspa	While you escaped to another nation
Pastollataña mikuchkanku cuy qina	They are eating grass, like guinea pigs
Wiksallaykipi manaña kaptin	When there is nothing in their bellies

While bin Laden is condemned for abandoning his "own people" (a reference, presumably, to Afghanistan and the widely reported famine that afflicted parts of the country in the winter following the ouster of the Taliban), the suffering of his American victims is rendered in somewhat more ambiguous terms in this song. Here, they are referred to not as mothers, fathers, and children, as in "Waqay Vida," but as "capitalists," the "bourgeoisie," and "gringos" who are worried that their "power may disappear" in the wake of 9/11. This relatively benign critique, representative of typical attitudes about the United States in the region, turns to outright condemnation of U.S. actions in the penultimate verses:

País pobrella qaykapikama	Poor countries, to what point
Explotado kasun Estados Unidoswan	will we be exploited by the United States?
Bolsas de valores bajaramullaptin	When stocks are down
Llapan dolarpas congelados kachkan	and dollars are frozen?
Ima llakillach kayllay llakiqa	How painful, this suffering
Enteru mundupas tristellañas kachkan	There is sadness all over the world
Afganistanllay llaqtallapipas	In Afghanistan
Llaparunatas prisionarullanku	They have taken everyone prisoner
Estados Unidos carcelllapipas	In a United States jail
Prisionerokunas torturasqa kachkan	The prisoners are tortured
Chullachullamantas qurqumullachkan	Taking them out one by one
Fusilasqaña wañullachun nispa	Killed by firing squad, they say

My focus here has been on the role of local, lived personal experiences of terror in framing understandings of 9/11, but "Tragedy in North America" also highlights the undeniable role that the national and transnational mass media played in informing attitudes about that event and its aftermath. Rumors of the torture and execution of Muslims in American-run prisons, for instance, were circulating in the transnational media long before photos from Abu Ghraib lent such allegations public credibility in the United States; their presence in this song, according to its composers, came directly from news stories they viewed on the Peruvian television stations Frecuencia Latina and Panamericana. The strong audience response to these verses at the Waswantu contest, confirmed in later conversations, indicated that the torture allegations were widely known (and condemned) in the region as a result of similar television and radio news consumption.

Nonetheless, I want to be clear, *pumpin* songs about 9/11 should not, indeed *cannot*, be reduced to mere local parroting of mass mediated news reports. Fajardinos are not, any more than other media audiences, simply passive receptors and re-transmitters of information and opinion; they select, interpret, critique, and evaluate news coverage in the process of watching TV or listening to the radio, and perhaps even more so, given that Peruvian stations routinely ignore the perspectives and concerns of those in rural provinces like Fajardo. Even "Tragedy in North America," whose themes we know are consciously drawn from television coverage of the "war on terror," reflects editorial choices and interpretations that are rooted far more deeply in local experiences and debates over violence and its effects than they are in national media discourse. By choosing to focus on the personae of Bush and bin Laden and their respective justifications of violence, as well as topics such as famine, torture, and First World exploitation, Nuevas Voces directed their listeners to aspects of the 9/11 story that most resonated with local experiences.

And in fact, beyond the differences in tone and rhetorical emphasis I have concentrated on here, the 9/11 *pumpin* songs are remarkably consistent in their overall politics, particularly in their blanket condemnation of violence. Judith Butler has recently encouraged us to ask whether "the experiences of vulnerability and loss [arising from terrorism] have to lead straightaway to military violence and retribution," or whether something else "might be made of grief besides a cry for war" (2004: xii–xiii). Without exception, these songs indicate that the culturally correct response to Butler's question in Fajardo, and to terrorist violence in general, is sadness and identification with the victims. No songs about either the Shining Path war or 9/11 call for victims to "fight back." This is not to say that blame is not cast: Osama bin Laden is named and condemned in almost all of the songs, in a manner reminiscent of how Abimael Guzmán is now blamed in certain songs for the violence of the 1980s and '90s. But the indiscriminate way in which the Peruvian state retaliated to the Shining Path insurgency has made people in Ayacucho all too aware of the human cost of combating terrorism with military action, a view which helps to explain the widespread condemnation by Fajardinos of the subsequent U.S. war in Afghanistan.

CONCLUSION: PEASANT COSMOPOLITANISM AND THE ETHICS OF EMPATHY

In 1983, in the wake of the brutal and confusing murder of eight journalists by indigenous peasants in the northern part of Ayacucho, an investigative commission headed by novelist Mario Vargas Llosa concluded that the deaths were the result of a tragic misunderstanding arising in part from the villagers' "cultural primitivism" and "archaism," and the continuing gulf between their Hobbesian world and the modern one that he viewed himself inhabiting (Vargas Llosa et al. 1983: 23). Whether that gulf ever truly existed, at least in the manner Vargas

Llosa saw it—and there were many who took issue with his claim[21]—the carnival songs of Ayacucho's Fajardo province two decades later present a radically different picture of Andean peasants, one in which they position themselves as global citizens, emergent cosmopolitans (Turino 2000; Appiah 2006), knowledgeable about and willing to comment on world affairs. Indeed, the terrorist attacks of September 11 presented to local songwriters a global topic about which they saw themselves as uniquely qualified to offer such commentary, given their own deep experiences with terror and political violence.

What I have attempted to highlight in this essay is the extent to which that experience shaped actual understandings of 9/11 in the Fajardo region, how 9/11 fit into established structures of feeling about violence and terror, and how in turn those understandings and feelings were publicly expressed through musical performance. From their language of identification with 9/11's victims to their numerous intertextual references to earlier songs and thus memories of local suffering, these songs are extraordinary not for their novelty but for the tremendous act of compassion and empathy that they represent, particularly toward "gringos"—people more typically viewed in rural Peru as simply imperialists and exploiters. These songs reflect an effort to place "their" and "our" experiences of terror on the same dialogic ground, promoting an ethics of empathy that challenges us here in the United States to join them in rethinking and decentering our collective debates over the meaning(s) of terrorism in the post-9/11 world.

Perhaps as was inevitable, the moment of empathy and attempt at mutual understanding did not last. By 2005, two years after the U.S. invasion of Iraq, attitudes toward the United States had hardened considerably. At the Waswantu contest that year, no songs commemorated 9/11, and the only song directly addressing the United States bluntly remarked:

Estados Unidos gringokuna	Gringos in the United States
Gozan ellos de nuestra pobreza	They live well off our poverty
Llamkankanchu derechos humanos	They don't work for human rights
Justiciata pobres manam kanchu	There is no justice for the poor[22]

Briefly realized in this most unlikely of places, Judith Butler's imagined post-9/11 "global political community," invoked in the opening epigraph of this essay, was already a thing of the past. Empathy, after all, is a difficult emotion to sustain even in the best of circumstances. It is virtually impossible when it is neither reciprocated nor acknowledged.

ACKNOWLEDGMENTS

My field research in Ayacucho, Peru, was conducted over eighteen months between January 2000 and April 2002, under the auspices of grants from Fulbright (IIE), the Wenner-Gren Foundation for Anthropological Research, and the UCLA International Studies Overseas Program, whose support I gratefully acknowledge. I also want to thank Gerard Béhague, Martin Daughtry, Steven Feld, Stacy Lieberman, Anthony Seeger, Christopher Waterman, and Deborah Wong for their comments and questions on different versions of this essay over the last few years. Abbreviated versions of this paper were delivered at the Society for Ethnomusicology annual meeting in Estes Park, Colorado, in November 2002, and at the thirty-seventh World Conference of the International Council for Traditional Music in Fuzhou and Quanzhou, China, in January 2004.

APPENDIX: 9/11 *PUMPIN* SONG TEXTS

1. *"Bin Laden"*

Written and performed by Voces de Colca ("Voices of Colca"), February 2002. In performance, the first two lines and the second two lines of each stanza were repeated.

Iskayllaway mileniopi	In the second millenium
Hermanullay paisanullay Fajardo masillay	Brother, countryman, fellowman from Fajardo
Enterullay mundurunapa imallaraq suertillanchik	People of the entire world, what will be our lot?
Kaynallaña miseriawan qaykallaraq destinunchik	With this misery, what will be our destiny?
Qawachkankichu rikuchkankichum	You see, you are watching
Hermanullay paisanullay Fajardo masillay	Brother, countryman, fellowman from Fajardo
Llaparuna llaparunata wañuchikta waqachikta	Among all humans, we are killing one another and making each other suffer
Llapan atiq llaqtakuna tercera guerra maskallaqta	The world powers are looking for World War Three
Yuyarillasun tragediata [2x: *desgraciata*]	We remember the tragedy [2x: misfortune]
Hermanullay paisanullay Fajardo masillay	Brother, countryman, fellowman from Fajardo

Chunka hukniyuq septiembreta hatun llaqta waqallaqta	On September 11th, the large country cried
Kuyasqallam wawallankuna wañullaptim chinkallaptim	Seeing its beloved children die and disappear
Chaypachallachum munduruna	For that reason, people of the world
Hermanullay paisanullay Fajardo masillay	Brother, countryman, fellowman from Fajardo
Todo poderoso nacionkuna bin Ladenpa kausallampi	The all powerful nations, for fault of bin Laden
Afghanistan llaqtallata wañuchichkan chinkachichkan	Are killing and disappearing the people of Afghanistan
Llaqtanchikpipas Perupipas	It's the same here in our Peru
Hermanullay paisanullay Fajardo masillay	Brother, countryman, fellowman from Fajardo
Mesa Redonda nillasqampi achka runa wañukuychkan	In Mesa Redonda they say many people died
Lliuchachallan Peruanukuna yawarllata waqallanchik	All Peruvians, we are crying tears of blood
Salvallasun mundunchikta	To save our world
Hermanullay paisanullay Fajardo masillay	Brother, countryman, fellowman from Fajardo
Sin envidia sin egoismo sin matanza kausallasun	We must live without envy, nor ego, nor massacres
Trabajallasun honradezwan llaqtanchikpa progresunpaq	We must work honestly for the progress of our people

FUGA

Kuyasqallay Fajardo masillay	Dear neighbors, fellow Fajardinos
Wayllusqallay Peruano masillay	Dear neighbors, fellow Peruvians
Imam pasachkan imana suceden enterullay mundurunata	What is happening to people all over the world?
Tanto odio, tanta venganza, tanta matanza, tanta miseria	So much hate, so much vengeance, so many massacres, so much misery
Wiraqucha Nostradamusqa	The wise man Nostradamus
Claruchallatan [2x: Ciertuchallatan] willawasqanchik	Told us clearly [2x: Told us certainly]
Kayllay mundupi llaparunaqa kikinchik puran tukunakusun	That in this world, all people will kill each other
Tercerallay guerra nisqampi llaparunalla chinkarillasunchik	When World War Three arrives, we will all disappear

2. "Injusticia en el Mundo" ("Injustice in the World")

Written by Medardo Quispe, performed by Mensajeros de Quilla ("Messengers of Quilla"), February 2002.

Chunka chunkaytam niwachkanchik	Over and over again we are told
Derechos humanos mundupiqa	about human rights in the world
Llapa runapa igualdadpaq	Equality for all people
Nispa nispalla engañawanchik	We are deceived by such talk
Chayna kaptinqa vida mia	If it was like that, my love
Sumaq kausaycha mundupiqa	Life would be great in this world
Mana chaynalla kallaptinqa	But it is not that way
Kaypi wakpipas sipinakuyllas	It's just massacres everywhere
11 de septiembre, 2001	September 11th, 2001
Estados Unidos llakillapi	The United States was in pain
Torres gemelas rupariptin	When the Twin Towers burned
Kausay infierno sufrimiento	A life of hellish suffering
Imapa kausampi Estados Unidos	What fault had the United States
Yawar mayupa chawpillampi	To be amidst a river of blood
Imapa kausampi Estados Unidos	What fault had the United States
Yanqaña rupaypa chawpillampi	To be amidst such fire
Injusticia sucia del mundo	What dirty injustice in the world
Desigualdad sucia del mundo	What dirty inequality in the world

FUGA

Yuyariya runakaskaykita	Remember that you are human
Yachaqtukoq kaskaykita	You who think you know all
Mundo del egoismo sucio	A world of dirty egoism
Mundo destruido por el hombre	The world destroyed by man

3. "Osama Bin Laden"

Written and performed by Alcones de Wamaqo de Cayara ("Falcons of Mt. Wamaqo of Cayara"), February 2002.

Osama bin Laden nispam runakunallas	People say that Osama bin Laden
Osama bin Laden nispam runakunallas	People say that Osama bin Laden
Enterullay naciontas mancharichimullan	Frightened the whole world
Chayllay tragediallay	With that tragedy
Iskaynin torrella tumbaykullaptinsi	With the fall of the two towers
Llakipiña tarikun wiraquchakunapas	The world's leaders were found in sadness

Chayllay tragediawan	With this tragedy
Umallantas raqchachkan	They are shaking their heads
Estados Unidos masiñallataqsi	Fellow people of the United States
Estados Unidos nacion llañataqsi	The people of the United States
Maskarawañas lluqsimun	Have come out with masks on [i.e., "with an attitude")
Challay barbasapata tarimusun nispa	Saying, we are going to find that bearded one
Chayman qinañataqsi Osama bin Laden	For that reason, Osama bin Laden
Habas ukuyllataña mandaykullasqaku	has sent fava bean farts [i.e., "explosives"]
Estados nacionman	to the States
Tayta Dios ninchikpa kastigunmi nispa	Saying it is God's punishment
Kachay kullasqaku	He let loose
Once de septiembre wata dos mil unutas	The 11th of September, of 2001
Once de septiembre wata dos mil unutas	The 11th of September, of 2001
Llapa apurunapas waqastillan purisqa	All the rich walked along crying
Chayllay llakillawan	With that tragedy
Manas puñuyllapas chayas qallachu	They couldn't sleep
Llapa gringotaqa	All of the gringos
Manas churillantapas qunqarqullasqañas	Unable to forget their children
Chayllay vidapiqa	That's how life was
Chaynachu manachu Hermanos Fajardinos	Is that so or is it not, brothers Fajardinos
Chaynachu manachu Hermanos Fajardinos	Is that so or is it not, brothers Fajardinos
Peru nacionllanchita afectaramullan	It affected our nation, Peru
Supa mankanchiktapas deqarqullarsunña	To the point that we've neglected our own issues
Miskiy puñuyllatapas manasa tarisunchu	We won't find sweet dreams
Chaysi kunanmanta cuentata qukusun	We must realize that from now on
Chilewan Brazilsi qikutakamuchkan	Because Chile and Brazil are hurrying up
Avion guerrallawan qariqarikachkan	Thinking they are big men with war planes

4. *"Tragedia en Norteamerica" ("Tragedy in North America")*

Written by Antonio Fernández Rodríguez and Raida Huamaní Gonzáles, performed by Nuevas Voces de Hunacapi ("New Voices of Huancapi"), February 2002.

Ima watach karqa año dos mil uno	What a year 2001 was
Ima killach karqa once de septiembre	What a month, the 11th of September
Estados Unidos nacionllapipas	In the United States
Iskay avionlla estrellarunampaq	Two planes crashed
Estados Unidos llaqtallapipas	In the United States
Torres gemelas wichiykullanampaq	In order to fell the Twin Towers
Wiraqucha Bushsi katkatataspa	President Bush trembled
Ustu kachasqa kaynaman waknaman	Moving about from here and there
Chaynama papayta pasarqa nispa	"It happened like this to my father," he said
Segunda guerrapi kallpachira nispa	"He had to run in WWII," he said
Chaynama papayta pasarqa nispa	"It happened like this to my father," he said
Segunda guerrapi katkatachira nispa	"He was scared in WWII," he said
Wiraqucha Bushsi embajadapi	President Bush, in the embassy
Rimanakuykuspa hukllataña piensasun	Thought and acted at once
Bin Ladenllata prisionamuy nispa	"Bin Laden must go to jail," he said
Llaqtanta wasinta bombardeyay nispa	"His country and home will be bombed," he said
Bin Ladenllata prisionamuy nispa	"Bin Laden must go to jail," he said
Llapan tropanta chinkachimuy nispa	"His troops must be eliminated ["disappeared"]," he said
Bin Ladenñataq contestamunsi	Bin Laden answered:
Kayllay liderman igualawaqchu nispa	"Are you my match as a leader?" he said
Chinkarusaqmi wañurusaqmi	"I will disappear, I will die," he said
Llapan burguesta chinkarachispay nispa	"eliminating ["disappearing"] the bourgeoisie"
Wañurusaqmi chinkarusaqmi	"I will disappear, I will die," he said
Capitalistata chinkarachispay ninsi	"eliminating the capitalists."
Llapallan gringos maskallawachkan	All of the gringos are in search of me
Poder ninchiktas chinkachinqa nispa	"Our power may disappear," they say
Llapallan gringos maskallawachkan	All of the gringos are in search of me

Apukayninchiktas chinkachinqa nispa	"Our wealth may disappear," they say
País pobrella qaykapikama	Poor countries, to what point
Explotado kasun Estados Unidoswan	will we be exploited by the United States?
Bolsas de valores bajaramullaptin	When stocks are down
Llapan dolarpas congelados kachkan	and all dollars are frozen?

Ima llakillach kayllay llakiqa	How painful is this suffering
Enteru mundupas tristellañas kachkan	There is sadness all over the world
Afganistanllay llaqtallapipas	In Afghanistan
Llaparunatas prisionarullanku	They have taken everyone prisoner
Estados Unidos carcel llapipas	In a U.S. jail
Prisionerokunas torturasqa kachkan	The prisoners are tortured
Chullachullamantas qurqumullachkan	Taking them out one by one
Fusilasqaña wañullachun nispa	Killed by firing squad, they say

FUGA

Umaykiya barbasapa	Your head, bearded one
sunquykiya chawar barba	your heart, stringy beard
Wawakunas waqallachkan mikuymanta	Children cry from lack of food
Runamasikis wañullachkan yarqaymanta	Your people are dying of hunger

Huk nacionman ayqiruspa	You escaped to another nation
Pastollataña mikuchkanku cuy qina	They are eating grass, like guinea pigs
Wiksallaykipi manaña kaptin	When there is nothing in their bellies
Barba sapa chawar barba	Bearded one, stringy beard
Pichqa watayuq wawakunapa, francotirador	Even five year olds are snipers

5. "Waqay Vida Llaki Vida" ("Life of Sadness, Life of Tears")

Written and performed by Santa Rosa de Huancaraylla, February 2002.

Hermanullay paisanullay yuyallachkanchikmi	Brothers, countrymen, we remember
Hermanullay paisanullay rikullarqanchikmi	Brothers, countrymen, we have seen
Enterullay continente Americanapi	In the entire American continent
Waqay vida llaki vida pasakullasqanta	A life of sadness and tears has been passing
Chayllay iskay jatun wasi wichiykullasqanta	Those two towers have fallen

Waranqantin runamasinchik chinkaykullasqanta	Thousands of people have disappeared
Chaynallataqsi hermanullay Lima capitalpi	In the same manner, our brothers in the capital of Lima
Chaynallataqsi paisanullay Mesa Redondapi	In the same manner, our countrymen in Mesa Redonda
Waqay vida llaki vida pasarqukullasqa	A life of sadness and tears has been passing
Hermanullanchik paisanullanchik	Our brothers, our countrymen
ninapi chinkarquptin	have disappeared in the fire
Waqay vida llaki vida pasarqukullasqa	A life of sadness and tears has been passing
Hermanullanchik paisanullanchik	Our brothers, our countrymen
ninapi chinkarquptin	Have disappeared in the fire
Yantallachum paqpallachum kallanmankukarqa	As if they were firewood or cabuya
Yantallachum paqpallachum kallanmankukarqa	As if they were firewood or cabuya
Ninallapa chawpillanpi uchpa yanankupaq	In the midst of the fire, they were reduced to ashes
Ninallapa chawpillanpi uchpa yanankupaq	In the midst of the fire, they were reduced to ashes
Enterullay centro Limas wichqakuykullasqa	All of the center of Lima was closed
Enterullay centro Limas wichqakuykullasqa	All of the center of Lima was closed
Wawallankuta churillankuta maskaspankuriptin	While boys and girls
Mamallankuta taytallankuta manaña tarispa	searched in vain for their parents

FUGA

Vidallanchik rantinallakanman	If we could just purchase our lives
Suertellanchik cambianallakanman	If we could just change our fate
Vidallanchik rantinallakanman	If we could just purchase our lives
Suertellanchik cambianallakanman	If we could just change our fate
Iskay kimsata rantirullaspanchik	We would buy two or three
Toda la vida kausakunanchikta	To live a full life
Iskay kimsata rantirullaspanchik	We would buy two or three
Wiñay wiñay kausakunanchikpaq	We would live eternally
Avionllay avion de guerra	Little plane, war plane
Avionllay avion de guerra	Little plane, war plane

Kutirimuspa apakullaway	Turning around, take me back
Vueltarimuspay pusakullaway	Turn around and return
Manasa mamallay kanchu	I no longer have my mother
Manasa taytallay kanchu	I no longer have my father
Maypiraq churiy nispa ninampaq	Who will say, "Where is my son?"
Maypiraq waway nispa ninampaq	Who will say, "Where is my daughter?"

REFERENCES

Appadurai, Arjun. 1996. *Modernity at Large: Cultural Dimensions of Globalization*. Minneapolis and London: University of Minnesota Press.

Appiah, Kwame Anthony. 2006. *Cosmopolitanism: Ethics in a World of Strangers*. New York and London: W. W. Norton and Co.

Baiocchi, Gianpaolo. 2002. "Media Coverage of 9-11 in Brazil." *Television and New Media* 3(2): 183–89.

Butler, Judith. 2004. *Precarious Life: The Powers of Mourning and Violence*. London and New York: Verso.

Cloonan, Martin. 2004. "Musical Responses to September 11th: From Conservative Patriotism to Radicalism." In *9/11—The World's All Out of Tune. Populäre Musik nach dem 11. September 2001*, edited by Dietrich Helms and Thomas Phleps, 11–32. Bielefeld, Germany: Transcript Verlag.

Comision de la Verdad y Reconcilición (CVR). 2003. *Informe Final de la Comisión de la Verdad y Reconciliación* (9 volumes). Lima, Peru: CVR.

Didion, Joan. 2003. *Fixed Ideas: America Since 9.11*. New York: The New York Review of Books.

Friedman, Thomas. 2005. *The World Is Flat: A Brief History of the Twenty-First Century*. New York: Farrar, Straus and Giroux.

Gorriti, Gustavo. 1999. *The Shining Path: A History of the Millenarian War in Peru*. Chapel Hill: University of North Carolina Press.

Gutiérrez Sanín, Francisco, Eric Hershberg, and Monica Hirst. 2002. "Change and Continuity in Hemispheric Affairs: Latin America After September 11." In *Critical Views of September 11: Analyses from Around the World*, edited by Eric Hershberg and Kevin Moore, 177–90. New York: The New Press.

Helms, Dietrich, and Thomas Phleps, eds. 2004. *9/11—The World's All Out of Tune. Populäre Musik nach dem 11. September 2001*. Bielefeld, Germany: Transcript Verlag.

Hershberg, Eric, and Kevin Moore. 2002. "Introduction: Place, Perspective and Power—Interpreting September 11." In *Critical Views of September 11: Analyses From Around the World*, edited by Eric Hershberg and Kevin Moore, 1–19. New York: The New Press.

Lincoln, Yvonna. 2003. "Grief in an Appalachian Register." In *9/11 in American Culture*, edited by Norman Denzin and Yvonna Lincoln, 63–66. Walnut Creek, CA: Altamira Press.

Lomax, Alan. 1968. *Folk Song Style and Culture*. New Brunswick: Transaction Publishers.

Mayer, Enrique. 1991. "Peru in Deep Trouble: Mario Vargas Llosa's 'Inquest in the Andes' Reexamined." *Cultural Anthropology* 6(4): 466–504.

Palmer, David Scott, ed. 1994. *Shining Path of Peru*, 2nd ed. New York: St. Martin's Press.

Piot, Charles. 1999. *Remotely Global: Village Modernity in West Africa*. Chicago and London: University of Chicago Press.

Poole, Deborah, and Gerardo Rénique. 1992. *Peru: Time of Fear*. New York: Monthly Review Press.

Post, Jennifer. 2006. "Introduction." In *Ethnomusicology: A Contemporary Reader*, edited by Jennifer Post, 1–15. New York and London: Routledge.

Ritter, Jonathan. 2002. "Siren Songs: Ritual and Revolution in the Peruvian Andes." *British Journal of Ethnomusicology* 11(1): 9–42.

———. 2003. "Cantando se recuerdan: Historia de una música testimonial." *Cuestión de Estado* 32: 80–82. Lima, Peru: Instituto de Diálogo y Propuestas.

———. 2006. "A River of Blood: Music, Memory, and Violence in Ayacucho, Peru." Ph.D. diss., University of California, Los Angeles.

Roseman, Marina. 2000. "The Canned Sardine Spirit Takes the Mic." *The World of Music* 14(2): 115–36.

Rubio, Luis. 2002. "Terrorism and Freedom: An Outside View." In *Critical Views of September 11: Analyses from Around the World*, edited by Eric Hershberg and Kevin Moore, 61–71. New York: The New Press.

Stern, Steve, ed. 1998. *Shining and Other Paths: War and Society in Peru, 1980–1995*. Durham and London: Duke University Press.

Turino, Thomas. 2000. *Nationalists, Cosmopolitans, and Popular Music in Zimbabwe*. Chicago and London: University of Chicago Press.

Vargas Llosa, Mario, Abraham Guzman Figueroa, and Mario Castro Arenas. 1983. *Informe de la comision investigadora de los sucesos de Uchuraccay*. Lima: Editora Peru.

Valdivia, Angharad. 2003. "What Is Over? Ruminations from One Who Has Already Lived Through Another September 11th." In *9/11 in American Culture*, edited by Norman Denzin and Yvonna Lincoln., 95–98. Walnut Creek, CA: Altamira Press.

Waterman, Christopher. 1990. "'Our Tradition Is a Very Modern Tradition': Popular Music and the Construction of Pan-Yoruba Identity." *Ethnomusicology* 34(3): 367–79.

Žižek, Slavoj. 2002. *Welcome to the Desert of the Real*. London: Verso.

NOTES

1. This and all other song texts in the essay have been translated by the author from originals in Quechua. The two verses excerpted here were the second and third verses of this song; see the appendix for a complete transcription.

2. "Glocalization," like "globalization" itself, first emerged as a term in the business world, where it referred to multinational corporations' practice of creating products that could be tailored to distinctly local and/or regional tastes. Academics today generally use the term in the opposite sense, as I have here, privileging the act of local appropriation, or as ethnomusicologist Jennifer Post has recently put it, emphasizing "how the global conforms to local needs through an historical process that bypasses and subverts hierarchies of power" (2006: 7).

3. The quoted phrase is taken from the introduction to John and Jean Comaroff's edited collection *Modernity and its Malcontents* (1993: xi), which lays out in much more extensive fashion some of the ideas about globalization and modernity referenced here; see also Appadurai (1996) and Piot (1999).

4. In addition to Hershberg and Moore's insightful collection (2002), the journal *Television and New Media* dedicated an entire issue (vol. 3, no. 2) to documenting and analyzing media coverage of 9/11 around the globe.

5. As Yvonna Lincoln notes in her work on the reception and meanings of 9/11 in rural Appalachia (2003), one needn't even cross national borders to find the kinds of cultural difference that affect readings of such terms.

6. Luis Rubio discusses these sentiments as "outsider" perspectives on 9/11 and the ensuing "war on terror" (2002: 61–65); Valdivia references them with respect to Chile (2002); Baiocchi for Brazil (2002); and Gutierrez et al. for Colombia (2002).

7. See, for instance, Helms and Phleps, eds., 2004.

8. I thank David Harnish for information on Indonesian shadow-puppet performances related to 9/11. Personal communication, January 2004.

9. Music, as a nonlinguistic mode of communication, is more open than most sorts of cultural texts to be read (heard) from afar and found meaningful, and a great deal of insightful scholarship is being produced today exploring how musical texts travel and acquire new meanings. Rather than an argument against the need for ethnography, however, I see this as a critical justification for it; if musical texts and performances always find their meaning in local circumstances, we need more attention than ever to those circumstances, be they where the music is first produced (my concern here) or where it is last heard.

10. The most authoritative and exhaustive account of the Shining Path conflict is contained in the final report of the Peruvian Truth and Reconciliation Commission (CVR 2003). Other important works in English that provide a good overview include Poole and Rénique 1992; Palmer, ed. 1994; and Stern, ed. 1998.

11. I explore the early history of these contests and their radicalization by the Shining Path in much more extensive form in Ritter 2002; 2003.

12. A. Quispe, interview with author in Ayacucho, 17 May 2000.

13. The songwriter quoted is Carlos Falconí, a prominent musician in the Ayacuchan *wayno* scene and author of some of the most powerful testimonial music of the 1980s. Further information on testimonial music, both *pumpin* and *wayno,* is contained in Ritter 2006.

14. Some aspects of this debate even made it into the North American press; see David Gonzalez, "Lima Street Vendors Caught Between Police and Poverty," *New York Times,* 6 January 2002.

15. Mayer provides a useful definition of "structural violence" as the term is understood in Peru, referring to "poverty, abuse, discrimination, racism, and arbitrariness and/or indifference by the state" (1991: 473).

16. The formation of the Truth Commission was first proposed by interim president Valentín Paniagua, who had been appointed president by the Peruvian Congress after the flight of former president Alberto Fujimori in November 2000. The actual appointment of the commission and initiation of their work took place under Paniagua's elected successor, Alejandro Toledo.

17. "Voces de Colca" is a venerable institution in the region, first formed in the late 1970s by the founder of the Waswantu song contest (who wishes to remain anonymous). Dozens of young women have passed through the group's ranks as singers, and it has recorded numerous commercial cassette tapes of *pumpin* music. In fact, due to this "professional" status, at the time of my fieldwork Voces had been banned from further competition in the song contests due to complaints from other groups, and had grudgingly settled for the prestige of performing an "exhibition" set as an honored guest. Consequently, the group (including me) did not compete that weekend, but did perform at every contest.

18. This is an excerpt, verses three through five out of a total of eight, from the uncharacteristically long song.

19. See the appendix for a complete transcription and translation of all five songs.

20. *Cabuya* is a type of large yucca plant, also referred to in Quechua as *paqpa,* whose broad spines are often dried and used for firewood.

21. Enrique Mayer provides a thoughtful deconstruction and critique of the Vargas Llosa report in his 1991 article for *Cultural Anthropology,* noting many of the report's inconsistencies and oversimplifications with regard to *comunero* (peasant) culture in northern Ayacucho.

22. The song was performed by the group Naranjitas de San José de Sucre. I thank Joshua Tucker for providing me with the DVD of the Waswantu contest from which this lyric was transcribed. The existence of a DVD of this contest for sale in Lima is, of course, further evidence of the continuing interpenetration of foreign, mass market technologies, and the always-local cultural phenomena that fill them with meaning.

9

EXPLODING MYTHS IN MOROCCO AND SENEGAL:

SUFIS MAKING MUSIC AFTER 9/11

Larry Blumenfeld

Why is music called the divine art, while all other arts are not so called? We may certainly see God in all arts and in all sciences, but in music alone we see God free from all forms and thoughts. In every other art there is idolatry. Every thought, every word has its form. Sound alone is free of form. Every word of poetry forms a picture in our mind. Sound alone does not make any object appear before us.

—**Hazrat Inayat Khan**[1]

It would be nice to think that, in the war against terror, our side, too, speaks of deep philosophical ideas; it would be nice to think that someone is arguing with the terrorists and with the readers of [Islamic philosopher] Sayyid Qutb. But here I have my worries. The followers of Qutb speak, in their wild fashion, of enormous human problems, and they urge one another to death and to murder. But the enemies of these people speak of what? The political leaders speak of United Nations resolutions, of unilateralism, of multilateralism, of weapons inspectors, of coercion and non-coercion. This is no answer to the terrorists. The terrorists speak insanely of deep things. The anti-terrorists had better speak sanely of equally deep things.

—**Paul Berman**[2]

The disconnect between last Tuesday's monstrous dose of reality and the self-righteous drivel and outright deceptions being peddled by public figures and TV commentators is startling, depressing. The voices licensed to follow the event seem to have joined together in a campaign to infantilize the public. . . . The unanimity of the sanctimonious, reality-concealing rhetoric spouted by American officials and media commentators in recent days seems, well, unworthy of a mature democracy.

—Susan Sontag[3]

The attacks of September 11, 2001, took place on the second day of the second week of the fall academic semester at Columbia University. At the time, I was a member of a small group of National Arts Journalism Program Fellows in Columbia's Graduate School of Journalism. In our weekly discussion groups, my colleagues voiced an acute awareness of the vast gray areas of identity and intent that seemed all but negated by the black-and-white posturing of politicians and media commentators immediately following 9/11. Among these lost fields of nuance were the complicated modern history of American military and other involvement in Iraq, Saudi Arabia, and throughout the Middle East; the volatility of the Israeli-Palestinian standoff and the withering of a once-promising peace process; the vastly different ways contemporary events and empirically verifiable historical facts are perceived in the West and the Middle East; and the diversity of opinion within both the United States and the Muslim communities abroad regarding the 9/11 attack itself and what constituted an appropriate response. Susan Sontag stirred controversy with her short essay in *The New Yorker* for her refusal to call the terrorists "cowards," perhaps a questionable choice on her part. But she was accurate in her portrayal of public voices that, in their unanimity and the simplicity with which they framed the event and its aftermath, appeared to stifle intelligent, open, and complex discussion of the issues at hand.

In discussions among the Columbia Fellows, one point repeatedly emerged: the roots of many of the problems underlying the standoff between radical Islamic fundamentalists and Western governments can be traced to deep and longstanding cultural rifts. This assertion led to the group's general conclusion regarding the current global impasse—namely, that cultural solutions had a chance to succeed where other means had not.

Such success would appear to hinge on the ability of both sides to look beyond the stereotypes that condition their perception of the other. Among the more powerful Western stereotypes—and one this essay seeks to interrogate—is the widespread belief that music is anathema to Islamic practice. This stereotype, which was reinforced by the post-9/11 increase in news reports about the Taliban's infamous anti-music policies in Afghanistan, ignores the central role music has always played in the mystical Islamic tradition of Sufism.[4] In fact, two of the most striking musical responses to 9/11 to come from Muslim nations were inspired by Sufi practices and thought: the Fez Festival of World Sacred Music, along with its offshoot colloquia and 2004 Spirit of Fez U.S. tour; and the recent career of Senegalese singer and bandleader Youssou N'Dour. In both instances Muslim performers used music to emphasize interfaith dialogue and understanding, and as such presented a powerful alternative to dominant Western images of Islam. In so doing, these musical events served as a sane, antiterrorist expression of the sort of "deep things" Paul Berman envisioned in the epigraph above, but emanating from a Muslim source. A close look at these two responses challenges our received wisdom concerning the Muslim world and its attitudes toward the West.

UP FROM MOROCCAN SOIL

The Fez Festival of World Sacred Music grew out of initiatives that predate the World Trade Center attacks by nearly a decade. The festival, launched under the patronage of Morocco's King Hassan II and currently enjoying the support of King Mohammed VI, is on one level a top-flight bazaar of the various musical expressions that accompany spiritual traditions, a nonpareil "world music" event. Entertaining as this has proved to be, the music has also provided a window into the deeper agenda of the festival's organizers: to encourage dialogue among different faiths in order to move toward a more enlightened approach to globalization.

The festival (and my experience of it) must be understood within the context of its setting. Among the oldest of Islamic holy cities, Fez, Morocco, has been a center of learning since two women founded Qaraouine University in the ninth century. It boasts a powerful history of tolerance: when Muslims and Jews were expelled from Spain in the fifteenth century, many immigrated to Fez. It is a city of remarkable contrasts, in which Internet cafes are tucked between ancient fortresses and donkeys pull carts past metered taxicabs. Like much of Morocco, Fez is a cultural crossroads, in which men and women in traditional djellabas (hooded robes) walk alongside teenagers in designer jeans.

Morocco is ruled by a monarchy, but its constitutional reforms and civil society stand in contrast to most Islamic states. Sufism, the mystical humanist face of Islam, is represented in Fez by the many brotherhoods active there. Embodied as it is in the tenor of both daily life and high-level policy making, the Moroccan Sufi spirit is akin to the voice of liberalism here—a force for moderation and inclusion.

Faouzi Skali, a Fez native and Sufi scholar, first initiated a film festival in the wake of the 1991 Gulf War. He dubbed it the Desert Colloquium, after Desert Storm. "At the time, all of our cultures were in great conflict, largely through the media," Skali told me in a 2002 interview. "I wanted to initiate a direct dialogue between peoples and cultures, not through the news media."[5] The first festival included several concerts of Sufi music, and the enthusiastic response generated by these performances convinced Skali that music could be a more potent tool for the type of exchange he sought to foster. "Music seemed more elemental," he explained, "and it got around barriers of language. It was no longer a question of what you thought or didn't think. It was a direct experience of the Other." Skali's comment echoes the Sufi mystic Hazrat Inayat Khan's idea regarding the exalted qualities of music, expressed in the first epigraph to this essay, and focuses their application to the problem of communicating across cultures in the incendiary political environment of the 1990s.

Beginning in 2000, Skali expanded his event to include "Fez Encounters," colloquia that spanned five mornings. These discussions, held in a dramatic museum courtyard, were punctuated with the trays of traditional mint tea that are ubiquitous in Morocco. When I attended the Fez Encounters in the Spring of 2002, just eight months after the 9/11 attacks, the tea's sweetness contrasted greatly with the mood of many of the academics, artists, authors, and nongovernmental officials in attendance. The French publisher Jean-Claude Petit spoke of access to spirituality as a "fundamental right" which had been somehow contorted in the post-9/11 world. Trinh Xuan Thuan, a Vietnamese-born astrophysicist, speculated on the roots of terrorism. James Parks Morton, an American minister, described an emergent vocation of "interfaith practitioners," a job description that, he argued, would soon enter common parlance in direct response to the post-9/11 political and social situation, much as the terms "psychotherapist" and "social worker" grew familiar in the wake of Freud's writings and of industrialized, urbanized societies. More recently, the annual Fez Encounters discussions have included among their participants the then-Prime Minister of Senegal Idrissa Seck as well as the Brazilian Minister of Culture (and celebrated singer-songwriter) Gilberto Gil. The smooth transition between these discursive colloquia and the musical performances that were the festival's most public manifestation helped solidify the relationship between the sharing of sacred musical traditions and the search for a new mode of political dialogue. That synergy of purpose was highlighted through the short musical interludes that preceded the commentary and roundtables, and was perhaps complicated when, once or twice, a discussion paused in deference to the muezzin's call to prayer.

Each evening after the colloquia's conclusion, I would wander through the dark, labyrinthine alleys of the city's walled Medina quarter, moving from one performance to the next. In Morocco, as in much of the Islamic world, exteriors can be deceiving. Stories are told, wealth and depth revealed, through interiors. Among the palaces hidden from street view in Fez's Medina is the Moqri Palace, with its intricate mosaic tiles and lovely courtyard. This was the setting for extended performances by various Sufi brotherhoods which held both sacred and secular appeal: teenage boys clapped wildly and danced as members of the Jilala brotherhood played wooden flutes, beat hand drums, and offered bent-toned chants into the early morning hours. Around the corner, another hidden treasure of a site, the Fez Hadara, hosted still more nightly performances, some of which extended the festival's emphasis on expressions of shared spirituality; one evening, for example, a drama enacted a communion between Moroccan and Senegalese Sufis. Though the singing and drumming styles of the Senegalese musicians sounded distinct from their Moroccan counterparts, the two groups related a single narrative, of Islamic roots in Senegal dating back to the eleventh century, and of important Senegalese connections to the Moroccan Tijani brotherhood forged in the early nineteenth century.

In addition to music from the Arab world and sub-Saharan Africa, the Festival featured a broad range of musicians from other continents. Free concerts of several of these groups were held at Bab Boujloud Square, just outside the Medina, and these drew throngs of local residents, many of whom could not afford the ticketed events. However unfamiliar the music may have sounded, audience members danced, clapped, and cheered as if it were their own. When the McCollough Sons of Thunder, a gospel-based brass band from Harlem, performed, audience members literally threw one another into the air in gleeful celebration. "Don't you feel it?" shouted out Elder Babb, the group's charismatic leader. The crowd cheered in response, never questioning Babb's specific reference.

I gained a more personal understanding of the efficacy of music as a tool to bridge cultural and religious rifts a year later, when I flew to Casablanca on my way to the 2003 Fez Sacred Music Festival just three weeks after terrorist bombings shook Morocco. Everywhere were public-service billboards bearing the Hand of Fatima—a symbol of protection for Muslims, Jews, and Christians. Scholars and cab drivers alike told me that the slogan, in Arabic and French—"Don't lay a hand on our country"—was directed at terrorists and fundamentalist Muslims. In my hotel room on my first night back in Fez, I was startled awake by the 3 a.m. muezzin's call to prayer, issuing from mosque minarets in all directions. I realized that I'd heard this before, right down to the vocal embellishments, from the Sephardic cantor in my childhood Brooklyn synagogue. Prior to that moment, I'd grasped intellectually music's ability to serve as a conduit connecting traditions; I'd witnessed such communication in Bab Boujloud Square as elsewhere. But when this awareness touched my identification with my own life and my home, when it happened on an unconscious level, the possibility that music could effect a broader cultural transformation seemed ever more real.

"THE SPIRIT OF FEZ" IN AMERICA

In 2004, the Fez Festival organizers decided to broaden their audience and attempt to reach Americans in their own backyards. The North American Director, Zeyba Rahman, an Indian-American woman of Sufi descent, organized an eighteen-city U.S. tour dubbed "The Spirit of Fez." As she explained in an interview at her Brooklyn, New York, home in 2005, "It was an effort to bring the message of the Moroccan festival directly to the hometowns of American audiences. On one level, we knew that this would be seen as a 'world-music' event with a mission underlining it. But on another level, we saw this as a way to translate the context and spiritual power that the music and its connected issues take on in Fez, and to transform otherwise neutral performance venues."

Rahman was correct in her assessment that the "Spirit of Fez" festival would be promoted and reported on chiefly in the customary contexts for so-called "world music"—as an eclectic aesthetic choice and/or as sociological and anthropological enrichment regarding "exotic" cultures. But, following the example set by Faouzi Skali in Fez, she had deeper ambitions: to create a visceral sense of interfaith sentiment and of enlightened global dialogue, and to transplant this seed to familiar American venues. When the "Spirit of Fez" tour convened in Washington, D.C., at the Coolidge Theater of the Library of Congress, for example, its main concert brought a multinational group of musicians and peace activists together with Moroccan dignitaries and officials of the World Bank. The Bank, an important sponsor of the event, clearly believed that its promotion of capitalism dovetailed with the festival's most overt raison d'etre—to develop a world-class venue for an eclectic collection of music performances. But the "Spirit of Fez" tour was also designed to spawn panel discussions at each venue modeled after Skali's colloquia, to "stimulate similar conversations in the West."

These conversations fused with the musical performances to produce fertile cultural exchanges that sought to bridge the painful cultural rifts of the post-9/11 world. Terrance Grace's impressionistic short film *Sawt-e-Sarmad: The Sound That Intoxicates Man*, which preceded and contextualized each concert, presented images of Sufis chanting and musicians singing intercut with talking heads of politicians and religious leaders, conflating the two endeavors. A quote from Rumi's Sufi devotional poetry appeared onscreen, then dissolved: "We have fallen into the place where everything is music."

The Washington, D.C., concert was opened by Gabriel Meyer, an Argentine-born rabbi's son, performing in a duet with recent U.S. immigrant Yacoub Hussein, the Palestinian son of a Sufi sheikh. As the two interwove Hebrew and Arabic calls to prayer, Meyer passed his frame drum to Hussein, scarcely missing a beat. The Algerian Jewish vocalist Françoise Atlan combined the strained intensity of Andalusian melismatics and the graceful purity of European plainsong through stunning renditions of fifteenth-century devotional songs. She was accompanied by the Moroccan oud master Farid El Foulahi, and the Lebanese-American percussionist Jamey Haddad. Hadra des Femmes de Taroudant, from a small village in southern Morocco, sat on a riser, singing folkloric wedding and funeral tunes while beating out complex patterns on small hand drums. After a short solo by Haddad, the Anointed Jackson Sisters, whose leader, Barbara Jackson, referred to the group from the stage as "just some country girls from North Carolina," demonstrated the dramatic range of African-American spirituals, ending with the raucous "God Is in the Building."

Commodified though it may be in our culture, music convinces in ways that tuneless words and beatless ideas cannot. That is the spirit of Inayat Khan's epigraph, and it is an idea that is in some ways put to the test by an event like the "Spirit of Fez" tour: can music drawn from diverse spiritual traditions, performed in languages foreign to the audience, still hold the visceral power it enjoyed in its original contexts? And more provocative, is it possible that this music communicates its purpose better, in fact, because it is removed from specific reference? That was certainly my impression at the Coolidge Theater, where the closing number, sung in Hebrew, Arabic, Spanish, and English successively by all of the evening's performers, capped an evening of touching collaborations and virtuosic performance. The stage, hopelessly overcrowded, became a metaphor for tolerance in a world where religions vie dangerously for dominance.

"It's one thing to march in a protest," Meyer told me in an interview after the concert. "But we also need spiritual activists. One thing that Western audiences sometimes need to be reminded of is the fact that it is important to have art rooted in transformation and healing in addition to art rooted only in aesthetics. The people who write treaties in Geneva are usually disconnected from the local indigenous cultures. I hope we can reach people at the level that CNN cannot touch, a level that exists before and after thought."

Despite the deep feelings of cross-cultural communion that concerts like this engendered, the "Spirit of Fez" tour was not free from the strain of political pressures. "During the buildup to the Iraq invasion, the Library of Congress expressed interest in the show," recalled Jean-Jacques Cesbron, the Columbia Artists Management agent responsible for booking the tour, during a 2004 telephone interview. "But they were concerned about the use of the word 'peace' in the materials." And after 9/11, it became so prohibitively difficult for Middle Eastern males to enter the United States that these concerts highlighted women as voices of Islam, which itself became a provocative element, for both non-Muslim audience members (whose assumptions may have been challenged) and Muslims (many of whom are sensitive to both the travel-restriction issues and the sight of women performing music in public).

The 2004 tour, which stretched from Orono, Maine, to Savannah, Georgia, to Berkeley, California, encountered no protests. And it stimulated dialogue of the sort not generally associated with world-music presentations. At Harvard University's Paine Hall, prior to one concert, an afternoon panel discussion included Dr. Diana Eck, head of the Pluralism Project, and Director of the Center for the Study of World Religions, along with religious leaders drawn from Islamic, Jewish, Christian, and interfaith centers. Discussion focused on the following questions: What are the fundamental differences between your religion and those of the other panelists and what are the similarities? Why is it that religion causes conflict? Is there something about religious faith and fervor that causes war? As wars between religions, cultures, and nationalities rage, what gives you hope?

On its face, the "Spirit of Fez" tour fits into a model of world-music presentation that is increasingly popular at universities and nonprofit performing arts centers. According to this model, world music is presented, not as exotic sounds for consumption, but as a vehicle for an alternative, "non-Western" ethics.[6] The U.S. tour, like the Moroccan festival it is drawn from, brought to bear music as a transformative and healing element connected directly to an expression of Islam that is at odds with the stereotypes common in post-9/11 America—namely, that Islam is governed by an essentially exclusionist and antimodern ideology that enables and even encourages terrorism. If this goal was achieved at all, it occurred on a nonliteral level. But the second element of the tour and festival, the colloquia it stimulated, functioned along the lines of most American arts-in-education models, using the music as springboard for dialogue—in this case, that which had been largely shut out of our political and media discourse.

TAKING A STAND IN SENEGAL: YOUSSOU N'DOUR

If you don't know where you're heading anymore, go back to where you came from.

—**Youssou N'Dour, "Wiri Wiri"**[7]

Had this man not shown up . . .

Islam would have sunk with shame into oblivion

Since religious people were being

Killed or deported by the colonialists

Their goal was to weaken Islam. . . .

Your knowledge and understanding are immense

You taught me tolerance and compassion.

—**Youssou N'Dour, "Shukran Bamba"**[8]

While the Fez Festival represents an organized, communal expression with Sufism at its core that preceded the 9/11 attacks and took on a deeper significance after them, the recent career of Senegalese singer Youssou N'Dour (Figure 9.1) is marked by a more direct and deeply personal response to 9/11, one informed in part by the performer's embedded (perhaps even, to some, hidden) roots in Sufism. To grasp the purpose and depth of N'Dour's responses to the tensions between the United States and the Islamic world, it is essential first to gain a sense of his career to date. N'Dour has been a star in his native Senegal for more than half his life. He has traveled widely during the past two decades, earning acclaim in Europe and the United States. But while his ballooning popularity in the West has greatly increased his mobility, N'Dour has remained connected to his native Dakar, where he still lives. And his music, however far and wide it has ranged in style and in reach, still speaks first and foremost of his home.

N'Dour's sinewy tenor, his dazzling vocal melismas, and his urgent, engaging lyrics (which frequently deal with issues of social responsibility and cultural memory) have become the face of *mbalax* (pronounced "um-balak"), the Senegalese popular music that blends centuries-old praise-singing and percussion traditions with

Figure 9.1 Youssou N'Dour. Photo by Galilea Nin, courtesy of Nonesuch Records.

Afro-Cuban arrangements and guitar-based Western pop. The band N'Dour has led since 1979, The Super Etoile, has held sway over Senegalese fans since its formation. They are widely considered to be among the most exciting African bands to hear in concert—a blend of rhythm, voice, and message that can be appreciated without translation.[9]

N'Dour had been issuing cassettes on Jololi, his Dakar-specific label, to the consistent pleasure of his Senegalese fans for twenty-five years, when he unexpectedly broke through to a much broader international audience, in large part due to his singing on Peter Gabriel's 1986 hit "In Your Eyes." N'Dour's 1990 release, *Set* (Virgin) earned him a reputation as "the next Bob Marley," a purveyor of an infectious type of "roots music" that would soon sweep across the globe. Others saw him as the good-looking poster boy for the nascent "world music" wave that swept international markets in the late 1980s. In fact, he was both and neither. "My music is like a spinning ball," N'Dour told me in an interview in New York in 2004. "It can turn in one direction, and then it comes back to origins."[10]

N'Dour's music is an amalgam of old and new, indigenous and foreign. He sings mostly in his native Wolof, with an occasional chorus in French. The instruments on his recordings have ranged from talking drum (a staple of Senegalese music) to electronic drum loops and synthesizers. Jimi Mbaye, the Super Etoile's lead guitarist, plays a Fender Stratocaster, but often plucks its strings in a style that sounds more like a *xalam* ("khaa-laam"), the Senegalese folk guitar. The music's jumpy six-beat rhythms and soaring, syncopated vocals simultaneously evoke ancient call-and-response refrains as well as contemporary calls to the dance floor. N'Dour's lyrics are heartfelt and traditional, his songs about basic things—the need for hard work, respect for women, love of god and of fellow man—and about more complicated issues, such as political struggles over electrical service in Dakar, or the need to remain connected to one's home. 1990's "Set"—meaning "clean" or "pure" in Wolof—was a motivating cry for young Senegalese to clean up their environment and to demand "transparency" in politics and business.

N'Dour likes to say that he wishes to motivate Western listeners to a new view of his native continent. "In spite of the images that one knows about Africa, the economic poverty," he told me in 2001, "there's a joy to living and a happiness in community, living together, in community life, which may be missing here in America. And I think America can learn from that."

In the aftermath of 9/11, and of the American invasion of Iraq, N'Dour's messages—bolder and more pointed than ever—have grown in their precision and potency for his Western audience. It would be difficult to think of a contemporary musician who has blended the personal and the political, the secular and the sacred, with greater depth and sensitivity in the period following 9/11.

In the spring of 2003, N'Dour cancelled what would have been the most ambitious U.S. tour of his career, in protest of the impending American invasion of Iraq. The statement publicly issued from N'Dour's "head office" to the press was heartfelt and nuanced:

> It is my strong conviction that the responsibility for disarming Iraq should rest with the United Nations. As a matter of conscience I question the United States government's apparent intention to commence war in Iraq. I believe that coming to America at this time would be perceived in many parts of the world—rightly or wrongly—as support for this policy, and that, as a consequence, it is inappropriate to perform in the U.S. at this juncture.[11]

"I know that I'm not Bruce Springsteen," N'Dour told me some months later during a telephone interview. "But it was a symbolic statement I wanted to make. I didn't make the decision simply because there was a war mounting against a Muslim country. I did it because the war that was mounting was unjust."

Even more profound, if less direct, was the statement made by N'Dour's 2003 CD, *Egypt*. As ethereal and exotic as this music may sound to the casual listener, it needs to be heard as a courageous personal pronouncement in a troubled and confusing time, a musical engagement with the emerging anti-Muslim stereotypes emanating from the West. Senegalese Islam is largely Sufi; through his original compositions for this album, sung in Wolof, N'Dour celebrated the caliphs, saints, and sages of his Sufi faith, "in order to praise the tolerance of my often misunderstood religion," he told me. The project began as a private thing, a recording N'Dour made for his friends and family to celebrate his faith and to combine Senegalese musical elements with the ouds, violins, and flutes N'Dour remembered from the recordings of Egyptian singer Umm Kulthum that his father used to play.

With *Egypt*, N'Dour offered a document of his introspective pilgrimage to the heartland of Sufi culture in his own country.[12] The compositions on *Egypt* marry Senegalese rhythmic, melodic, and harmonic elements with arrangements from the repertoire of Egyptian and Arab orchestral sound. Recording with traditional Senegalese instrumentalists and singers in Dakar and Fathy Salama's sparkling Cairene Orchestra, *Egypt* references the historical link between the great seats of Islamic learning to the North and West Africa's outposts of Sufi thought. With the album, N'Dour built a symbolic bridge from sub-Saharan Africa to the continent's Arabic north. And he fashioned a corrective pronouncement about Islam directed at the whole world designed to counter the stereotype of Muslims as exclusionist fundamentalists bent on destroying all traces of modernity.

As N'Dour explained to both the BBC and Al-Jazeera in interviews, "*Egypt* is an album which praises the tolerance of my religion, which has been badly misused by a certain ideology. At a time when there is a debate on Islam, the world needs to know how people are taking over this religion. It has nothing to do with the violence, with terrorism."

"I think that Sufism fits all over the world," N'Dour told me in 2005. "The concept is not anything that fits standard Western ideas; it's always related to culture, to music, to religion. It is a dominant religion in Senegal. The music that it creates calls into question the idea that the Muslim religion is only a matter for Arabs—that it belongs only to the Arabs. In the West, you have always associated the Islamic faith 100 percent with Arab culture. This in itself is a fundamentalist attitude and is mistaken."

N'Dour went further in a statement he wrote in the program book for the American live premiere of his *Egypt* project at Carnegie Hall in October, 2004:

I would be happy if this album, and our performances throughout America, could serve as a gateway toward knowledge of the real face—or faces—of our faith, of Islam. The Muslim world—like the Jewish and Christian communities worldwide—is remarkably diverse, as an aggregation of geographies, peoples, cultures, and social and religious practices. A billion Muslims live their faith in a billion ways, probably.

In Senegal, we live as Muslims in a certain way, defined by, and nourished by, our several Sufi turuq [Arabic for 'ways' or 'pathways']. These communities of believers trace their spiritual legacies back to the great Sufi masters of the eleventh to the nineteenth centuries, but they have evolved in a modern West African environment where religion fits hand-in-glove with daily life, politics, and the rest. So it is this 'Senegalese way' of Islam, and I prefer to say 'of Muslim culture', which we are presenting with the songs of Egypt.

"'Duty' and 'art' almost always go poorly together," N'Dour continued:

But there are exceptions. Desperate times call for—not desperate, I'm sorry—but noble measures. Rabbi Hillel, who was evidently the same kind of teacher as the shaykhs I celebrate in the songs of Egypt, famously said in the *Pirkei Avot*: 'If I am not for myself who will be for me? If I am for myself alone, what am I? If not now, when?' So who better than Muslim artists to assume a kind of duty now—to protect Islam, and all the beautiful cultures of Islam, from its slanderers at both poles of the malicious, ignorant, ideologically inane morass of speech which passes for a 'dialogue of religions' in these challenging times?

Like most non-Western musicians who have enjoyed the spotlight and exposure of status within the "world music" community, N'Dour has straddled many identities. He is a pop singer and the front man of a band that plays rhythmically intense, danceable music (often with choruses that are catchy enough to transcend language barriers). He is an attractive and articulate media presence who helped create a veritable "Afropop" industry. And he has blended these roles with his inherited responsibilities as a griot to become a forceful political voice on issues of African, and, in recent years, global concern.

When he cancelled his American tour in the face of the American invasion of Iraq, N'Dour called up both recent and distant memories for his American audience: the many American performers who boycotted South Africa in the 1980s in protest of apartheid; or how Louis

Armstrong caused a stir in 1957 when he rebuffed President Eisenhower and canceled a U.S. State Department tour to the Soviet Union because of riots in Little Rock, Arkansas, over school integration. Moreover, N'Dour identified sub-Saharan Africa with the Arab-centric image of Islam in the West, announcing his solidarity and challenging American ideas. With *Egypt*, N'Dour took a further step. He personalized the issue, exposing himself and even taking career risks (*Egypt* is not the sort of music his American or African fans were necessarily hungering for) and attempted to tap the musical core of his Sufi faith to speak his mind.

It is worth noting that N'Dour brought his *Egypt* tour to eight American venues during the Muslim holiday of Ramadan. Shortly after his first tour stop, at Carnegie Hall, I asked N'Dour whether there was special meaning to this timing. "It's very interesting," he replied. "There was a big debate on Senegalese radio. With professors, Islamic leaders, musicians and rappers—about making music and performing during Ramadan. I'm sorry, but I don't remember reading anywhere that you can't play music after sundown during Ramadan. People like me have decided to ask ourselves, 'Why?' Maybe we'll do something different. Maybe it is time to do some things differently."

CAN VOICES CARRY?

With his Sufi sensibilities, N'Dour has contributed a thoughtful voice to the highly charged multinational discourse on the cultural rift that divides the post-9/11 world, one that criticizes both the United States for its militarism in Iraq and the Muslim world for its tolerance of militant fundamentalism, while simultaneously pointing the way toward a more nuanced understanding of Islam. The Fez Festival, too, contributes to this project, moving both music and discourse beyond the boundaries of commemoration and political outrage.

These expressions harness two very different forces with potential to transcend borders and beliefs: ancient modes of Sufi (and in N'Dour's case, Senegalese griot) expression, and the contemporary frame of world-music communication. On both levels, they offer potential and purpose to alter the prevalent frame surrounding U.S.-Islam relations. Whether these sane voices emanating from the Muslim world will inspire similar calls for tolerance on either side of the vast cultural rift that so troubled my colleagues and me in Columbia in 2001 is an open question. How deeply they stimulate positive dialogue and how far they reach beyond enlightened entertainment will depend on how success-fully they drown out national anthems and fundamentalist calls. In the meantime, however, the music and talk coming from N'Dour's Dakar and Skali's Fez continue to ring with the promise of reconciliation and the potential to shatter myths that are at the root of much misunderstanding in the post-9/11 world.

ACKNOWLEDGMENTS

This essay owes deeply to the wisdom and guidance of two editors, Robert Christgau and Jeanne Carstensen, to the passion of one publisher, Alecia Cohen, to essential knowledge shared by Zeyba Rahman and Thomas Rome, and to pianist Randy Weston, who first pointed me toward Morocco.

NOTES

1. Hazrat Inayat Khan, *The Mysticism of Sound and Music: The Sufi Teachings of Hazrat Inayat Khan,* Boston: Shambala Publications, 1996, 1.
2. Paul Berman, "The Philosopher of Islamic Terror," *The New York Times Sunday Magazine,* 23 March 2003.
3. Susan Sontag, "The Talk of the Town," *The New Yorker,* 24 September 2001.
4. At a public discussion I moderated, "Music in the Islamic World Today," hosted by the Brooklyn Academy of Music in connection with a presentation of Sufi music, I asked panelist Peter J. Awn, professor of Islamic Religion and Comparative Religion at Columbia University, to frame Islamic attitudes about music and the influence of Sufism on this issue. He commented as follows: "It's true that in Islam, there is a historical ambivalence toward music. But if you look at the origins of Islam what you find front and center is recognition of the power of sound. The Koran itself is a collection of sounds. So where does the ambivalence about music come from? It's in how this power of sound is managed by individuals who hear it. Music without text or music with poetry has the power to raise all sorts of emotions that conservative elements find dangerous. Not to say that music per se is bad, but what does it do to emotions? Sufism as it evolves in Islam recognizes this power and enhances it for exactly the same reason, saying, "Look, this is a unique avenue to explore, and if we put it within the proper context of spiritual practice it can be an essential if not critical means of achieving the goal of mysticism, which is union with God. Islam in its extraordinary cultural diversity has had an ability to take classical forms and embed them within the local context. Historically, a main entrée into local cultures has been the power of Sufis. Sufis tended to be much more willing to embrace local practices. Sufism is the bridge for a whole range of philosophical traditions and cultural traditions, especially into Asia, and music, adapted and influenced by local

cultures, has been a primary vehicle." (BamTalk: Music in the Islamic World Today" was held 7 May, 2005 at the Brooklyn Academy of Music's Hillman Attic Studio. In addition to Professor Awn and myself, the participants included the musicians Hassan Hakmoun and Rashid Ahmed Din, and Fez Festival of World Sacred Music North American Director Zeyba Rahman.)

5. Portions of my interviews with Faouzi Skali, Gabriel Meyer, and Jean-Jacques Cesbron appeared in "Weapons of Mass Sedition," *The Village Voice*, 30 March 2004, 29.

6. In his 2004 review of the tour, for example, critic Jon Pareles referred to it as "Part concert tour, part peace mission." Jon Pareles, "Songs of peace, from many perspectives," *New York Times*, 8 March 2004.

7. From the song "Wiri Wiri," on N'Dour's 2000 album *Joko: The Link*, Nonesuch 79612-2. Original lyrics in Wolof, English translation contained in the liner notes.

8. From the song "Shukran Bamba" on N'Dour's 2004 album Egypt, Nonesuch 79694-2. Original lyrics in Wolof, English translation contained in the liner notes. Lyrics reprinted with the permission of African Broadband Broadcasting.

9. Note, for instance, Kalefa Sanneh's review of a Youssou N'Dour concert in New York in 2005, in which he wrote, "To a crowd full of non-Wolof speakers, Mr. N'Dour's devotional music might sound an awful lot like dance music; sometimes ecstasy translates more clearly than piety. (As it happened, Mr. N'Dour had played an exhilarating set of dance music—the mbalax songs that first brought him fame—the night before, in Zankel Hall, with his band, Super Étoile.)" Kalefa Sanneh, "From a Senegalese Superstar, an International Hybrid of Music Inspired by Islam," *New York Times*, 28 October 2005.

10. Portions of my interviews with Youssou N'Dour appeared in "Not Your Father's Ramadan," Salon.com, 26 October 2005.

11. Youssou N'Dour issued this statement regarding the tour cancellation as a media advisory on March 7, 2003, through African Hypertext, his U.S. management company.

12. N'Dour's musical engagement with Sufi themes was complemented in 2005 by his pilgrimage to Fez, Morocco, during which he visited sites of historical importance to his Sufi roots and performed the music of *Egypt* at the Festival of World Sacred Music.

10

CORRIDOS OF 9/11:

MEXICAN BALLADS AS
COMMEMORATIVE PRACTICE

John Holmes McDowell

In the immediate aftermath of the terrorist attacks of September 11, 2001, the makers of Mexican ballads known as *corridos* created a rich body of narrative songs commemorating and commenting on these events. In this essay, I examine these "9/11 *corridos*" and the dynamics of their cultural production in a zone of what I term "commemorative practice," taking note of stylistic and functional features that link this specific corpus to the larger *corrido* tradition, and ascertaining the range of attitudes they express toward the events of 9/11 themselves. I propose that we regard the 9/11 *corridos* as mediated ballads of mass communication, performed on a global stage and addressing issues of international consequence, a far journey from their point of origin as local ballads responding to matters of primarily local and regional interest.

Remarkably, these ballads of global commentary evince a broad stylistic fidelity to the contours of the genre in its previous and more restricted orbits, indicating the staying power of a sung verse-narrative matrix that has persisted over the centuries and across oceans and national boundaries. *Corrido* makers, or *corridistas*, express a variety of attitudes toward 9/11, suggesting that the process of commemoration as practiced in this unofficial and noninstitutional venue is open to competing formulations of shared memory. I see in the emergence of 9/11 *corridos*, then, the appropriation of a familiar expressive resource, the *corrido* itself, in an effort to try out interpretations of calamitous events deeply affecting the general public. My objective is to pinpoint the role of commemorative song in this interpretive process, with regard to both timing and function: At what stage do these songs enter the picture? And what is accomplished in this medium by virtue of properties inherent to the song tradition itself?

THE REALM OF FOLK COMMEMORATION

Folklorists and ethnomusicologists, by the very nature of what they study, have a useful perspective to offer on the variety of public reactions to the devastating events of September 11, 2001. In the immediate aftermath of the attacks, and in the ensuing weeks and months, people in the United States and elsewhere drew on traditional models to craft verbal, material, and musical responses across a range of mostly casual and unofficial communications, a realm I will refer to as "folk commemoration." Expressive forms at the core of our disciplines—songs, stories, legends, jokes, and artistic displays—clearly played a prominent role in such commemoration during the painful adjustment to a post-9/11 reality, and our subjects of study and expertise consequently gained a new relevance and importance.[1]

We are now at a sufficient distance from 9/11 that we can begin to obtain some perspective on the sequence of these public responses, from early moments when the wound was raw, to the present, when it has partially healed (at least for those of us who experienced its events from a distance). It was amply apparent even in the initial aftermath of 9/11 that a variety of traditional expressive forms, ranging from the ludic through the ceremonial to the reflective, were being employed in many communities to sort through powerful emotions and sift for viable shoots of meaning. Informal discourse was a crucial venue; in conversations and electronic exchanges among friends and family, stories were being shared—of miraculous escape, of unfortunate fatality, of mundane activities interrupted—that began to shape the interpretive frames within which the events would be understood and remembered more broadly.

In this mix of popular artistic responses, the arena of commemorative song has not yet received the attention it merits, particularly in areas beyond the pop music mainstream. Songs that tell a story, such as ballads, of course have a long and intimate connection to newsworthy events in the annals of oral tradition. Typically, I think, their purpose is not so much to narrate the event in the manner of the "reporter on the beat," but rather to assess and communicate its deeper meanings.

This was certainly the case with many musical responses to 9/11, which tended to minimize descriptions of "what" had happened in favor of emotional appeals, and in doing so played a vital role in shaping and testing public perceptions of how the attacks should later be commemorated and collectively remembered. The Spanish-language *corrido* recordings released in the United States and Mexico in response to 9/11 were a distinctive part of this repertoire of popular music responses, speaking to and for a particular segment of the (North) American populace, and as such offer a compelling window into the process of individual and collective commemoration through song.

The first *corridos* dealing with 9/11 began to appear on the airwaves in northern Mexico and the southwestern regions of the United States within weeks of the attacks, reaching their collective peak during the final months of 2001. My inventory is by no means complete, but based on the materials in my possession, including cassette and CD recordings released on both sides of the border, as well as journalists' reports and Web sites documenting the phenomenon, I estimate that a dozen or more 9/11 *corridos* were in general circulation by December of 2001, of which perhaps a half-dozen received significant attention from popular music audiences in both Mexico and the United States. This tally does not include more informal or local compositions that failed to register in the public record, and there were no doubt a good many of these.

Commercial 9/11 *corridos* emerged primarily from the two popular music zones along the U.S./Mexico border, what we might call the *western axis* running from the Mexican states of Colima and Sinaloa northward into Los Angeles, California, and the *Tex-Mex axis* running from Monterrey, in the state of Nuevo León, northward into San Antonio, Texas. As a consequence, one could hear 9/11 *corridos* in the jaunty western style of *banda* music and in the melodious *conjunto* style typical of *norteño* and the Tex-Mex sound.[2] In addition, some of these *corridos* were performed in an old-timey string-band style, rounding out the variety of musical idioms employed in these recordings. According to press accounts, 9/11 *corridos* enjoyed airplay in some areas from mid-October 2001 into February of 2002 and beyond. These accounts paint a picture of a veritable 9/11 *corrido* craze in such cities as Monterrey, Laredo, San Antonio, and Los Angeles during this time, with people seeking out tapes and CDs and requesting these songs on their favorite radio shows.

FROM THE LOCAL TO THE GLOBAL CORRIDO

The composers and musicians who created this stock of *corridos* drew on a ballad genre that is practically atmospheric in Mexico, utilizing a platform for social commentary that has accompanied Mexican history since at least the middle of the nineteenth century (Paredes 1993). The *corrido* is the traditional ballad of Mexico, a faithful companion to the Mexican people as they have created their history as a nation, and as they have wandered north across the border with their powerful neighbor in search of jobs and adventure. *Corridos* are performed by *trovadores* and *juglares*, popular composers and musicians, in settings both private and public, in *conjuntos* or ensembles ranging from a singer with guitar to full-scale mariachis and brass bands. *Corrido* singers launch tuneful melodies on major-key progressions (with the exception of Mexico's Costa Chica, where some *corridos* are in minor keys) shifting from tonic to dominant and back to tonic, sometimes with the insertion of a strophe moving to the subdominant as well. Meters can be duple or triple, in full or cut time, and instrumental interludes punctuate the singing of verse stanzas, which is often done in sonorous two- or three-part harmony.

Corridos render the experiences and the ideals of Mexicans as they have weathered revolution, government corruption, migration, the immigrant life, violence stemming from the drug business, and most recently, the scourge of international terrorism. Taken as a whole, this balladry is a remarkable chronicle of Mexican history told from the vantage point of the common man and woman. In villages, towns, and cities of the Mexican homeland, and in near and distant outposts across the northern borders, *corridistas* and those who perform their songs commemorate notable events in the taut poetry and sweet sonority of this traditional ballad form.

The scope of *corrido* production and consumption has always been primarily local and regional, but moments in the history of the genre foreshadow the kind of global commentary that manifested itself in the 9/11 songs. During the Mexican revolution (1910–30), hack poets and journalists tuned into the stories reaching the cities to churn out ballads by the dozens (Tinker 1961; Paredes 1993). These journalistic ballads emanated for the most part from Mexico City publishing houses in the form of broadside sheets (*hojas sueltas*), often with striking woodcut designs, and were mass-produced and sold at marketplaces throughout the nation (Figure 10.1).

The broadside *corrido* typically tells its tale through descriptive verse, but often closes with a moral framing the narrative as exemplary, or attaches a sentimental tag that can touch on the maudlin. Some of this production reads as a schematic account of events, much like the conventional news report in the papers, with the moral or sentimental conclusion tacked on at the end. Musical scores are rare, but the

Figure 10.1 "Versos de Valentín." FG0099 Mexican Popular Prints 099-019-0099. Courtesy of the Center for Southwest Research, University Libraries, University of New Mexico.

broadsides often carried instructions to sing the song according to a specific well-known tune.

The truly global *corrido*, as evidenced in the 9/11 corpus, did not fully emerge until the advent of the necessary mass communications infrastructure. While *corridistas* commented on international events in some of the broadside *corridos* distributed during the Mexican revolution, and on occasion in subsequent decades, with several songs

Homenaje
al
Mártir de la
Democracia
•

Grabación 221

Homenaje
a
John F. Kennedy

Letra y Música de José A. Morante

Como homenaje sincero
canto su vida y su muerte
del hombre que el mundo llora
porque fue un gran Presidente.

Kennedy tuvo la dicha
de demostrar su valor
en la guerra que pasara
el año cuarenta y dos.

Fue comandante de un barco
en las islas del Oriente;
nunca soñaba que un día
llegara a ser Presidente.

Anduvo por todo el mundo,
no hubo enemigo capaz
de atentar contra la vida
de este gigante de paz.

En la Alemania cautiva
sobre el cercado se vio
brindarle un gran homenaje
por la esperanza que dio.

México le abrió sus brazos
como a ninguno jamás;
y Kennedy hizo justicia
regresando el Chamizal.

Kennedy se vino a Texas
y a San Antonio llegó,
entre homenajes y fiestas
a su pueblo conquistó.

Iba por Austin y Houston
a saludar su nación
porque era grande de todo
sobrado de corazón.

El 22 de noviembre,
no se me podrá olvidar,
porque sin causa o razones
su destino fue fatal.

En Dallas se le esperaba,
lo grande de la ocasión;
nunca hubo presentimiento
de una horrorosa traición.

En su carro iban su esposa,
y el señor Gobernador;
los dos iban saludando
cuando un balazo sonó.

Alzó los brazos al cielo
sin saber qué le pegó;
se oyó otra bala certera
y el Presidente cayó.

Su fiel esposa al momento
con su cuerpo lo cubrió,
y al señor Gobernador
la otra bala le pegó.

Esta es la historia más negra
que al mundo entero enlutó
cuando la vida de un grande,
un asesino truncó.

Derechos de Autor Reservado.

Figure 10.2 "Homenaje a John F. Kennedy" *corrido* broadside by José Morante. Reprinted with permission of the Center for Mexican-American Studies, University of Texas at Austin.

addressing episodes in the Second World War, for instance, a new plateau was reached with the slew of *corridos* released in the southwest of the United States in the early and mid-1960s commemorating the life and death of John F. Kennedy (Figure 10.2). The assassination of Kennedy, a great hero among Mexican-Americans, stimulated the production and broadcast of some seventeen different *corridos* in a variety of styles, ranging from folk to literary; these were recorded in Houston, San Antonio, Austin, and smaller cities of the Rio Grande valley, as well as in Los Angeles, Miami, and Mexico City (Dickey 1978).

Not coincidentally, the Kennedy *corridos* emerged at a moment when the tools of mass communication had become widely accessible, even in areas of ethnic marginalization. According to Dan Dickey, in the decades following WWII, a homegrown commercial music industry developed in the American Southwest:

> In the 1950s and 1960s, because of the greater availability of local recordings of *conjuntos*, the influence of Mexican records and radio, and because of the increasingly higher economic status of most Mexican Americans, Spanish language radio stations began broadcasting in many communities in South Texas. . . . These stations were outlets for the local recording companies' products (1978: 19).

Dickey further notes that "many *corridistas* themselves started their own recording companies in Texas to produce their own *corridos* as well as to record commercially-profitable *conjuntos*" (1978: 20). As a consequence, *corridistas* had wider access to recording studios to cut and produce their 45rpm singles and radio stations catering to a Chicano listening public gave them airtime, responding to the wishes of their growing audience. In short, the *corrido* of greater Mexico had become a vehicle of mass communication, attaining a wide audience across a large swath of the Spanish-speaking United States.

The public-speaking platform for social and political commentary that was consolidated in the popular Kennedy songs was used repeatedly in following years, in *corrido* recordings that addressed the deaths of Martin Luther King Jr. and Robert Kennedy, and on other noteworthy events such as the moon walk, the Patty Hearst case, hurricanes and tornados, prominent homicides, and train wrecks (Avitia Hernández 1998). The 9/11 *corridos* signal yet another level in this extension of the *corridista*'s voice and audience, now speaking to a broad demographic that crosses the northern zones of Mexico and the American Southwest, and also includes people of Mexican origin or Mexican-American cultural identity throughout the rest of the United States and even into Canada. The *corridos* of 9/11 can be seen as successors to the Kennedy *corridos* in that they feature the *corridista* as social critic whose voice, expounding on events with resonance beyond the ethnic community, is projected to a mass audience through the medium of commercial recording and transmission.

I've indicated here that the 9/11 *corridos* fit within a certain trajectory of the genre as a site of broad political commentary over the last half-century, but a number of questions remain. How true to other conventions of the genre are these mediated ballads of global commentary?

Figure 10.3 El As de la Sierra's *Soy Ranchero* CD cover (2001). Reprinted with permission of Titan Records.

How are the events of 9/11 rendered or referenced in their verses, and what attitudes or positions about the attacks are revealed? And more generally, how does the medium of popular music contribute to ongoing processes of memory formation in the aftermath of cataclysmic events? In formulating a preliminary response to these questions, I argue that the 9/11 *corridos* are a legitimate manifestation of the genre and deeply implicated in a process of testing a master narrative of the events they address.

THE 9/11 *CORRIDOS*

I will focus here on five 9/11 *corridos* that offer trenchant responses to the tragedies of that day, beginning with a brief description of each and returning to analyze their texts in a more sustained manner (complete song texts for all five songs are contained in the appendix to this chapter).[3] This sample, while small, provides a reasonable cross section of 9/11 *corrido* production, including three examples that endorse, in varying degrees, what we might call the "official" story line as pronounced by leading politicians and the mainstream media in the United States in the aftermath of the attacks, as well as two examples that depart from this position to a greater extent.

The first *corrido*, "Tragedia en Nueva York," was composed and performed by El As de la Sierra (The Highland Ace), in September of 2001 on his CD and cassette *Soy Ranchero* ("I Am a Country Boy") (Figure 10.3).

El As, based in Los Mochis, Sinaloa, is characterized by music journalist Elijah Wald on his "Corrido Watch" Web page as "a hardcore

narcocorrido singer in the style of Chalino Sánchez," one of the found-
ers of the subgenre.[4] Wald reports that El As was in Los Angeles preparing a CD of *ranchera* songs when the planes struck the towers and
was able to add his take on the 9/11 events to that set of songs and get
them into production quickly. Wald speculates that El As may have
been trying to soften his image by producing a collection of songs that
do not deal with the drug business. In "Tragedia en Nueva York," he
depicts the 9/11 attacks as the beginning of the new century's first war,
noting the many deaths and wondering about the mentality of people
who would carry out such deadly acts. He names the Taliban as likely
suspects and, weeks before the invasion of Afghanistan, predicts the
destruction of their "country."

Filogenio Contreras and Lalo de la Paz are the authors of "Once
Negro" ("Black Eleventh"), the second *corrido* in our sample. Performed
by Los Estrellas del Bravo on their cassette *El Once Negro*, the song was
released in Monterrey, Nuevo León, about one month after the terrorist attacks. Contreras, who was sixty-nine years old at the time and is
based in Monterrey, has written hundreds of songs, including ballads
about California's Proposition 187 and about the murder of Selena, the
star singer from Corpus Christi, Texas.[5] He offered this explanation for
writing his 9/11 corrido:

> I want the people to hear my words, and in the world, wherever
> the music is heard, I want them to know that Mexico is lament-
> ing a lot, that everyone is lamenting the situation in which a lot
> of Americans, and so many people of different nations, including
> Mexicans, were killed.[6]

"Once Negro" makes note of the fact that the Twin Towers had been a
center of the global financial industry, and it includes vivid depictions
of the confusion and suffering brought about by the attacks, including a
striking metaphor of the seemingly solid towers collapsing like "castles
of cards."

José Guadalupe Paredes began writing his *corrido*, "El Terror del
Siglo" ("The Terror of the Century"), the third in our sample, just hours
after the 9/11 attacks.[7] According to a later story in the *Los Angeles
Times*, the ballad was recorded by Grupo Imperio Norteño at Discos
Acuario in Long Beach, California, and has a companion video including footage of the collapse of the Twin Towers. Paredes, fifty-eight years
of age at the time, had been a machine-shop worker at an aerospace
factory until illness forced him to retire. His *corrido* briefly depicts the
attack on the towers and warns in closing that the United States is now
surrounded by dangers on all sides.

Rigoberto Cárdenas Chávez, the author of our fourth *corrido*, "Bin Laden, el Error de la CIA" ("Bin Laden, the CIA's Mistake"), recorded by Los Soberanos del Norte, lives in the Mexican state of Colima and was thirty-nine years old when 9/11 occurred. In a Reuters report filed a month after the attacks, Cárdenas stated, "from when I saw the news on television, I began to write the words of a new song."[8] In contrast to the first three songs, his finds a measure of poetic justice in the attacks, and observes, philosophically, that the "most perverse of all creatures" is the human being. In this version of events, bin Laden, trained by the United States to commit acts of violence, eventually turns his tactics against his former teachers.

The final example, "El Corrido de Osama bin Laden" ("The Corrido of Osama bin Laden"), was composed and performed by Andrés Contreras, who is characterized by Elijah Wald on the "Corrido Watch" Web site as "the unofficial bard and *corridista* of the Zapatista rebellion." Contreras's song, self-recorded and distributed on cassette, takes a definitive stance against the United States, adopting the disdain toward Mexico's northern neighbor more typical of the border ballads documented and analyzed by the great *corrido* scholar Américo Paredes (1958; 1976). For example, in the song's preamble, Contreras resurrects the classic insult, *esos gringos patones*, "those big-footed gringos," a common epithet in the ballads of border struggle of the early decades in the twentieth century. He further spices his song with spoken interludes heaping scorn on the *pinches gringos*, "damned gringos," and praise on Osama and his associates. The final spoken segment concludes, with admiration, that Mexican heroes such as Francisco Villa and Joaquín Murieta, and even the Nicaraguan rebel Sandino, were less adept than Osama in exterminating gringos. Contreras, who calls himself *el juglar de los caminos*, "the bard of the byways," devotes most of the *corrido* to celebrating the scare that Osama has brought to the Americans, who, he claims, are receiving "in their house" the treatment they have meted out to others.

CONTINUITIES OF STYLE AND FUNCTION

In my recent study of *corridos* and violence on Mexico's Costa Chica (McDowell 2000), I discuss a set of stylistic features and functional roles that characterize the social aesthetic of the genre. Across time and space, *corridos* have retained an expressive profile marked by meta-narrative framing devices, vivid descriptive passages, and striking episodes of reported speech. These elements are implicated in a complex commemorative exercise involving three takes on the violence they address: celebration, regulation, and healing. Given the broader scope of their political content and the different sort of "community" they address, it is worth exploring whether (and if so, how) these stylistic and functional elements persist in the 9/11 *corrido* repertoire.

In terms of musical properties, they all fall well within the *corrido* tradition, marked by ¾-time, major keys, and melodies that ride a simple harmonic progression from the tonic to the dominant and back again, with an occasional stanza inserted that moves to the subdominant. Some are in a rapid ¾ time, as in El As's *corrido*, while others are slower; singing may be by a solo voice or, more often, two voices separated by thirds. Typically, the melody is covered between stanzas, in part or in full, by a lead instrument, usually accordion or guitar in the *conjunto* versions. All of these musical elements are standard in the *corrido* repertoire, and in this sample they persist across the shift from *banda* to *conjunto* to string-band arrangements.

In the poetry, too, we encounter the expected *corrido* elements. The verse comes in octosyllabic lines organized into stanzas of four, six, or eight lines, with rhyme or assonance occurring on the even-numbered lines. The composers remain rooted in the direct vocabulary of the *corrido,* and draw amply on the stock of traditional formulas and formulaic expressions that populate these ballads. As one expects, these authors have a story to tell, but they do not deliver it in a linear fashion. Instead, the narrative unfolds in a series of scenes that index and highlight a tale that is already known, in an effort to bring out significant patterns of action, attitude, and emotion. *Corrido* discourse, in general, is marked by the insertion of original formulations of fresh content into a largely traditional stock of conventional formulaic lines and phrases. Many formulas are scattered throughout the texts of these 9/11 ballads, giving their poetry the distinctive flavor of the *corrido.*

Setting the tone are the familiar opening and closing gambits, moments when the singer addresses the audience directly and acknowledges the performance framework itself. The traditional opening formula, in which the *corridista* announces his intent to sing the *corrido,* is curtailed somewhat in the 9/11 songs, as is common in commercially recorded *corridos* of recent years. However, "Tragedia en Nueva York" by el As de la Sierra makes a nod in this direction by including in the first stanza the imperative verb *miren,* "you (pl.) look," in the line *miren como empezó,* "look how it got started," which briefly acknowledges the fact of performance. A similar strategy appears in the famous "Corrido de Gregorio Cortez," the object of a seminal study by Américo Paredes (1958), which marks this metanarrative moment by the phrase, *miren lo que ha sucedido,* "look what has transpired."

Two of the *corridos* in our sample include a rendering of the closing formula, the *despedida* or leave-taking. One of them, "El Terror del Siglo," makes use of the conventional closer, *ya con ésta me despido,* "now with this I say farewell." El As de la Sierra delivers a more customized closing, with these lines:

Me da tristeza cantarles	It grieves me to sing to you
pero lo tenía que hacer.	but I just had to do it.

Numerous formulaic lines and phrases within the body of the narratives clearly signal a link to the larger tradition. El As de la Sierra, for example, periodically inserts the polite term of address *señores,* gentlemen, echoing a practice that has been standard since the days of the Mexican revolution, and he makes use of a typical formula for citing the day and time of the event:

Un martes negro, señores	It was a black Tuesday, gentlemen
las ocho quince serían.	it would have been about 8:15.

It is El As, as well, who draws on the emotive framing device, *no me quisiera acordar,* "I'd rather not remember," present in so many *corridos* at poignant moments in the narrative.

Throughout the corpus of Mexican and Mexican-American *corridos,* one finds a tendency to insert episodes of reported speech into the narrative, arguably to situate the listener in the midst of the action and thereby accentuate the drama of the moment. On this point, as with the less frequent use of framing formulas, the present selection of 9/11 *corridos* strike a slightly divergent posture. "El Corrido de Osama bin Laden," alone among our sample of five, makes conventional use of reported speech. Contreras employs this device twice in his *corrido,* once to heroic and once to comic effect. In the first instance, he has Osama offer money to those who will help him and pronounces his hopes of doing bodily harm to his enemies:

Decía Osama bin Laden	Osama bin Laden said
con millones en la mano:	with millions in his hand:
"Se los doy al que me ayude	"I give this to those who will help me
a matar americanos,	to kill the Americans,
con mis bravos mujaedines,"	with my brave mujahadeen,"
decía con voz en cuello:	he said at the top of his voice:
"No pierdo las esperanzas	"I have not yet lost hope
de cortarles el pezcuello."	of slitting all their throats."

We can note right away the play on the standard *corrido* formula, *con su pistola en la mano*, "with his pistol in his hand," chosen as the subtitle for the classic study by Américo Paredes (1958). Clearly Osama is a different kind of hero, one who wields loose money rather than handguns as his weapon of choice. This playful mood persists as the poet takes liberty with the word *pezcuello*, evidently a mixing of *pescuezo* ("neck") and *cuello* (also "neck"). Later in the *corrido* the humor broadens in an alleged conversation between George Bush and his wife, which turns on a near appearance of the word *culo*, "ass," which I try to capture in a rough English equivalent:

George Bush, bastante asustado	George Bush, very alarmed
le pregunta a su mujer:	inquires of his wife:
"¿Cómo le hago con bin Laden	"What can I do with bin Laden
que él ya nos pasó a torcer?"	who has already come to tweak us?"
Su mujer le contestó	His wife answered him
con bastante disimulo:	in a manner oh so sly:
"Vete para Afganistan	"Get you to Afghanistan
para que le des el cul ..."	so you can give him your as ..."
... pables son estos gringos	... suming the guilt are the gringos
de todo lo que les pasa ...	for all that happens to them ...

The authors of the remaining *corridos* in our sample find means other than reported speech to involve listeners in their narrative webs, for example by inserting vivid descriptive passages as well as striking images and metaphors. The descriptive power of the genre is present in this passage from "Once Negro," which evokes the "nightmare" of bodies hurtling toward the ground from the upper stories of the towers:

Parecía una pesadilla	It seemed to be a nightmare
mujeres y hombres llorando,	women and men were crying,
cuerpos envueltos en llamas	bodies wrapped in flames
por las ventanas saltando.	jumping out of the windows.

Earlier in the same *corrido* we encounter this telling image:

Once negro de septiembre	Black eleventh of September
del dos mil uno presente,	of the present year 2001,
como castillos de naipes	just like castles of cards
cayeron las gemellas potentes.	the powerful twins came down.

The first two lines of this stanza repeat a venerable *corrido* formula for conveying the date of a narrated event, while the two last lines offer a compelling metaphor comparing the falling towers to collapsing card castles.

These tactics, with their gritty evocation of experience and unfolding of imaginative vistas, connect us to the stylistics of the traditional *corrido* even as they mark the mass-mediated *corrido* as a distinctive branch of the tradition. This stylistic loyalty plays into the voicing of celebratory, regulatory, and therapeutic motifs, present to differing degrees in the 9/11 sample. *Corridos* have universally celebrated heroic action, resistance to tyranny, and forceful self-defense; this tendency to celebrate the resolve of history's underdogs pervades the *corrido* of Andrés Contreras and creeps into the others in the form of grudging praise for the authors of the attacks—even when they refer to these perpetrators as cowards! The regulatory process surfaces in repeated warnings to the effect that the exercise of violence has its consequences, whether desired or not. Here the theme of Osama bin Laden coming back to haunt the Americans seems especially poignant. The therapeutic tendency of *corrido* discourse abides in performance, in live or mediated venues, where their meditation on violence in sonorous tonalities has a potentially restorative effect.

These stylistic and thematic continuities enhance the commemorative impact of the 9/11 *corridos,* allowing them to powerfully evoke the past and propose tentative framings of its meaning. The literature on collective memory stresses the importance of the communicative medium; as Edward Casey has it, "[i]t is as if this past were presenting itself to me translucently in such media—as if I were viewing the past in them, albeit darkly: as somehow set within their materiality" (2000: 219). Felicitous commemoration draws most readily on familiar expressive forms whose presence seems necessary and whose purpose appears to be self-evident. There is, moreover, a ritual flavor to commemorative action, which adds solemnity to linkages with the past. The deployment of conventional verbal forms in a rich musical texture fuels the perception that events are being memorialized in natural and appropriate ways.

FORMULATING 9/11

The *corridistas* who have assumed the authority and responsibility to reflect on the events of 9/11 do not speak with a single voice. A range of orientations can be observed in this sample, falling into three main categories: those that enunciate some version of the official story

(Examples 1–3 in this chapter's Appendix); one that takes a more neutral stance (Example 4); and one that takes the side of those who attacked on 9/11 (Example 5). It is important to notice that although a range of positions is articulated, the weight of opinion leans decidedly toward the official story in the commercial releases. The contribution of Andrés Contreras, on the other hand, with its sympathy for the Taliban, was produced informally and consequently had only a limited release within local outlets. Among the commercially released songs, the ballad by Rigoberto Cárdenas is the only one that deviates in some respects from the official story by imputing some level of responsibility to the Americans. Even here, though, we should note that this *corrido,* performed in an old-fashioned style with acoustic guitars, comes across as the vernacular cousin of the slick productions emerging from the commercial recording studios.

What are the contours of this official story as replayed in the majority of 9/11 *corridos*? These narratives are framed as laments lodged in a world of black and white, of terrorists and victims—the Twin Towers are portrayed as beautiful (though fragile), the victims are innocents, the attackers cowardly, and the quest for vengeance is a natural and legitimate response by the injured party. The word *cobardes,* "cowards," resonates in this portion of the corpus as a verbal assault on the authors of the 9/11 attacks, as it did in speeches made by Western leaders in the days and weeks after September 11, 2001. This word and what it signifies, naturally, carry a particular sting in the heroic worldview of the Mexican ballad. Typical of this usage is this stanza near the end of the *corrido* by El As de la Sierra:

Los que iniciaron la guerra	Those who began the war
prepárense pa' perder,	should prepare themselves to lose,
el país de esos cobardes	the country of those cowards
puede desaparecer.	could completely disappear.

In "El Terror del Siglo," José Guadalupe Paredes accuses the *terroristas cobardes* "cowardly terrorists," of "leaving a terrible mark," and the authors of "Once Negro" mention *el cobarde atentado,* "the cowardly attack." The authors of "Once Negro" even go so far as to pronounce a bond of solidarity between Mexico and the United States; referring to a worldwide voice of outrage, they state that:

Mexico también se ha unido	Mexico has also joined the cause
sus dolencias ha dado	sending its condolences
al gobierno americano.	to the American government.

Expressions of solidarity with the neighbor to the north are hard to come by in the Mexican *corrido* repertoire, whose authors are far more likely to endorse the kinds of sentiments that exude from the voice of Andrés Contreras (Example 5). The sympathies expressed in this portion of the sample suggest a realignment of sentiment, with more people in the border regions now having a stake in what happens in the United States.

What messages are conveyed in those songs that depart from the official story? As already noted, "Bin Laden, el error de la CIA," proposes a more neutral reading of 9/11. In this ballad, composer Rigoberto Cárdenas Chávez makes little reference to the terrorist attacks. Instead, his attention is fixed upon bin Laden, characterized as a star pupil of the CIA:

La graduación con honores	The graduation with honors
con traición les ha pagado.	he has repaid them with betrayal.

Pursuing a theme that received much attention on the street if not from official outlets, Cárdenas presents Osama bin Laden as a product of CIA training, which is now targeted against its source. In keeping with the heroic tone of the traditional *corrido*, he proposes a heroic vision of the Taliban:

llevan a Dios por cobija	they carry God as their blanket
y se olvidan de su cuerpo.	and they forget about their bodies.

At this juncture, his *corrido* takes an interesting turn with parts of two stanzas and another full stanza addressing bin Laden in the second person, as if the *corridista* were in dialogue with him, a device utilized in a classic *corrido* of the Mexican revolution, "Siete Leguas," composed by Graciela Olmos as a paean to Pancho Villa's favorite horse (and an inquiry into his soul). Again, reflecting a habit of thought that is common in the tradition, Cárdenas refuses to stand in judgment of the controversial figure:

bin Laden a ti te culpan	bin Laden, it's you they are blaming
que la guerra has iniciado.	that you have started a war.

No soy Dios para juzgarte	I am not God to judge you
pero tendrás tus motivos.	but you must have your reasons.

Here the *corridista* signals his distance from conventional judgments and voices a grudging respect for a character whose behavior is outside the law. The *corrido* tradition favors those who stand against authority, which is customarily depicted as corrupt beyond repair. A genre forged in revolution, it readily embraces the bold hero, assimilating even bandits, outlaws, and drug dealers, to this heroic vision. In this regard, the *corridos* by Cárdenas and Contreras, framing Osama bin Laden in heroic terms, adhere most closely to the *corrido* ethic. The Cárdenas ballad concludes with these lines:

Por cielo, mar y por tierra	By air, sea and by land
Osama te andan buscando,	Osama they are looking for you,
bin Laden el terrorista	bin Laden the terrorist
la CIA te ha preparado,	the CIA has trained you,
ese fue el error más grande	that was the biggest mistake
del gobierno americano.	of the American government.

Once again the government of the United States is invoked, but in this instance the argument is more in keeping with the *corrido* heritage of expressing an adversarial relationship between the North American neighbors.

If Cárdenas skirts the official story, Andrés Contreras presents its antithesis. His *corrido* goes beyond the suggestion of poetic justice and argues explicitly that the gringos got what was coming to them. The mood is one of celebration rather than lamentation. Osama bin Laden is portrayed in the manner of the glamorous Mexican revolutionary, acting in good conscience to inflict pain on oppressive powers while cleverly foiling their attempts to corral him. Contreras holds that the gringos have only themselves to blame; the key moral construct appears in these lines:

Lo que ellos han hecho al mundo	What they have done to the world
se lo hicieron en su casa.	was done to them in their house.

The pain and suffering of the victims, the loss of innocent life, and the expectation of severe retribution related in the first songs are absent or reversed in this formulation of 9/11. For Andrés Contreras, it is the gringos—and specifically George Bush—rather than the attackers who tremble as they play the part of the *cobarde*.

UNFINISHED COMMEMORATIVE PRACTICE

I close by inquiring what contribution these popular ballads make to the processing of calamitous world events such as the 9/11 attacks. I see them as part of a larger arena of commemorative practice, ranging from stories and legends that emerge in the immediate aftermath of such events to the solid memorials and monuments placed on the landscape once a consensus has taken shape regarding their meaning. Within the informal, unofficial, or vernacular subset of this practice, a variegated terrain of traditional and popular expressive forms, the creation of commemorative songs occupies a distinctive niche, transitional both in regard to the permanence of the cultural artifact and the stability of the interpretive lens. The making of songs about disasters and calamities comes neither at the beginning of the process of memory formation nor at its end, but is positioned somewhere in the middle, since composing and singing songs presupposes some degree of prior processing but also signals an ongoing process of memory construction.

It seems probable that commemorative song has a distinctive role to play among the expressive resources employed for testing schemes of remembering in the aftermath of public tragedies like the 9/11 attacks. With exacting musical and poetic requirements, songs are not as quick to appear on the scene as casual stories, new or adapted legends, tendentious jokes, spontaneous shrines, and other conventional expressive forms closer to hand or more readily fabricated. At the same time, commemorative songs, with their sensuous acoustic properties and telling images, have the potential to reach people at a deep emotional level. As instances of fully realized commemorative discourse, such songs draw people into special realms of experience and profoundly shape their consciousness (McDowell 1992). The core features of this discursive mode are a highly patterned expressive medium and a deeply resonant message content. These features, working together, can create for performers and their audiences the illusion of moving beyond the ordinary into a realm of exalted reality.

It is this potential for transcendence, I believe, that bestows on these measured and allusive forms their essential role in processing the flux of actual events into the more or less steady constructions of social memory. Yet ballads launched in the aftermath of dramatic happenings and circulating in social gatherings or through the mass media are most likely to be contributions to a continuing dialogue, not definitive or final statements. They are fleeting rather than permanent memorials, composed in evanescent sound, not enduring stone and steel. Indeed, we can appreciate from this vantage point, now five years beyond 9/11, the ephemeral nature of these *corridos*, as they have faded from the active performance and listener repertoire. Still, even as I write this, I hear on a Spanish-language radio station out of Indianapolis a 9/11 *corrido* that I hadn't heard before, perhaps released on a recent CD, suggesting a recursive dimension to the treatment of global events in popular music, with successive waves of sung commemoration, each connecting to a different phase of memory processing. Moreover, we must allow that especially strong contributions may obtain a permanent place in the repertoire.

The 9/11 *corridos* illustrate very well both the special efficacy of sung commemoration and its imperfect character as memorialization of the past. In regard to the former, these *corridos* weave together descriptive, emotive, and interpretive elements to fashion a complex artistic response to their subject matter. Their musical and poetic profiles reinforce the perception of a significant encounter with truth. They draw their audiences into the narrative frame by inserting passages of reported speech or highly charged descriptive passages. Using such formulas as *no me quisiera acordar*, "I would rather not recall," the *corridista* dramatizes emotional involvement in the story. Memorable comparisons—the collapsed castle of cards in "Once Negro"—capture pivotal nuances of meaning. Judgments are delivered in propositions emanating from the *corridista* as chronicler of the human condition: the attackers are cowards, their deeds will be avenged, the gringos got a dose of their own medicine, the work of the CIA came back to haunt them. Elements of celebration, meditation, and therapy interact in this corpus to ensure its vitality as a locus of folk commemoration.

The presence of divergent interpretations underscores the location of the 9/11 *corridos* in a zone of unfinished commemorative practice. In such close proximity to the events they commemorate, they cannot be expected to achieve consensus, though they certainly work to move a population in that direction. It may well be that the *corridos* of 9/11, tilting as they do towards the official story (at least the more commercial versions), lend additional solidity to that master narrative. But we must not lose sight of the ever-present tendency of this genre to contest official stories. In our 9/11 sample, two *corridos* stake out independent positions, and even the three conformist *corridos* contain lines that hint at contrary sentiments, such as thinly veiled admiration for the cleverness or stoutness of the attackers.

On balance, it makes sense to view the 9/11 *corridos*, and much commemorative song in general, as located at the more formalized end of a spectrum of expressive forms deployed in the early phases of processing and constructing shared memories after cataclysmic world events. As examples of commemorative practice, these musical and poetic compositions enter an ideological setting that is already partly defined by other discourses, both official and unofficial. The moment is still early, and the situation still fluid, so different schemes of interpretation can be launched. The cache of commercial, mass-mediated songs is most likely to follow the contours of the official story, if our sample of 9/11 *corridos* is an accurate guide. In this guise these compositions may contribute to the hardening of the official story into a consensual store of memory. But the counterhegemonic potential of these genres is always lurking around the edges, and in the right circumstances, songs will emerge to challenge the official story and propose a different understanding of our collective history.

APPENDIX: 9/11 CORRIDO SONG TEXTS

Example 1. *"Tragedia en Nueva York"*

Composed and recorded by El As de la Sierra, on *Soy Ranchero*, Titan Records TNCD 9908 [CD], TNC 9908 [cassette], Sinaloa, Guadalajara, and Pico Rivera, CA, 2001. This new English translation is by the author, from the Spanish text in the CD lines notes. Lyrics reproduced with the permission of Titan Records.

La guerra ya comenzó	The war has now begun
en los Estados Unidos,	in the United States,
y miren como empezó	and look how it got started
con aviones dirigidos	with airplanes targeting
a esas torres tan hermosas	those two beautiful towers
el terrorismo ha surgido.	terrorism has reappeared.
No me quisiera acordar	I would rather not remember
de imágenes tan violentos,	those images so full of violence,
ni me quiero imaginar	nor do I wish to imagine
en cuanta gente está muerta,	how many people are dead,
de luto está el mundo entero	the entire world is in mourning
esto es inicio de guerra.	this is the beginning of war.
Que mentes tan criminales	How criminal those minds
o tal vez sean desquiciados,	or maybe just unbalanced,
de qué paises vinieron	from which countries did they come

estos planes tan malvados,	those plans so full of malice,
dicen que son Talibanes	they say they are Taliban
los que están involucrados.	the ones who are involved.
La primer guerra del siglo	The first war of the century
señores ya comenzó,	gentlemen, now has begun,
el que organizó el ataque	those who organized the attack
no sabe en que se metió,	have no idea what they got into,
el que resulte culpable	whoever turns out to be guilty
ay, pobrecita nación.	ah, I pity his poor nation.
Que planes tan estudiados	Such plans so carefully made
al secuestar cinco aviones,	to hijack five jet airplanes,
con dieciocho terroristas	with eighteen terrorists
hicieron operaciones,	they did their operation,
Washington y Nueva York	Washington and New York
el blanco de esos traidores.	the targets of these traitors.
Un martes negro señores	On a black Tuesday, gentlemen
las ocho quince serían,	it would have been eight-fifteen,
cuando en las torres gemelas	when against the Twin Towers
un avión estrellaría,	an airplane came to crash,
la gente se imaginaba	the people they were thinking
que un accidente sería.	it must be an accident.
La gente de Nueva York	The people of New York
sin saber lo que pasaba,	not knowing what it was,
mirando arder esa torre	watching that tower burn
otro avión se aproximaba,	another plane came in close,
como a los quince minutos	about fifteen minutes later
con la otra torre chocaba.	it crashed the other tower.
Me da tristeza cantarles	It grieves me to sing to you
pero lo tenía que hacer,	but I just had to do it,
los que iniciaron la guerra	those who started the war
prepárense pa' perder,	you'd better get ready to lose,
el país de esos cobardes	the country of those cowards
puede desaparecer.	could completely disappear.

Example 2. *"Once Negro"*

Composed by Filogenio Contreras and Lalo de la Paz; recorded by Los Estrellas del Bravo on their cassette *El Once Negro*, Mexico y su Música CLD-051, Centro Casetero, Monterrey, 2001. This new English translation is by the author, from the transcription of the Spanish lyrics.

Todo el mundo se estremece	All the world is trembling
con tristeza y ay, con dolor,	with sadness and ah, with pain,
al escuchar la noticia	upon hearing the announcement
por radio y televisión,	on radio and television,
derribaron las dos torres	they brought down the two towers
orgullo de Nueva York.	the pride of New York City.
Cuatro aviones comerciales	Four commercial airlines
secuestrados en las pistas,	kidnapped on the runways,
usados como misiles	employed just like missiles
por cobardes terroristas,	by cowardly terrorists,
la primera entra de centro	the first one comes straight in
la segunda hecha cenizas.	the second one turned to ashes.
Once negro de septiembre	Black eleventh of September
del dos mil uno presente,	of the present year 2001,
como castillos de naipes	just like a castle of cards
cayeron las gemellas potentes,	the powerful twins came down,
llevando miles de vidas	taking thousands of lives
de personas inocentes.	of completely innocent people.
Destrozaron las dos torres	They destroyed the two towers
bolsa y centro financiero,	center of financial markets,
el atentador no sufrió	the attacker did not suffer
otro atentado certero,	another well-aimed attack,
hubo muertos por doquiera	there were bodies everywhere
pero no como el primero.	but not like the first one.
Parecía una pesadilla	It seemed to be a nightmare
mujeres y hombres llorando,	women and men were crying,

cuerpos envueltos en llamas	bodies wrapped in flames
por las ventanas saltando,	jumping out of the windows,
otro avión en Pennsylvania	another plane in Pennsylvania
le falló en el cuarto blanco.	failed to hit the fourth target.
Todo el mundo enardecido	All the world inflamed
con coraje ha protestado,	with anger has protested,
México también se ha unido	México too has joined in
sus condolencias ha dado	and sent its condolences
al gobierno americano	to the American government
por el cobarde atentado.	for the cowardly attack.

Example 3. "El Terror del Siglo"

Composed by José Guadalupe Paredes; recorded by Grupo Imperio Norteño on an untitled cassette released by Cintas Acuario. This new English translation is by the author, from the Spanish original as posted on the "Corrido Watch" Web site (http://elijahwald.com/corridowatch.html).

Las predicciones locales	All the local predictions
ya estaba prognosticado,	they were already foretold,
a los Estados Unidos	the entire United States
en minutos lo enlutaron.	in minutes they had them mourning.
Se esperaba cualquier cosa,	They expected almost anything
pero no lo que ha sucedido,	except what has come to pass,
famosas torres gemelas	the famous Twin Towers
en segundos han caído.	fell in a matter of seconds.
Un día once de septiembre	On the eleventh of September
cuando nadie lo esperaba,	when nobody was expecting it,
habían sonado las nueve	it had just rung nine o'clock
el terrorismo llegaba.	terrorism was arriving.
Miles y miles de humanos	Many thousands of human lives
de diferentes naciones,	from several different nations,

han quedado cancelados	have been cancelled out
por esas crueles acciones.	because of those cruel actions.
Cuatro aviones estrellaron	Four planes came crashing
por diferentes lugares,	into different places,
terrible huella dejaron	they left a terrible mark
los terroristas cobardes.	the cowardly terrorists.

Ya con ésta me despido,	Now with this I take my leave
pero hay que estar preparado,	but one must be prepared,
en los Estados Unidos,	in the United States
de peligro están rodeado.	they are surrounded by danger.

Example 4. "Bin Laden, el Error de la CIA"

Composed by Rigoberto Cárdenas Chávez; recorded by Los Soberanos del Norte on an unknown cassette. This new English translation is by the author, from the Spanish original as posted on the "Corrido Watch" Web site (http://elijahwald.com/corridowatch.html).

Bill Clinton lo dijo en prensa	Bill Clinton said it in the press
que dio la orden de matarlo,	he gave the order to kill him,
su gobierno no cumplió	his government did not follow through
y el error están pagando,	and they are paying for that error,
la graduación con honores	graduating with honors
con traición les ha pagado.	with betrayal he paid them back.

Saben que él es poderoso,	They know he is a power
que tiene mucho dinero	that he has plenty of money,
los talibanes lo siguen,	the Taliban follow him
para enfrentarse al mundo entero,	to take on the entire world,
llevan a Dios por cobija,	they bring God as their blanket
y se olvidan de su cuerpo.	and forget about their bodies.

Por cielo, mar y por tierra	By air, sea and by land
su huella están buscando,	they are seeking his track,
la CIA de Estados Unidos	the US CIA
a causa del atentado,	on account of those attacks,

bin Laden a ti te culpan	bin Laden, they blame it on you
que la guerra has iniciado.	that you have started the war.
No soy Dios para juzgarte	I am not God to judge you
pero tendrás tus motivos,	you must have your motives,
dinero llama dinero	money calls to money
y a ti te quieren los gringos,	and the gringos are wanting you,
como un tesoro te buscan	they seek you like a treasure
si te encuentran serán ricos.	if they find you they'll be rich.
Nostradamus lo predijo	Nostradamus foresaw it
el dragón ha despertado,	the dragon has come to life,
inicios del fin del mundo	the beginning of the end of the world
es lo que estamos mirando,	that's what we are seeing,
el animal más perverso	the most perverse of creatures
de la tierra el ser humano.	on this earth, the human being.
Por cielo, mar y por tierra	By air, sea, and by land
Osama te andan buscando,	Osama they are looking for you,
bin Laden el terrorista	bin Laden the terrorist
la CIA te ha preparado,	the CIA has trained you,
ese fue el error más grande	that was the biggest mistake
del gobierno americano.	of the American government.

Example 5. *"Corrido de Osama bin Laden"*

By Andrés Contreras, released on self-produced cassette tape titled *Intifada 2001*. This new English translation is by the author, from the Spanish original as posted on the Corrido Watch Web site (http://elijahwald.com/corridowatch.html).

Allá por Saudi Arabia	Over in Saudi Arabia
un valiente hombre nació,	a valiant man was born,
lo que nadie había hecho	what nobody else had done
él hacerlo atrevió,	he would dare to do it,
en varios lugares	in a number of places
a los gringos atacó,	he attacked the gringos,
y siempre que lo hizo	and every time he did it

muchos soldados mató.	he killed many soldiers.
Aunque es gran millonario	Though he is a big millionaire
eso nada le importó,	that meant nothing to him,
y toda su fortuna	and all of his fortune
a la lucha dedicó,	he dedicated to the struggle,
el gobierno americano	the American government
con él mucho se asustó,	became very fearful of him
y para poder matarlo	and in order to kill him
miles de tropas mandó.	it sent in thousands of troops.
Osama bin Laden,	Osama bin Laden
no te dejes agarrar	don't let yourself get caught,
mira que si te atrapan,	look, if they can trap you
seguro te han de matar,	they will kill you for sure,
tu cabeza tiene precio	your head has a price on it
muchos lo quieren cobrar,	many would like to cash in,
por todo lo que has hecho	for all that you have done
no te van a perdonar.	they will not forgive you.
Un una saltamontañas	In a mountain hideaway
con el frío de la chingada,	with one hell of a chill,
tranquilo espera bin Laden	bin Laden calmly waits
a que llegue la avanzada,	for the arrival of the advance,
los que se topen con él	those who come across him
vivos no regresarán,	will not return alive,
en una bolsita negra	in a little black bag
a su país volverán.	to their country they will return.
Ora, gringo criminal	Now, criminal gringo
el diablo se te apareció,	the devil has appeared to you,
hombre de barba y turbante	a man with beard and turban
asustote que te dió,	quite a fright he gave you,
hasta el modito de andar	even the way you travel
Osama te lo quitó,	Osama took from you,
y nomás de oirlo hablar	and just hearing him speak

temblorina que se dió.
Osama bin Laden
no te dejes agarrar,
mira que si te atrapan
seguro te han de matar,
tu cabeza tiene precio
muchos lo quieren cobrar,
por todo lo que has hecho
no te van a perdonar.

Helicópteros y aviones
con potente artillería,
bombardean al Taliban
sea de noche o sea de día,
muchos miles de soldados
los han mandado a buscarlo,
solo que los pobrecitos
ruegan a Dios no encontrarlo.

Decía Osama bin Laden
con millones en la mano:
"Se los doy al que me ayude
a matar americanos,
con mis bravos mujaedines,"
decía con voz en cuello:
"No pierdo las esperanzas
de cortarles el pezcuello."

George Bush, bastante asustado
le pregunta a su mujer:
"Cómo le hago con bin Laden
que él ya nos pasó a torcer?"
Su mujer le contestó
con bastante disimulo:
"Vete para Afganistan

it gave you the shivers.
Osama bin Laden
do not let them catch you,
look, if they can trap you
they will kill you for sure,
your head has a price on it
many will want to cash in,
for all that you have done
they will not forgive you.

Heliocopters and airplanes
with heavy artillery,
are bombing the Taliban
be it by day or by night,
many thousands of soldiers
they have sent to search for him,
it's just that those poor fellows
ask of God that they not find him.

Osama bin Laden said
with millions in his hand:
"I give this to those who will help me
to kill the Americans,
with my brave mujahadeen,"
he said at the top of his voice:
"I have not yet lost hope
of slitting all their throats."

George Bush, very alarmed
inquires of his wife:
"What can I do with bin Laden
who already came to tweak us?"
His wife answered him
in a manner oh so sly:
"Get you to Afghanistan

para que le des el cul . . ."	so you can give him your as . . ."
. . . pables son estos gringos	. . . suming the guilt are the gringos
de todo lo que les pasa,	for all that happens to them,
lo que ellos han hecho al mundo	what they have done to the world
se lo hicieron en su casa,	was done to them in their house,
y vuelven los bombaderos	and the bombers now return
allá por Afganistan	there in Afghanistan,
andan buscando a bin Laden	they are looking for bin Laden
pero no lo encontrarán.	but they will never find him.

REFERENCES

Avitia Hernández, Antonio. 1998. *Corrido Histórico Mexicano*. Mexico City: Editorial Porrúa.

Casey, Edward. 2000. *Remembering: A Phenomenological Study*. Bloomington: Indiana University Press.

Dickey, Dan William. 1978. *The Kennedy Corridos: A Study of the Ballads of a Mexican American Hero*. Austin: University of Texas Center for Mexican American Studies.

Ellis, Bill. 2001. "A model for collecting and interpreting World Trade Center jokes." *New Directions in Folklore* 5. Available at http:// www.temple.edu/isllc/newfolk/journal_archive.html.

Grider, Silvia. 2001. "Preliminary observations regarding the spontaneous shrines following the terrorist attacks of September 11, 2001." *New Directions in Folklore* 5. Available at http://www.temple.edu/isllc/newfolk/journal_archive.html.

McDowell, John. 1992. "Folklore as commemorative discourse." *Journal of American Folklore* 105: 403–23.

———. 2000. *Poetry and Violence: The Ballad Tradition of Mexico's Costa Chica*. Urbana: University of Illinois Press.

Paredes, Américo. 1958. *"With His Pistol in His Hand": A Border Ballad and Its Hero*. Austin: University of Texas Press.

———. 1976. *A Texas-Mexican Cancionero: Folksongs of the Lower Border*. Urbana: University of Illinois Press.

———. 1993 [1958]. "The Mexican Corrido: Its Rise and Fall." In *Folklore and Culture on the Texas-Mexican Border*, edited by Richard Bauman, 129-41. Austin: University of Texas Center for Mexican American Studies.

Peña, Manuel. 1985. *The Texas-Mexican Conjunto: History of a Working-Class Music*. Austin: University of Texas Press.

Simonett, Helena. 2001. *Banda: Mexican Musical Life Across Borders*. Middletown, CT: Wesleyan University Press.

Tinker, Edward. 1961. *Corridos and Calaveras*. Austin: University of Texas Press.

Wald, Elijah. 2001. *Narcocorrido: A Journey into the Music of Drugs, Guns, and Guerrillas*. New York: Rayo (HarperCollins).

ACKNOWLEDGMENTS

An earlier draft of this paper was given at the annual meeting of the American Folklore Society, Rochester, NY, in October 2002. I'd like to recognize the many students and colleagues who have heard me talk on this topic and offered valuable feedback.

NOTES

1. Several folklorists—Bill Ellis (2001) with respect to jokes, Silvia Grider (2001) with respect to spontaneous shrines, for example—stepped forward with thoughtful discussions of this prolific popular reaction to 9/11.
2. See Simonett 2001 for a detailed history of the *banda* tradition, and Peña 1985 for a classic study of *conjunto*.
3. I thank my sister Maura Kealey, Ethan Sharp, and Elijah Wald for delivering into my hands some of these tapes and CDs. Also, see Wald (2001) for portraits of El As and Andrés Contreras.
4. See Elijah Wald's Corrido Watch Web site at http://elijahwald.com/corridowatch.html.
5. Associated Press, "Mexican Songs Chronicle Attacks," *New York Times*, 21 October 2001.
6. Translated by the author from the Spanish original in Julie Watson, "Radio mexicana transmite canciones sobre ataques terroristas," *El Imparcial*, 17 February 2002.
7. Jennifer Mena, "Commentary Set to Sad, Satiric Song," *Los Angeles Times*, 5 November 2001.
8. Translated by the author from the Spanish original in Leticia Lozano, "Rancheros mejicanos componen balada sobre bin Laden," *Reuters*, 15 October 2001.

11

"I'LL TELL YOU WHY WE HATE YOU!"

SHA'BĀN 'ABD AL-RAHĪM AND MIDDLE EASTERN REACTIONS TO 9/11

James R. Grippo

Nine days after 9/11, George W. Bush declared, "Either you are with us, or you are with the terrorists," a statement that foreshadowed the "lengthy campaign" his administration would make on "every terrorist group of global reach." "Americans are asking," Bush said in the same speech, "why do they hate us? They hate our freedoms—our freedom of religion, our freedom of speech, our freedom to vote and assemble and disagree with each other."[1] This essay, analyzing the songs of Egyptian singer Sha'bān 'Abd al-Rahim and other Middle Eastern perspectives to 9/11, challenges Bush's understanding of "they" and proposes some different answers to the question "Why do they hate us?"*

Although the events of 9/11 were two years distant when I arrived in Cairo, Egypt, in 2003 to begin research for my dissertation, they were still very much on the minds of many local residents, and they formed a recurring theme in our conversations. Like the citizens of all nations, Egyptians exhibited a wide range of perspectives on 9/11, but that particularly tense year, during which the United States and the "Coalition of the Willing" extended their "War on Terror" from Afghanistan into Iraq, did seem to synchronize these perspectives somewhat. My Egyptian friends and acquaintances appeared relaxed, lighthearted, and even blasé at times, but, almost uniformly opposed to the war

---

* All Arabic symbols are based on the standard for Arabic transliteration (American Library Association, Library of Congress [ALA-LC]).

in Iraq, they often voiced an uneasiness or disappointment with the way current affairs were unfolding. Nonetheless, in 2003 most of these people continued to make a distinction between the U.S. administration and its citizens (at least when they were talking to me), asserting that Bush was "bad" while the American people were "good."

Presently, writing and researching in Egypt has afforded me the opportunity to listen to what Egyptians have to say about the volatile topics of 9/11 and its far-reaching aftermath.[2] In 2003, I was deeply moved by their sincerity as well as humbled by those who felt the need to apologize to me, an American, for the horrible acts of 9/11. By contrast, as I revise this essay, in the summer of 2006, apologies of this type have long ceased. While my Egyptian interlocutors generally remain captivated by American popular culture and continue to enjoy the company of most Americans, many voice a mistrust of, if not outright contempt for, the way 9/11 has been used to advance a U.S. foreign policy that, in the words of the Project for a New American Century, "boldly and purposefully promotes American principles abroad," a policy that has metastasized into wars and other interventionist activities, particularly in the Middle East.[3]

In this essay, I discuss ways in which the events surrounding 9/11 have reverberated in Egyptian popular music and culture, focusing on the politically charged musical genre known as *sha'bī*. Commonly associated with Cairo's working class, *sha'bī* has a long history of bawdy humor and trenchant social critique; it is frequently characterized as giving a voice to "the homeless, the orphaned, the sickly, [and] the unemployed."[4] After providing a history of *sha'bī*'s development and its position relative to other popular genres, I devote the bulk of this essay to one of contemporary urban *sha'bī*'s foremost practitioners of social commentary and political dissent, the Egyptian singer Sha'bān 'Abd al-Rahīm. In this essay, then, rather than charting the ideological positions of a vague mass of cultural "others" on the Western academic map, I strive to present, in as vivid a manner as possible, a single prominent voice from the Middle East, one that communicates a critical perspective on 9/11 and on post-9/11 developments.

EGYPT'S SOCIOECONOMIC DESCENT AND THE RISE OF EGYPTIAN *SHA'BĪ*

In order to understand the rise of *sha'bī*, one must first situate it within the recent social and musical history of twentieth-century Egypt. For much of the twentieth century, Cairo was the musical center of the Arab Middle East, producing superstar singers, composers, and musicians who enjoyed fame comparable to (and sometimes exceeding) kings and presidents throughout the region. Egyptian legends, such as Umm Kulthūm, Muhammad 'Abd al-Wahhāb, 'Abd al-Halīm Hāfez, and Farīd al-Atrash, produced and reinvigorated a pan-Arab art music which came to be referred to as *al-mūsīqā al-'arabiyya*.[5] This genre, which developed from nineteenth-century practice, is characterized by the sophisticated use of melodic and rhythmic modes (*maqām* and *īqā'*) within vocal and instrumental forms, and of experimentation using a wide variety of compositional and performative idioms, "provided that these idioms do not transcend the boundaries of Arabic music styles as perceived by native musicians and audiences" (El-Shawan 1980: 86). By the mid-twentieth century it was commonly performed in large orchestras featuring pan-eastern Arab instruments such as *'ūd* (lute), *qānūn* (plucked zither), *nāy* (reed end-blown flute), and *riqq* (tambourine), as well as a Western string section (violins, cellos, double bass). While it was strongly associated with elitist cosmopolitan sectors of Egyptian society, *al-mūsīqā al-'arabiyya*, particularly during the period when the above prominent singers were active, was also an extremely popular music.[6] *Al-mūsīqā al-'arabiyya* was performed and recorded using a long song form (*al-ughinyya*), where it was common to hear several modal modulations, rhythmic changes, and thematic colors (*alwān*) in a piece that lasted between twenty minutes to an hour. Performances were regularly broadcast on radio (beginning in the late 1920s) and later on television (as of 1960), while recordings were distributed first on cylinders and records (during the first decade of twentieth century), followed later by cassettes, videos, CDs, DVDs, and, most recently, numerous Web sites (Racy 1976: 25; El-Shawan 1980: 94–5; 112).

This climactic era of *al-mūsīqā al-'arabiyya* preceded a period of political instability and economic deterioration in Egypt. By 1966, Prime Minister Gamal Abdel Nasser's newly created Ministry of Culture had assumed state control of giant media industries such as television and cinema (Wahba 1972: 29).[7] Abdel Nasser quickly and effectively crushed opposition forces such as the existing aristocracy, communists, and political Islamists, thereby establishing a "majority fraction of the rural and urban petty bourgeoisie" who, in turn, idolized their leader (Aoude 1994: 3). After Egypt's 1967 defeat to Israel in the Arab-Israeli war and failed attempts to unify the pan-Arab world, however, confidence in Nasser's regime declined dramatically. Widespread depression, insecurity, and anger plagued Egyptians, who found themselves living under a government that could neither protect them (from Israel) nor stimulate economic development. Although the regime made enormous efforts to encourage private enterprise, foreign and local capitalists were not enticed to invest in Egypt's dauntingly bureaucratic industrial complex; agitating this already volatile situation, the state compensated its deficits by increasing taxes that were largely borne by the working classes (Aoude 1994: 2–7). After Abdel Nasser's fatal heart attack in 1970, Anwar al-Sadat further fanned the flames of discontent by 1) establishing diplomatic ties with Israel and reestablishing ties with the United States; 2) increasing the national debt through dependence on loans from the World Bank, International Monetary Fund, and the U.S.; and 3) trying to squash opposition in the public sector, specifically labor unions and other leftist factions.

Al-Sadat's Open Door policies (*infitāh*; literally "opening"), a set of economic directives based on market economics, like Abdel Nasser's attempts at free enterprise, failed miserably. According to Marie-Christine Aulas, "As Sadat began to implement the new, more laissez-faire policies of *infitāh*, opposition developed among the working class, the intelligentsia, the state bureaucracy and other sectors of society" (1982: 8). Further contributing to the decline of Egypt's socioeconomic situation in the 1970s was the exportation of 10 percent of its most skilled laborers to the burgeoning oil-rich Arab Gulf countries (Wahba 2004: 184), pushing Egypt, once the industrial leader of the Middle East, into a downward spiral of debt, fragmentation, and social unrest.

It was within this chaotic milieu during the late 1970s that *al-mūsīqā al-ʿarabiyya* began to be superseded by a new urban musical style known as *shaʿbī*. In addition to Abdel Nasser's death and the economic hardships that followed, Egyptians mourned the loss of their most beloved singer, Umm Kulthūm, in 1975 (Farīd al-Atrash died a year earlier and ʿAbd al-Halīm Hāfez two years later), signifying the end of a legendary era of *al-mūsīqā al-ʿarabiyya*. At the same time, by the 1980s, Egypt's industrial laborers, either returning from Arab countries or fulfilling a local demand for contractual labor, began enjoying the fruits of extra money and time to spend on entertainment. The majority of the working class in Cairo consisted of migrants from Upper Egypt, the Delta, and other surrounding villages or hamlets. Although familiar with *al-mūsīqā al-ʿarabiyya*, many were more accustomed to the folksy sounds and entrancing grooves of their own region's traditional religious and secular music. Many lower-rung nightclubs started catering to this reinvigorated working class by hosting bands featuring faster, rougher songs. A new music influenced by folk and art music elements, along with an emerging working class identity informed by the harsh urban realities of Egypt's economic and cultural decline, began to blossom.

Sha'bī, the term that was commonly given to this music, literally means "folk," "traditional," and "popular" in Arabic (Badawi and Hines 1986: 466).[8] The term represents a complex cultural formation, one perhaps most easily defined as the antithesis of Egypt's elite cosmopolitanisms, encompassing cultural corollaries of the working class such as its styles of dress, particular neighborhoods,[9] and the atmosphere of public events such as weddings. From the perspective of the cultural elite, the term often serves as an index for what is seen as the cultural backwardness of the uneducated masses. However, *sha'bī* also evokes for many Egyptians a sense of local identity, tradition and heritage, and the aura of authenticity that is referred to as *asīl*. In its focus on the quotidian and the topical, urban *sha'bī* also draws upon a long tradition in Egypt of using music as a vehicle for criticism, dissent, and even comic relief. Given this contentious history, it is not surprising that one of Egypt's most popular *sha'bī* singers, Sha'bān 'Abd al-Rahīm, is both the most politically brazen and the most derided by cultural elites.

Sha'bī musicians and composers draw on specific elements of Egyptian folk and art music (*al-mūsīqā al-sha'biyya* and *al-mūsīqā al-'arabiyya*). With regard to folk music, the use of *mawwāl* (pl., *mawawīl*), a vocal genre featuring melodic improvisations in a specific mode (*maqām*) using colloquial poetic texts, is one of the dominant influences. Double entendre, indirect metaphor (*kanāya*), and popular slang are also frequently employed by singers to convey folk wisdom (*hikmat al-sha'b*), commonplace topics, socially charged issues, and innumerable variations of romantic and religious themes to their listeners. *Sha'bī* employs three or four primary rhythms (*maqsūm, maqsūm dūmmeyn, wāhda wa nūss,* etc.) played on *al-tabla* (a goblet-shaped drum), *al-duff* (a frame drum), and *al-mazhar* (a large frame drum with cymbals). These rhythms, explicitly Egyptian in character, are also used in *al-mūsīqā al-sha'biyya* and *al-mūsīqā al-'arabiyya*, although these genres utilize many more rhythmic modes. In addition, a number of aspects of art music, including the use of instrumental devices such as preludes (*muqaddima*), accentuation between sung lines (*lāzma*), and arranged margins for improvisation (*taqsīm*) within compositions, are common to *sha'bī*. In some of the *sha'bī* songs of Muhammad Rushdī, Muhammad Qandīl, and Ahmad 'Adawīya, for example, a condensed version of the long song, featuring the devices just mentioned as well as stately string-dominated orchestras and separate movements, can be discerned.

What then differentiates *sha'bī* from *al-mūsīqā al-'arabiyya* and *al-mūsīqā al-sha'biyya* is, as A. J. Racy demonstrated decades ago regarding the "popular-art" distinction, "a matter of degree and interpretation" (1981: 6). Racy outlined a comparative model that regarded

Cairo's music as "a group of overlapping and interconnected musical domains" centered around one "multifaceted" central domain of art, or *fann*, music (1981: 11–12). Inasmuch as *sha'bī* contains elements from both folk and art music domains, it is characterized more accurately by what it is *not*. It is *not* based on oral and lineal tradition, like *al-mūsīqā al-sha'biyya*, and is *not* performed in a compositionally intellectual manner in large orchestras or small ensembles using acoustic art music instruments associated with *al-mūsīqā al-'arabiyya*.

Like the residents of Cairo's *sha'bī* districts, *sha'bī* music can be identified by the class of people who perform it, *what* they have to say, and *how* they say it. In the early 1970s, musicians hailing from Cairo's vibrant working-class neighborhoods, particularly Shubra, Sayyida 'Aysha, and neighborhoods around Muhammad 'Ali street began to attract attention while performing at local life-cycle celebrations, such as weddings and circumcisions, and the lower rungs of the nightclub and cabaret business on Pyramid Street (*shāri' al-haram*). As *sha'bī* music developed and fused with an urban vernacular sensibility featuring a new textual and musical language, more songs were composed using short repetitive refrains and dramatic rhythmic shifts from fast to slow (or vice versa) to create a lively party atmosphere. Often employing a brass section (some configuration of trumpets and trombones), the overall timbre and presentation of *sha'bī* is raucous and rough. While the poets of *al-mūsīqā al-'arabiyya* wrote about love and the pains and joys of life in idealized, even esoteric terms, the lyrical content of *sha'bī* emphasizes instead a vernacularized "thick description" of Egyptian street culture (Geertz 1973). Currently, the genre is commonly presented as a quintessential "music of the people."

The undisputed king of *sha'bī* is Ahmad 'Adawīya, a performer who achieved enormous success throughout Egypt after emerging from the *sha'bī* underbelly of the Cairo nightclub scene in the early 1970s. His first commercial release, "*Is-sah indah imbuh*" (1974) (similar to "goo goo gaa gaa," imitating baby-speak), sold over one million copies in part due to the rise of a local "cassette culture," a feat that had not been accomplished by any singers before him.[10]

'Adawīya was seminal in establishing the standard for modern *sha'bī* that would be followed by hundreds of performers after him. 'Adawīya introduced a new *sha'bī* style that relied on heavy amplification (often with effects such as delay and reverb); used faster, driving meters; and employed freer and bolder lyrics. Lyrical content, perhaps *sha'bī*'s most salient feature, began to feature the exigencies of street culture, sex, politics, and unrequited love, delivered in a vernacular slang often considered tasteless and vulgar by the Egyptian cultural elite. The bawdy lyrics and unabashed presentation of an "undesirable," "low-class" culture challenged the matrix of permissibility regulated and enforced by the guardians of Egypt's dominant modernist ideology and the Islamic infrastructure: though 'Adawīya was selling millions of albums, and even appeared in several films from the mid 1970s to the 1980s, virtually no trace of him or other *sha'bī* musicians could be found on television or radio, the two primary forms of Egyptian mass media at the time. Hasan 'Abdallah, a *sha'bī* music producer, explains that it "could be because of their social and educational background and their *baladī* [rural] appearance—it's not appealing to the elite."[11] 'Adawīya's influence can be heard, nonetheless, in the works of many stars, such as Ramadān al-Brins, Tāriq al-Shaykh, 'Abd al-Bāsat Hamūda, Hasan al-Asmar, Sha'bān 'Abd al-Rahīm, and Hakīm.

Currently, *sha'bī*, with its funky, realist, mirrorlike portraits of urbanized village culture, enjoys success throughout Egypt and, facilitated by a booming local and pirated cassette industry, the Arab world. Despite the genre's broad popularity, Egypt's entertainment industry remains equivocal with regard to *sha'bī*. 'Adawīya's enormously popular songs, for example, are still not played on the radio. The industry does not hesitate, however, to embrace certain of his successors who have a cleaner and cooler image and sound, such as Hakīm and Rīco.

IGNITING THE FUSE: SHA'BĀN 'ABD AL-RAHĪM'S EXPLOSION TO STARDOM

In the fall of 2000, a relatively unknown veteran *sha'bī* singer, Sha'bān 'Abd al-Rahīm, stormed into the popular culture of the twenty-first century with the release of his song "I Hate Israel" (*Anā Bakrah Isrā'īl*).[12] The song made him an overnight success as it boomed out of public spaces (cassette stalls, shops, car stereos, etc.) all over Egypt, the Arab world, and especially Palestine. His brazen sociopolitical commentary and satire, as well as his contentious *sha'bī* background and appearance, turned him into the unlikely hero of millions of Egyptians and Arabs. Together with lyricist Islām Khalīl, 'Abd al-Rahīm mobilized the music's potential to tap into the "pulse of the Egyptian-Arab street" by politicizing songs, often to the point of ridiculousness (Gordon 2003).[13]

Impelled by the success of "I Hate Israel," 'Abd al-Rahīm released several overtly political albums and accompanying music videos in 2002: *Amrīka Yā Amrīka* (America O America), *al-Kurah Shay' Qalīl Yā Isrā'īl* (Hate Is a Trivial Thing O Israel), and *Al-Darab fī al-Irāq* (Bombing

Iraq).[14] Unlike "I Hate Israel," the title track to "America O America" was less an attack and more an appeal to the United States to rein in its imperialist policies. I have highlighted some excerpts below:[15]

America O America, the people live in pain.	Amrīka yā amrīka, il-nās 'āysha fī ālām.
The whole world wants love and peace.	Il-'ālam kulluh 'āwiz il-hubb wi-s-salām.
America O America, you made us suffer for a long time.	Amrīka yā amrīka, ta'abnā min zamān.
We got angry over Iraq, Bosnia and Chechnya.	Za'alanā 'al al-'irāq wa bōsnya wa shīshān.
America O America, don't speak of another war, enough.	Amrīka yā amrīka māta'ūlsh tānī harb, kifaya.
We love peace but we're tough like iron.	Ehna binahibb il-salām lakin 'awwitnā hadīd.

The album *al-Kurah Shay' Qalīl Yā Isrā'īl*, a veritable rallying cry for the ongoing Palestinian intifada (popular uprising), was released immediately after the footage of the killing of twelve-year-old Muhammad al-Dūra by Israeli snipers horrified and outraged Egyptian, Arab, and international television audiences.[16] And finally, *Al-Darab fī al-Irāq*, which featured 'Abd al-Rahīm on the cover in front of the Statue of Liberty and a fighter jet dropping bombs, criticizes the United States for invading Afghanistan, threatening to invade Iraq, and supporting the Israeli occupation of the West Bank and the Golan Heights, and demands that Israel be submitted to international inspection instead. The cassette album, video clip (or *fīdyūclīb*, as they're called in the eastern Arab world), and song made an enormous impact in the Middle East. The song begins powerfully:

Enough, enough!	Kifāya, Kifāya
Enough of your excuses.	Kifāya ba'a talākīk
Enough of your excuses, our patience is wearing thin.	Kifāya ba'a talākīk, khalās il-khul' da'
Just check out Israel and leave Iraq alone. . .	Mā tashūfū isrā'īl wa tasībkū min al-'irāq. . .
. . . attacking in plain sight, they didn't even respect any elders	. . . wa il-darb 'aynī 'aynak, mābyahtaramūsh kabīr.
Sharon makes a pool, and the blood falls like rain.	Sharon khallāhā birka, wa il-dam zayy il-matar.

Perhaps even more compelling is the *fīdyūclīb*, which shows graphic stock news footage—taken during the first Gulf War, and prior to that, in Palestine—of charred Iraqi corpses, giant explosions, weeping women, and dead bodies carried out from bombed-out buildings. (The video came out ten days before the U.S. invasion of Iraq on March 20, 2003.) Superimposed over these are images of key politicians, such as George W. Bush, Colin Powell, and Ariel Sharon shaking hands, giving speeches, or smiling. As the focus shifts between the news footage and ʿAbd al-Rahīm, he openly questions the United States' push for war, asking if America seeks to partition Iraq in order to take control of its oil, and wondering what military intervention might follow the campaigns in Afghanistan and Iraq.

After the release of the song and video, ʿAbd al-Rahīm rapidly became the talk of the town; he was invited to appear on television talk shows (an honor usually reserved for "respectable" performers), and even to star in films. By the beginning of 2003, seemingly everyone, whether they liked him or not, knew his songs. Later, ʿAbd al-Rahīm reached new heights of polemics with the release, in 2003, of the song and animated music video "Yā ʿAmm ʿArabī" (literally, "O Arab Uncle" but commonly translated as "O Fellow Arab" or "Hey Arab Leaders").[17] The song urges the disaffected and largely silent Arab leaders to action while asserting that George W. Bush and Ariel Sharon are global imperialist bullies divvying up the world like a pie. "O Fellow Arab," like "America O America" and "Bombing Iraq" calls into question and boldly challenges the interventionist policies of the United States and Israel. Most of these songs were made into music videos and featured on satellite music channels ("Melody Hits" and "Mazzika," mainly) within weeks of the events that inspired them. This timeliness is seen as one of Shaʿbān ʿAbd al-Rahīm's principal virtues: according to a daily news Web site, the artist "does not allow any colossal incident to pass by without making a suitable song in the same expeditious manner that he and his listeners are accustomed to."[18] "O Fellow Arab" is an animated music video featuring hand drawn art in simple but bold colors similar to the style used in *The Simpsons*. The song text and a number of stills from the video are reproduced below:

Yā ʿAmm ʿArabī (O Fellow Arab 2003)

Mawwāl:	Mawwāl:
a) He drew a line of the road for his brothers, sisters and children	Rasamluh khatt il-tarīq l-ikhwānuh wa ʿayyāluh.
b) And he made a quadrilateral committee to discuss his business.	Wi ʿamal-luh lagna rubāʿyya wa tashūf-luh aʿmāluh.

c) The Road Map didn't work and the committee members didn't agree on anything.

Kharīta mā-it'amaltsh wa il-lagna mā-ittfa'tsh.

d) And that's what our friends want, he's always thinking (O night = O yeah).

Wa da illī sahābnā 'āyizuh, tamalli 'ala bāluh (yā layl).

Song:

Song:

1. Heads or tails, America and Israel

Il-sūra wa il-kitāba amrīka wa isra'īl.

2. They made the world like a jungle, and then ignited the fuse.

Dūl khallū il-dunyā ghāba wa wala'ū il-fatīl

3. America spreads its wings and doesn't care.

Amrīka faraduh ganāh-hā mā'ādsh yahimmahā.

4. She doesn't find anyone to prevent or stop her.

Mish lā'iya had yahūsh-hā w-lāhad yalmahā

5. Then (Bush) talks about Iran and, after a while, Syria.

Shwaya ya'ūl irān wa b'ad shwaya sūrīyā.

6. And he makes his talk short if anyone mentions Korea.

Wa ya'sarnī il-kalām law had 'āl-luh kūrīya.

7. O People, O Mankind, it wasn't but a tower.

Mākānsh hitta borg yā nās yā khalq huwa.

8. And certainly its owners were the ones that made it fall.

Wa bil-tā'kīd sahābuh homā illī wa'ū'uh.

9. With terrorism as an excuse, for years America and Israel have acted as bullies.

Bahigit il-irhāb ba'a linā kam sana amrīka wa isrā'īl wakhdinihā fatawina.'

10. They still offended Syria and bombed Lebanon.

ā'adīn yadā yi'ū fī sūrīyā wa yidrabū fī lubnān.

11. And from one direction Israel and the other, America.

Wa il-yama isrā'īl wa il-tāniya amrīka.

12. Two long arms extended over the whole area, still destroying and usurping it.

Iyīdayn tawīla itamadat 'ala il-hita kulahā 'amāl takharrab fīhā wa tafarra' fīhā.

13. Who said it's just a cloud (something that will pass), who said this is a looming cloud?

Mīn illī 'āl sahāba, mīn illī 'āl dī ghuma?

14. We need to take a stand, we need a nation of Islam!

Hakāyitnā 'āyizuh wa 'afa hakāyitnā 'āyizuh umma!

15. The people everywhere were offended and complained.

Il-nās fī kul hita itadāyu'ū wa ishtakū.

16. O Fellow Arab when do you intend to do something?

Yā 'amm 'arabī imta nāwīīn tatharakū?

17. Silence is a big mistake and has become useless.

Sukūt mā'ādsh nāfiʿ mā huwa akbar ghalta.

18. And tomorrow everyone will make a map (Road Map).

Bukra kul wāhid hayt'amaluh khārta.

19. O Fellow Arab when will you wake up from that which you are in?

Yā 'amm 'arabī imta hatfuʾ min illī inta fīh?

20. A flood is coming upon you and you are not aware of it.

Gāyy il-tūfān 'alayk wa mā'intash dāra bīh.

21. Everybody's sitting and silent, depending on each other to do something.

Il-kul 'āʿid sākit 'al b'ad kulluh ittakal.

22. Day and night Sharon still lures (us into) a fight.

Nahār wa layl shārōn 'amāl sigur shakal.

23. He's a liar all his life, accustomed to lying and hypocrisy.

Kidāb tūl 'umruh wākhid 'ala il-kidb wail-nafāʾ.

24. And there are no secreting of weapons nor tunnels.

Walā fī silāh mitharrab walā hita fī anfāʾ

25. (He's) a person who hates himself and his lies are countless.

Insān biyikrah nafsuh wi kidbuh mālūsh hasr.

26. Every time he falls he blames Egypt.

Wi kul hudr tiyākhduh yigīb fī sīra masr.

27. Egypt is none of your business so take yourself a good picture.

Mālaksh da'ūh bi-masr wa iʿīl linafsak sūra.

28. This is Egypt, 'Mother of the World," and (remember) the victory and the crossing (of Sinai).

Dī masr umm il-dunyā wa in-nasr wa il-'ubūr.

29. Our president is very precious to us, he's in our hearts, and at the time of his speech we all became worried.

R'aīsnā ghālī 'alaynā wa guwwa 'albinā, wi sā'ia il-khitāb 'ili'nā kullinā.

The music video begins with President Bush (carrying a rolled-up piece of paper) and Prime Minister Sharon marching next to a long wall with four childlike figures following close behind (Figure 11a.1). Bush and Sharon have guns strapped to their hips and are accompanied by a group of children who bear a strong resemblance to Dick Cheney, Donald Rumsfeld, George Bush Sr., and Benjamin Netanyahu (wearing pink diapers and a *kippah*). While they walk, 'Abd al-Rahīm's *mawwāl* begins after a short instrumental introduction featuring the brass and rhythm sections. Bush unrolls the paper to reveal a map of the Middle East, signifying Bush's Road Map for Peace, and the "children" gather around and cheer as Bush draws the Star of David in the center of the map (Figures 11a.2 and 11a.3).

Figure 11a Yā ʿAmm ʿArabī ("O Fellow Arab") video-clip stills, group 1. Courtesy of Al-Wadi lil Intag al–Fanni.

The song begins with the lines, "Heads or tails, America and Israel" (line 1), as a coin spins, revealing the flags of both countries on each side. ʿAbd al-Rahīm makes his appearance, superimposed over the animated scenes, sometimes addressing the characters directly. He adds to the poignancy of the lyrics with facial expressions and hand gesticulations expressing mostly exasperation and frustration.

The video continues with literalist interpretations of the lyrics. For example, while he sings, "America spreads its wings and doesn't care"

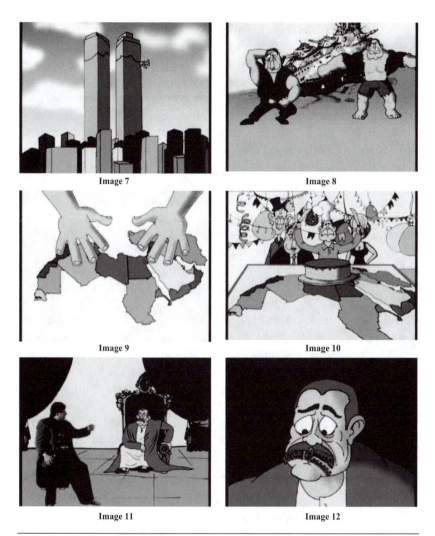

Image 7 Image 8

Image 9 Image 10

Image 11 Image 12

Figure 11b Yā 'Amm 'Arabī ("O Fellow Arab") video clip-stills, group 2. Courtesy of Al-Wadi lil Intag al–Fanni.

(Line 3), viewers see giant wings reaching toward Earth, which then morphs into hands and grab it. Likewise, "They made the world like a jungle, and then ignited the fuse" (Line 2) shows Bush and Sharon wiring the Earth with explosives (Figure 11a.4), after which it blows up in their faces. Perhaps 'Abd al-Rahīm's most brazen remark, "And certainly its owners were the ones that made it fall" (Line 8), claims that America and Israel are responsible for the 9/11 attacks. These lyrics are accompanied by scenes of Sharon pushing a button (Figure 11a.5) that causes a commercial airplane to come to life (Figure 11a.6) and then crash into the Twin Towers (Figure 11b.7). Bush and Sharon are then portrayed as hulking bullies (Figure 11b.8) as 'Abd al-Rahīm sings, "With terrorism as an excuse, for years have America and Israel acted as bullies" (Line 9). Again alluding to the imperialist activities of the United States and Israel 'Abd al-Rahīm sings, "From one direction Israel and the other, America. Two long arms extended over the whole area, still destroying and usurping it" (Lines 11 and 12). The accompanying scenes show two long arms extending over the Middle East (Figure 11b.9), pulling it off the globe and into a cake, which Bush proceeds to slice into pieces (Figure 11b.10); a caricature of Tony Blair stands in the rear wearing a black top hat.

As the song and video come to a close, 'Abd al-Rahīm appeals directly to the Muslim-Arab world, calling for a nation of Islam, or *umma* (Line 14), and criticizing Arab leader for their silent acquiescence regarding U.S./Israeli aggression (Lines 16, 17, and 19). Facing the camera, 'Abd al-Rahīm calls for an *umma*, while the flags of the Arab world pass behind him. In the next scene (Figure 11b.11), 'Abd al-Rahīm reproaches "*'amm 'arabī*," a regal-looking mustached man in a large throne, acting out physical signs of frustration and exasperation. While he sings about how silence is a mistake and has proven to be useless, the accompanying scene shows the throned Arab leader with a closing zipper for a mouth (Figure 11b.12). If somehow the lyrics and images of the "*Yā 'Amm 'Arabī*" video clip weren't enough to arouse Arab-Muslim fervor, the last scene features a portrait of Sheikh Ahmad Isma'īl Yāsīn, the cofounder and leader of Hamas who was assassinated by an Israeli helicopter gunship on March 22, 2004, causing an international uproar.

"LET THEM DRINK OF THE CUP"
—ARABS RESPOND TO 9/11

'Abd al-Rahīm's songs underscore two widespread opinions in the Middle East regarding the events and aftermath of September 11, 2001. First, the presentation of America and Israel as "two faces of the same coin" is extremely common. A second related outlook portrays the United States and Israel as global "bullies," dividing and conquering the Middle East one piece at a time. Whether caused by a long history of U.S. intervention in the Middle East, voluminous anti-U.S and anti-Israel propaganda, or by the sheer magnitude of grim news reports detailing Israel's apartheid-like domination over the Palestinian people, many Egyptians confirmed these views in conversations with me. Indeed, "O Fellow

Arab" soared to the top of the Arab music charts within four days of its video debut on the Cairo-based Melody Hits satellite channel, and could be seen daily on monitors in Cairo's main downtown subway station, Anwar al-Sadat. Following a long line of *sha'bī* singers who have used their craft to enlarge sociopolitical criticism, Sha'bān 'Abd al-Rahīm has become the latest to sit on this controversial throne.

Conversations and interviews with Egyptians from all walks of life about 9/11 reveal, as one would expect, opinions from disparate extremes and everything in between. Cameron S. Brown's informative article "The Shot Seen 'Round the World: The Middle East Reacts to September 11th" (2001) summarized the earliest statements from the Egyptian/Arab press regarding the attacks. By discussing popular and official reactions to 9/11 from a variety of news sources, Brown demonstrated that Middle Eastern reactions in 2001 ranged from "exuberant support to outright condemnation; from saying that the United States deserved these attacks for its errant foreign policies (especially in the region), to claiming that Israel had actually perpetrated the attack" (2001: 69). Among the numerous quotes in Brown's article, one of the harshest yet most poignant responses to 9/11 was expressed by Ali 'Uqleh 'Ursan, chairman of the Syrian Arab Writers Association:

> The deaths of the innocent pain me; but the eleventh of September—the day of the fall of the symbol of American power—reminded me of the many innocents whose funerals we attended and whose wounds we treated . . . I remembered the funerals that have been held every day in occupied Palestine since 1987 . . . I remembered Tripoli [Libya] on the day of the American-British aggression, and the attempt to destroy its leader's house as he slept; then, his daughter was killed under the ruins . . . I remembered the oppression of the peoples in Korea and Vietnam . . .
>
> . . . I began to say to myself, when I saw the masses fleeing [in] horror in the streets of New York and Washington, "Let them drink of the cup that their government has given all the peoples [of the world] to drink from, first and foremost our people . . ." I [felt] that I was being carried in the air above the corpse of the mythological symbol of arrogant American imperialist power, whose administration had prevented the [American] people from knowing the crimes it was committing . . . My lungs filled with air and I breathed in relief, as I had never breathed before.[19]

Hosni Mubarak, Egypt's current president, in an interview with United Press International, was asked what motives were behind the terrorist attacks. Mubarak, who, according to Brown, is "a close American ally and major beneficiary of U.S. foreign aid," also could not hold back his criticism of U.S. Middle East foreign policies, specifically regarding Israel:

> The feeling of injustice... Muslims everywhere see America giving arms to the Israelis to kill Muslims and America not putting any conditions on the arms it gives free to Israel. Muslims see the media taking the side of Israel whatever it does. Public opinion is seething against an America which continues to support Israel irrespective of Sharon's policies that are designed to prevent the Palestinians from having their own state. Go to all the so-called moderate states in the region, from Jordan to Saudi Arabia, Kuwait, Qatar and Oman. Their leaders have told me that their streets are on the verge of boiling over.[20]

The notion that U.S. foreign policies were erroneous, and that the attacks offered the opportunity and potential for reflection and reform, was expressed by mainstream intellectuals throughout the Arab world in 2001. Hasan Nafi'ah, chairman of the political science department at Cairo University, acknowledged, "What happened . . . [will] push the United States to reconsider and reflect on why it is being the object of all that violence and antipathy. That kind of violence has its roots and causes. It is necessary to look for the causes."[21]

The wide range of published Egyptian and Arab opinions regarding 9/11 is too vast to present in this essay, but the statements above accurately summarize the majority of voiced and printed perspectives that I have witnessed in Egypt. It should be emphasized that the sources above were published within weeks of 9/11, whereas the majority of opinions in the months and years following were primarily reactions to the United States response, namely, the invasions of Afghanistan and Iraq, threats against Syria and Iran, and, most recently, support for Israel's invasion of Lebanon on July 12, 2006. Essentially, this response was perceived by many Muslims as a contemporary "crusade" against Islam, a term Bush himself used in a press conference on the South Lawn days after the 9/11 attacks.

The music of Sha'bān 'Abd al-Rahīm embraces all of these heated and heartfelt reactions to 9/11 and beyond, loudly repeating them for all to hear. As previously mentioned, 'Abd al-Rahīm is currently the most popular, or infamous, sha'bī singer in Egypt. He is also the first person people here refer to when asked about musical reactions to 9/11. The key to 'Abd al-Rahīm's success, or the "Shabaan Phenomenon," is his reliance on current events and trends as well as his rearticulation of a popular consensus.[22] Often quoting directly from "main news headlines," his songs appropriate controversial topics, such as smoking marijuana and cigarettes, taxes, and, as explored here, issues of American and Israeli aggression.[23]

By celebrating the working-class connotations of sha'bī, 'Abd al-Rahīm presents himself as the quintessential "salt of the earth," or *ibn al-balad* (literally, "son of the country"). He makes no effort to conceal his family trade (foot-operated laundry presser, or *makwāgī*); the fact that he lives with his mother and extended family in a small village, Mit Halfa; or that he has suits made to match his upholstery and wears two wristwatches on one arm. 'Abd al-Rahīm's public persona is that of a clownlike bard who rarely takes himself or his songs seriously, maintaining a delicate balance between the powerful Egyptian archetypes of "fool" and "hero" (Grippo 2006). Happily contradicting himself in interviews and admitting to not knowing much about the subjects of his songs, 'Abd al-Rahīm cleverly plays the fool card when backed into corners by critical interviewers. At the same time, he humbly accepts the "heroic" praise that is directed toward him for his bold statements against the United States or Israel. The archetypal "fool" in Middle Eastern folklore is *Jōha* (*Gōha* in Egypt), known endearingly as the wise fool or trickster; like 'Abd al-Rahīm, he "is portrayed as either very stupid or miraculously clever, a resistance figure who thumbs his nose in the face of authority and capitalist rulers" (Abdelsadek 2002). Similarly, in Egyptian cinema and theater, the protagonist, or *batal* (which also means hero or lead actor) is often a bumbling, cowardly, or comical character. Embracing this dual archetype, 'Abd al-Rahīm explains how "presenters like to make fun of me when I appear on TV because I'm an ironer, but that's OK with me. Who am I to complain when the same people hire me for their weddings because I'm fashionable, then pay me thousands to open my mouth?"[24]

Whether embracing provocative global current events or popular local issues, 'Abd al-Rahīm actively pursues sensationalism in a "shock and awe" strategy of music production. With one foot in a culture-specific locality (Egyptian sha'bī), and another foot in a wider mass-mediated globalism (current events), 'Abd al-Rahīm unites both with blunt statements that resonate in a popularized local discourse. To some Egyptians he has become a hero, the "voice of the people," not only by saying what seems to be on everyone's mind, but also by producing such songs within the context of an otherwise predominately vapid and overcautious, self-censoring entertainment industry. His humble village upbringing, together with his discourteously candid lyrics, sung in local slang, appear to endear as many to him as are repulsed. "My songs are simple and that's why people love me," 'Abd al-Rahīm explains. "They understand the words, because this is how we talk on the streets. You don't need to be educated to enjoy one of my songs."[25] Abdel Hamid, a driver in Cairo, told BBC News, "His words are good because he tells the truth and fears nothing."[26]

Sha'bān 'Abd al-Rahīm, the current figurehead of *sha'bī* music culture, has managed to penetrate the Egyptian popular music industry, thereby both winning and losing the hearts and minds of countless Egyptians and Arabs who receive him as either a fool or a hero. His songs reflect stereotypes and attitudes that are common in the popular Arab media, attitudes that provide a different answer to George W. Bush's rhetorical question, "Why do they hate us?" Rather than an abstract antipathy toward America's freedoms, artists such as 'Abd al-Rahīm present in their music an acute critique of concrete American policies in the Middle East.

In many ways, the response to 9/11 that is embedded in 'Abd al-Rahīm's music and videos can be characterized as a reaction to a reaction: namely, the U.S. invasions of Afghanistan and Iraq. The initial outpouring of sympathy and support that I experienced in 2003, at least on an individual level, has been eclipsed by critical attitudes toward U.S. interventionist policies. This evolution of sentiment has fueled (and been fueled by) the ascendance of musical polemicists such as 'Abd al-Rahīm, and controversial, politically charged genres like *sha'bī*. Paying close attention to this music reveals much about the profound complexities of the region and the challenges Americans face as they struggle to position themselves in a chaotic and critical post-9/11 world.

ACKNOWLEDGMENTS

Excerpts of song lyrics by Islam Khalil courtesy of Al-Wadi lil Intag al-Fanni.

REFERENCES

Abdelsadek, Nafisa. 2002. "Persianate Children's Literature: Social and Political Perspectives." Work in progress for doctoral thesis at University of Edinburgh, available at http://www.geocities.com/zimbbo/chapter1.htm.

Aoude, Ibrahim G. 1994. "From National Bourgeois Development to Infitah: Egypt 1952–1992." *Arab Studies Quarterly* 16(1): 1–23.

Aulas, Marie-Christine. 1982. "Sadat's Egypt: A Balance Sheet." *MERIP Reports* ("Egypt in the New Middle East") 107: 6–18, 30–31.

Badawi, El-Said, and Martin Hines. 1986. *A Dictionary of Egyptian Arabic*. Beirut, Lebanon: Library du Liban.

Brown, Cameron S. 2001. "The Shot Seen 'Round the World: The Middle East Reacts to September 11th." *Middle East Review of International Affairs Journal* 5(4): 69–89.

El-Shawan, Salwa. 1980. "The Sociopolitical Context of *al-Musika al-Arabiyyah* in Cairo, Egypt: Policies, Patronage, Institutions, and Musical Change (1927–1977)." *Asian Music* 12(1): 86–129.

Geertz, Clifford. 1973. *The Interpretation of Culture*. New York: Basic Books.

Gordon, Joel. 2003. "Singing the Pulse of the Egyptian-Arab street: Shaaban Abd al-Rahim and the Geo-Pop-Politics of Fast Food." *Popular Music* 22(1): 73–88.

Grippo, James R. 2006. "The Fool Sings a Hero's Song: Shaaban Abdel Rahim, Egyptian Shaabi, and the Video Clip Phenomenon." In *Journal of Transnational Broadcasting Studies* 16 (June–Dec.), available at http://www.tbsjournal.com/Grippo.html. Cairo: American University of Cairo; and Oxford: St. Anthony's College, University of Oxford.

Manuel, Peter. 1993. *Cassette Culture, Popular Music and Technology in North India*. Chicago and London: University of Chicago Press.

Racy, Ali Jihad. 1976. "Record Industry and Egyptian Traditional Music: 1904–1932." *Ethnomusicology* 20(1): 23–48.

———. 1981. "Music in Contemporary Cairo: A Comparative Overview." *Asian Music* 13(1): 4–26.

Wahba, Jackline. 2004. "Does International Migration Matter? A Study of Egyptian Return Migrants." In *Arab Migration in a Globalized World*, 179–99. Geneva: International Organization for Migration.

Wahba, Magdi. 1972. *Cultural Policy in Egypt*. Paris: Unesco.

DISCOGRAPHY

'Abd al-Rahīm, Sha'bān. 2000. *Anā Bakrah Isrā'īl*. Cairo: al-Wādī lil-Intāj al-Fannī. Audiocassette.

———. 2002. *Al-Darab fī al-Irāq*. Cairo: al-Wādī lil-Intāj al-Fannī. Audiocassette.

———. 2002. *Al-Kurah Shay' Qalīl Yā Isrā'īl*. Cairo: al-Wādī lil-Intāj al-Fannī. Audiocassette.

———. 2002. *Amrīka Yā Amrīka*. Cairo: al-Wādī lil-Intāj al-Fannī. Audiocassette.

———. 2003. "Yā 'Amm 'Arabī." On *Illī Khāyaf Yarūh*. Cairo: al-Wādī lil-Intāj al-Fannī. Audiocassette.

———. 2005. *Kilmat Haqq*. Cairo: unreleased video.

NOTES

1. Address made to a Joint Session of Congress, on September 20, 2001.
2. This essay is currently being written in Egypt on a Fulbright-Hays dissertation fellowship. Previously, I have conducted fieldwork in Egypt in 1998, 1999, and 2003.

3. See the Project for a New American Century's "Statement of Principles," datelined June 3, 1997, and available at www.newamericancentury.org. The "Statement" is signed by a veritable "who's who" of conservatives: Elliott Abrams, Gary Bauer, William J. Bennett, Jeb Bush, Dick Cheney, Eliot A. Cohen, Midge Decter, Paula Dobriansky, Steve Forbes, Aaron Friedberg, Francis Fukuyama, Frank Gaffney, Fred C. Ikle, Donald Kagan, Zalmay Khalilzad, I. Lewis Libby, Norman Podhoretz, Dan Quayle, Peter W. Rodman, Stephen P. Rosen, Henry S. Rowen, Donald Rumsfeld, Vin Weber, George Weigel, and Paul Wolfowitz.

4. Mohamed El-Assyouti, "Man on the Street," *Al-Ahram Weekly*, February 2001 (no. 520), 3–14.

5. For more on *al-mūsīqā al-ʿarabiyya* see El-Shawan 1980.

6. For example, Umm Kulthūm's monthly radio broadcasts on the first Thursday of every month were famous for clearing the streets of Cairo, as people sought out radios in coffee shops and homes.

7. Radio was previously nationalized in 1934 (Wahba 1972: 67).

8. The translation of shaʿbī as "popular," it must be emphasized, relies on the latter term's archaic English and French meaning "of the people," as opposed to its modern connotations of wide acceptance and technological mediation (although these, it could be argued, are increasingly salient aspects of contemporary shaʿbī). Because of the inherent polysemy of the term "shaʿbī" I am regularly confronted with passionate appeals from Egyptian intellectuals to use the term "shaʿ'iyya" (widespread) instead of "shaʿbī" because of the latter term's associations with Egyptian folk music (al-mūsīqā al-shaʿbiyya). I continue to use "shaʿbī" due to the fact that the people who produce and consume this music use this term. Moreover, out of all the named subgenres of al-mūsīqā al-shaʿbiyya there is only one genre labeled "shaʿbī"—the genre discussed here. These topics will be examined at length in my dissertation.

9. Government subsidized low-income housing developments, for instance, are called masākin shaʿbiyya (Badawi and Hines 1986: 466).

10. Scott Bortot, "Shaabi Album Misses a Couple Beats," *Middle East Times*, 25 February 2000. I take the phrase "cassette culture" from Manuel 1993.

11. Yomna Kamel and Rahsa Mehyar, "The Unsung Heroines of Shaabi Music," *Middle East Times*, 21 April 2000.

12. Since the release of this song, Shaʿbān ʿAbd al-Rahīm has received semi-international notoriety due to reports appearing on CNN and the BBC (among others), as well as on various news and blog Web sites.

13. Some of ʿAbd al-Rahīm's songs, for instance, are literally quotations from newspaper articles.

14. For more on these music and video releases, see Grippo 2006.

15. This and all following lyric translations are by the author.

16. The twelve-year-old Al-Dūra was killed while his father tried to shield him from the snipers. The horrific scene was captured by a France 2 cameraman and aired repeatedly on Palestinian television.

17. These are the common translations found in English language press and Web sites. However, "yā ʿamm" literally means "paternal uncle," but is also widely used as an informal address to males meaning "mate" or "buddy" (Badawi and Hines 1986: 603).

18. Mohamed ʿAbd al-Rahman, "Shaʿbān yughanī didd al-danmark" (Shaʿbān sings against Denmark). In *īlāf il-yom*, 14 February 2006; available at http://www.elaph.com/ElaphWeb/Music/2006/2/128176.htm.

19. Originally published in *Al-Usbuʿ al-Adabi* [Arabic], 15 September 2001; translated in *Middle Eastern Review of International Affairs*, Special Dispatch 275, September 25, 2001; and quoted in Brown 2001: 74.

20. Originally published by Middle East News Agency [*MENA*], 17 September 2001; translated by Foreign Broadcast Information Service [FBIS] and quoted in Brown 2001: 75.

21. Originally published in *Al-Akhbar*, 13 September 2001; translated by FBIS and quoted in Brown 2001: 78.

22. Tarek Atia, "Shabaan!," *Al-Ahram Weekly*, 18–24 January 2001 (no. 517).

23. Mohamed El-Assyouti, "Man on the street," *Al-Ahram Weekly*, February 2001 (no. 520), 3–14.

24. Nicole Veash, "Pop Crooner Hits Sour Note with Egyptian Elite," *The Christian Science Monitor*, 18 January 2002.

25. Ibid.

26. *BBC News*, "Arabs Rock to Antiwar Song," 11 March 2003. Available at http://news.bbc.co.uk/2/hi/middle_east/2839795.stm.

12

9/11 AND THE POLITICS OF MUSIC-MAKING IN AFGHANISTAN

Veronica Doubleday

Greedy people want our country

And enemies have interfered with us.

They think about colonizing us

Through political games and support of different military groups.

—Malang Kohestani, 2003

For people in Afghanistan, the events of September 11, 2001, are remembered primarily as the trigger that prompted massive U.S. military action in their homeland. As the Taliban regime persisted in "sheltering" Osama bin Laden that autumn, the United States retaliated by invading the country, establishing a long-term military presence and promoting an uneasy political transition that continues to evolve today. While the hunt for bin Laden and Al Qaeda members was cited as justification for the war, ultimately it was the Afghan people who were caught in the crossfire, and who have accounted for the greatest number of its casualties.

The changes wrought by military interventions extend well beyond the tragic statistics of body counts. One of the various unforeseen effects of the U.S.-Allied military campaign in Afghanistan has been a significant alteration of the country's musical landscape.

Most prominent, the ousting of the Taliban regime ended a period of severe music censorship, rooted in their imposition of an extreme interpretation of Islamic law.[1] This development was widely reported in the Western press, as coalition forces were eager to portray their campaign as a "humanitarian war" against the Taliban, and the end of music censorship in Afghanistan thus emerged as a key symbol of the war's "just cause" and success.[2] Less discussed in the press were the actual efforts to revive music in the country, which emerged on two key fronts. First, exiled professional musicians began to return to the country, hoping that once again they would be able to make a living by playing music. Second, a number of other interested individuals and institutions began the difficult work of creating and supporting projects, particularly educational initiatives, capable of regenerating Afghanistan's ailing but historically rich musical culture.

For many reasons, Afghan musical culture today remains in a state of flux. Decades of war, the exodus of many musicians, and periods of restrictive censorship have contributed to a decline in both the quantity and quality of musical performances, even as many new influences have penetrated the country's musical culture in recent years. Western influences are noticeable, and the themes of some songs reflect the experiences of conflict and recent world events.

In contrast with some of the articles in this volume, however, post-9/11 music in Afghanistan does not commemorate the lives lost in the United States on that day, for a number of reasons. First, Afghan people do not mark September 11, 2001, as an important date, and they have very little sense of the cost of human life in the 9/11 attacks. Rather, the significant (and clearly 9/11-related) moment occurred in December 2001, when the Taliban rulers departed from Kabul. Second, when it comes to mourning the dead, Afghan people have many martyrs of their own. The current U.S.-led "war on terror" has cost thousands of Afghan lives, including those of many innocent civilians who died in the initial U.S. bombing strikes. What is more, these are only the most recent casualties of political violence in the country; prior to 9/11, more than two decades of conflict had already taken the lives of at least a million people (Johnson and Leslie 2004: 3).[3]

Few people in Afghanistan are likely to commemorate those lost on 9/11 for another reason, also recognized by many foreign political analysts: namely, that Western countries bear much historical responsibility for creating and fueling the forces that engineered those events. The United States in particular supported Islamic fundamentalist movements during the Cold War against the Soviet Union, and this had the ultimate effect of promoting the kind of autonomous terrorism embodied in Al Qaeda.[4] Many Afghans are keenly aware of this history of foreign political interference, and the destructive impact that it has had on their country.[5]

In this article I draw on the work of ethnomusicologists, anthropologists, filmmakers, and political analysts, as well as my own long-term involvement with Afghanistan, Afghan people, and Afghan music, to present a portrait of music and politics in the country before and after 9/11. Tracing the roots and reconfiguration of traditional poetic themes that include religious piety, patriotism, lament, satire, and ridicule, I argue that the politicization of Afghan music largely began with the period of armed conflict in 1978. By comparing preconflict song texts with material recorded in 2003, I also illustrate how Afghan social consciousness as a whole has broadened during this period. Turning to the post-9/11 era specifically, I focus on two important social themes in contemporary Afghan musical culture: the impact of the Afghan diaspora on music inside Afghanistan and the continuing power play between conservative Islamic values and secularized modernity, including how that struggle is playing out in recent music educational initiatives in Kabul. I conclude with an overview of the state of Afghan music in the post-9/11 world, and the ongoing impact—musical, cultural, and otherwise—of the fallout from that fateful day.

MUSIC IN AFGHAN HISTORY

In Afghanistan, as in many other Islamic cultures, "music" is rather narrowly defined. The term *musiqi* refers solely to instrumental music, or singing accompanied by instruments. Singing or chanting, such as lullabies, Sufi chants, Koranic cantillation, and the Islamic call to prayer, are considered separate, non-"musical" phenomena, and this important conceptual distinction has shaped public policies and had a tremendous effect on the status of music and musicians.[6] In contrast, music-making with instruments is associated with celebration and enjoyment, especially weddings. Significantly, music is not to be played after someone has died, and ideally, a forty-day mourning period is observed in which no music should be heard. These notions about appropriate contexts for music-making had a considerable impact in the politicized (not to mention violent) environments of the 1980s and 1990s.

Further discussion of music's place in this turbulent history requires at least a cursory overview of recent Afghan history itself. In this essay, I will refer to the relatively peaceful decades preceding the pro-Soviet coup d'état of April 1978 as the "preconflict" period. The "conflict period" that began in 1978 has not really ended, as military action, political violence, and pro-Taliban insurgencies are ongoing. Within this long era of conflict, the "communist period" (1978–92) was marked by strife pitting Islamist resistance forces (mujahideen) against the communist government. In 1992, amidst the collapse of the communist regime, the mujahideen leaders formed an Islamist coalition government, marking the beginning of the "coalition period" (1992–96), but civil war continued between rival factions. The Taliban movement emerged from Pakistan in 1994, gradually sweeping across the country and taking Kabul in 1996. "Taliban rule" (1996–2001) refers to the years when the Taliban controlled Kabul and much of the rest of Afghanistan (but never the extreme northeast). The U.S.-led military campaign in Afghanistan was initiated in October 2001, and the "Karzai period" began in early 2002, with Hamid Karzai's inauguration as leader of the interim government. Karzai was later elected president, and at the time of this writing (May 2005), is still in power.

Each successive stage of the conflict period has had a significant impact on musical practices. After the 1978 coup and throughout the communist period, violent conditions led many people to flee the country, including many professional musicians, although some stayed in Kabul to work for the state radio and television stations. Successive communist governments promoted music for propaganda purposes, while the mujahideen groups tried to prohibit civilian music-making in areas that they held. They argued that in conditions of war, when so many families had martyrs to mourn, music-making was forbidden. In any case, in such grim circumstances, many people simply lost the heart for music. Beginning in 1992, the Islamist coalition government severely restricted music broadcasting, and the roots of official music censorship took hold. These policies reached their most extreme form under the Taliban, when musicians were penalized and sometimes even beaten and imprisoned, musical instruments were publicly destroyed, and it became illegal to play or listen to music. In short, the Taliban tried to erase music from everyday life. The only melodious sounds they officially allowed were religious singing and *taranas* (commonly termed "chants"), consisting of male unaccompanied singing, sometimes with new lyrics about Taliban heroes.[7] In Taliban-held areas very little live music-making existed otherwise, although some people defiantly continued to play in secret.

THE EMERGENCE OF POLITICIZED SONGS

As implied by the special place accorded vocal music even under Taliban censorship, sung poetry is an important aspect of Afghan culture, practiced and appreciated across all levels of society. Prior to the 1978 coup, however, Afghan music-making was not generally concerned with social or political themes. Rather, the most important topic addressed by singers and poets was love: romantic love, mystical love, the sorrow of separation from loved ones, and love for the homeland and countryside. Consequently, the literature on Afghan music in the 1960s and 1970s rarely refers to songs with social or political themes.[8]

After 1978, professional singers were encouraged by ensuing regimes to address more topical and politicized themes, as all political entities, including eventually the Taliban, attempted to capitalize on the power of sung texts. Often new poetry would be set to existing melodies, though existing poetry (sometimes adapted) could also acquire a new significance and popularity.[9] We know little about the pro-communist propaganda songs of state radio and television in the 1980s, due to a lack of scholarship and/or reporting on the topic, and these songs have fallen into disuse along with the communist ideals they espouse, which have no place in today's Afghanistan.[10] In contrast, a number of the rousing songs that appealed to the mujahideen still have some currency, as they express heroic, devotional, and Islamic ideals that are still relevant and cherished by a significant segment of the population.

Mujahideen songs of the communist era typically extol the virtues of those fighting a "holy war" (*jihad*) against "unbelievers." In Badakhshan in 1996, Jan van Belle recorded one such example that dated to the communist period whose lyrics, by singer-composer Mehri Maftun, are strongly religious and forcefully anticommunist.[11] Maftun bluntly states that Afghanistan has fallen into the hands of Satan, and that the government is "the slave of Russia." In a passionate style, with percussive accompaniment on his own *dambura* (long-necked lute), he rouses fighters to bravery, using Arabic invocations to God as a refrain and drawing on the language of love poetry:

Mujahed! mujahed! feda-ye peykar-e tu

Mubariz! mubariz! khoda madadgar-e tu

Mujahed! mujahed! I sacrifice myself to your person/figure

Fighter! Fighter! May God be your helper![12]

Pious wishes, invocations, and prayers are common tropes in these newly composed Islamic political songs, which began to be performed publicly after the 1992 fall of the communist regime. In 1994, I recorded another such song in Herat, *Khoda-ye mehraban* ("O kind God"), performed by a band led by the well-known professional singer-harmonium player Mahmud Khushnawaz.[13] The singer told me that it had been composed in Kabul two or three years previously. The chorus runs:

Khoda-e mehraban darbarat ast kalan

Arezu o hawas darim arami Afghanistan. Allah! Allah! Allah!

O kind God, your court is great

Our wish and desire is for peace in Afghanistan. God! God! God![14]

The chorus also asks for help from the Prophet Muhammad's son-in-law and follower, Hazrat Ali, who is known in Afghanistan as a healer and "Problem-solver." Interestingly, two years later van Belle recorded this same song in Mazar-i Sherif, sung by the professional singer Hassan Besmil and accompanied by a band. It had obviously achieved fairly wide currency as a public expression of pious desires.

The most typical poetic themes emerging from the Islamic resistance movement were prayer, lament, patriotism, and heroism. The long tradition in Afghanistan of solo heroic epics lent itself well to political treatment. In the past, epics provided singers with the opportunity to explore idealized social values through telling stories about mythical heroes. Under present circumstances, singers turned their attention instead to contemporary heroes and their feats in battle. Outside the immediate war zone, across the border in Pakistan, Afghan professional singers were able to elaborate on this art form, and they recorded sung narrations of modern battle epics on commercial audiocassettes. A single song describing a battle might take up an entire forty-minute audiocassette. The mujahideen enjoyed listening to these epics, which were performed in an intense martial style, with the sounds of real gunfire or tabla drums imitating guns and rockets.

Male singers and poets have been largely responsible for composing new political music, but some interesting female songs also emerged from the refugee camps of Pakistan. These were composed and recorded (with musical accompaniment played by men) by girls from a school run by the Revolutionary Association of the Women of Afghanistan (RAWA) in Quetta. One example is very much within the tradition of Pashtun heroic and patriotic poetry:

Zerah dai Asia chai qahraman dai

Da watan mu gran Afghanistan

Soak cai puh yerghal der ta ragheli dee

Goad aw puh ghashuno mot wateli dee

So cha baturan dai watan kai shori

Bia puh kazho strego soak nagori

The heart of Asia [Afghanistan] is a hero.

This country dear to us is Afghanistan.

Those who have come to assault you

Have left limping with their teeth broken.

As long as your brave sons are in the country

No one will look at you [Afghanistan] with bad intentions.[15]

In the atmosphere of post-Taliban Kabul, patriotic songs are genuinely popular. They seem to express people's desire to feel unified and secure in a national identity. A prime example is the much-loved and ubiquitous Pashto-language song *Da zemu ziba watan* ("This is our beautiful country"), which has become something like the unofficial national anthem.[16]

Da zemu ziba watan

Da zemu leila watan

Da watan mu zan dai

Da Afghanistan

This is our beautiful country

This is our lovely country

This country is very dear to us

This is Afghanistan[17]

Composed and popularized in the preconflict period by the great Pashtun radio singer Awal Mir, it enjoyed a resurgence of popularity in the 1980s among Pashto-speaking Afghan refugees in Pakistan.[18] In Kabul it is now played when President Karzai makes official speeches, and it regularly crops up in all kinds of musical performances. There are three versions in John Baily's film *Kabul Music Diary* (Baily 2003).[19] Known among all ethnic groups, its meaning transcends Pashtun nationalism and expresses warm emotions about Afghanistan as a homeland, asserting that such feelings are central to every Afghan.

A different sort of proud and militant nationalism is contained in the songs recorded in the post-9/11 era by Malang Kohestani, a remarkable poet-singer who was filmed by the anthropologist David Edwards in 2003. Kohestani's home region of Istalif is strategically situated north of Kabul, close to the Panjsher Valley and the site of a great deal of fighting. Kohestani described himself to Edwards as a "*mujahed*," and explained that local people enjoy songs that refer to the recent struggles. The following verse expresses a defiant confidence and patriotism similar to the RAWA song quoted above:

Lashkar-e najat-e meihan

Afghanistan zadeim

Yak musht o yak parchegi o

Mardom-e azadeim

Az Sikander ta Britania

Har biganei

Tarikh-e dandanshekan darim

Jawabash dadeim

We are the liberation army of this country

We are from Afghanistan,

A single fist and united,

We are a free people.

From Alexander to Britain,

And all invaders,

We have a teeth-breaking history

And we have defeated them all![20]

In another verse of this song, a mother tells her child to grow up prepared to struggle for the homeland which, interestingly, is personified as a beloved female:

Jawan shu farzand-e man

Dar nabard o ruzegarat

Kamarat mahkam beban

Ba tu shiramra ke dani

Dar maqamat sar baland

Yak madarat man mibashum

Madar-e digar watan

Grow up my child,

Prepare yourself for the struggle of your time.

Take pride

In the milk I gave you.

Your mother I am;

Your other mother is your homeland

Islamic and patriotic songs such as these that emerged during the decades of conflict remain current and popular, expressing a continued concern with Islamic values and nation-building. They are not the only thematic treatments of Afghanistan's long-running conflict in its music, however; songs of lament, dealing with the traumas of death and destruction that inhabit the popular memory, are also widespread.

THE POETRY OF LAMENT

Lament themes have a strong presence in Afghan culture, prominent in the poetry and expressive arts of both Persian and Pashto speakers.[21] The folklorist Benedicte Grima makes the general point that the "tragic esthetic" is "deeply rooted in Indo-Iranian perception and world-view" (1993: 143). In the past, however, lament poetry was normally concerned with love: love of a person who had died or gone far away, or love for one's distant homeland.

The Persian-language northern genre of quatrains known as *falak*, for example, laments the trials of fate, taking its name from "the wheel of fate" (*charkh-e falak*). The ethnomusicologist Mark Slobin quotes a quatrain, sung around 1970 by the Badakhshani singer Baba Naim (who then lived in Kabul), which alludes to the flight of refugees from the Soviet Republic of Tajikistan (Kulab) to Afghanistan (Balkh) in the

1920s and '30s. This example shows how historical events may be retained in the poetic memory for many decades (and, indeed, centuries):

Charxe felak mara dar Balx awordi

Kulab budim mara dar Balx awordi

Janam dar Kulab budim u mixurdim abe shirin

Az abe shirin bar abe talx awordi

O wheel of fortune, you spun me around

I was in Kulab, you brought me to Balkh

Dear, I drank sweet water in Kulab

You brought me from sweet water to bitter[22]

Other laments mourn tragic heroes, and they may convey messages about social values. One example is an old Herati song about a bandit called Asadullah Jan, who was eventually caught and killed.[23] In the song the bandit's mother tells her dead son that he sealed his own fate by defying the king's authority:

Ku takht-e tu ku bakht-e tu Asadullah jan

Ku madar-e kambakht-e tu akh amir- e madar

Sad bar goftum yaqi mashu Asadullah jan

Be padashah yaqi mashu akh amir-e madar

Where's your throne, where's your luck, Asadullah Jan?

Where's your unlucky mother, o prince of your mother?

A hundred times I told you not to be rebellious, Asadullah Jan

Not to rebel against the king, o prince of your mother[24]

During the conflict period, the lament genre was reconfigured as an appropriate means of mourning the dead and the losses of war; numerous songs were composed lamenting the ruin of Afghanistan itself. One example was recorded on video in 1997 at a public concert in the United States organized by the Afghan-American community in Virginia. The visiting singer was Ustad Amir Mohammad, a respected Kabuli *ustad* (master-musician), with a remarkable new version of his classic Persian-language song *Chaharbeiti Shomali*.[25] ("Shomali" refers both to an area near Kabul that was devastated and to a melody type.) In the well-known original, recorded by John Baily in 1974, Amir Mohammad used traditional folk quatrains about unrequited love: the pain of separation, and of waiting, chiding his loved one for her cruelty and faithlessness. This is the first verse:

Gham-e eshqat biaban parwaram kard

Hawayat morgh-e bi bal o param kard

Mara gofti saburi kon saburi

Saburi khak-e alam ba saram kard

Sadness at love for you has made me frequent the desert

Your air has made me into a bird without wings or feathers

You told me to wait, to wait

Waiting has brought me a world of unhappiness[26]

The new version laments the ruin of Kabul, using the language of traditional love poetry and personifying Kabul as a beloved:

Shomali jang shod o shahr-e kalanat

Ba bala-e sarash mehr-e jahanat

Bia ziyarat konim Seyed Jafar Agha

Hamishe dastegir-e bikasanat

Chera Kabul tura weiran namudan

Tanatra bi sar o saman namudan

...

Ala ai Kabul-e nazdana-ye man

Chera atash zadi dalanan-e man?

Keshidam saleha bar-e ghamanatra

Chera az man gerefti khana-ye man?

Sarosar Kabulam weiran gashte

Hame pir o jawan diwana gashte

War came to the Shomali area and its principal city [Kabul].

May the love of heaven come down onto Kabul.

Let's go and pray at the shrine of Seyed Jafar Agha,

Who always supports the dispossessed.

Why did they ruin you, Kabul?

Why did they leave you bereft like this?

....

Alas, o Kabul, my sweetly alluring one,

Why did you [i.e., enemies] set fire to my alleys?

For years I've carried the weight of your grief

Why did you take my house away?

All of Kabul has turned to ruins,

Old and young alike have gone mad.[27]

Visiting a privately run orphanage in Kabul in 2002, John Baily recorded another lament for Kabul. The young girl who sang it had learned it in the state orphanage where she had previously lived. Such songs may have partly been composed in order to touch the hearts of visitors. This one, in Pashto, has the poet's name, Haidari, in the last verse. Like the previous lament from Amir Mohammad, it names specific areas of Kabul:

Golan rishigi lagidelai pre khazan jan jan

Puh lambu swazi Kabul jan jan jan

Kote Sangi toti toti dai

Da Chihilsutun puh gham akhtah dai

Khe ratapai hadirei di

Uran awijar de tarikhi Darulaman jan jan

Puh lambu swazi Kabul jan jan jan

Tortsu ba da jang o jagre wi

Zamun puh sarba ba mele wi

Kala sare kala tau di wi

Haidari wai khodaya tah she mehraban

Puh lambu swazi Kabul jan jan jan

Flower petals are falling as though it's autumn, dear, dear

Beloved Kabul blazing, dear, dear, dear

Kote Sangi is in bits and pieces

Misery has been inflicted on Chihilsutun

I'm aware that it's a graveyard

Historical Darulaman is ruined and destroyed

Beloved Kabul is blazing

How long will this war and fighting continue?

How long will they have fun doing deals over our heads?

How long will this blowing hot and cold continue?

Haidari says O God, please be kind

Beloved Kabul is blazing[28]

Given its prominence in Afghan culture, the sung lament lends itself well to the expression of pain resulting from forced migration and other emotional hardships of war. Haidari's song also sounds a note of anger, especially in its mention of powerful people doing deals at the expense of Afghanistan's innocent civilians.[29] Its concluding lines, however, are pious, praying for God's mercy.

SATIRE AND RIDICULE

Anger at the ruin and exploitation of Afghanistan is perhaps best expressed through open criticism, and singers have occasionally satirized and ridiculed specifically targeted enemies. For much of the conflict period, however, it was not safe for singers to take too many risks. In this section I will focus mainly on material from the preconflict and post-9/11 periods.

Satire and ridicule are significant elements in Afghanistan's expressive culture, normally occurring less in songs than in stories, jokes, poems, and comic dramas. Verbal inventiveness and wit are esteemed, and poetry and storytelling have long been used to highlight contro-versial social issues. In her study of Herati storytelling, Margaret Mills illustrates many satirical commentaries on social issues, and she notes a populist tendency to "lodge legitimacy of judgment with common people" (1991: 24).[30] Allusions to corruption and social inequalities were also important in Herati satirical folk dramas performed by low-status barber-musicians who used instrumental music, singing, and sometimes puppetry in their plays. The 1977 study by anthropologist Hafizullah Baghban shows that these plays covered particularly sensi-tive social topics: domestic issues such as arranged marriages, polygamy, divorce, and "liberated women," as well as broader social dichotomies between the strong and weak and rich and poor. Verbal play was also a feature of the teahouse culture of northern Afghanistan, where singers engaged in competitive and satirical performances focused on socially topical themes (Slobin 1976: 161–75).

In times of repression, Afghan audiences have become adept at interpreting coded messages. For instance, even under strict Taliban censorship it was occasionally possible for singers to covertly ridicule the regime. Ordered by the Taliban to sing on the radio, the noted singer Nairiz chose this text:

Ba khabar bash ke in khalq khodayi darad

Akher in naleh-e makhluq sedai darad

Ah-e mazlum be zudi migirad zalemra

Har amal ajre o har karda jazai darad

Remember the people are protected by God

Their cries will be heard at last

Their oppressors will be punished

Since wrongdoing brings retribution[31]

The Taliban liked this song, apparently not understanding that it could be referring to them as the "oppressors." Because of its subversive message, the song enjoyed great popular success.[32]

In present-day Afghanistan, singers now have more freedom to express political ideas that are not necessarily pious and/or conform-ist, and themes relating to the traumatic experiences of conflict, dis-placement, and political upheaval are at the forefront of people's minds. I will illustrate this radical change of Afghan social consciousness by comparing songs in the satire/ridicule vein from two northern singers, the first recorded in 1972, and the second—Malang Kohestani, discussed above—in 2003.

In 1972, the ethnomusicologist Lorraine Sakata recorded the poet-singer Islam in the city of Faizabad, in Badakhshan. Islam was an amateur musician of some verbal talent who composed his own material and accompanied himself on the *dambura*.[33] He used direct accusations in his texts, poetically addressing a local "traitor":

Ai setam paisha-ye bad kar tura migoyam

Khain-e khalq o del awar tura migoyam

Man ke reshwat khori hgadar tura migoyam

Ai daghal parwar-e taraz tura migoyam

O oppressor, I'm telling you

Traitor, offender of hearts, I'm telling you

O bribe-taker, I'm telling you

Deceitful one, I'm telling you[34]

He identified his target by listing specific family possessions:

Pedarat kuti Parwan be khoda dasht nadasht

Tamiri sorkh ba paghman ba khoda dasht nadasht

Motar laine-ye laghman na khoda dasht nadasht

Hama shab yak labak man ba khoda dasht nadasht

Pas tura kar o fari motar-e walga zi kojast

Qasri shash manzela-ye sar ba sar ya zi kojast

Did your father have a building in Parwan, by God, or not?

Did he have a red building in Paghman, by God, or not?

Did he have a bus line to Laghman, by God, or not?

Did he have a morsel of bread every night, by God, or not?

Then where did you get your Volga car and splendor?

Where did the six-story building come from?

The singer also claimed that the man lacked certain socially recognized, admirable qualities:

Rahm o ensaf o morowat tu nadari chi konam

Pai dar marka-ye jahl tu gozari chi konam

Khuni mazlom zadai mast o khomari chi konam

Dar sar-e shana-ye iblis tu sawari chi konam

You don't have mercy, justice, kindness, what should I do?

You always join the ignorant ones, what should I do?

You have tasted the blood of the oppressed and are intoxicated by it, what should I do?

You are riding on the devil's shoulder, what should I do?

The entire song is a powerful invective against an individual, criticizing his evil qualities and even linking him with the devil. The song's references—to particular towns, to the (Soviet-made) Volga car, to a particular building—locate both its protagonist and antagonist as neighbors living in a shared milieu.

The singer of the second, post-9/11 example, Malang Kohestani, has already been mentioned as self-professed *mujahed* from a heavily affected conflict area. He belongs to a similar critical tradition, but his songs have a much broader content, displaying a remarkably informed view of international political interference in Afghanistan. For the filming, he simply sat on the ground surrounded by people and accompanied himself on a long-necked lute (Figure 12.1).

Kohestani's first song contained a mocking attack on Osama bin Laden and the Taliban, focusing especially on their personal cowardice. Cowardice is a shameful quality in Afghanistan; the Herati anthropologist Baghban ranks it third in his list of "unmanly" qualities (after miserliness and inhospitality) (Baghban 1977 vol.1: 212 n. 33).

Koja shodi bin Laden?

Khod meshi dar mushkhane

Chi amal kardi ke tura

I dunia midawanad

Figure 12.1 The poet-singer Malang Kohestani filmed in the Kapisa/Parwan area as he sings about Osama bin Laden. Photo by Greg Whitmore (2003).

Koja shodan washiha?

Ba tofang o topkhane?

Koja shod Radio Shariat?

Har shab mikhand tarane

Yake me didi zura

Rafti be Tora Bora

Dar gurekhtan bin Laden

Be khod nadari jura

Where are you, bin Laden?

You are hiding in a mousehole!

What have you done

That the world is running around after you?

Where are the savages [Taliban],

With their guns and cannons?

What happened to Radio Shariat,

Playing those chants [*tarana*] every night?

Once you saw the force against you,

You ran away to the Tora Bora [mountains]

Bin Laden, in fleeing

You have no rival!

Animal imagery is quite common in Afghan rhetoric, and elsewhere in the song Kohestani describes the brave Afghans as mountain lions. Bin Laden, on the other hand, is ignominiously likened to a mouse, which is fearful, tiny, and insignificant.

Kohestani's second song addressed another enemy: Pakistan, the neighboring state that created the Taliban movement and exported religious zealotry to Afghanistan for its own ends.[35] Again, Kohestani pressed the theme of cowardice:

Koja shodan chopanan?

Koja shod ghulha-ye biaban?

Koja shodan muy-kashalan?

Datsunharam midawand

Where did the country bumpkins ["shepherds" i.e., Taliban] go?

Where did the desert ogres go?

Where did the dirty long-haired Taliban go?

Who used to drive the Datsun trucks?

The two singers (Islam and Kohestani) use notably similar techniques of social criticism, scorning or ridiculing their victims, and identifying them by means of personal markers, such as the rich man's Volga car, or the Taliban's hallmark Datsun trucks. Both singers also criticize their targets on the grounds of unmanly behavior. There is, however, an importance difference: whereas the earlier singer's target was a local person, Kohestani's songs address internationally known political entities such as bin Laden and the Taliban.

Kohestani's third song further enlarged the compass of his wrath, railing against interference by other nations:

Hawahakhan keshwar-e mastan

Dast-e razi e namude har dushman

Dar sareshan ast fekr-e estemar

Siahsatbazi o guru karde be kar

Az zaman-e Sikander o Russha

Az Britania o ham Chengisha

Hame nobat resid be Pakistan

Chechen o Arabha hamra eshan

Greedy people want our country

And enemies have interfered with us.

They think about colonizing us

Through political games and support of different military groups.

From the times of Alexander, the Russians,

Britain and Genghis Khan's people.

Now came the turn of Pakistan,

And Arabs and Chechens with them.

The United States is a significant omission in Kohestani's song about political interference in Afghanistan, which may reflect an Afghan ambivalence towards the U.S. presence. While many Afghans are grateful to see the end of Taliban rule, they are also aware that bin Laden originally received significant U.S. backing when he entered Afghan politics in 1980.[36] People are also angry about the U.S. treatment of Afghan prisoners in Guantanamo Bay and in prisons inside Afghanistan.[37]

Kohestani's songs have reached a reasonably wide audience in Afghanistan, as he has sung for Mazar-i Sherif's radio and television station, but unfortunately we do not know if many other singers are composing and performing such songs. My main point, however, is to illustrate the striking contrast between the Afghan worldviews of 1972 and 2003. The earlier singer's focus is strictly local (although one suspects that if he were alive today he would have plenty to say about wider political issues), whereas Kohestani's songs refer to historical and international aspects of Afghan politics.

Kohestani's songs illustrate the extent to which many people in Afghanistan have become politically aware of their circumstances, particularly in the post-9/11 era. Three factors help to explain this politicization. First, the presence in Afghanistan of many foreign people and organizations (for purposes of military intervention, diplomacy, journalism, humanitarian aid, etc.) has brought numerous Afghans into contact with new people, ideas and projects. Second, there has been a great increase in the scope of the media, with new radio stations and television channels and the wide availability of imported videos and DVDs. These have brought news and film footage of the outside world into people's homes. Third, the significant displacement of Afghan people within and outside the country has broadened people's perspectives. This final point is crucial. Family life is central to Afghan culture, and family ties with Afghans living in Pakistan, Iran, Europe, North America, and Australia have had a significant impact on both Afghan political consciousness and Afghan musical culture. It is to these diaspora issues that I now turn.

THE IMPACT OF THE AFGHAN DIASPORA ON MUSIC

The exile of musicians had a serious impact on morale and on musical standards inside Afghanistan. Most of the musicians who have settled in Europe and North America have little realistic prospect of ever visiting Afghanistan again, but many of them continue to perform and make commercial recordings. Several important musical figures died abroad, including Ustad Rahim Bakhsh, a great classical singer, who died in Pakistan; the singer Ustad Amir Mohammad, who died while traveling from Pakistan to Iran; Ustad Hashem, the famed tabla master, singer, multi-instrumentalist, and composer, who died in Germany; and Ustad Malang Meshrabi, the virtuoso *zirbaghali* (goblet drum) player, who died in France. The loss of so many skilled and knowledgeable musicians has been devastating for Afghan musical culture.

Despite the attendant dangers, throughout the conflict period Afghan civilians have continued to move across the borders with Iran and Pakistan, visiting one another and doing business. A steady flow of messages, news, and recorded music into and out of the country has resulted. The two-way flow of videos of weddings was especially significant in keeping people in touch with changing musical tastes. The fall of the Taliban in 2001 dramatically opened up these international communications, allowing numerous Kabuli musicians to return from exile in Pakistan. Since then, the traffic of music cassettes, CDs, and videos has become more open and extensive. Many families in Iran and Pakistan have returned home, bringing new tastes and ideas with them, and Afghans who had settled in Europe and North America are now able to visit the country, although they rarely return permanently.

The music coming into Afghanistan from the Afghan diaspora has introduced certain new features, particularly the use of new instruments. Afghan musicians in North America and Europe found it hard to obtain certain traditional Afghan instruments, such as the *rubab*, *tanbur*, or *dutar* (types of plucked lute), and they adopted keyboards and drum machines in their place.[38] After 9/11, with the opening of markets, Western instruments became available inside Afghanistan as well, and they are now popular among the younger generation. Following the diaspora trends, young Afghan musicians inside Afghanistan are also incorporating Western electronic effects and harmonies into their music, and some Afghan singers have even partially modified their style of vocal production in favor of a more Westernized sound. At weddings in Kabul and other cities, clients now want Westernized Afghan pop music with a fast dance beat, emulating Afghan weddings in the United States. A parallel trend for Westernized sounds in Iranian-American pop, known as *los angelesi*, is also filtering into Afghanistan. If they have the means, urban amateur musicians try out electric guitars or electronic instruments. In Kabul, musical instrument shops display hand-painted signs depicting keyboards,

Figure 12.2 Hand-painted signboard of a Kabul music shop, showing traditional and modern instruments side by side. Photo by John Baily (2002).

synthesizers, and guitars beside traditional instruments like the *rubab* (Figure 12.2).

Most recordings of Afghan music produced in Europe and North America incorporate some degree of innovation, but not all of it is Westernized. Some demonstrate influences from Indian music, such as a CD recorded in 2002 in Delhi by the New York–based veteran radio singer Hafizullah Khyal. His voice is accompanied by a range of Indian instruments: sitar, *sarod*, Indian-style violin, *sarangi*, flute, tabla, and *dholak*, with keyboards and Bollywood-style arrangements (Khyal 2002). A CD of the California-based female singer Mahwash, entitled *Radio Kaboul*, was produced in France in 2003 as an interesting "homage" and memorial to musicians of the past. She is accompanied by Afghan musicians and instruments supplemented by an Indian tabla player and a French disciple of Hariprasad Chaurasia playing Indian *bansuri* flute (Mahwash 2003). This influence of North Indian music on Afghan music reinforces a long-term relationship dating from the 1860s, when the king of Afghanistan imported Indian musicians to his court (see Baily 2000).

The flow of musical influences has been reciprocal, and Afghans abroad have been eager to watch and listen to music recorded in Afghanistan, especially by performers they knew in the past. Afghans are accustomed to sending and receiving personal greetings and messages through the medium of audiocassettes and videos, and singers have been known to exploit this possibility in their songs. In 1996, Jan van Belle recorded one such song from the northern singer Hassan Besmil. It is a lament, stating that no one in Afghanistan has been untouched by the war, pleading for Afghans to forget their ethnic differences and stop fighting, and also appealing to those outside Afghanistan for support and help. Besmil's last verse mentions explicitly that the cassette would be sent to "Germany" (via van Belle).[39]

The return of Afghan professional and amateur musicians from abroad is obviously important for the rebuilding of Afghan musical culture. Many are unable to return on a permanent basis, but it is now possible for diaspora musicians to give concerts or work on fixed-term contracts. In 2004–5, the activities of one greatly respected individual had a significant impact on the hereditary musician community. Ustad Asif Mahmood, who has lived in London since 1990, went to Kabul in 2004 on a year's paid returnee scheme organized by the International Office of Migration (IOM), a nongovernmental organization (NGO). He is the most esteemed tabla player from Kabul's hereditary musician community, and his return was thus greatly appreciated by fellow musicians. Funded by IOM to work at Radio Afghanistan, he succeeded in galvanizing the demoralized musicians into a more creative and optimistic state. His work has included training musicians, arranging new pieces, and composing new material himself, but he has been hampered by a lack of funds, instruments, skilled singers and instrumentalists, composers, and necessary technical equipment and support.

Concert appearances are also very welcome. In 2004 the popular U.S.-based Afghan singer Farhad Darya sang for a huge and rapturous audience in Kabul's football stadium. It was an emotive occasion, as the concert—a once-forbidden public event—took place at the very site where the Taliban had previously staged public executions. Such events remain fairly rare, however, as Darya and other diaspora musicians fear reprisals by the still-powerful antimusic lobby. The singer Mahwash has said that if she returned to give a concert, "They would kill me." Her fears are understandable; before migrating to California, she received death threats from the mujahideen. In any case, it is always a big emotional step for exiled Afghans to return to their birthplace after many years of destruction and change.

CONSERVATIVE ISLAMIC VALUES VERSUS SECULARIZED MODERNITY

At present two important opposing trends are at work with regard to music: the continued assertion of Islamist antimusic attitudes and the proliferation of modern, secular, Westernized influences. The power play between forces of conservatism and modernization is a familiar feature of Afghan history, and to understand the dynamics of the present situation it is necessary to look briefly back to the past.

Antimusic attitudes existed in Afghanistan long before the Taliban movement, but in the decades preceding the 1978 coup, religious arguments about the immorality of music had relatively little influence. At that time music was much enjoyed, and secular values were in their ascendance. This was particularly evident in the modernizing agenda of government broadcasting policies and, since its inception in the 1940s, radio broadcasting has been an important indicator of the politics of music-making in Afghanistan.[40] As Baily notes, the radio station "started to replace the royal court as the principal patron of musicians, and as the institutional sponsor of new developments in music" (2000: 808). Radio Afghanistan employed a large number of skilled professional musicians to compose, arrange, rehearse, and perform new pieces. The singer Hossein Arman describes the 1950s and 1960s as "a very creative era" for radio music, with everyone "conscious of participating in the building of a national cultural identity."[41] In the late 1960s and early 1970s, Slobin observed that the Afghan people enthusiastically embraced Radio Afghanistan as a regular presence in their lives, paying most attention to "the music, rather than the spoken programming" (1976: 28).[42]

Conservative attitudes toward music reasserted themselves strongly during the communist period. Television was a new medium in Afghanistan at the time, and the government used it to promote the Marxist cause. Musicians and dancers were pressured to perform patriotic pieces on television, and the public display of alluring female performers particularly upset conservative viewers, especially since communist ideology was widely felt to be alien and atheistic. The public violation of local Islamic norms of behavior fueled negative attitudes toward music, and the mujahideen capitalized on this. Their antimusic rhetoric masked a certain hypocrisy, however, as they used singing and, significantly, instrumental music, to further their own cause. To mention but one example, the mujahideen tried to force the female Pashtun singer Naghma to sing for their cause, but without appearing in public. She refused, and continued to sing for the communists, and one night they killed her sister, mistaking her for Naghma herself.[43]

After 1992, the Islamist coalition government removed the female presence from radio and television altogether, but some selective music broadcasting continued. Later, under the Taliban, Radio Afghanistan was renamed "Radio Sharia [Islamic law]." Conventional music was completely prohibited, but the radio regularly broadcast unaccompanied songs performed by male singers. Many of these *taranas*, as I have already discussed, had new texts that praised Taliban heroes and denigrated their enemies.

During the U.S.-led military campaign of 2001, as each important Afghan city fell, the jubilant sound of music once again blared out from its local radio station, and the sound of this broadcast music was a clear signal that the Taliban had fled. As widely reported in the international media, the demise of the Taliban was indeed greeted with music and dancing in the streets. Unfortunately, this freedom has not persisted in all areas, and the antimusic lobby has gradually reasserted itself through threats and acts of public intimidation. A 2003 Human Rights Watch report, for instance, describes how in Paghman, an area close to Kabul, the governor publicly beat up shopkeepers who were listening to taped music. He also sent soldiers to beat and humiliate Kabuli musicians who had come to play at a wedding.[44]

President Karzai's Ministry of Information and Culture has been cautious in its music broadcasting policies. Under pressure from fundamentalists, it completely banned singing by women on radio and television until January 2004.[45] Then, with the ratification of the new Afghan constitution, the state television station took the bold step of broadcasting old footage of two female singers. The Supreme Court immediately ordered this exposure of female performers to be stopped, and the deputy Chief Justice, Fazl Ahmad Manawi, declared: "We are opposed to women singing and dancing as a whole and it has to be stopped."[46] As Johnson and Leslie point out, this view was based on no existing law and with no case before the courts (2004: 171).

The ban on female broadcasting was lifted in March 2004, but coverage of female performers on state radio and television to date has still been very limited. This is partly due to a dearth of trained female singers. Although two amateur female singers have offered to sing at the radio station, their standard of performance was considered to be too low, and in 2005 no women were being trained.[47] In the present political climate, very little video archive material of female singers is suitable for broadcasting. Images from the communist period are too eroticized for contemporary Afghan audiences, as female singers' heads were uncovered, and they usually wore un-Islamic Westernized clothing and heavy makeup.

In contrast to state broadcasting, private sector radio and television and satellite television are all booming in Afghanistan. Videos of foreign films also enjoy great popularity, although many of the screened images are controversial. Scenes from Bollywood films, for instance, with their scantily dressed female singing and dancing, attract adverse comment.

The hardline lobby that opposes music and female rights is still powerful, as evidenced by one shocking and widely publicized incident that occurred in 2005. Shaima Rezayee, a twenty-four-year-old female television presenter, was murdered, and, although the murderer was never identified, her death was related to her "shameful" image on television. She had hosted a "racy" music program on Tolo TV, a controversial MTV-style private station that was the brainchild of a returnee Afghan from Australia. Two months before her death the managers dismissed her, under pressure from mullahs who were disgusted by her music show. Their objections were not surprising, since the show screened eroticized performers, such as Madonna, and Turkish and Iranian pop stars (the latter from Los Angeles). After the murder, the deputy minister for information and culture told a foreign interviewer that "the government prided itself on not censoring the show" but had been compelled to ask Tolo TV for changes with regard to Rezayee's program. Mullahs and members of the Supreme Court were reportedly still incensed after losing the battle to have women removed from the nation's television screens in 2004.[48]

These opposing forces of conservatism and modernism are still battling over the issue of female public performance. At the same time, the hardships experienced by women under Taliban rule have made liberal Afghans and foreign aid workers all the more eager to promote female interests with regard to music. In an interesting development, an NGO called the Institute for Media Policy and Civil Society has created four provincial female community radio stations. The first was established in Mazar-i Sherif in 2003, and the others are in Kunduz, Maimana, and Herat. They broadcast women's phone-in discussions and play recorded music from a computer (on random play, without announcements), although they hope to expand their music coverage.

MUSIC EDUCATION INITIATIVES IN KABUL

Due to the high media profile of Taliban censorship, the international aid community has supported several music-education initiatives, with the Goethe Institute and the Polish Mission especially active. The Goethe Institute has organized projects at Kabul University's music department, sending equipment and making provisions for teachers to work with students, while the Polish Mission has supported music classes at other venues. As with many aid agencies, the Polish Mission wished to incorporate girls into their projects, since female rights for education were denied under Taliban rule. The problems they encountered are instructive, both for understanding current cultural dynamics in Afghanistan as well as for other entities interested in promoting such initiatives in the country.

The Polish Mission began operations in 2002, financing the rebuilding and reopening of Kabul's Arts High School (*Lycee Honari*), which in the 1970s had offered a normal school curriculum plus specialist training in Western classical music and other arts. The current school director, however, did not want to compromise his school and refused to admit girls, so the Mission withdrew support. The Mission then forged a partnership with an NGO working for Afghan women, and succeeded in establishing a music class for fifteen to twenty girls. No female teacher could be found, so they employed a man (who had actually been trained in Western music). After three months local mullahs objected, and, bowing to local pressure, the NGO director asked the Mission to discontinue the project.

Eventually the Polish Mission found two workable venues. One was a large orphanage whose female director wanted her girls' music class to learn to play Afghan instruments. The Western-trained teacher taught Afghan music on the harmonium and tabla, although he could not play them well himself. The classes were popular, but it seemed unlikely that the pupils would reach a very high standard. The other venue was an Afghan NGO for girls, where the two male teachers were skilled players of tabla and *rubab*, but did not work efficiently together. Although circumstances are not ideal, it is an achievement to set up music courses for girls, and the pupils are challenging gender conventions about the use of musical instruments.

As these examples demonstrate, while it is clearly preferable for women to teach girls in Afghanistan, it is hard to find women with the necessary skills and confidence. In July 2003, the BBC's correspondent Kylie Morris interviewed a woman named Najiba Samin, who was then giving female singing classes. Eight pupils had enrolled, but an armed guard had to stand at the door to protect the class against "extremists." In the interview Samin expressed considerable psychological tension, and by 2004 the course had been discontinued.[49]

Kabul University may become the most significant venue where girls can learn music in a coeducational context, but the music program is in its infancy. In April 2003 a broad four-year music degree course was inaugurated (of the sixteen pupils, one was female). The students currently enter with minimal knowledge of music, however, and there is an urgent need for good teachers in a range of instruments—an inevitable outcome of the repression of music under Taliban rule.

A separate humanitarian initiative in the post-9/11 era worthy of mention focuses specifically on Afghan art music, which has suffered

Figure 12.3 Ustad Ghulam Hussein teaching *rubab* and demonstrating the skill of his seven-year-old son in a music class organized by the Aga Khan Trust for Culture in Kabul (Photo by Veronica Doubleday, 2004).

considerably in recent decades due to a lack of patronage and the exodus of musicians. With the return of some musicians to Kabul after 2001, the Aga Khan Trust for Culture organized an education program featuring four significant and respected *ustad*s as its teachers: Ustad Salim Bakhsh (vocal/harmonium), Ustad Amruddin *(delruba)*, Ustad Ghulam Hussein *(rubab)*, and Ustad Wali Nabizada (tabla).

The project was partly aimed at younger members of the hereditary musician community. All the teachers have brought in their sons, and many other pupils come from Kabuli professional musician families (Figure 12.3). The students are motivated and often talented, but most of them are hampered by a lack of funds to purchase instruments on which to practice at home.

In short, these are early years for the rebuilding of Afghanistan's music culture, and its future will depend on securing funding and continued institutional backing.

MUSIC IN THE POST-9/11 KARZAI ERA

At this point, only a general assessment may be made about the present situation of music in Afghanistan. For years very little fieldwork on music has been undertaken, and only scanty information is available about conditions in the provincial cities and countryside.[50] Most is known about music in Kabul, through short research trips and journalistic reports, but sustained fieldwork is necessary to gain a proper understanding of how musical practices have developed and changed.

Many old venues for music-making have simply been lost. The excellent urban concerts performed each evening of the month of Ramadan, once a musical highlight of the year during the preconflict era, have disappeared. Similarly, the urban theaters that were once common sites for live music have now long been closed. Other possible losses include the musical culture of teahouses in northern Afghanistan. This suffered a decline during the 1990s, when van Belle reported that owners were unable to afford the cost of hiring musicians (2000: 831), and we do not know if this tradition has survived.

Economic hardship continues to affect musical institutions. Since the fall of the Taliban, Kabul's state radio station, formerly a hotbed of musical creativity, has functioned with extremely limited resources. In 2002, facilities for recording music were very restricted, so musicians were rehearsing pieces that had no immediate prospect of being broadcast.[51] The valuable radio music archive, mercifully intact after the Taliban years, did not possess reel-to-reel tape recorders with which to play the music, although tapes could be sent to another section for broadcasting. In 2005, at the time of writing, facilities are a little better, but still extremely basic.

Tastes have also changed, and many outside influences have filtered into Afghan music. In the past, live amateur music-making was a valued form of domestic entertainment, but television and video culture has to some extent replaced it in the post-9/11 era. Patronage patterns are also changing. At urban weddings, which were previously one of the main contexts for serious traditional art music, families now want the kind of fast dance music they have seen on videos of weddings in the United States.

People in Kabul comment that there is a generation gap in terms of musical tastes. Members of the older generation prefer the kind of music that existed before the conflict years, whereas younger audiences are enamored of Western pop culture and Westernized music broadcast on commercial radio and television stations. There is also a gap between traditionalists who seek to discourage many forms of music, and liberals who embrace change and want to participate in twenty-first-century globalized culture.

It remains to be seen what will be resurrected in this uncertain milieu, and it is unclear to what extent the politicized music of the past decades will remain relevant and popular. By way of comparison, Naila Ceribasic reports that in postwar Croatia popular music "mainly reverted to its traditional themes of either happy or unhappy love" (2000: 233). If peaceful conditions are maintained, it is likely that romantic love will regain its ascendancy in Afghan song texts. My sense is that patriotic songs will probably remain popular for some time, to help heal the wounds of war and to assert a sense of unified identity in a politically fragmented country. The lament theme has deep roots in Afghan culture, and verses lamenting the experiences of conflict will likely endure within traditional performance genres. If conditions are safe, more critical and satirical songs may be composed. As to the continued popularity of Westernized styles, much depends upon the role of the West in Afghanistan's political and economic future.

CONCLUSIONS: THE IMPACT OF 9/11 ON MUSIC IN AFGHANISTAN

At the beginning of this article I mentioned three significant effects of the post-9/11 U.S. military actions on the musical culture of Afghanistan: the easing of musical censorship, the return of exiled Afghan musicians, and the founding of new initiatives to regenerate the country's musical culture. Having examined the situation of music in some detail, I will conclude with some final comments on each of these points.

First, with regard to music censorship, it is clear that Taliban-era repression had a number of serious and long-term effects on Afghan musical practices. Stretching well back before Taliban rule, the normal process of musical transmission had been halted and disrupted by the decades of conflict, but the years of Taliban prohibition were especially crushing. A generation of young people has grown up having very little experience of live musical performance, and in some areas Taliban-style antimusic attitudes persist. Nonetheless, there is a strong desire among many people to listen to music today, and many musicians have demonstrated a continued desire to maintain their hereditary profession.

The easing of censorship has also greatly broadened the scope of music being played and heard in Afghanistan. There is a virtually unregulated free market in recorded music, and independent radio and television stations are popular with the younger generation. The importation and copying of recorded music, videos, and DVDs from outside Afghanistan has also fostered an increased demand for Western instruments such as guitars, keyboards, and synthesizers. Despite such developments, censorship issues remain a problem for the Afghan government, and the Islamist antimusic lobby is particularly opposed to female public performance.

My second point concerns the post-9/11 return of professional musicians from exile. This has been crucial to the restoration of musical normality in Afghanistan, and was an essential step toward reestablishing musical standards, particularly in art music. The professional circumstances of these musicians, however, leave much to be desired. Public resources are scarce, and the state radio and television stations are in a state of poverty, housed in crumbling buildings without basic equipment or reliable electricity. Patronage is a problem for some professional musicians, as traditional music is in far less demand at weddings than previously. There is, however, a thirst for music, and some musicians are offering private music lessons as an additional source of income. Given these constraints, it is also significant that not all musicians have returned from exile; though many have moved back from Pakistan and Iran for economic and family reasons, they rarely return to settle from farther afield. The rift between diaspora musicians and their relatives and former colleagues inside the country remains as a source of pain and potential resentment and guilt.

Third, on a more positive note, in the Karzai era it has become possible for musicians and aid agencies to support initiatives to revitalize Afghanistan's musical culture. Although operating on a small scale at this stage, there is opportunity for tremendous expansion. Music education classes appear to have a dual function: not only do they disseminate musical knowledge, they also function as a symbol of optimism and change for the good.

The regeneration of Afghanistan's musical culture will not, however, be a simple process. Afghan officials have become wary of the ideological or economic self-interest that is potentially attached to offers of humanitarian aid, and mistrust has delayed or derailed some projects.[52] Various agencies have sought to help digitize the Radio Afghanistan music archive, for instance, but to date the Afghan authorities have not reached any partnership agreement. They appear hesitant due to an understandable concern over safeguarding their national musical heritage from copyright theft. As a result, however, the music archive is still in urgent need of digitization.

The institutional structures of the country that might support musical activities remain severely impaired and impoverished. After years of bombing, rocket attacks and neglect, the radio and television stations, universities and schools are in a state of poor repair and lack the resources to rebuild (Figure 12.4).

Figure 12.4 A broken grand piano affords entertainment for two boys in a ruined Kabul ballroom which the Ministry of Information and Culture's Music Department now uses as a rehearsal space. Photo by Veronica Doubleday (2004).

There is also a shortage of skilled Afghan personnel to staff music initiatives at this point. Furthermore, the advent of foreign agencies operating in Kabul, including military and diplomatic personnel, security firms, journalists, and aid workers, has raised rents and salaries, making funding issues even more critical. In short, the rebuilding of Afghanistan's musical culture needs more support if it is to succeed.

The presence of a large community of foreigners has had other effects, too. Foreign residents have become significant patrons, and the Kabuli *ustad*s are in demand at embassy parties. Members of the aid community, including returnee Westernized Afghans, have also brought new perspectives to ideas about gender roles in Afghanistan. In some quarters this is welcomed, and in others it is resented. The initiatives to help girls learn musical instruments previously assigned to men are laudable, and it remains to be seen to what extent gendered roles do change along more egalitarian lines.

In the aftermath of U.S. military and political intervention, Afghanistan's future remains fragile and unpredictable. The U.S. "war on terror" in Afghanistan is not over, and the Taliban movement is not dead; for several years now there has been a resurgence in southeastern Afghanistan. As I write this in 2005, in Kandahar a mullah who spoke out against the Taliban has recently been assassinated, and his funeral was then targeted with a bomb that killed and injured many people.[53]

In the future, much will depend on the actions of the United States, its allies and enemies, interested neighboring states, the international peacekeeping forces, and the policies of the United Nations and NGOs.

In 2003 Kohestani reminded his audience of Afghanistan's poverty, and correctly pointed out that those who interfered in Afghan politics have a duty to provide compensation:

Dar qazawat-e i jahan-e bashar

Arz-e bichareganad kard nokar

Hawahakhan ke chi sar zakhm zadan

Mahram gozarad o jezire konan

For the people of this world to judge,

I am expressing the complaints of the poor.

The greedy ones who have inflicted wounds

They should apply healing ointment and provide compensation.

Afghanistan has been destroyed by decades of war, and it sorely deserves the "compensation" for which Kohestani asks. After years of repression, musicians and musical institutions need support. As the Herati musician Ustad Rahim Khushnawaz said in 2002, likening his musical culture to a sick patient, "it still needs injections." Ultimately, however, the main task of the international community needs to be the preservation of peace in the region for, above all, the constant, destructive presence of armed conflict needs to end if Afghanistan's remarkable musical culture is to regenerate fully and flower again.

REFERENCES

Arnold, Alison, ed. 2000. *The Garland Encyclopedia of World Music*. Volume 5: South Asia: The Indian Subcontinent. New York and London: Garland Publishing.

Baghban, Hafizullah. 1977. "The Context and Concept of Humor in Magadi Theater." Ph.D. diss., University of Indiana.

Baily, John. 1988. *Music of Afghanistan: Professional Musicians in the City of Herat*. Cambridge: Cambridge University Press.

———. 2000. "Music and the State." In *The Garland Encyclopedia of World Music*, Volume 5: South Asia: The Indian Subcontinent, edited by Alison Arnold, 804–11. New York and London: Garland Publishing.

————. 2001a. *"Can You Stop the Birds Singing?" The Censorship of Music in Afghanistan.* Copenhagen: Freemuse.

————. 2001b. "Afghanistan." In *The New Grove Dictionary of Music and Musicians*, 2nd ed., edited by Stanley Sadie, vol. 1, 182–90. London: Macmillan Press.

————. 2003. *Kabul Music Diary.* London: Goldsmiths College. DVD.

————. 2004. "Music Censorship in Afghanistan Before and After the Taliban." In *Shoot the Singer! Music Censorship Today*, edited by Marie Korpe, 19–28. London: Zed Press.

————. 2005. *Tablas and Drum Machines.* Unreleased film.

————. (forthcoming). "Music and Censorship in Afghanistan, 1973–2003." In *Music and the Play of Power: Music, Politics and Ideology in the Middle East, North Africa and Central Asia*, edited by Laudan Nooshin. Aldershot: Ashgate.

Broughton, Simon. 2002. *Breaking the Silence. Music in Afghanistan.* London: Songlines Films. DVD.

Ceribasic, Naila. 2000. "Defining Women and Men in the Context of War: Images in Croatian Popular Music in the 1990s." In *Music and Gender*, edited by Pirkko Moisala and Beverley Diamond, 219–38. Urbana and Chicago: University of Illinois Press.

Doubleday, Veronica. 2000. "Afghanistan." In *World Music: The Rough Guide Volume 2: Latin and North America, Caribbean, India, Asia and Pacific*, edited by Simon Broughton and Mark Ellingham, 3–7. London: Rough Guides.

————. 2003. "Chaharbayti." In *South Asian Folklore: An Encyclopedia*, edited by Margaret A. Mills, Peter J. Claus, and Sarah Diamond, 104–5. New York and London: Routledge.

————. 2005. "Music in Afghanistan." In *Afghanistan: A Companion and Guide*, edited by Bijan Omrani and Matthew Leeming, 648–54. Hong Kong: Odyssey.

————. 2006 [1988]. *Three Women of Herat.* London: I.B. Tauris.

Grima, Benedicte. 1993. *The Performance of Emotion Among Paxtun Women: "The Misfortunes Which Have Befallen Me."* Karachi, Lahore and Islamabad: Oxford University Press.

Halliday, Fred. 2002. *Two Hours That Shook the World: September 11, 2001: Causes and Consequences.* London: Saqi Books.

Johnson, Chris, and Jolyon Leslie. 2004. *Afghanistan: The Mirage of Peace.* London: Zed Books.

Khyal, Hazifullah. 2002. *Carwaan-e-amr.* CD. Available at www.h-khyal.com.

Koepke, Bruce. 2002. "Finding a Balance between Religious Orthodoxy and the Maintenance of Afghanistan's Performative Traditions." In *Afghanistan: A Country Without a State?*, edited by Christine Noelle-Karimi, Conrad Schetter, and Reinhard Schlagintweit, 65–76. Frankfurt: IKO Verlag fur Interkulturelle Kommunikation.

Mahwash. 2003. *Radio Kaboul.* Accords Croises / Harmonia Mundi. CD.

Mills, Margaret A. 1991. *Rhetorics and Politics in Afghan Traditional Storytelling.* Philadelphia: University of Pennsylvania Press.

Misdaq, Nabi and John Baily. 2000. "South-Eastern Afghanistan." In *The Garland Encyclopedia of World Music,* Volume 5: South Asia: The Indian Subcontinent, edited by Alison Arnold, 833–41. New York and London: Garland Publishing.

Neubauer, Eckhard and Veronica Doubleday. 2001. "Islamic Religious Music." In *The New Grove Dictionary of Music and Musicians,* 2nd ed., edited by Stanley Sadie, volume 12, 599–610. London: Macmillan Press.

Rahimi, Fahima. 1986 [1977]. *Women in Afghanistan / Frauen in Afghanistan.* Liestal: Stiftung Bibliotheca Afghanica.

Rashid, Ahmed. 2000. *Taliban: Islam, Oil and the New Great Game in Central Asia.* London and New York: I.B. Tauris Publishers.

Sakata. Hiromi Lorraine. 2002 [1983]. *Music in the Mind: The Concepts of Music and Musician in Afghanistan.* Washington D.C.: Smithsonian Institution Press.

Slobin, Mark. 1970. "Persian Folksong Texts from Afghan Badakhshan." *Iranian Studies* 3(2): 91–103.

———. 1976. *Music in the culture of Northern Afghanistan.* Viking Fund Publications in Anthroplogy No. 54. Tucson: University of Arizona Press.

Van Belle, Jan. 2000. "Northern Afghanistan." In *The Garland Encyclopedia of World Music,* Volume 5: South Asia: The Indian Subcontinent, edited by Alison Arnold, 825–32. New York and London: Garland Publishing.

———. 2005. *Mehri Maftun: Music from Afghan Badakhshan,* CD. Leiden: Pan Records [Pan 2105].

ACKNOWLEDGMENTS

I am indebted to many people for help in my work with Afghan music. My husband, John Baily, has been a constant source of information about recent developments in Afghan music (inside and outside Afghanistan), and he kindly read a late draft of this article. I am grateful to David Edwards, Greg Whitmore, and Jan van Belle for sending me audio recordings and song texts from their fieldwork in different parts of Afghanistan. Thanks also go to Mark Slobin for inviting me to a symposium on Afghanistan in 2004, where I saw Edwards's film footage. I also wish to thank Nabi Misdaq, Yama Yari, and Leila Zazayery for help with translating song texts. The Aga Khan Music Initiative in Central Asia funded my trip to Afghanistan in 2004, where numerous individuals offered invaluable support. Thanks go to the Polish Mission for showing me their music projects.

NOTES

1. For music censorship in Afghanistan, see Baily 2001, 2004, and forthcoming, and Broughton's 2002 BBC film (for which Baily was the consultant).
2. As Chris Johnson and Jolyon Leslie point out, the idea that the war was "fought only for the best of motives" characterized most Western press coverage, and although it was Al Qaeda and not the Taliban that planned and executed the 9/11 attacks, "the terrorism of one was easily elided with the oppression of the other" (2004: 84–5).
3. Many Afghan deaths were not officially recorded, and the real figure is likely to be much higher.
4. This argument is outlined in Halliday 2002: 37 (qualified with further points about political responsibility).
5. Johnson and Leslie point out, "While the West caricatures Afghans as war-loving people, recent conflict has been largely fueled by others." In 1980–89 the annual mujahideen military-aid allocations of the U.S. administration for the war were about $2.8 billion (Asia Watch 1991, cited in Johnson and Leslie 2004: 3).
6. There is an extensive literature on this topic; see Neubauer and Doubleday 2001.
7. Baily (2001a) has an accompanying CD with two tracks of Taliban chants (Tracks 9 and 10).
8. For Afghan music prior to the conflict period, see Slobin 1976, and Slobin's Web site http://afghanistan.wesleyan.edu, Sakata 2002 [1983], Baily 1988, and Doubleday 2006 [1988]. For more recent overviews of Afghan music, see Baily 2001b (revision of Slobin 1980), Doubleday 2000 and 2005, and articles in the *Garland Encyclopedia* (Arnold ed. 2000).
9. An example of adaptation by the Pashtun singer Shah Wali Khan is discussed in Misdaq and Baily 2000: 836–40.
10. Research has not been done on the pro-communist songs. At the time it was too dangerous to do fieldwork, and today it is difficult to gain access to the archive material at Radio Afghanistan.
11. For biographical information about Mehri Maftun, see van Belle 2005.
12. Persian text from van Belle's unpublished recording (1996); translation mine.
13. For biographical information on the Khushnawaz family, see Baily 1988. The portable Indian hand-pumped harmonium is commonly used by urban singers (and was originally taken to India by Christian missionaries).
14. Persian text from my own unpublished recording (1994); translation mine.
15. Quoted in Misdaq and Baily 2000: 841.
16. The idea of *Da zemu ziba watan* as an unofficial national anthem is widespread (Harun Youssefi, pers. comm. 2005), though an official national anthem is in preparation (Ustad Asif, pers. comm. 2005).
17. Pashto text from the orphanage performance in Baily 2003; translation as in subtitles.

18. Awal Mir was a famous singer from Peshawar, in Pakistan, who came to the Kabul radio station in 1970, where he lived and worked until his death in 1982. His songs were very popular during his lifetime (Abdul-Wahab Madadi, pers. comm. 2005). In the refugee context in Pakistan the song carried additional undertones of Pashtun nationalist separatism.
19. The three versions occur in the following chapters of the DVD: 7, "The children of Khorasan House [orphanage]"; 8, "Kabul University's Department of Music" (an instrumental version), and 10, "A concert at Kabul University" (in the final act).
20. These and the following Persian texts from Kohestani are taken from film footage shot in the Parwan/Kapisa areas by David Edwards and Greg Whitmore in 2003. At the time Maliha Zulfiqar did rough translation into English. Yama Yari helped me with the Persian textual transcription, and we have refined the translation.
21. "Expressive arts" includes women's stories of misfortune and grief, as discussed in Grima 1993.
22. Quoted in Slobin 1970: 100.
23. I have been unable to establish when Asadullah lived, but it was probably in the twentieth century.
24. Persian text and my own translation from my unpublished recording of Zainab Herawi in Herat (1977).
25. *Chaharbeiti* is a common type of quatrain in Afghanistan, and it also refers to a generic song type (see Doubleday 2003).
26. Quoted in Baily 1988: 85–6.
27. Persian text from private video recording of a concert in Virginia, 1997. The Persian textual transcription and translation were done with the help of Leila Zazayery and Yama Yari.
28. Pashto text from Baily 2003, Chapter 7; transcription and translation were done with the help of Nabi Misdaq.
29. The text refers to people "picnicking" or "partying" (*mele*) "over our heads," meaning at our expense, as explained by Nabi Misdaq.
30. As early as the 1930s the "traditional satirical poetry of a famous wit and raconteur" was published in Herat (Mills 1991: 79, n. 8).
31. Text quoted in Broughton's 2002 film. I did the transcription and a new translation with help from Yama Yari.
32. Information from a scene in Broughton's 2002 film.
33. I obtained additional information on this singer from Sakata (pers. comm. 2005).
34. These Persian and English texts are quoted from Sakata 2002: 153–54.
35. In 1997 Pakistan provided the Taliban with an estimated $30 million in aid. The political analyst Ahmed Rashid points out that the issue of Kashmir was a prime reason behind its support, since pro-Pakistani insurgents were being trained inside Afghanistan for anti-Indian operations in Kashmir (Rashid 2000: 183–84).

36. At bin Laden's first mujahideen camp in Peshawar, volunteers were trained by Pakistani and American officers, using weapons supplied by the Americans (Rashid 2000: 132).
37. In May 2005 riots against the U.S. treatment of prisoners in Guantanamo Bay started in Jalalabad and spread to other parts of Afghanistan.
38. This phenomenon is documented in Baily's 2005 DVD, *Tablas and Drum Machines*.
39. Unpublished recording (van Belle 1996). The cassette was in fact destined for Holland, not "Germany."
40. Baily 2000 describes the beginning of radio in Afghanistan.
41. Quoted in the booklet to the CD *Mahwash: Radio Kaboul* (2003).
42. Margaret Mills points out that many Herati people could not easily understand the language of Radio Afghanistan, and this problem would apply to other provincial areas, so music was more accessible than speech (Mills 1991: 88).
43. Naghma describes this incident in Broughton's 2002 film, and her statement is also cited in Baily forthcoming.
44. Cited in Baily, forthcoming.
45. Women had a presence on radio from its very early years. For information on this and other aspects of Afghan women's history, see Rahimi 1986 [1977].
46. J. Alexander Thier, "Attacking Democracy From the Bench," *New York Times*, 26 January 2004.
47. Ustad Asif pers. comm. (2005).
48. Catharine Philp, "The Woman Killed for Pop Music," *The Times* (U.K.), 20 May 2005.
49. In 2004 in Kabul I heard that Najiba Samin had succumbed to mental illness.
50. During the Taliban period, van Belle and Koepke did research in northern areas not under Taliban control (see, for instance, Koepke 2002). In Herat in 2004 live music traditions seemed to be in a reasonably healthy state. Male professional musicians were playing traditional and Westernized styles, and three women's bands were allowed to entertain women in wedding halls where correct standards of gender segregation were guaranteed.
51. See footage in Baily 2003: Chapter 5.
52. See discussion in Johnson and Leslie 2003: 106–8.
53. This incident was widely reported; see, for example, Catharine Philp, "Police Chief Among Dead in Mosque Attack," *The Times* (U.K.), 31 May 2005.

CONTRIBUTORS

Gage Averill, Dean of Music at the University of Toronto, is an ethno-musicologist specializing in popular music of the Caribbean. His books on Haitian popular music and power (Chicago, 1997) and barbershop harmony (Oxford, 2003) have won book prizes from the Society for Ethnomusicology, the Society for American Music, and the Association for Recorded Sound Collections. He has written on applied ethno-musicology, steel bands, diasporic music, culture industries, world music ensembles, Alan Lomax, music and militarism, and music in peace and conflict. He has consulted for the Ford Foundation, the NEA, and the Organization of American States, as well as for films, festivals, and copyright law cases.

Larry Blumenfeld writes regularly about music and culture. His work has appeared in the *Wall Street Journal,* the *Village Voice,* the *New York Times,* and *Salon.com.* In 2006 to 2007, he was a Katrina Media Fellow with the Open Society Institute, documenting the challenges facing New Orleans musical culture. He was previously a fellow in the National Arts Journalism Program at Columbia University's Graduate School of Journalism. He is the former editor-in-chief of *Jazziz* magazine, and former editor of *Global Rhythm* magazine. His work as producer and recording annotator includes *Brazil: A Century of Song* (Blue Jackel 1995) and *Echoes of the Forest: Music of the Central African Pygmies* (Ellipsis Arts 1994).

J. Martin Daughtry earned a Ph.D. in ethnomusicology from UCLA in 2006. His work has been published in *Ethnomusicology, ECHO,* and, most recently, the Routledge collection *Ethnomusicology: A Contemporary Reader* (2006). He is pursuing research projects on music and ethics within the Russian intelligentsia; ethnographic approaches to the writing of history; and musical nationalism in the former Soviet

315

Union. He currently teaches at the University of Maryland, College Park, and will join the music faculty of NYU in fall 2007.

James Deaville is Associate Professor for Music in the School for Studies in Art and Culture of Carleton University. He has published extensively on Liszt and his circle in Weimar. In addition to books with Pendragon and UMI, he has also contributed chapters in books published by (among others) Cambridge, Princeton, Yale, Routledge, and Ashgate presses. His articles have appeared in *American Music, Die Musikforschung, Journal of Musicological Research, 19th Century Music Review,* and *Echo,* as well as entries for the new editions of the *New Grove Dictionary of Music and Musicians* and MGG.

Veronica Doubleday is a visiting lecturer in the School of Historical and Critical Studies at the University of Brighton. Since her fieldwork in Afghanistan in the 1970s, she has been involved continuously with Afghan music, specializing in women's music and gender issues. Her publications on Afghanistan include her narrative ethnography, *Three Women of Herat* (reprinted in 2006), numerous articles, and a CD of her field recordings of women's music. She is an accomplished performer of Afghan music, singing and playing the frame drum, and regularly gives concerts with her husband John Baily and with noted Afghan performers.

Susan Fast is Associate Professor of Music at McMaster University. Her work focuses on constructions of identity in popular music performance. She is author of the book *In the Houses of the Holy: Led Zeppelin and the Power of Rock Music* (Oxford, 2001), a collection of essays exploring the body in performance, gender and sexuality, cultural appropriation/hybridity, and ritual/mythology in rock music. Her publications also include articles on Live Aid and cultural memory, constructions of authenticity in U2, and Tina Turner's gendered and racialized identity in the 1960s. Her current project, funded by the Social Sciences and Humanities Research Council of Canada, investigates normative genre boundaries in mainstream popular music.

Bryan Garman received his Ph.D. in American Studies from Emory University and is author of *A Race of Singers: Whitman's Working-Class Hero from Guthrie to Springsteen* (University of North Carolina, 2000). A past recipient of the Olmstead Prize for Excellence in Secondary School Teaching from Williams College, he is currently Head of School at Wilmington Friends School in Wilmington, Delaware.

Reebee Garofalo is a professor in the College of Public and Community Service at the University of Massachusetts, Boston, and an internationally known scholar of popular music studies. Garofalo's most recent book is *Rockin' Out: Popular Music in the USA*, 3rd Edition (Prentice-Hall, 2005). He is also coeditor of *Policing Pop* (Temple, 2003); editor of *Rockin' the Boat: Mass Music and Mass Movements* (South End Press, 1992); and coauthor of *Rock 'n' Roll Is Here to Pay: The History and Politics of the Music Industry* (Nelson-Hall, 1977). In addition, he has lectured internationally and written numerous articles on digital downloading, copyright, racism, censorship, the political uses of music, and the globalization of the music industry.

James R. Grippo is a Ph.D. candidate in ethnomusicology at the University of California, Santa Barbara (UCSB). With over twelve years experience performing Middle Eastern music on the *'ūd* and *qānūn* in the United States and Egypt, his research focuses on Egypt's dynamic music cultures, specifically *sha'bī*, a relatively new form of subcultural popular music. Currently completing the final stages of his dissertation research, James and his family have been living in Cairo for the past two years on Fulbright Fellowships.

John Holmes McDowell is Professor of Folklore and Ethnomusicology at Indiana University, working primarily in Mexico and the Andes of Colombia and Ecuador, where he attends to commemorative practices and other artistic traditions of indigenous and marginalized populations. His most recent monograph is *Poetry and Violence: The Ballad Tradition of Mexico's Costa Chica* (University of Illinois, 2000). In addition, he has published two monographs on the indigenous peoples of Andean Colombia, both with University Press of Kentucky: *Sayings of the Ancestors: The Spiritual Life of the Sibundoy Indians* (1989) and *"So Wise Were Our Elders": Mythic Narratives of the Kamsá* (1994).

Kip Pegley is Associate Professor of Music at Queen's University, Kingston, Ontario. Her book *"Coming to You Wherever You Are": MuchMusic, MTV and the Construction of Youth Identities* is forthcoming from Wesleyan University Press (2008). Her current work explores changes to and functions of mass-mediated music during periods of international conflict.

Jonathan Ritter is Assistant Professor of Ethnomusicology at the University of California, Riverside. He has conducted extensive field research on indigenous and Afro-Hispanic musical cultures in Andean

South America, focused most recently on how musical expressions are implicated in the work of cultural memory and social activism during times of political violence. Ritter received his Ph.D. in ethnomusicology from UCLA in 2006, with a dissertation chronicling the role of music in mediating and commemorating the violence that devastated Ayacucho, Peru, during the years of the Shining Path insurrection.

Martin Scherzinger is Associate Professor of Musicology and Music Theory at the Eastman School of Music, and currently a research fellow at the Princeton University Society of Fellows. His current research includes large-scale projects on the political hermeneutics of absolute music as well as the globalization of musicology and music theory. His awards include fellowships from AMS 50 (2000), ACLS (2003–04), Paul Sacher Foundation (2006), Tuck Foundation (2006), and the SMT Emerging Scholar Award (2003–04).

Peter J. Schmelz is Assistant Professor of Musicology at the University at Buffalo (State University of New York), where he teaches courses on twentieth-century music, Russian music, and music after 1945 (including both popular and art music and their intersections). He is in the process of completing a monograph tentatively titled "*Such Freedom, If Only Musical*": *Unofficial Soviet Music and Society, 1956–1974*. Professor Schmelz has also recently initiated a Cold War and Music study group within the American Musicological Society.

Peter Tregear, until recently a fellow and lecturer in music at Fitzwilliam and Churchill Colleges, Cambridge, is currently Dean of Trinity College at the University of Melbourne, Australia. His research interests include the reception history of Beethoven's works, Australian music history, and music and politics in the Weimar Republic. His critical study of the music of Ernst Krenek will be published by Scarecrow Press in 2007. Also active as a conductor and singer, Peter was awarded the Sir Charles Mackerras conducting prize in 2003.

INDEX

A

'Abd al-Halīm, Hāfez, 257, 258
'Abd al-Rahīm, Sha'bān, 259, 261–272
  as "hero" and "fool," 271
  popularity of, 269, 270
  post-9/11 songs, 261–268
'Abd al-Wahhāb, Muhammad, 257
Abu Ghraib, 84, 194
AC/DC, 15
Adams, John
  Death of Klinghoffer, 96, 106–112, 168
  On the Transmigration of Souls,
    155–156, 161, 169
'Adawīya, Ahmad, 260–261
Adorno, Theodor, 165, 166, 167, 169
Aerosmith, 98
AFL-CIO, 23
Afghanistan, 277–314
  antimusic lobby, 299–301, 306
  censorship, 278, 301, 306; *see also*
    Censorship
  circulation of music, 297
  diaspora, 296–299, 307
  foreign music patrons, 308
  history, 279–280
  humanitarian projects, 278
  lament in, 285–289
  mass media in, 296
  music education in, 302–304, 307
  politicized songs in, 281–285
  post-9/11 music in, 304–309
  return of exiled musicians, 278
  satire in, 289–296
  Westernization, 297–298, 300
  influence of Indian music, 298
Afghanistan war, *see* U.S. military action

Aga Khan Trust for Culture, 304
Agency, 180, 194–195
Aguilera, Christina, 5
al-Atrash, Farīd, 257, 258
Album cover art, 20–21
Ali, Hazrat, 282
Ali, Mohammed, 7
Allende, Salvador, 181
Allen, Stuart, 29
Al-mūsīqā al-'arabiyya, 257, 258
Al Qaeda, xxvi, 8, 72, 129, 238, 277
al-Sadat, Anwar, 258
Alterman, Eric, 101
"America the Beautiful," 7, 40
Amruddin, Ustad, 304
Anderson, Benedict, 157
Anderson, Laurie, xii
Anointed Jackson Sisters, 215
Anticapitalism, 20
Anti-Flag (punk group), 20
Appiah, Kwame, 196
Arman, Hossein, 300
Atlan, Francoise, 215
Attali, Jacques, 27
Audio-viewers, 43, 67n. 3
Auricularity, 50, 69n. 28
Averill, Gage, xxviii
Axis of Justice (activist group), 23

B

Bach, Johann Sebastian, 52, 155, 159
Backstreet Boys, 5, 6, 95
Bagdikian, Ben, 14
Baghban, Hafizullah, 290, 292
Baily, John, 284, 287, 288, 300

S

Sadler, Barry, 3, 125
Sakata, Lorraine, 291
Salama, Fathy, 220
Samin, Najiba, 303
Santa Rosa of Huancaraylla, 190–193
Schauer, Frederick, 100
Schechter, Danny, 44–45
Schlessinger, Laura, 104
Seal, 6
Seck, Idrissa, 212
Sellars, Peter, 110
Sendero Luminoso, see Shining Path
Senegal, 212, 213, 217–223
SFX Entertainment, *see* Clear Channel
    Entertainment
Sha'bī, 256, 259–272
    as anti-cosmopolitan, 259
    criticizing U.S. and Israeli policies,
        262, 268, 272
    emergence of, 258
    musical characteristics, 259–260
    reception, 261
    satire in, 261–268
    video, 263–268
Shallot, Jeffrey, 107
Sharon, Ariel, 263
Sheffield, Rob, 75
Shining Path, 182–185
Simon, Paul, 6
Simmons, Russell, 23
Sinatra, Frank, 5
Skali, Faouzi, 212
Sleater-Kinney, 19–20
Slobin, Mark, 285, 300
Smith, Stephen A., 138
Smith, Will, 7
Smits, Jimmy, 34
Sontag, Susan, 210
Sparxx, Bubba, 22
Spearhead, 19
Spivak, Gayatri Chakravorty, xxviii
Springsteen, Bruce, 5, 6, 71–89
    allusions in his songs, 79–83
    and American history, 71, 83
    approval of Bush administration, 9
    Devils and Dust, 71, 84
    endorsement of John Kerry, 23, 76, 84
    mythologizing of, 75

performance in "America: A Tribute
    to Heroes," 29, 35
political activism, 71, 83–84
The Rising, 19, 71, 73, 75–83
"Star Spangled Banner, The," 5, 12
Stevens, Cat, 19, 96, 115n. 3
Stevens, Ray, 11
Sting, 6
Stipe, Michael, 5, 6, 22, 103
Street, John, 125
Strokes, The, 6, 18
Stockhausen, Karlheinz, xvi, xxii, xxxin.
    5, 96
Sufism, 77, 211, 220
    and music, 213, 215
    Youssou N'Dour's interaction with,
        217; *see also* N'Dour, Youssou
Sunderland, Mark, 97–98
Swed, Mark, 111
System of a Down, 19, 97, 98, 136

T

Taliban, 108–109, 124, 233, 239, 240,
    277, 308
    emergence of, 280
    policies, 280,
Taruskin, Richard, 107–112, 168
Taylor, James, 23
Telecommunications Act (1996), 13, 14
Televisual authority, 34
Terrorism
    artistic strategies for reducing, 110,
        168
    as performance, xv–xvi, xxxn. 2
    as physical and symbolic violence, xx
    domestic (pre-9/11), xiv–xvi, 20
    in Latin America, 180–181, 182–184
    media constructions of, 45
Thuan, Trinh Xuan, 212
Tichi, Cecilia, 124
Tippin, Aaron, 10, 126, 136
Tommasini, Anthony, 106, 110
Tours, politically charged
    "Rock for Change Tour," 23
    "Tell Us the Truth Tour," 23
Trick Daddy, 98
Truth and Reconciliation Commission
    (Peru), *see* Peru, Truth and
    Reconciliation Commission
    (CVR)